Ellen Harmon White

Ellen Harmon White

White

American Prophet

Edited by

TERRIE DOPP AAMODT,
GARY LAND, AND
RONALD L. NUMBERS

OXFORD
UNIVERSITY PRESS

OXFORD

UNIVERSITY PRESS

Oxford University Press is a department of the University of Oxford.
It furthers the University's objective of excellence in research, scholarship,
and education by publishing worldwide.

Oxford   New York
Auckland   Cape Town   Dar es Salaam   Hong Kong   Karachi
Kuala Lumpur   Madrid   Melbourne   Mexico City   Nairobi
New Delhi   Shanghai   Taipei   Toronto

With offices in
Argentina   Austria   Brazil   Chile   Czech Republic   France   Greece
Guatemala   Hungary   Italy   Japan   Poland   Portugal   Singapore
South Korea   Switzerland   Thailand   Turkey   Ukraine   Vietnam

Oxford is a registered trademark of Oxford University Press
in the UK and certain other countries.

Published in the United States of America by
Oxford University Press
198 Madison Avenue, New York, NY 10016

Library of Congress Cataloging-in-Publication Data
Ellen Harmon White : American prophet / edited by Terrie Dopp Aamodt,
Gary Land, and Ronald L. Numbers.
pages cm
Includes index.
ISBN 978-0-19-937386-4 (pbk. : alk. paper)—ISBN 978-0-19-937385-7 (cloth : alk.
paper)   1. White, Ellen Gould Harmon, 1827-1915.   2. Seventh-Day Adventists—United
States—Biography.   I. Aamodt, Terrie Dopp, 1954-   II. Land, Gary, 1944-   III. Numbers,
Ronald L.
BX6193.W5E45 2014
286.7092—dc23
[B]
2013039954

To Julius Nam,
Whose vision for this book inspired us all

Contents

Contents

Foreword

Grant Wacker

THE VICTORIAN ERA was exceptional, and so was Ellen White. In America, as in Britain, the era enjoyed a long life, stretching from the 1830s to the 1910s. More important, it marked the transition from a pre-modern to a modern way of life. White's own life (1827–1915) spanned those years and then some. Even so, the last three months of a single year, 1844, served as the pivot for everything else. When the Lord failed to return on October 22, as White and other followers of William Miller had predicted, she did not lose heart. Fired by a vision that took place sometime in late December, White played the principal role in transforming a remnant minority of Millerites into the sturdy sect that soon came to be known as the Seventh-day Adventists. Today that flourishing denomination posts nearly twenty million adherents (including approximately eighteen million baptized adults) globally and one of the largest education, hospital, publishing, and missionary outreach programs in the world.

White can be understood only in the context of the era's technological achievements, social structures, cultural assumptions, and religious aspirations. To be sure, she cannot be reduced to her age, for she brought extraordinary "gifts and graces," as her Methodist parents might have said, to her work. And in crucial ways she cut against the grain of the age too. But the era provided the basic ingredients of her life and legacy, and that is the place we first need to look in order to gain an understanding of White's historical significance.

All eras witness change, but Victorian America witnessed a degree of change that remains unparalleled. It progressed from the effervescence of the Second Great Awakening to the stable ordering of the Industrial Revolution—a process that one historian described as a movement from "boundlessness to consolidation," and another as the "quest for order."

Allowing for countless important exceptions, the turmoil of Jacksonian democracy grew into the middle class respectability of the Gilded Age. The fervor of the Methodist campground settled into the decorum of the Methodist retreat center. And the nostalgic evocations of Winslow Homer genre paintings evolved into the jarring presentations of the Ash Can School.

The transformations that marked the technological realm are perhaps the most visible ones today. The horse drawn carriage yielded to the steam locomotive and automobile. Domestic and trans-Atlantic print communication veritably exploded, and an avalanche of religious tracts, penny novels, and newspapers made their appearance.

Society, too, saw striking changes. Piecework at home yielded to mass production on the assembly line. Business assumed corporate hierarchical structures, research universities appeared, and America looked abroad for new venues for its economic and military energies. Other social changes followed a more erratic trajectory, but the results proved equally dramatic. Though slavery disappeared, Jim Crow, with its bitter racism and widespread lynching, followed. Americans found that translating equalitarian ideals into equalitarian practice was harder than they had supposed. Similar complexities marked the slow but inexorable redefinition of gender roles. Before the Civil War, women, or at least middle-class white women, knew that their place was in the home. After the war, the boundary between the domestic and the market spheres grew porous. Private women spoke about public matters, albeit inconsistently and often in the face of fierce opposition.

In matters of culture, the Victorian Era posted transformations equally far reaching. Puritan visions of a distant, transcendent God who predestined humans to their ultimate fate gave way to evangelical visions of a comforting, proximate God who invited humans to embrace a loving and often sentimentalized Jesus. The shift to a more "maternal" Savior did not mean that Victorians were any less certain of themselves than their Puritan forbearers had been, but they expressed their values in more vernacular and accessible forms.

And then there was a new awareness of time, symbolized by the creation of time zones, reliable clocks, and unforgiving railroad schedules. Time counted, both on the assembly line, where it was money, and in the larger scheme of things, where the present surpassed the past, and the future the present, in all things truly important.

The growing awareness of time translated into an enhanced awareness of the urgency of personal discipline. Character did not come cheap; it required relentless seriousness. Thoughtful men and women measured art, music, and even recreation by a moral yardstick: did it produce character? Did it make people aware of the passage of time and their accountability for it? Assuming that the health of the body influenced the health of the mind, they turned their attention to diet and drink and the dire consequences of undisciplined sexual expression.

And finally, there were the changes in religious structures, ideas, and practices. Long ago the historian Winthrop S. Hudson said that the nineteenth century was the Age of Methodism. Hudson exaggerated, of course. He did not mean that everyone was Methodist—far from it—but that the Low Church, non-liturgical, Jesus-centered piety that Methodism represented grew to predominate. In that milieu, flesh became words, torrents of words, in print and in the pulpit. Liturgy receded as pen and voice proceeded.

Ellen White shared that world: its technology, social structures, cultural assumptions, and religious ideals. Her achievement is unimaginable without the technology of the railroad, the steamship, and, above all, the printing press.

A compulsive traveler, she made twenty-four trips by train from Michigan to California. Widowed in 1881, she spent nearly two years traveling in Europe and then ventured on to Australia. "Down under," White invested another eight years expanding the church's reach into a worldwide medical and missionary endeavor. But it was in the realm of words written and printed that White left her most enduring mark. By one scholar's tabulation, White's published and manuscript corpus exceeded 100,000 pages. Allowing for duplication, the sum totaled more than 70,000 pages. One book alone, *Steps to Christ*, published in 1892, eventually saw circulation of an estimated 100,000,000 copies in more than 165 languages.

In the realm of public social arrangements, White again proved a child of her age. Not totally, to be sure. The Civil War scarcely registered on the horizon of her consciousness. But slavery did. She found it a stench in the nostrils of the Lord. Though she remained doubtful that the war or any human endeavor would eradicate a custom so heinous—only the Lord would destroy it at the end of time—she called fellow Adventists to do all they could, short of volunteering for service to kill, to bring about its demise. White's attitude toward venerable gender divisions followed a similar protocol. Though she never, or at least never explicitly, advocated woman's ordination, let alone suffrage, she fervently supported woman's involvement in the manifold ministries of the church. Similarly, she advocated woman's involvement in a wide range of reform endeavors, including, most conspicuously, temperance. In all of these respects—slavery, vocation, and reform—she mirrored her times. If as a young woman she honored the boundaries of domesticity, as a mature one she blurred those boundaries as she moved cautiously yet inexorably from the private into the public spheres.

Religion is more complex, and precisely for that reason, both more interesting and more important. The young White, fired with visionary experiences, bespoke the "Shouting Methodist" traditions of the early nineteenth century. The views and actions of the mature White, however, traced a move toward decorum and respectability that the majority of her Methodist contemporaries followed as well. In her hands, the fiery and judgmental Lord of the 1840s became the intimate and maternal Jesus of the 1910s.

More significant, in White's ministry the movement's spiritual weight shifted from Adventism to *Seventh-day* Adventism. If the early White preached an exhilarating expectation of Christ's imminent return, the later one preached an equally exhilarating enjoyment of Christ's presence in the sacrament of seventh-day worship. At the same time, the warrant for Adventists' widely heralded concern for the health of the physical body—expressed in abstemious habits of eating, sex, and recreation—shifted from visions and Old Testament exegesis to prescriptions dictated by contemporary medical science. Here, the historian Jonathan M. Butler says that White possessed a remarkable ability to make people feel bad about themselves, and they loved it. The evidence suggests, however, that increasingly she made people feel a bit less bad about themselves and they loved it—and her—even more.

Ellen Harmon White: American Prophet provides the basis for most of the preceding paragraphs. The book's respectful yet contextualizing thrust represents the tip of the historiographical arrow in Ellen White studies. That approach has been hard won. Though White never claimed inerrancy for her visions and writings, she left little doubt that she expected them to be taken as authoritative interpretations of Scripture. Yet most Adventists soon saw her pronouncements less as "authoritative interpretations" than as the direct word of the Lord himself speaking through White's voice and pen. By the 1940s her spoken and published words enjoyed a status very close to fundamentalist inerrancy.

Nonetheless, questions about the originality of White's work arose as early as the 1880s. As the decades passed, those questions not only persisted but also grew stronger—and darker. By the 1970s, historians reared in the church yet trained in secular graduate schools claimed that White had pirated much of her work. Some perceived serious factual errors and demonstrable changes over time, both of which were difficult to square with conventional notions of infallible and immutable divine revelation. Predictably, the church took none of these charges lying down and mounted its own defenses. The result is a historiographical debate today as spirited as any in the field of American religious studies.

This volume approaches White's legacy through a wide range of topics and perspectives. With deft strokes, Butler provides a biographical portrait that focuses less on well-known factual details than on broad patterns of influence between White and her cultural environment. Taves, in turn, explores the enduring import of White's "enthusiastic" early Methodism, along with recurrent charges that she employed the anti-Christian, if not Satanic, tools of Mesmerism. Sharrock looks at the construction and dissemination of White's earliest means of community formation, her "testimonies." Looking at White's competitors, Graybill asks how White emerged from a field of visionaries as the sole voice of authority. Patrick assesses White's extraordinary—some said preternaturally extraordinary—literary output, along with the bitter debates about plagiarism, while Aamodt details White's charismatic speaking style. Greenleaf and Moon cover the sweep of her contribution to institutional Adventism and capture the surprising progressivism of her contributions to elementary, secondary, and collegiate education. Guy perceptively takes up the paradoxical—which is to say, systematically non-systematic—character of her theological writings, and Haloviak traces the practical qualities of her theology. Butler's second piece exhibits the relentlessly this-worldly effects of White's putatively other-worldly eschatology. Looking beyond formal theological claims, Numbers and Schoepflin analyze the brain/mind nexus in White's anthropology and investigate both the sources and the influence of her views of health, diet, and sexuality. Different aspects of the great political controversies of the day—slavery, race, war, gender, and suffrage—receive thoughtful treatment in the chapters by Morgan, Anderson, and Vance. McArthur's analysis of White's seemingly utilitarian, if not philistine, views of art, music, and recreation ironically finds resonances with modern cultural criticism. Willey takes up the extensive and culturally resonant mourning rituals that accompanied her demise and that of her husband, James. White's legacy in a variety of spheres occupies McGraw's and Valentine's careful attention. Land concludes, appropriately enough, with a survey of the historiography of White studies, a minefield of surprises, happy and otherwise.

Some of the authors in this work identify with the Adventist tradition, some with other streams in the great Christian river, and some with no religious tradition at all. The reader will be hard-pressed to know which is which, since they all adhere to the most rigorous standards of critical yet appreciative historical inquiry. Taken together, they show how White was both a product and a producer of her age. They also show that however one judges the role of supernatural inspiration, White ranked as one of the most gifted and influential religious leaders in American history, male or female. *Ellen Harmon White: American Prophet* tells her story in a new and remarkably informative way.

FIGURE 0.1 Ellen Harmon White (Courtesy of the Ellen G. White Estate, Inc.)

Acknowledgments

THIS VOLUME ORIGINATED with discussions among members of the Association of Seventh-day Adventist historians in 1998. In 2007 four scholars (Julius Nam, Terrie Aamodt, Gary Land, and Ronald L. Numbers) began to lay plans for a conference and subsequent book providing a scholarly introduction to Ellen Harmon White.

On October 22–25, 2009, a group of scholars—Adventists, ex-Adventists, and non-Adventists—met at the Regency Hotel in Ellen White's hometown of Portland, Maine, for a weekend conference on the 165th anniversary of the Great Disappointment of 1844. In addition to the contributors to this volume, the participants included

Beverly Beem, Walla Walla University
Margaret Bendroth, Congregational Library
Roy Branson, Loma Linda University
Merlin D. Burt, Andrews University
Paul S. Boyer, University of Wisconsin-Madison
Michael Campbell, Wichita, Kansas
Vern Carner, Tularosa, New Mexico
Joseph Conforti, University of Southern Maine
Jeff Crocombe, Helderberg College
Heather Curtis, Tufts University
Lisa Clark Diller, Southern Adventist University
Ruth Alden Doan, Hollins University
J. Spencer Fluhman, Brigham Young University
Joan Francis, Washington Adventist University
Robert C. Fuller, Bradley University
Susan Gardner, Southwestern Adventist University
John T. Grayson, Mount Holyoke College
Kendra Haloviak, La Sierra University

Ginger Hanks Harwood, La Sierra University
Joan D. Hedrick, Trinity College
George R. Knight, Andrews University
Judson Lake, Southern Adventist University
Ronald Lawson, Queen's College, CUNY
Theodore N. Levterov, Loma Linda University
Marilynn Loveless, La Sierra University
Bernadette McCauley, Hunter College, CUNY
Julius Nam, Loma Linda University
W.G. Nelson, Kettering College of Medical Arts
Craig Newborn, Oakwood University
Donald R. McAdams, Center for Reform of School Systems
Jon Paulien, Loma Linda University
Shawn Francis Peters, University of Wisconsin-Madison
William S. Peterson, University of Maryland
Amanda Porterfield, Florida State University
Jon H. Roberts, Boston University
Gregory Schneider, Pacific Union College
Ciro Sepulveda, Oakwood University
Jean Silver-Isenstadt, National Physicians Alliance
Randall J. Stephens, Eastern Nazarene College
Alden L. Thompson, Walla Walla University
William V. Trollinger, University of Dayton
Daryll Ward, Kettering College of Medical Arts
Woodrow Whidden, Adventist International Institute of Advanced
    Studies
Charles Reagan Wilson, University of Mississippi

For financial support we are grateful to the following Seventh-day Adventist institutions: Andrews University, Avondale College, Kettering College of Medical Arts, La Sierra University, Loma Linda University, Pacific Union College, Southwestern Adventist University, and Walla Walla University. The American and New England Studies Program at the University of Southern Maine and the Maine Humanities Council provided additional support, as did the John and Mildred Medic Wuchenich Family Foundation, the Lindgren Foundation, T. Joe and Barbara Willey, Thomas and Betty Zwemer, James and Priscilla Walters, Carl Shin and Esther Suh Young Son, Glenn L. Foster, David and Constance Wilbur, Lawrence and

Arleen Downing, Lawrence and Betty Jeanne Longo, Marilynn Loveless, and E. Gary and R. Marina Raines.

The editors also wish to thank Montgomery Buell for editorial support, the Walla Walla University Faculty Research Grants Committee for assistance with photo reproduction and indexing, Katrina Greer and Victoria Buell for copyediting, Rosa Jimenez and Chris Drake for assistance with logistics and photo preparation, and Nicholas Jacobson for preparing the index. We are grateful to Arthur Patrick, Michael Campbell, and Jere Fox for their suggestions on the manuscript and to our editors at Oxford University Press, Cynthia Read and Marcela Maxfield.

Contributors

Terrie Dopp Aamodt is professor of history and English at Walla Walla University. She earned a Ph.D. in American and New England Studies at Boston University. She studies the intersections between religious history and American culture, the topic of her book *Righteous Armies, Holy Cause: Apocalyptic Imagery and the Civil War* (2002). She has written book chapters and presented conference papers on Ann Lee, Harriet Beecher Stowe, and Ellen White.

Eric Anderson is president of Southwestern Adventist University in Keene, Texas. A graduate of Andrews University, he earned a doctorate in history at the University of Chicago under the tutelage of John Hope Franklin. He has written or contributed to several books on southern and black history, including *Race and Politics in North Carolina, 1872–1901: The Black Second* (1981) and *Dangerous Donations: Northern Philanthropy and Southern Black Education, 1902–1930* (1999), coauthored with Alfred Moss of the University of Maryland.

Jonathan M. Butler obtained a Ph.D. in church history at the University of Chicago and authored *Softly and Tenderly Jesus Is Calling: Heaven and Hell in American Revivalism, 1870–1920* (1991). Most of his scholarly publications, however, have focused on Millerism and Adventism, including a groundbreaking essay, "Adventism and the American Experience," in *The Rise of Adventism* (1974). He also coedited (with Ronald L. Numbers) *The Disappointed: Millerism and Millenarianism in the Nineteenth Century* (1987).

Ronald Graybill formerly served as an associate director at the Ellen G. White Estate and then for several years as chair of the department of history at La Sierra University. In 1982 he completed his doctoral dissertation at the Johns Hopkins University, "The Power of Prophecy: Ellen

G. White and the Women Religious Founders of the Nineteenth Century." He has written numerous journal articles, as well as the volumes *Ellen White and Church Race Relations* (1970) and *Mission to Black America: The True Story of Edson White and the Riverboat* Morning Star (1971). He retired in 2010 from his position as the community benefit director at Loma Linda University Medical Center.

Floyd Greenleaf is emeritus professor of history at Southern Adventist University. He is the author of *The Seventh-day Adventist Church in Latin America and the Caribbean* (1992), *In Passion for the World: A History of Seventh-day Adventist Education* (2005), and *A Land of Hope: the Growth of the Seventh-day Adventist Church in South America* (2011). He is coauthor of the standard Seventh-day Adventist denominational history textbook, *Light Bearers: A History of the Seventh-day Adventist Church* (2000), an updated edition of the volume first written in 1979 by Richard W. Schwarz.

Fritz Guy is research professor of philosophical theology at La Sierra University, where he also served as president from 1990 to 1993. After earning a Ph.D. in Christian theology from the University of Chicago, he wrote or edited several books: *Meeting the Secular Mind: Some Adventist Perspectives*, co-edited with Humberto M. Rasi (1987), *Thinking Theologically: Adventist Christianity and the Interpretation of Faith* (1999), *Understanding Genesis: Contemporary Adventist Perspectives*, co-edited with Brian Bull and Ervin Taylor (2006), *Christianity and Homosexuality: Some Seventh-day Adventist Perspectives*, co-edited with David Ferguson and David R. Larson (2008), and *God, Sky and Land: Genesis 1 as the Ancient Hebrews Heard It*, cowritten with Brian Bull (2011).

Bert Haloviak retired in 2010 as director of the office of archives and statistics at the Adventist world headquarters in Silver Spring, Maryland. While there he established online access to many nineteenth- and twentieth-century Adventist periodicals and other documents of historical interest, including the full text of the 1919 Bible Conference transcription. He has taught courses in Adventist history and the books of Daniel and Revelation at Washington Adventist University.

Gary Land retired in 2010 after forty years with the Andrews University Department of History and Political Science, serving as departmental chair from 1989 to 2010. He received his Ph.D. in American history from the University of California, Santa Barbara. He is the editor of *Adventism in America: A History* (1986), *The World of Ellen G. White* (1987), Everett

N. Dick's *William Miller and the Advent Crisis* (1994), and the author of *Historical Dictionary of the Seventh-day Adventists* (2005). He coauthored, with Calvin W. Edwards, *Seeker after Light: A. F. Ballenger, Adventism, and American Christianity* (2000), and is currently completing a biography of the early Adventist pioneer Uriah Smith.

Benjamin McArthur is professor of history at Southern Adventist University. He earned his Ph.D. in American cultural history at the University of Chicago. He has authored two books, *Actors and American Culture, 1880—1920* (1984) and *The Man Who Was Rip Van Winkle: Joseph Jefferson and Nineteenth-Century American Theatre* (2007).

Paul McGraw is professor of history at Pacific Union College. He specializes in American religious history with a specific focus on Adventist history and the development of the designation "cult." He earned a Ph.D. in American history at George Washington University with a dissertation titled "Born in Zion?: The Margins of Fundamentalism and the Definition of Seventh-day Adventism." He is currently working on a biography of the Adventist church historian LeRoy Edwin Froom.

Jerry Moon is professor and chair of church history at the Seventh-day Adventist Theological Seminary, Andrews University. His Adventist Studies dissertation at Andrews examined the relationship between Ellen White and her youngest son, William C. White, who was her closest professional colleague after the death of her husband, James, in 1881. It subsequently appeared as *W. C. White and Ellen G. White: The Relationship between the Prophet and Her Son* (1993). He is co-editor (with Denis Fortin) of *The Ellen G. White Encyclopedia* (2014).

Douglas Morgan is professor of history and political studies at Washington Adventist University. He has a Ph.D. in American religious history from the University of Chicago. He is the author of *Adventism and the American Republic: The Public Involvement of a Major Apocalyptic Movement* (2001) and *Lewis C. Sheafe: Apostle to Black America* (2010).

Ronald L. Numbers is Hilldale Professor Emeritus of the History of Science and Medicine and of Religious Studies at the University of Wisconsin-Madison, where he has taught for the past four decades. After earning his Ph.D. in the history of science from the University of California, Berkeley, he taught briefly at Andrews University and Loma Linda University. He has written or edited more than thirty books, including *Prophetess of*

Health: A Study of Ellen G. White (3rd ed., 2008), *The Creationists: From Scientific Creationism to Intelligent Design* (expanded edition, 2008), and *Galileo Goes to Jail and Other Myths about Science and Religion* (2008). He is past president of the History of Science Society, the American Society of Church History, and the International Union of History and Philosophy of Science.

Arthur Patrick (1934-2013) was an honorary senior research fellow at Avondale College of Higher Education in Australia and was director of the Ellen G. White/SDA Research Centre for the South Pacific Division of Seventh-day Adventists from 1976 to 1983. He earned a D.Min. degree in biblical studies from Christian Theological Seminary and a Ph.D. from the University of Newcastle in Australia. Over the years he sought to interpret the accumulating data relating to Ellen White. He also supported Avondale's initiative to offer a Ph.D. in Adventist Studies, for which it received government accreditation in 2006.

Rennie B. Schoepflin is professor of history and director of semester conversion, California State University, Los Angeles. He obtained a Ph.D. in the history of science from the University of Wisconsin-Madison. His research interests focus on the historical interactions of religion, science, and health. His publications include *Christian Science on Trial: Religious Healing in America* (2003) and numerous articles on the history of science and religion and on Adventist studies.

Graeme Sharrock holds graduate degrees from Andrews University and the Divinity School of the University of Chicago. His chapter in this volume condenses portions of an extensive research project on the development of Ellen White's "testimonies" for his forthcoming University of Chicago Ph.D. dissertation.

Ann Taves is professor of religious studies at the University of California at Santa Barbara, where she holds the Virgil Cordano OFM Endowed Chair in Catholic Studies, and past president of the American Academy of Religion. Her most recent books include *Religious Experience Reconsidered: A Building Block Approach to the Study of Religion and Other Special Things* (2009) and *Fits, Trances, and Visions: Experiencing Religion and Explaining Experience from Wesley to James* (1999). The latter includes a chapter on the visions of Ellen White.

Laura Vance teaches sociology and directs the gender and women's studies program at Warren Wilson College in North Carolina. Her research explores gender ideology and sexual norms in Seventh-day Adventism and Mormonism. She is the author of several articles on the topic and of *Seventh-day Adventism in Crisis: Gender and Sectarian Change in an Emerging Religion* (1999).

Gilbert Valentine is chair and professor of educational leadership at La Sierra University. He has written several books on Adventist history, including *W. W. Prescott: Forgotten Giant of Adventism's Second Generation; The Struggle for the Prophetic Heritage: Issues in the Conflict for Control of the Ellen G. White Publications, 1930–1939* (2006); and *The Prophet and the Presidents: Ellen G. White and the Processes of Change, 1887–1913: A Study of Ellen White's Influence on the Administrative Leadership of the Seventh-day Adventist Church* (2011).

Grant Wacker is professor of Christian history at Duke University. Trained at Stanford and at Harvard universities, he has co-edited or authored six books, including the award-winning *Heaven Below: Early Pentecostals and American Culture* (2001), and numerous articles in academic journals and popular magazines. A winner of two distinguished teaching awards, Wacker served as president of the Society for Pentecostal Studies in 1995 and the American Society of Church History in 2008. He also served as a senior editor of the quarterly journal *Church History: Studies in Christianity and Culture* from 1998 to 2005. Wacker is working on a cultural biography of the Protestant evangelist Billy Graham, titled *Billy Graham and the Shaping of Modern America.*

T. Joe Willey received his Ph.D. in neuroscience from the University of California, Berkeley, and later worked as a postdoctoral fellow at the State University of New York, Buffalo, with Sir John Eccles, Nobel Prize laureate in medicine. He also held a joint appointment at the Brain Research Institute at UCLA. He conducted research on the brain and taught neuroscience at the Loma Linda University School of Medicine. In 2009 his book *A Beast in the Garden: Who Were the Confused Races of Man Created by Amalgamation of Man and Beast* was published. Now retired, he contributes articles to *Adventist Today* on Adventism in the nineteenth century.

Ellen Harmon White

I

A Portrait

Jonathan M. Butler

ELLEN GOULD HARMON White (1827–1915) mentioned Queen Victoria only once. In a sermon she preached in Washington, D.C. in 1889, she bemoaned the buzz for the monarch on the occasion of her visit to the nation's capital two years earlier in the golden jubilee of her reign. "During the jubilee, the queen's name was on every lip," the prophet complained. "How I desired that Jesus might be as highly honored, and his name be spoken with as much praise."[1] White's allusion to Victoria suggested that more than an ocean separated the American prophet from the British queen. Yet despite obvious and vast differences between them, the charismatic leader of a global church and the queen of the British Commonwealth were women whose lives paralleled each other in remarkable ways.

Both enjoyed the gift of longevity. Queen Victoria (1819–1901) lived to be eighty-one years old, Ellen White to eighty-seven. Victoria ascended the throne in 1837, Ellen's tenth year, but White lived fourteen years beyond the queen's death. Victoria had inherited the throne by bloodline, the old-fashioned way, as the last monarch in the House of Hanover, while White had become the leading figure within her Victorian religious sub-culture by the even older "divine right" of a prophetic calling. At eighteen years of age, Victoria had become England's queen as the daughter of Prince Edward Augustus, Duke of Kent, and the granddaughter of King George III. At seventeen, Ellen Harmon, a hat-maker's daughter from New England, had "risen higher and higher above the earth" by way of a first vision that would exalt her to a kind of religious royalty. While one owed her status to Britain's aristocratic tradition, the other was a product of America's Jacksonian democracy.

In their own distinctly different ways, however, these two contemporaries became magisterial figures. The prophet's Seventh-day Adventist Church was never more than an obscure enclave of Victoria's world, unknown to Victoria and most of her subjects. Yet White, preaching in her nation's capital, seemed unimpressed by Victoria's celebrity. Indeed, inspired by the millennial impulse of her American Protestantism, the prophet regretted the "bustle of preparation for the coming of England's queen" in Washington, D.C.; she urged people instead to prepare for "the coming of Christ." For those with the ears to hear her sermon, *Jesus* would be the royal that mattered, not Victoria.

White's American context also differed from Queen Victoria's British setting. In England, somewhat ironically, the Queen's most *Victorian* of subjects lived at the margins of genteel society and political influence. In White's America, on the contrary, Victorians came to dominate their social, economic, and political world. For this reason, Daniel Walker Howe has suggested that Victorian culture may have been "experienced more intensely in the United States than in Victoria's homeland."[2] Though White throughout her life remained at the margins of mainstream American culture, it might also be argued that she became more Victorian in a sense than Queen Victoria herself. Indeed, she emerged as another of those homegrown American religious figures whose life and career blurred the distinction between marginal and mainstream.[3] And by any measure, she belongs in the company of other notable nineteenth-century American women.

The American Victorian era emerged in the 1830s, during Ellen Harmon's childhood, from the furor and ferment of the greatest evangelical revival in American history. And Victorianism can be understood as a taming and ordering of Second Awakening religious, cultural, and social impulses, much as White's prophetic career proved to be a more stable and durable outgrowth of her early trance experiences. From the mid to late nineteenth century, evangelical Protestantism came to sustain a culture-shaping role in America, especially in the way that it sought and succeeded in imposing its Protestant values on society; and White alternated as outsider and insider relative to this value system. Throughout her life, White, like all her contemporaries, witnessed an era of profound and pervasive change in the United States, probably the single most transformative period in the nation's history. Americans like White were no longer content with a vertically structured Calvinist cosmos, and they exchanged it for a horizontally oriented world marked by romantic values and intense experience. Despite the fundamental changes in her life and those of other Americans, however, these nineteenth-century Protestants were just as sure of themselves as their grandparents had ever been of God. White was hardly alone when she asserted that "we have the truth." The changes had led to no loss of certitude.[4]

To describe these self-assured, even smug, Victorians is therefore to set the stage for White's life and career and to understand her at the deepest level. "In ancient times God spoke to men by the mouth of the prophets and apostles. In these days He speaks to them by the testimonies of His Spirit," White wrote, referring to her own messages.[5] Just as the classic Hebrew prophets had been called to speak to an ancient world, and the Apostles had been chosen to spread first-century Christianity in the Pax Romana, White had been selected as "the Lord's messenger" to declare God's "last-day" message to the Victorian world. There was no mistaking her sense of mission, for White saw herself as a prophet who was blessed—gifted—in two unique ways. She had seen in vision the most complete understanding of Christianity yet revealed. And her era provided an ideal "fullness of time" in which to preach and write that message. Like so many prominent women of her time, White found her quintessential calling as a writer (see Chapter 5). In pursuing a prolific publishing career, she took full advantage of the dramatic expansion of print communication and the great increase of literacy among her contemporaries. But she did more than disseminate the word; she spread her people. In this she benefitted by being a New Englander who followed the migratory path of others in her subcultural zone, traveling from Maine to upstate New York to Michigan heralding her message. And this geographic diaspora, which strung Seventh-day Adventists from the Northeast to the Midwest, was held together less by a sense of common space than uncommon time. In this White insisted that their faith was all in the name "Seventh-day Adventist."

In her preoccupation with time—both the time for worship and the time of the end—White's seventh-day sabbatarianism resonated with the contemporary importance of weekly Sabbath observance, but worshipping on Saturday rather than Sunday set Adventists apart from—and above—her generation. Her Adventism drew on the historical consciousness of her age as well, in that she saw all ages prior to hers as incomplete stages on the way to her own. Her world mattered like none before it because *her* world marked the end of *the* world.

To prepare for this imminent end meant to build character. And as character builders, Adventists would appear very much like other nineteenth-century Protestants but would make an ardent effort to surpass them. Every page White wrote and every sermon she delivered urged Adventists to the highest possible moral ground in readiness for Christ's coming. And as was typical of the period, she did this by embracing morals with more ardor than theology, the experiential over the ideological. She wrote impromptu letters or "testimonies" (eventually published as *Testimonies for the Church*) rather than systematic theological tomes. And in her crucial *Conflict of the Ages* series she cast Adventism as an epic story rather than as a set of ideas. As a prophet and literary figure, she was most herself when flooding Adventist homes with advice literature on child nurture and education, diet and health, self-improvement and sanctification, personal etiquette and social ethics.[6]

In order to stand morally spotless before their heavenly Judge, Adventists must listen to their "mother." For White had become the spiritual mother of this latter-day Israel and had transformed her community into a cult of domesticity. Though always known warmly and respectfully as "*Sister* White," she was, without any doubt, the one and only founding *mother* of her church. Her domestic agenda for Adventists turned them into a home, a family, over which she reigned as the spiritual queen. All the while, however, her charismatic status within Adventism would remain a paradox. She gave the "brethren" their due. She knew "her place" as a demure and submissive figure relative to the founding fathers of her church. But her insistence that she was merely a "lesser light," both to the brethren and to the Bible, would prove the means by which she assumed a singular and unsurpassed importance within her community. In the course of her stellar and ever-ascendant ecclesiastical career, she parlayed her position within the conventional "woman's sphere" into something more; she mounted a public stage of considerable influence and power. Within Seventh-day Adventism and beyond, she served as another illustration, if unintentionally, of the triumph of a domestic feminism (see Chapter 15).[7]

To encapsulate her life within her nineteenth-century context is both modest and ambitious. It is easy enough to sketch her story in the form of an insular narrative, but to begin to interpret her life calls for the more complex demands of cultural biography. To view the Adventist prophet as a Victorian woman can be a way of understanding and appreciating her achievement without unduly celebrating or derogating it. White's portrait belongs in the Victorian room of an American art museum, so to speak, but neither as a bland derivative work nor as a burlesque piece.

The Prophet in Her Place

From her petit bourgeois background, Ellen Harmon was in a sense adopted into Victorian culture, not born a Victorian. She therefore came to embrace aspects of the new culture with all the ardor of the "born again." At about nine years of age, however, it looked like Harmon would not live to see most of the nineteenth century when, as she later wrote, "an accident happened to me which was to affect my whole life." A classmate, "angry at some trifle," struck her on the nose with a stone that spread its ruin throughout her face, at least for a time. Her mother later told her that, after the injury, "Ellen noticed nothing, but lay in a stupid state for three weeks." Her father, on returning from business in Georgia, found his bedridden daughter so physically disfigured by the trauma that he could not recognize her. This childhood "misfortune" left her with a host of physical disorders and put an end to her formal schooling, which would always distress her. Throughout the remainder of her paradoxically long life, she considered herself a "great sufferer from disease." In her diaries, letters, and autobiographical writings, she would chronically complain of a whole panoply of physical and psychological problems: weakness and fainting, breathing difficulties and lung pains, "heart disease," loss of sight and loss of consciousness, "inflammation of the brain," paralysis and lameness, stomach trouble, dropsy, and rheumatism, as well as melancholy and severe depression. Clearly she was deeply ensconced in the cult of frailty, but her maladies probably had less to do with her call to prophesy than did her religious background.[8]

The "Shouting" Methodism of Harmon's childhood and adolescence sustained the spirit of a Second Great Awakening that paved the way to Victorian America (see Chapter 2). It also laid the spiritual groundwork for White's career as a prophet. In the Chestnut Street Church where her father served as a Methodist exhorter, the Harmon family favored the "Shouters" in the backless benches of the church's gallery, not the quieter members in the pews below. Though Ellen Harmon, along with several in her family, later forsook Methodism for Millerism and ultimately became mother of her own church, in many respects the Adventist prophet would remain a child of Methodism her entire life. Long after the "Shouters" of her childhood church had been muted, White would be exclaiming "Glory, Glory, Glory," as she vaulted into vision among the Seventh-day Adventists.[9]

Without leaving Methodism for Millerism, however, Harmon might never have embraced Jesus or heard the call to prophesy. First came her conversion to an evangelical Jesus. Like so many in her day, especially young women experiencing revival fervor, Harmon abandoned the "old rules" of the Calvinist-Federalist era, which for her meant discarding God as a sovereign for God as a beneficent Father. In a conversion narrative typical of her times, Harmon provided all the gloomy and glorious details of her personal transformation. Vacillating in her mid teens between faith in one kind of God and faith in another, she ultimately eschewed allegiance to a remote, harsh, and arbitrary deity and embraced an immanent, personal, and loving Jesus. Indeed, her new God may have been more like her mother and less like any father she knew.[10]

Harmon found this more maternal Jesus, ironically, after hearing a man named William Miller—known affectionately as old "Father" Miller—speak in her hometown of Portland, Maine in 1840. And by way of Millerism, Harmon not only came to Jesus, she found her calling. To pass as she did from the receding shadows of Colonial Puritanism's "old rules" to the "new rules" that enveloped mid-nineteenth-century American Victorianism involved traversing the "no rules" of Romantic revivalism and "freedom's ferment." The Millerite movement, inspired by Miller's own rules of prophetic interpretation, plunged Harmon into a millenarian vortex of "no rules" that proved an ideal milieu for the birth of a prophet. When the world did not end "about 1843," as Miller had predicted, Harmon gravitated to a younger, less educated, and more "radical" movement within the larger movement that looked for Jesus to come on October 22, 1844. After the failure of that date, known to heartsick Millerites as the Great Disappointment, Harmon's first vision in December of 1844 explained the delay. Two months later, her second vision implored a frail, introverted, seventeen-year-old girl to pursue prophesying among disheartened Millerites.[11]

Looking back on that time, she would declare it "the happiest year of my life." God had imparted the "gift of prophecy" on her, and she had been rescued from the miseries of this world by envisioning a new heaven and new earth. Her life without prospects had become the life of a visionary. In the reckless excitement of that moment, however, Harmon could not have imagined the new order that a Protestant culture would soon impose or the significant role she would play in that culture. However extraordinary her prophetic gifts, she could not have predicted that her life or her world would last some seventy more years.[12]

Harmon was the fragile trance figure of a motley group of ephemeral millenarians. She would be transformed into the full-fledged, incredibly forceful prophet of a viable and durable church. A comprehensive explanation for her success story should no doubt include a variety of factors rooted in her life and her times, but none of them was more important than her marriage to James White. If Harmon might never have budded into a millenarian visionary without hearing William Miller preach, she most certainly would never have flowered into her church's prophet without marrying White. Their critics had faulted the unmarried couple for traveling together unchaperoned to preach Adventism and share Harmon's visions. But they chastised them even more for their marriage in 1846, as it implied that the world's end was not so imminent after all. By way of marriage, however, the Whites drew a bold line between themselves and what they had come to see as the excesses and fanaticism of millenarianism. They had snubbed "promiscuous" (mixed) foot washing and "holy kisses," as well as scandalous "spiritual wifery," for the institution of a bourgeois and respectable marriage. And their marital institution would prove paradigmatic for the institutional church they would found together.[13]

Theirs would be the marriage of two religious traditions as well. A nineteen-year-old "Shouting" Methodist, whose upbringing had predisposed her to charismatic phenomena, had married a twenty-five-year-old Christian Connexion school teacher and minister who, by background, was generally resistant to visionaries. For the Whites as a couple, their marriage had been "arranged" by religious circumstances and would assume a fairly distinct social division of labor along gender lines. In her husband, the visionary had taken on a promoter, the artist had retained an agent, and, ultimately, the writer had acquired an editor and publisher. Throughout their marriage, in one way or another, James White supported his wife's visions but *her* visions exclusively; he would promote one visionary *at the most*.[14]

In her home state of Maine, Harmon's initial visions seemed indistinguishable, in phenomenological terms, from those of numerous female visionaries; yet she transcended this sorority of seers and asserted herself as a singular figure, while the others would swoon and fall facedown in obscurity.[15] She would later account for her success and their failure in starkly supernatural terms: she spoke for God; they were pawns of Satan. But the more mundane explanation lay in the fact that she married James White and the others did not. The Ellen White the world would see would be a refracted glimmer in her husband's eye. And he refused to endorse a romantic medium given to outlandish displays of emotion. He idealized instead his visionary wife as the sentimental woman of the 1840s, slim, pale, and spiritually transparent, whose visions unveiled another world as surely as her demure clothing revealed character.[16]

For James White, to describe his young wife in trance was to depict the then fashionable sentimental woman, a prototype of the Victorian woman:

> In passing into vision...she seems to drop down like a person in a swoon, or one having lost [her] strength; she then seems to be instantly filled with superhuman strength, sometimes rising at once to her feet and walking around the room. There are frequent movements of her hands and arms, pointing to the right or left as her head turns. All these movements are made in a graceful manner. In whatever position the hand or arm may be placed, it is impossible for anyone to move it. Her eyes are always open, but she does not wink; her head is raised, and she is looking upward, not with a vacant stare, but with a pleasant expression.[17]

In James White's irenic portrait of a lone visionary, there was nothing reminiscent of what had once been a turbulent mural of romantic men and women convulsed by the spirit, rolling on the ground, barking and howling at otherworldly sights. A Victorian woman, the "weakest of the weak" as Adventists dubbed her, took on "superhuman strength." Though timorously delicate in manner, it was "impossible for anyone to move" her.[18]

As a prophet, she accessed not only "superhuman strength" but the human strength of the men in her emerging movement, and this combination of the divine and the human—the woman's gift and the men's prowess—would always involve a *quid pro quo*. The Whites, as a couple, added Joseph Bates, a grizzled fifty-five-year-old sea captain, as the third member of their founding triumvirate. The prophet impressed Bates with her vision of the planets and their moons that no ordinary woman could have known. Bates in turn convinced the Whites of the truth of the seventh-day Sabbath. In the subsequent Sabbath Conferences of 1848, the "brethren" hammered out Scripture-based church doctrines on the

Sabbath, the sanctuary, and conditional immortality in arcane discussions that the woman confessed she could not understand. "During the whole time I could not understand the reasoning of the brethren," she regretted. "My mind was locked, as it were, and I could not comprehend the meaning of the scriptures they were studying."[19] But this lent all the more credibility to her subsequent visions that clarified for them an opaque Bible. Studious men had reasoned their way through the Scriptures but could not reach agreement based on the Scriptures alone. They needed the revelations of an inspired woman to resolve the impasses among them on points of faith.

Once God had bridged this gender gap, however, the doctrines had been established, and they could then be disseminated. "I have a message for you," she told her husband. "You must begin to print a little paper and send it out to the people."[20] In his wife's vision that he should become a publisher, James White had been thrown into a briar patch; he therefore had no trouble seeing God's hand in his wife's message. In 1849 he produced *The Present Truth* and followed in 1850 with the *Advent Review and Sabbath Herald*, in which written versions of his wife's visions were featured. The following year the Whites moved to Saratoga Springs, New York, where James published *A Sketch of the Christian Experience and Views of Ellen G. White*, a collection of her earliest writings. Moving to Rochester, New York, in 1852, the Whites continued their writing and publishing blitz from a rented house, shared with editorial colleagues, where a printing press would be their most important piece of household furniture.[21]

Criticism of the couple, however, revolved around an apparent imbalance of power that had developed between them and how that might affect the church as a whole. The prophet had not stayed within her "proper place" relative to the Bible. Rather than the Bible occupying a head-of-household position within the Adventist family, as the brethren maintained, the church's doctrines appeared tied to a woman's apron strings. And a Victorian husband took the criticism personally, as if perhaps the charges reflected poorly on his marriage. As a result, he became defensive. In the summer of 1851, he unilaterally decided to exclude his wife's vision-based writings from the widely circulated *Review and Herald* and confine them to a bi-weekly *Extra* with a more limited circulation. Since only one *Extra* was ever published, this move resulted in a five-year moratorium on the prophet's ministry.

In his effort to keep the prophet in her proper place, White undercut any meaningful place at all for her in the movement. Curtailed by her husband, she grew discouraged and experienced fewer and fewer revelations. Indeed, she came to believe that she was finished as a prophet and would devote herself to homemaking and childrearing. Her two young sons, Henry (b. 1847) and James Edson (b. 1849), who had sporadically been left with other families while she pursued her prophetic ministry, were brought home for proper mothering while her husband continued his work with the *Review and Herald*. The birth of a third son, William (b. 1854) would further solidify her role as a mother. Even so, as late as 1855, the still exasperated editor would protest, "What has the REVIEW to do with Mrs. W.'s views?" This may have been the Christian Connexion minister in him still preaching, as well as an embattled male reasserting himself. But White would soon learn that *his* idea for his wife's "proper place" in the church was not the *church's* idea for her after all. Church members no longer saw the prophet through her husband's eyes, if they ever had; they saw her through their own.[22]

The Prophet as "New Woman"

By November of 1855, when the Whites and the publishing association moved to Battle Creek, Michigan, the collective judgment of the church regarding their spurned prophet had judged James White and found him wanting. The first known photographic image of the young couple (Figure 1.1) was made about this time. The brethren "went before the assembly and sorrowfully confessed the church's unfaithfulness in ignoring God's chosen messenger." But clearly they blamed the prophet's husband for neglecting the visions. "To say they are of God, and yet we will not be tested by them, is to say that God's will is not a test or rule for Christians, which is inconsistent and absurd." They would rectify the problem by replacing James White as editor of the *Review and Herald* with a twenty-three-year-old new convert, Uriah Smith. And for her part, the prophet quickly pressed her advantage, predicting that God would once again look with favor on His people. The spiritual lesson could not have been clearer. In the last half decade, church members had languished without the *vox deus* among them; they would now prosper by once again listening to God's voice in their midst. The demand to hear the voice of God from above had come from the *vox populi* below. It had taken the democratic impulses of a Jacksonian past for such an inauspicious visionary to be taken seriously in the first place. In the new moral order of the mid-nineteenth century, however, her adherents wanted her

FIGURE I.I James and Ellen White in Battle Creek, Michigan, ca. 1857. This ambrotype is the earliest known photograph of James and Ellen White (Courtesy of the Ellen G. White Estate, Inc.).

elevated to a more authoritative religious status. The people's will was to hear God's absolute will through the prophet. And the prophet would accommodate them. "I saw that God would soon remove all light given through visions," she told a little church in Roosevelt, New York, "unless they were appreciated."[23] To channel God's will to the people, the prophet adopted letter-writing as the literary genre at the heart of her charismatic discourse. She termed the messages "testimonies." They harked back to her Methodist roots and, strictly speaking, echoed the exhortations that her father had once delivered orally at Chestnut Street, not the testimonials evoked by him at his Methodist social meetings. Indeed, through her testimonies, White transformed all of Adventism into a kind of social meeting in which her prophetic utterances proved highly personal, probative, and often reproachful (see Chapter 3).[24]

Her *Testimonies* initially formed the very definition of her prophetic ministry. They were God's words to her people and were ignored at the people's spiritual peril. "To defy the words of the Lord, spoken through his instruments, will only provoke his anger," she insisted solemnly. "To dissect them to suit your ideas, claiming that God has given you ability to discern what is light from heaven, to what is the expression of mere wisdom," would prove equally perilous. Adventists were God's chosen people or just another church; they were real Christians or "nominal Christians." And how they viewed God's latter-day prophet and her *Testimonies* had everything to do with who they were. The *Testimonies* were "light from heaven" or they were "mere wisdom." There was no middle ground for this Victorian woman. She was prophet or fraud, Madonna or painted lady.[25]

White wrote her *Testimonies* from her own home, and they found their way into virtually every Adventist home. She shaped Adventism into a domestic religion with her concern for child nurture and education, diet and health, marriage and family. Typically Protestant, Adventists eschewed iconography on the walls of their homes. But White's books and pamphlets, periodical articles and letters were invested with iconic value on the tables and bookshelves of Adventist parlors and on the bed stands in Adventist bedrooms. To be sure, many of her *Testimonies* could have served as devotional literature in any Protestant home. She wrote about being "thy brother's keeper," proper Sabbath practice, faith in God, repentance, preparing to meet the Lord, lessons from the parables, duty to the poor, and family religion. But Victorian homes demarcated sharply between the "front regions" of the parlor and the "back regions" of the kitchen, the closets, and the bedrooms. And as a prophet, White refused to be confined by the conventional "social geography." She proved stunningly clairvoyant in seeing through walls, as it were, into the back regions of the home and commenting on how Adventists lived their private lives. She unmasked faults in their personal child-rearing practices, their hygiene and eating habits, their outward appearance and their internal thoughts, their spiritual hypocrisy, and even their sexual improprieties. Though these highly invasive *Testimonies* had to disturb their individual recipients, they doubtless titillated the general reader with glimpses into the hidden lives of *other* Adventists. Adventist ministers spoke more traditionally from the pulpit to the pew. The prophet followed Adventists home and told their deepest spiritual secrets. Church members believed in her for her uncanny ability to betray them in public.[26]

Had White restricted her ministry to her *Testimonies*, however, she would have remained a private woman enmeshed in the private lives of her church members. But she wanted more for herself and for them. As a prophet, she would no longer stay barricaded within the boundaries of the so-called "woman's sphere." In fact, she would illustrate just how porous the partition was between a private woman and the public stage. The critical moment for her came in a two-hour vision in Lovett's Grove, Ohio, in the spring of 1858. In this vision, she saw beyond the walls of the Victorian Adventist home and above its gabled roofs. She envisioned the cosmic history of the world and Adventism's crucial place in its climactic end. Based on what she would call her "great controversy" vision, White claimed her right to know and opine on the world outside the home. She would no longer limit herself to the domestic writing of informal letters; she would build a professional literary career by writing formal history. In a very real sense, her cosmic vision would lead to a career move. Between 1858 and 1864, she produced four small volumes entitled *Spiritual Gifts*, beginning with *The Great Controversy between Christ and His Angels, and Satan and His Angels*. From 1870 to 1884, she greatly revised and expanded this work into *The Spirit of Prophecy*, also in four volumes. Her Ohio vision had been a dazzling, cinematic view of salvation history. And whatever her literary efforts revealed in the way of historical prowess, they demonstrated that she had largely obliterated the gender-based distinction between her private sphere and the public stage. In the peculiar idiom of the inspired prophet, she had equated her divine right as a visionary with a "woman's right" to enter a man's world.[27]

Despite her scrutiny of the world's past and future, she saved particular attention for the church. Indeed, "the church, enfeebled and defective though it may be," she later wrote, "is the only object on earth on which Christ bestows His supreme regard."[28] In the early 1860s, a Millerite mentality still persisted, opposing within Adventism the very notion of a church. Anti-bureaucratic, anti-clerical, anti-business, reluctant Adventists railed against a move from come-outerism, a movement away from organized denominations, to corporation. Millerites, however, never had to pay the bills. James White did, and he faced huge financial stresses. He held a full-time job as president of the Publishing Association, but to make ends meet he had to moonlight selling Bibles, concordances, and Bible dictionaries, as well as his wife's books. The impoverished couple had their fourth baby boy, John Herbert, in 1860. It was a difficult delivery for Ellen, who was left with a weak back and lame legs. Three months later, the baby contracted erysipelas and died in intense pain.[29]

The grief-stricken Whites were in no mood for criticism about their plan to organize a church. Both as publisher and as prophet, they fretted in the face of their opposition. The publisher remarked caustically, "I have not yet been able to find in God's book any suggestion in regard to [a] power press, running tents, or how Sabbath-keepers should hold their Office of publications." The prophet chafed at splinter groups that dug from her earliest visions evidence that she had contradicted both the Bible and herself. She answered the divisive elements within the church with repeated calls for "Gospel Order." John Loughborough, her most ardent apologist, insisted that Adventism would be in disarray without an ecclesiastical identity centered on the prophet. "How do you manage in forming a church about taking in members," he complained, "who use tea, coffee, and wear hoops, and some who do not believe in Sister White's visions?" In the eyes of their critics, James White was too dictatorial to be an organization man and his wife too flawed to be a prophet. But in the end, the first family of Adventism (see Figure 1.2) would prevail. In 1861, the Publishing Association was incorporated and, two years later, the church was incorporated, too, under its new name, Seventh-day Adventist.[30]

No sooner had Seventh-day Adventism been formally organized than it underwent a profound institutional and ideological transformation inspired by the prophet. In 1863, in the wake of a vision on sex, diet, and dress, she launched a health-reform movement within Adventism (see Chapter 11). Placing Adventists on a steady diet of health reform

FIGURE 1.2 James and Ellen White ca. 1865 with sons William Clarence (Willie), b. 1854 and James Edson (Edson), b. 1849 (Courtesy of the Ellen G. White Estate, Inc.).

only increased White's appetite for success in other venues. In 1872, she began to do for education what she had done for health (see Chapter 7). In the same year, White also admonished the church to look for an institutional presence far beyond Battle Creek by advancing foreign missions, beginning in Europe. In each Adventist colony, the chronically ill prophet wanted a sanitarium, the undereducated woman desired a school, the writer insisted on a publishing house, and of course the religious figure required a church. By her late forties, the prophet had refashioned Seventh-day Adventism into the mirror image of her life as a Victorian woman.[31]

As Adventism flourished throughout the world, the Whites endured serious marital problems at home. James suffered a paralytic stroke at age forty-four in 1865, the first of several that proved personally devastating to him as a churchman and as a family man. His wife had always been the one, it seemed, with the more serious health problems. Incapacitated by a variety of physical maladies, she would nevertheless go into vision or stand up, with assistance, to speak to a congregation, and suddenly she would undergo a miraculous healing. Speaking as a prophet typically proved self-therapeutic for her. Her workaholic husband, in contrast, had been debilitated by the demands of his career. Despite his wife's admonition that he should take better care of his health, he persisted in working himself into an early grave. After perhaps as many as five strokes, the once gifted leader, the caring father of two surviving sons, and a devoted husband now cast an ugly shadow of himself. Depressed and paranoid, harsh and irrational, he lashed out at his colleagues, spewed venom on his growing boys—Edson and Willie—and repeatedly castigated his wife.

Though the first family had once collaborated in leading the church, it had become apparent to the middle-aged James that he had now decreased, while his wife, in her late thirties, had increased. In the past, he had valued her *Testimonies* when they did his bidding in advancing the cause. They now disgusted him. "I shall use the good old head God gave me until He reveals that I am wrong," he scolded. "Your head won't fit my shoulders. Keep it where it belongs, and I will try to honor God in using my own. I shall be glad to hear from you," he added disingenuously, "but don't waste your precious time and strength lecturing me on matters of mere opinion." A relentless barrage of such toxic sentiments left his wife dispirited, and she sought solace in a female confidante. "I can but dread," she wrote her best friend Lucinda Hall, "the liability of James's changeable moods, his strong feelings, his censures, his viewing me in the light he

FIGURE 1.3 Ellen White in Oakland, California, ca. 1880 (Courtesy of the Ellen G. White Estate, Inc.).

does." However, she continued to express her love for James. The couple's correspondence exposed their marital separation. "I do not think my husband really desires my society," Ellen confided to Lucinda. "He charges a good share of his unhappiness upon me." Tellingly, the prophet surmised, "I think he would be satisfied if he had the entire control of me, soul and body, but this he cannot have." Indeed, in the wake of her fractured marriage, no one ever again would control the prophet as her husband had once done; her confidence as an individual pervaded portraits such as Figure 1.3.[32]

The Prophet as Matriarch

In August of 1881, James White's funeral evoked a solemn spectacle for Seventh-day Adventists. Resembling all the grandeur of a state funeral, the event drew 2,500 mourners to the Battle Creek Tabernacle to hear eulogies for their founding father, laid to rest at sixty years of age. No one had been more important than James White for the origins and development of the denomination. No one had mattered more in the life and career of Ellen White than her husband. She had emerged from the primordial soup of early Adventist enthusiasm by becoming, in large part, his creation as a prophet. Though both credited the supernatural for her call to prophesy, he had served his young wife as something of a benign Svengali. Without him, she may well have been buried in an unmarked grave of American religious history. With him she played an integral role, both ideologically and institutionally, in the co-founding of a church. With him she transcended her own expectations—and his—as a religious leader.

In the days following his funeral, she looked into a future without James at her side and saw only darkness and despair. Escaping to their summer home in Colorado brought no relief; it only intensified her mourning. Overwhelmed by her loss, she recalled nothing of the unhappy dénouement to their thirty-four-year marriage. "I miss Father more and more," she mused. "Especially do I feel his loss while here in the mountains.... I am fully of the opinion that my life was so intertwined with my husband's that it is about impossible for me to be of any great account without him."[33] Life had never been easy with him; it would be even more difficult without him. In the first generation of Adventism, she had been an ensemble figure; now she must perform solo. To be of "any great account" over the next three and a half decades, she must find her own voice as Adventism's charismatic leader. Her path from fragile, teenage visionary to prophet had been often unsteady, even perilous. To complete her journey from malleable prophet-wife to singularly powerful matriarch, she would face obstacles at least as daunting.

Despite her popularity as a speaker (see Chapter 6), White felt increasingly called to write. She would be less God's voice than His "pen of inspiration." Seeing the Reformation sites in Europe while visiting the Old World from 1885 to 1887 had seized her with a sense of déjà vu. She had witnessed these places and people in vision and was inspired to elaborate on them further in writing. More than ever, she would stand as a prophet on a platform made of books. And like other female Victorian writers, she would access a wider audience by writing history, not according to the canons of traditional male historians but history as women wrote it, from a "divine viewpoint." In writing this history, she saw herself as a "time traveler," a tourist transported on the supernatural wings of angels. Gazing on the stone monuments of the Reformers, she knew that she had been shown in vision these real-life Protestant heroes in action.[34]

Putting it on paper, however, plagued her with the author's anxiety. Ever mindful of her limited schooling, she complained, "I am not a grammarian" but "the Lord will help me...to become a scholar in the science" of writing.[35] Self-admitted problems with grammar, though, proved to be a gross euphemism, masking her far deeper inadequacies as a would-be author. And evidently the Lord would do only so much to help. Extensive editorial assistance was necessary. The degree to which her husband may have aided her as not only an editor and publisher but perhaps, at times, as co-writer was evidenced in the large literary staff needed to replace him and the nature of its work.

White first obtained her son Willie to head her literary staff. Though he had aspirations of filling his father's shoes as an administrator, she saw a higher calling for him. "The Lord appointed him as my helper," she wrote, and an acquiescent Willie in turn employed what he deftly termed "Mother's copyists." They were "entrusted with the work of correcting grammatical errors, of eliminating unnecessary repetitions, and of grouping paragraphs and sections in their best order." The "copyists" included "Sisters Davis, Burnham, Bolton, Peck, and Hare," with others to follow. The prophet relied most heavily on Marian Davis, whom she called her "bookmaker," which appears to have been no exaggeration. Her assistants were to make no substantive changes in her inspired writing, but they gingerly mined material from her previously published articles, pamphlets, and books to produce her major five-volume literary work, the popular *Conflict of the Ages* series, and her other best-selling books in this period. Both White and her son promoted the prophet's publications based on proclamations of her independence as an inspired writer. The "Spirit of prophecy" could not be ghost written (see Chapter 5).[36]

Though her inspiration may have benefitted from the perspiration of others, her books were promoted as if the products of God alone. And there was every indication that not only the public but also the prophet herself came to believe her own press. White invested colporteuring, by which her books were sold door to door, with the highest of callings. *The Great Controversy*, published in 1888, was to be not only distributed to Adventists but also worn out by their non-Adventist neighbors, who would buy and read it.[37] The lavishly illustrated volume became a marketing marvel, lifting White to the ranks of a best-selling author of books.

In 1888 she not only published *The Great Controversy*, but she also attended a historic General Conference conclave in Minneapolis, Minnesota, where she preached the gospel as it had never been done among Adventists. Delivering nine seminal sermons on righteousness by faith, she abandoned Adventism's legalistic old guard from Battle Creek—led by Uriah Smith, aged fifty-six, and G. I. Butler, fifty-four—for a new gospel heralded from the California coast by two young Turks—Dr. Ellet J. Waggoner, thirty-eight, and Alonzo T. Jones, thirty-three. The fierce and often uncivil debate in Minneapolis between the law and the gospel exposed a deep division within Adventism between modern and traditional, California and Midwest, minority and majority, experience and doctrine, "Spirit of prophecy" and the brethren. "Let the law take care of itself," White argued. "We have been at work on the law until we get as dry as the hills of Gilboa.... Let us trust in the merits of Jesus."[38] The debate may have unearthed, retrospectively, an old marital quarrel between James White and his widow. Butler, the General Conference president, channeled the posthumous voice of the patriarch in declaring that if James White were alive "those young men...would have heard thunder around their ears...that would have made them tingle."[39]

But the prophet now sang solo and in a new, more lyrical voice. Her husband had articulated the "old landmarks" in the flinty language of the law and a Jesus who kept the law as a human being like the rest of us. The prophet saw a seductive "new light" in righteousness by faith in a divine Christ, elevated to Trinitarian status. In theological terms, her Methodist experience had trumped her late husband's Christian Connexion doctrine. "I see the beauty of truth in the presentation of Christ in relation to the law as the doctor has placed it before us."[40] The gospel may have been nothing new for the prophet personally; she may have understood the gospel in this way since adolescence. But the early decades of the Adventist movement nonetheless consisted of legalists who were "dry as the hills of Gilboa." If Ellen Harmon's conversion to an evangelical Jesus as a single, teenage girl, defined her as a person, her adolescent rebirth experience hardly defined her Adventist followers.[41]

With what amounted to White's reconversion to Christ in the late 1880s, the sixty-one-year-old matriarch insisted on redefining Adventism in a way that made an evangelical experience a condition of being Adventist. No longer the submissive wife but her own woman, she took a bolder, more outspoken stance. Where once she had been a consensus figure whose visions endorsed the majority against the minority in doctrinal matters, she now aligned herself with a minority against the majority. She risked division on traditional Adventist doctrine to lead Adventists toward a new evangelicalism. And in doing so, her authority imposed a heavier hand. Once the label "Sister" White had implied an egalitarian role for her within Adventism. Now "Sister," in her case, suggested an elevated position. Among believers, she was not just another female sibling; she was far more like a mother. And she invested all her matriarchal authority in a new gospel for Adventism. This was the means by which Adventists would be righteous enough to stand in the last days—the righteousness of Christ. This was the message she would take on the road with her new protégés, Waggoner and Jones, to Adventists at large. This would be her theme, too, in a literary rebirth with such Christocentric books as *Steps to Christ* (1892), *The Desire of Ages* (1898), *Thoughts from the Mount of Blessing* (1896), and *Christ's Object Lessons* (1900). In these books, the gospel according to Ellen White distanced itself from much of old-school Adventism and muted the voice of her late husband.[42]

Just when her larger-than-life authority seemed to have eclipsed her beleaguered brethren, she left them behind and traveled to Australia in 1891. Surprisingly, this did not lessen her hold on Adventist leadership or the rank-and-file. In Australia, the prophet discovered what she called "a new world, a second America" that would serve as a laboratory for her to develop ideas and institutions on which the church would soon model itself. She had gone on an errand into the wilderness from which, in just less than a decade, she would become a beacon in the outback for the American church back home. She had gone to a place where she could dream again, and the future church would realize her dream.[43]

White had always flourished on the frontier. She had not only pursued it across the New England zone to Battle Creek but, by 1885, she had also traveled by train between Michigan and California twenty-four times. Her frontier experience, as well as life as a widow, had encouraged her to take on more diverse roles for herself. Flouting the stereotypes, she believed that a woman should be able "to harness and drive a horse" and use "the saw and hammer as well as the rake and hoe."[44] As a prophet, she should be as well suited as any man for overseeing a church's organization. On the Australian frontier her leadership style shifted from that of a vicarious charismatic influence to a hands-on organizational force. She harnessed and drove Australian Adventists, as it were; she also told them what and where to build, as well as when and how to hoe and rake. In selecting their site for a college in New

South Wales, Adventists needed rich soil to support their manual training program. The brethren believed the Brettville Estate was so barren
that if a rabbit-sized bandicoot crossed it, "he would find it necessary
to carry his lunch."[45] But White saw in a night vision that God would
prosper the land, so the property for Avondale College was purchased.
The prophet then micromanaged the college's Bible-based curriculum
and its manual training. She determined the crop rotation. And she
ordered the tennis courts dug up to expand the farmland. In the 1,450
acres acquired for an Adventist colony, she justified her own generous
forty-acre plot for her Sunnyside home as an investment that would
profit the educational program. She poured her own royalties into
scholarships for students, who would study their Bibles, work the farm,
and not play any tennis.[46]

For the church at large, she envisioned a new organizational level
between local conference and General Conference—the union conference.
She placed the mantle of leadership for Australia on a promising new
protégé, the thirty-something Arthur G. Daniells, who became the president of the Australasian Union Conference. White and Daniells formed
the ideal symbiotic relationship of charisma and order. Happily for her,
Daniells never made an organizational move without the backing of one
of her *Testimonies*. Back home in America, in contrast, her voice seemed
to have been muffled by the vast ocean between. A new, young, female
prophet, Anna Phillips, had surfaced with her own visions and "testimonies." The mercurial A. T. Jones, whom White had so recently embraced
in Minneapolis, saw Phillips as a successor to the aging prophet. White,
however, would not be the woman scorned by her former ally. By mail
she summarily dismissed Phillips as a pretender. [47] White also opposed a
"Holy Flesh" movement in Indiana that looked for the outpouring of God's
Spirit in the last days to save them from sin and from physical illness.
White saw this as a resurgence of the excesses surrounding Adventism's
beginnings. Any manifestations of the Spirit would flow through her. The
rest was fanaticism.[48] Having served in Australia from 1891 to 1900, it was
time for the one, true, contemporary prophet to return to America to put
the Adventist house in order, with her new man of the hour in tow. "I must
be true as a needle to the pole," Daniells later wrote, "to the counsels of the
Spirit of Prophecy."[49]

In 1901, the Seventh-day Adventists convened in Battle Creek as important a General Conference session institutionally as the 1888 meetings
in Minneapolis had been for them ideologically. Once again the now

seventy-four-year-old matriarch placed herself at the heart of the action. Her handprints were all over its agenda. She rejected "kingly power" for a more representative leadership and called for sweeping changes in the church's bureaucratic structure. She also successfully promoted Daniells to leadership of the reorganized church. After all, Daniells had been most enthusiastic in expressing his appreciation for White, in whom "we have a definite, certain voice to speak to us."[50]

In the way of organizational problems, the prophet-writer reserved her harshest criticisms for the publishing houses that were "contemptible in the sight of God, contemptible."[51] Their greed had cost her, as well as others, their royalties. The health-minded prophet decried the fact that the ministry and the medical work had drifted apart, with Adventist church headquarters now overshadowed by an ever-expanding Battle Creek Sanitarium, its budget exceeding that of the entire General Conference. Though the good Dr. John Kellogg had once been as close as a son to her, she had become alarmed by the fact that his medical work was no longer just an "arm" of the church but more like its whole body. She had once placed her blessing on Kellogg's urban medical missionary work; but, unfortunately, his social Christianity had become more social than Christian, more medical than missionary, and more engrossed with the poor than the upper classes. Kellogg quickly sensed in White's turn-of-the-century *Testimonies* the handwriting on the wall. In this matriarchal church, he had become the odd man out, disowned by his surrogate mother and an adversary to the new man of the house, Daniells.[52]

In the wake of White's return to America, Battle Creek, in a few short years, would no longer be the bureaucratic hub of Adventism. The aging prophet had pulled off nothing less than a revolution. The Battle Creek Sanitarium still belonged to Kellogg, but the doctor had been "disfellowshipped." And his Sanitarium lingered as no more than a "white elephant," so to speak, in the Adventist consciousness. The Battle Creek physicians protested that White's revered *Testimonies* had been used as political tools against them. In their view, her sacrosanct *Conflict of the Ages* series had been largely the plagiarized product of a literary empress without clothes (see Chapter 5).[53] Their arguments, however, fell on deaf ears among Adventists at large. At White's insistence, the church's headquarters were reestablished in Takoma Park, Maryland, near the cosmopolitan Washington, D.C., and as far from the Battle Creek physicians as possible. With her encouragement, Battle Creek College was moved to the rural Berrien Springs, Michigan, more closely conforming to the prophet's ideal.

The Pacific Press, near her new home in northern California, became the prophet's exclusive publisher, providing her a more substantial cut of the royalties. With one property after another in California, White declared, "This is the very place God has shown me" for a sanitarium.[54] In Loma Linda, California, she chose the property, raised the funding, and pressed for the building of a sanitarium and medical school that would showcase Seventh-day Adventism for generations to come.

For the last fifteen years of her life, White resided at her own evocation of paradise, a country estate at the upper end of Napa Valley, California, called "Elmshaven" for the generous grove of elm trees on the grounds, where she was photographed in her 80s (see Figure 1.4). Her Victorian home was an imposing two-story residence, with first- and second-story porches, vaulted ceilings, and high arched windows. Her attic was expanded into a spacious writing room with a cozy wood-burning fireplace and a big bay window overlooking an orchard of 2,000 plum trees. Her large staff of nurses, housekeepers, and editors lived in an eight-room

FIGURE 1.4 Ellen White in her eighties, at her home, Elmshaven, in St. Helena, California (Courtesy of the Ellen G. White Estate, Inc.).

building north of the home. For nearly seventy years she had looked for the end of the world, but at the very end of her life she seemed most preoccupied with her literary immortality.[55]

The octogenarian prophet had twenty-four books in circulation with two other book manuscripts in press. She had published over 5,000 periodical articles and more than 200 tracts and pamphlets. In addition to this, her typewritten materials included correspondence and general manuscripts that approximated 40,000 pages. Two thousand more handwritten letters, diary entries, and other documents numbered roughly 20,000 typewritten pages. All in all, her literary production consisted of more than 100,000 pages.[56] Even allowing for the fact that a sizeable portion of her writing was recycled from letters to articles, pamphlets to books, she produced roughly 70,000 pages. This meant a staggering output averaging about three pages a day, every day, for seventy years.

But had White's one-woman publishing juggernaut been enough to immortalize her? Before her death in 1915, she offered her own definitive answer. "Whether or not my life is spared," she commented, "my writings will constantly speak, and their work will go forward as long as time shall last." Clearly sensing that the end for her was near, she took heart in her literary afterlife. "My writings are kept on file in the office, and even though I should not live, these words that have been given to me by the Lord will still have life and will speak to the people."[57] Whatever prophecies may have failed her in the past, this one seems secure. For among some 18 million Seventh-day Adventists throughout the world, she is still read as their best-selling author. Her words "constantly speak" to them, as though she were their living contemporary with divine discernment into every aspect of their daily lives.

White's importance to so many people for so many years has been truly remarkable. She came such a long way from the invalid girl who made hats for her father to a Victorian lady who mothered a prospering church, a church that in turn was good to her. Despite her insistence on being its only prophet, she remained surprisingly self-deprecating. She emphasized that she was the "lesser light" directing her people to the "greater light" of the Bible. Yet, as something of a double entendre, her own life was the triumphant achievement of a woman who herself grew from a lesser to a greater light. Historians of nineteenth-century religious women now recognize that piety and purity need not result in submissiveness and domesticity. In the antebellum phase of her career, White may have come closest to embodying the so-called "cult of true womanhood" in which her docile compliance became a matter of church doctrine.[58] In the long run, however, White's prophetic career proved to be anything but compliant and narrowly domestic. As a prophet, she empowered herself as a woman. She wielded her femininity as a formidable weapon for purifying individuals and transforming institutions. Ultimately, the "domestic sphere" served less to confine her than to catapult her to the wider recognition and power of a more "public stage." For this she deserves serious recognition. The length and breadth of White's life and career suggest that there is far more to her than has met the eyes of historians. From a self-effacing young woman who kept within "her place," to her own version of a "new woman," to a matriarch of extraordinary accomplishments, White's lifetime of longing for another world placed its indelible and historic mark on this world. The woman who once shouted "Glory!" at the sight of heaven had earned her own glory on earth.

NOTES

1. Ellen White's sermon, entitled "The Christian's Calling Honorable," preached January 25, 1889, was soon published in *Signs of the Times* 14 (1889): 209–10.
2. Daniel Walker Howe, ed., *Victorian America* (Philadelphia: University of Pennsylvania Press, 1976), 4.
3. R. Laurence Moore draws attention to this aspect of the American landscape in *Religious Outsiders and the Making of Americans* (New York: Oxford University Press, 1986).
4. I am particularly indebted to Daniel Walker Howe's introduction, "Victorian Culture in America," 3–28, in *Victorian America*, ed. Howe; and Richard D. Brown, "Modernization: A Victorian Climax," ibid., 29–44.
5. Ellen G. White, *Testimonies for the Church*, 9 vols. (Mountain View, CA: Pacific Press, 1948), 4:147–48 (Testimony No. 27, 1876); and ibid., 5: 665 (Testimony No. 33, 1889).
6. George R. Knight provides a popular glimpse at White as a writer in *Meeting Ellen White: A Fresh Look at Her Life, Writings, and Major Themes* (Washington, DC: Review and Herald Publishing Assn., 1996), 91–127.
7. See Steve Daily, "The Irony of Adventism: The Role of Ellen White and Other Adventist Women in Nineteenth Century America" (D.Min. diss., Claremont School of Theology, 1985).
8. The first few chapters of White's autobiography, *Spiritual Gifts*, 4 vols. (Battle Creek, MI: James White, 1858, 1860, 1864), vol. 2 (1860), provide detailed information on her early life. For a chronology of White's illnesses, see Ronald L. Numbers, *Prophetess of Health: A Study of Ellen G. White*, 3rd. ed. (Grand Rapids, MI: Eerdmans, 2008), 291–319.

9. For Ellen Harmon's Methodist background, see Ronald Graybill, "Adventist Roots in Methodist History" (unpublished paper, White Estate, 1974); and Ann Taves, *Fits, Trances, and Visions: Experiencing Religion and Explaining Experience from Wesley to James* (Princeton, NJ: Princeton University Press, 1999), 153–65. For White's comment on her father, see Ellen G. White, "They Sleep in Jesus," *Advent Review and Sabbath Herald*, 31 (1868): 29, hereafter referred to as *Review and Herald*.

10. Ellen White described Miller's impact on Portland, Maine, in *Testimonies*, 1: 14 (Biographical Sketch). For the torments of her spiritual experience in adolescence, see Ellen G. White, "Communications," *Youth's Instructor*, 1 (December 1852): 20–22; see also Ellen G. White, *Life Sketches of Ellen G. White* (Mountain View, CA: Pacific Press, 1915), 30. Note that White's name as published in her books, Ellen G. White, used the initial of her middle name, Gould (her mother's family surname), rather than her maiden name (Harmon) as her primary self-identification.

11. A more extended analysis of this material appears in Jonathan Butler, "The Making of a New Order: Millerism and the Origins of Seventh-day Adventism," in *The Disappointed: Millerism and Millenarianism in the Nineteenth Century*, ed. Ronald L. Numbers and Jonathan M. Butler (Bloomington: Indiana University Press, 1993), 189–208. The scenario of "old rules" through "no rules" to "new rules" is taken from Kenelm Burridge, *New Heaven, New Earth: A Study of Millenarian Activity* (New York: Shocken Books, 1969), esp. 105–116.

12. White, *Life Sketches*, 59. I elaborate on Ellen Harmon's early years in Jonathan M. Butler, "Prophecy, Gender, and Culture: Ellen Gould Harmon [White] and the Roots of Seventh-day Adventism," *Religion and American Culture*, 1 (1991): 3–29.

13. Ellen White did her part in repressing the church's collective memory regarding its "no rules" origins in *Spiritual Gifts* (1860), 40–42. In sharp contrast to her account, however, is the recorded testimony of spirited "no rules" practices in Frederick Hoyt, ed., "Trial of Elder Dammon Reported in the *Piscataquis Farmer*," *Spectrum: Journal of the Association of Adventist Forums*, 17 (August 1987): 29–36 (hereafter referred to as *Spectrum*).

14. See the entry on "James Springer White" in Gary Land, ed., *Historical Dictionary of the Seventh-day Adventists* (Lanham, MD: Scarecrow Press, 2005), 323–26.

15. Frederick Hoyt and Ronald Graybill name the female Millerite visionaries that they have located in Maine newspapers (in addition to Ellen Harmon) as Dorinda Baker, Emily Clemons, Mary Hamlin, and Phoebe Knapp, in Jonathan Butler, Ronald Graybill, Frederick Hoyt, and Rennie Schoepflin, "Scandal or Rite of Passage? Historians on the Damon Trial," *Spectrum*, 17 (August 1987): 38–39.

16. On the difference between romanticism and sentimentalism in fashion, see Karen Halttunen, *Confidence Men and Painted Women: A Study of Middle-Class Culture in America, 1830–1870* (New Haven: Yale University Press, 1982), 79–81.

17. James White, *Life Incidents in Connection with the Great Advent Movement* (Battle Creek, MI: Seventh-day Adventist Publishing Assn., 1868), 272.
18. Early Adventist historian John N. Loughborough used the phrase "weakest of the weak" in *The Great Second Advent Movement: Its Rise and Progress* (Washington, DC: Review and Herald Publishing Assn., 1909), 306.
19. Ellen G. White, *Selected Messages*, 3 vols. (Washington, DC: Review and Herald Publishing Assn., 1958, 1980), 2: 207.
20. White, *Life Sketches* (1915), 125.
21. The story of Adventism's early publishing is told in Richard W. Schwarz and Floyd Greenleaf, *Light Bearers: A History of the Seventh-day Adventist Church*, rev. ed. (Nampa, ID: Pacific Press, 2000), 69–82.
22. Though I make my own use of his narrative, Numbers documents White's moratorium as a prophet in *Prophetess of Health*, 72–73.
23. "Business Proceedings of the Conference at Battle Creek, Michigan," *Review and Herald*, 7 (1855): 76; EGW to the Church in Roosevelt and Vicinity, August 3, 1861 (R-16a-1861, White Estate); the primary documentation cited here appears in Numbers, *Prophetess of Health*, 74, notes 54 and 55.
24. White, *Life Sketches* (1880), 222.
25. White, *Testimonies*, 4:179 (Testimony No. 2, 1876); ibid., 5: 691 (Testimony 33, 1889).
26. For samples of Ellen G. White's domestic devotional writing, see *Testimonies*, 1: 113–310 (Testimonies Nos. 1–8, 1855–1862); *Adventist Home* (Nashville, TN: Southern Publishing Assn., 1952); *Child Guidance* (Nashville, TN: Southern Publishing Assn., 1954); *Messages to Young People* (Nashville, TN: Southern Publishing Assn., 1930). For a collection of her letters on sexual misconduct, see *Testimonies on Sexual Behavior, Adultery, and Divorce* (Silver Spring, MD: Ellen G. White Estate, 1980).
27. White, *Spiritual Gifts*, 1: 5–219 (1858).
28. Manuscript 155, 1902, in Ellen G. White, *Sons and Daughters of God* (Washington, DC: Review and Herald Publishing Assn., 1955), 13.
29. Numbers, *Prophetess of Health*, 93.
30. For their chapter on "Organizational Birth Pangs," see Schwartz and Greenleaf, *Light Bearers*, 83–99; the James White comment is cited ibid., 91; Loughborough, *Review and Herald* 23 (1861), cited in Arthur L. White, *Ellen G. White*, 6 vols. (Washington, DC: Review and Herald Publishing Assn., 1981–1986), 1: 457.
31. Schwarz and Greenleaf introduce Adventist missionary outreach in *Light Bearers*, 141–44.
32. Knight explores the story of their marriage and its collapse in *Walking with Ellen White*, 69–78. Ronald Graybill probes their marriage in even greater depth in "The Power of Prophecy: Ellen G. White and the Women Religious Founders of the Nineteenth Century" (Ph.D. dissertation, Johns Hopkins University, 1983), 38–48.

33. Letter 17, 1881, in *Ellen G. White, The Retirement Years* (Washington, DC: Ellen G. White Estate, 1990), 161–62.

34. For examples of White's déjà vu experiences at European Reformation sites, see D. A. Delafield, *Ellen G. White in Europe, 1885–1887* (Washington, DC: Review and Herald Publishing Assn., 1975), 273, 566–567.

35. White, *Selected Messages*, 3:90.

36. Letter 328, 1906, cited in Knight, *Meeting Ellen White*, 78; White, *Selected Messages* 3: 91–92. For descriptions of White's book production relative to her son Willie and her literary assistants, see Herbert E. Douglass, *Messenger of the Lord: The Prophetic Ministry of Ellen G. White* (Nampa, ID: Pacific Press, 1998),108–123; Knight, *Meeting Ellen White*, 78–81; and Jerry Moon, *W. C. White and Ellen G. White: The Relationship between the Prophet and Her Son* (Berrien Springs, MI: Andrews University Press, 1993), 221–26.

37. White, *Life Sketches* (1915), 217; *Testimonies* 4: 390.

38. George R. Knight, *A User-Friendly Guide to the 1888 Message* (Hagerstown, MD: Review and Herald Publishing Assn., 1998), 95. White's sermons in Minneapolis have been republished in Ellen G. White, *1888 Sermons* (New York: Teach Services, 2000).

39. Knight, *A User-Friendly Guide to the 1888 Message*, 48.

40. Ibid., 55.

41. Woodrow W. Whidden, II, traces the development of White's soteriology in *Ellen White on Salvation* (Hagerstown, MD: Review and Herald Publishing Assn., 1995).

42. For an apologetical account of the 1888 Conference, including White's role in it, see LeRoy Froom, *Movement of Destiny* (Washington, DC: Review and Herald Publishing Assn., 1971).

43. For White's Australian years, see Arthur L. White, *Ellen White: Woman of Vision* (Hagerstown, MD: Review and Herald Publishing Assn., 2000), 274–370; and White, *Ellen G. White*, vol. 4. See also Milton Hook, "The Avondale School and Adventist Educational Goals" (Ph.D. dissertation, Andrews University, 1978); and Hook, "The Avondale School: A Holy Experiment," *Adventist Heritage*, 7 (Spring 1982): 34–45.

44. Ellen G. White, *Education* (Mountain View, CA: Pacific Press, 1903), 216.

45. A. L. White, *Ellen G. White: Woman of Vision*, 307.

46. Ibid., 332–33. Ellen White made her disparaging comments on tennis in *Counsels to Parents, Teachers, and Students* (Mountain View, CA: Pacific Press, 1913), 350.

47. Lowell Tarling, *The Edges of Seventh-day Adventism* (Barragga, NSW, Australia: A Galilee Publication, 1981), 87; White, *Ellen White: Woman of Vision*, 348–54.

48. Tarling, *The Edges of Seventh-day Adventism,* 74–83; Calvin W. Edwards and Gary Land, *Seeker after Light: A. F. Ballenger, Adventism, and American Christianity* (Berrien Springs, MI: Andrews University Press, 2000), 103–7.

49. A. L.White, *Ellen White: Woman of Vision,* 423.

50. White, *Testimonies,* 8:232–33 (Testimony No. 36, 1904); for an overview of Adventism's reorganization, including the stresses leading up to it, see Richard W. Schwarz, "The Perils of Growth, 1886–1905," in Gary Land, ed., *Adventism in America,* rev. ed. (Berrien Springs, MI: Andrews University Press, 1998), 77–111; see also Schwarz and Greenleaf, *Light Bearers,* 241–72.

51. Manuscript 43, 1901, cited in White, *Ellen White: Woman of Vision,* 385.

52. Richard W. Schwarz focuses on the conflict between Kellogg and the church in *John Harvey Kellogg, M.D.* (Nashville, TN: Southern Publishing Assn., 1970), 174–92; and "The Kellogg Schism: The Hidden Issues," *Spectrum* 4 (Autumn 1972): 23–39.

53. For the theological turmoil of this period that turned on conflicting understandings of the prophet's inspiration, see Bert Haloviak, "Pioneers, Pantheists, and Progressives: A. F. Ballenger and Divergent Paths to the Sanctuary," unpublished paper, General Conference of Seventh-day Adventists, June, 1980 (General Conference Archives, Silver Spring, MD).

54. White, *Ellen White: Woman of Vision,* 408.

55. White, *Ellen G. White,* 6: 378–86.

56. Knight, *Meeting Ellen White,* 83.

57. White, *Selected Messages,* 1: 55 (1958).

58. See Barbara Welter, "The Cult of True Womanhood: 1820–1860," *American Quarterly,* 18 (1966): 151–174.

2

Visions

Ann Taves

AMONG THE CAMP meeting songs that have come down to us from the early nineteenth century, there is one titled simply "The Methodist." From it we learn not only that John Wesley's followers in America were "despised...because they shout and preach so plain," but also that they proudly referred to themselves as "shouting Methodists." Though the shout tradition with its rich biblical imagery, exuberant worship, and stress on the felt presence of God was embraced by substantial numbers of early American Methodists, it was not exclusive to them. Rather it is a tradition that emerged in the context of late-eighteenth-century revivals in the Chesapeake Bay region and radiated from there into Virginia and the Carolinas to the south, Kentucky to the east, and north into New Jersey, Pennsylvania, and, in the 1790s, into New England.[1]

When Methodist preachers steeped in the shout tradition entered New England, the leadership of the more established Congregationalist and Presbyterian churches responded with dismay. Though New Englanders had a long history of revivals, they disliked the Methodists' enthusiastic style of worship, their uneducated preachers, and their all-round lack of respectability. In response to this populist challenge, the clergy looked back to the colonial awakening in New England, reclaiming Jonathan Edwards as the father of a tradition of sober revivals, a staunch critic of enthusiasm and excess, and, in the language of the early national period, an unequivocal opponent of "fanaticism."[2]

The phenomena that the more "respectable" sort branded as "fanatical" typically involved claims regarding the presence of God that the respectable folks felt were too bold. Where critics heard noise and confusion at

FIGURE 2.1 An early nineteenth-century Methodist camp meeting. Responses of worshipers in both Methodist and Adventist camp meetings ranged from devout to ecstatic; note the worshiper in the foreground who has been "slain by the spirit" (Library of Congress, Prints & Photographs Division, LC-USZ62-2497).

revivals and camp meetings, those prone to shouting spoke of the power of God descending as the unsaved cried out in distress and the newly saved shouted with joy. In their accounts of such meetings, shouters often described overpowering emotions that led them to fall under the weight of their sins and rise shouting praises to God, as illustrated in the early 19th century print of a Methodist camp meeting (Figure 2.1). In the throes of conversion or sanctification, a few offered more dramatic accounts of falling into trance, journeying to heaven in the manner described by St. Paul, and dreams and visions in which they had direct encounters with Jesus or God. While opponents characterized such claims as fanatical, shouters viewed them as the essence of religion and characterized their critics as "formalists," that is, Christians who understood the form of religion but failed to grasp its substance.

In the late 1820s, in the context of the Second Great Awakening, clergy eager to discredit "fanaticism" began applying explanations advanced to account for the experiences supposedly caused by mesmerism and animal magnetism to the unusual phenomena associated with revivals. Methodists, especially shouting Methodists, figured prominently in these discussions of the "influence of the imagination on the nervous system," since, following John Wesley's lead, they often resisted naturalistic explanations and attributed unusual experiences to "a supernatural influence, either good or bad."[3] In light of the evident sincerity of those who made such claims, naturalistic accounts of the powers of animal magnetism provided critics with a way to account for experiences that people attributed to the power of God in psychological terms without accusing them of lying or seeking to deceive. As public demonstrations of the power of mesmerism became more common in the 1830s and 1840s, mesmerism became widely available as a way to account for unusual experiences.

Tensions between these two sides of the revival tradition informed the Millerite movement from which Seventh-day Adventism eventually emerged. Although the Millerite movement drew from many denominations and ultimately reflected a wide spectrum of views regarding unusual experiences, Ellen Gould Harmon grew up as a Methodist, and her responses to William Miller and the Great Disappointment of 1844 were shaped by the visionary culture of shouting Methodism. Though the details are somewhat sketchy, we know that Harmon was raised in the Chestnut Street Methodist Church in Portland, Maine, where her father was an exhorter. Sometime during her childhood, a conflict erupted between advocates of "shouting" and advocates of instrumental music, which was won by the latter. The Harmons most likely sympathized with the shouters but did not withdraw from the church.[4]

Ellen Harmon heard William Miller lecture on the imminent second coming of Christ in Portland in 1840. She was deeply impressed by Miller's warnings, and she brought her newly awakened anxiety with her to a Methodist camp meeting where she began to "seek the Lord." Shortly thereafter, she experienced conversion at a prayer meeting. Sometime in her twelfth year, she was baptized, presumably after the traditional six months of probation, and became a formal member of the Methodist church. After attending Miller's second course of lectures in Portland in 1841, Harmon decided she was "not ready for Christ's coming" because, in her words, she had not experienced "the soul-purifying [i.e., sanctifying] effects of the [advent] truth." For the next year or so, she attended both adventist meetings and Methodist class meetings and experienced no contradiction in doing so. She described herself as all the while "hungering and thirsting for holiness of heart," suggesting that she did not distinguish between the purification of soul that she sought in preparation for the second coming and the Methodist experience of sanctification.[5]

Millerism became a subject of great concern in the Methodist conferences of the northeast during the early 1840s. It came up at the Maine annual conference in both 1842 and 1843. By the end of 1843, records of the Maine conference indicate that eight or ten ministers in full connection and three on trial were reproved by the conference and told to abstain from advocating "the peculiarities of Millerism." Portland was the center of advent-oriented Methodism in the conference. Gerschom Cox, Harmon's former minister at the Chestnut Street church, was the most prominent adventist in the conference. As presiding elder of the Portland district and editor of the *Maine Wesleyan Journal*, he was in a position both to promote and protect the Millerite movement in the Portland area. By 1842, Cox's efforts were so successful and, in the eyes of the conference, so detrimental to the church that he was appointed to Orrington, a town outside Bangor. There, a Methodist source recounts, he continued to teach "the doctrines of Miller, to the damage of the strong and flourishing society in that place."[6] The removal of Cox as presiding elder led to the expulsion of Harmon and other Portland-area Millerites from the Methodist church in 1842.

Methodists and Adventists

Between 1842 and 1844, adventist lecturers, known up until that time primarily for their rationalistic exposition of the prophetic texts of the Bible, turned to the Methodist revival tradition as a means of proclaiming their message. By 1842, a year before the predicted Second Coming, the ranks of both believers and opponents had grown dramatically. The growing opposition within the denominations made it more difficult to hold meetings in churches, while burgeoning numbers made it harder to find rental halls suitable for the largest adventist gatherings. At the adventist General Conference held in Boston in 1842, the Millerites, a majority of whom were by that time come-outers from Methodism, voted to adopt the camp-meeting as a means of holding large gatherings and effectively spreading the advent message.[7]

In recasting the camp-meeting for their own purposes, adventists downplayed communion and love feasts, potentially divisive rituals in a movement that had come out from a variety of Protestant traditions, and substituted the by-then traditional adventist lecture with its detailed exegetical charts for the traditional camp-meeting sermon. Despite adventist leaders' efforts to avoid any hint of enthusiasm, adventist camp-meetings did not lack for emotion. Although adventist lectures were rationalistic in tone, their content evoked strong emotional responses. Indeed, while the Millerites' rationalistic exegesis, precise predictions, and pre-millennial eschatology were novel, their effect was to intensify and often revitalize traditional evangelical fears of damnation and longings for the felt-presence of God and heaven.[8]

Adventist emotions were caught up in camp-meeting hymns and spiritual songs, rapidly amended and abridged where necessary to reflect adventist theology. In many cases little adaptation was needed. Much of the practical theology and ritual of the Methodist camp-meeting was appropriated without change. Millerite camp-meetings, for example, continued the shout tradition's focus on Jerusalem, the Jerusalem prefigured in the camp and the new heavenly Jerusalem soon to come. As adventists circled the camp before departing, they typically sang the traditional camp-meeting spiritual "Jerusalem." A song of longing and expectation, tinged with this-worldly sorrow and otherworldly hope, it played off inverse images of departing the camp to return to the world and departing the world for heaven. In the interplay of images, the sorrow of departure from the camp was transformed into longing for the second coming where "we shall our Jesus meet,/And never, never part again." The longing and hope were caught up in the concluding lines of the chorus in a call-and-response dialogue ("What, never part again? No, never part again") popular among both Millerites and Methodists.[9]

Conversion and sanctification remained central to the adventist camp-meeting, the urgency of both only enhanced by the advent message. As at Methodist camp-meetings, convicted sinners came forward to the mourner's bench or the anxious seat and were directed from there to prayer tents after the sermon was over.[10] Those already converted sought sanctification or, as they more commonly put it, strove to "consecrate" themselves more fully in preparation for the coming advent. Milton Perry argues that the adventist camp meetings were less emotional, and in particular gave less evidence of "physical exercises," than Methodist camp meetings. Nonetheless, he presents considerable evidence to the contrary. At a camp-meeting in Kentucky in 1844, for example, the newspaper reported that "the mourners or converts, of whom there were a very large number, threw themselves in the dust and dirt around the pulpit, and for nearly an hour, men and women were praying, singing, shouting, groaning, and weeping bitterly."[11] In the prayer tents, in particular, there was seemingly little restraint. There, the New York Herald reported, "men and women [were] down in the straw lying and sitting in every conceivable posture; praying, shouting, and singing indiscriminately with all their might."[12] The power of God manifested itself at smaller meetings as well. Hiram Edson reports that during a meeting in his home in 1844 a number of people were "so deeply convicted" that they attempted to leave before succumbing to the advent message. While two left, "the third one fell upon the threshold; the fourth, the fifth, and so on, till the most of the company were thus slain by the power of the God." All then lay on the floor, uttering "agonizing cries and pleading for mercy."[13]

In light of the antipathy of the movement's most prominent leaders toward any displays of Methodist-style "enthusiasm," Perry evinces some puzzlement in the face of the abundant evidence of "emotional and ecstatic experiences" among the Millerites.[14] I suspect that he is right in finally attributing the prevalence of such experiences to the disproportionate numbers of Methodist preachers and people in the ranks of the Millerite movement. But knowing that not all Methodists were "shouters," we might also speculate that adventism, especially after it appropriated the camp-meeting tradition, had a disproportionate appeal to those Methodists most steeped in the shout tradition. Ruth Alden Doan has emphasized the supernaturalism inherent in the Millerite movement. "For most Millerites," she points out, "mention of 1843 served as a reminder of a supernatural order so real as to be almost palpably, physically present."[15] For "shouting Methodists," early adventism undoubtedly aroused or intensified traditional longings for the felt-presence of Jesus-in-heaven and precipitated renewed attention to sanctification as a means of preparing for his imminent return. Viewed in light of their intense concern for sanctification, adventist come-outers from Methodism had features in common with both "respectable" holiness advocates, such as Phoebe Palmer, and the more radical holiness "come-outers" of the late-nineteenth century.[16]

The early religious experiences of Ellen Harmon make a great deal of sense when viewed in relation to the Methodist shout tradition. While some scholars have questioned her mental health, her religious experience was not unlike that of the Methodist itinerant preacher Benjamin Abbot. In both cases, dreams and trances played a significant role. Where Abbot had a long and tortuous conversion experience accompanied by significant dreams and a relatively unanguished trance-based sanctification experience, Harmon's conversion was relatively uneventful and her experience of sanctification long and tortuous. The latter process was accompanied by dreams and ended in trance. Her experiences presupposed and elaborated on the shouter's typological reading of the Bible. [17]

Harmon's first dream was set in the heavenly temple in the New Jerusalem. All who entered the temple were expected to "come before the lamb and confess their sins, and then take their place among the happy throng who occupied the elevated seats." In her dream, Harmon was "slowly making [her] way...to face the lamb, when the trumpet sounded, and the building shook, and shouts of triumph went up from the saints in that building" and she was left "alone in the place in great darkness."[18] Here imagery prominent in the shout tradition—the temple, the trumpet, and shouts of triumph—blended with the Adventist imagery of an imminent end.

In the second dream, she met face to face with Jesus, again it seems within the heavenly temple.

> As I entered I saw Jesus, so lovely and beautiful. His countenance expressed benevolence and majesty. I tried to shield myself from his piercing gaze. I thought he knew my heart, and every circumstance of my life. I tried not to look upon his face but still his eyes were upon me. I could not escape his gaze. He then, with a smile, drew near me, and laid his hand upon my head, saying, "Fear not." The sound of his sweet voice, caused me to feel a thrill of happiness I never before experienced. I was too full of joy to utter a word. I grew weak, and fell prostrate at his feet. And while lying helpless, scenes of glory and lasting beauty passed before me. I thought I was saved in heaven. At length my strength returned. I arose upon my feet. The loving eyes of Jesus were fixed upon me still, and he smiled upon me. His presence filled me with such holy awe that I could not endure it.[19]

Here we have an encounter with Jesus that begs to be described as "mesmerizing." The effect of Jesus' gaze stands out. It pierced her heart and seemed to know every circumstance of her life. She tried to shield herself from it, to turn herself away from his face, but his eyes did not leave her and she could not escape it. He broke the spell with a smile and a touch. Harmon, thrilled by the sound of his voice, filled with joy, and unable to utter a word, responded to his presence in the manner of the shout tradition. She fell prostrate and lay helpless while scenes of heavenly glory passed before her eyes.

Shortly after recounting these dreams to her mother and a Methodist minister who was preaching to "the Advent people in Portland," she experienced sanctification at a prayer meeting. There, apparently for the first time, she entered into trance and "the burden and agony of soul" that she had so long felt finally left her. As she described it:

> Wave after wave of glory rolled over me, until my body grew stiff. Everything was shut out from me but Jesus and glory, and I know nothing of what was passing around me. I remained in this state of body and mind a long time, and when I realized what was around me, everything seemed changed. Everything looked glorious and new, as if smiling and praising God.[20]

Here again in its language and imagery and in its use of trance, Harmon's experience of sanctification was entirely in keeping with the Methodist shout tradition.

Although White would not have denied her Methodist heritage, it was largely presupposed in her account. She emphasized the importance of her faith in the imminent second coming of Christ, and indeed her "Methodist" narrative was infused with this expectation. Harmon's expulsion from her Methodist class meeting was precipitated by her refusal to abandon her adventist understanding of her sanctification experience. After testifying in her class meeting shortly after Gershom Cox left Portland for Orrington, her new presiding elder asked Harmon "if it would not be more pleasant to live a long life of holiness here, and do others good, than to have Jesus come and destroy poor sinners." Harmon responded by expressing her longing for the second advent, adding that then "sin would have an end, and we should enjoy sanctification forever."[21]

While this exchange prefigured later controversies over the meaning of holiness, it was only after she left Methodism that Harmon faced opposition as a "shouter." The "shouting Methodist" in Ellen Harmon, in other words, stands out in sharpest relief for us, as indeed it did for her, not while she was among Methodists, where it was still reasonably well accepted, but in adventist meetings filled with "come-outers" from a variety of other Protestant denominations. In a section of her *Experience and Views* titled the "Opposition of Formal Brethren," White recounted the conflict that emerged between herself and the adventist "formalists" at the Portland adventist meetings in 1842. Here, in the unmistakable cadences of the shout tradition, she wrote:

At times the Spirit of the LORD rested upon me in such power that my strength was taken away. This was a trial to some of those who had come out from the formal churches....They did not believe that any one could be so filled with the Spirit of the LORD as to lose their strength.... But soon one of the family which had been most forward in opposing me, while praying fell prostrate like one dead. His friends feared he was dying; but...he regained his strength to praise GOD, and shout with a voice of triumph....While attending an evening meeting I was much blessed, and again lost my strength. Another of the family mentioned, said he had no faith that it was the Spirit of GOD that was upon me.... Bro. R. was immediately prostrated, and as soon as he could give utterance to his feelings, declared that it was of GOD.[22]

As Malcolm Bull and Keith Lockhart have noted, "the intense desire for experience of the divine presence is an aspect of Mrs. White's experience that is often overlooked."[23] While Bull and Lockhart look to St. Teresa and the Catholic mystical tradition for a point of comparison, it was Methodism, and above all the Methodist shout tradition, that provided Ellen Harmon with an initial sense of the form that an experience of the divine presence might take.

Fanatics

While many outsiders viewed the Millerites as fanatics, most adventists did not view fanaticism as a serious threat to their movement until after the Great Disappointment. After October 22 passed, seemingly without event, many left the movement. Those who remained were divided and confused. Within a month prominent leaders, such as Joshua V. Himes, publicly admitted not only that their calculations had been wrong, but that they had erred in attempting to anticipate a definite date. The radicals who rejected this conclusion were typically branded as "fanatics" by the more moderate adventists who renounced dates. The radicals, while remaining committed to the idea of a definite date, differed with respect to particulars. Some sought new dates; others sought to find meaning in the apparent uneventfulness of October 22. Between November 1844 and April 1845, moderates and radicals battled for the loyalties of those who remained in the movement.[24]

In April 1845, probably in response to widely publicized reports of fanaticism in Maine, the moderates held a convention and formed a new denomination, the Advent Christian Church. The new denomination abandoned camp meetings and revivals and denounced the fanaticism of their opponents. They specifically rejected the practices associated with the radicals, stating "we have no confidence in any new messages, visions, dreams, tongues, miracles, extraordinary revelations, impressions, discerning of spirits, or teachings not in accord with the unadulterated word of God."[25]

While the moderates returned to a more traditional understanding of the second coming, the radicals forged ahead in their efforts to understand the significance of October 22. Relying on biblical exegesis and visions, the radicals did not suffer for lack of creative insights into the Great Disappointment. Indeed their problem, as the moderates clearly discerned, was that they had too many solutions and no way to adjudicate among them. Ellen G. White emerged out of this period of exegetical and visionary "enthusiasm" as the prophetess of a new denomination, the Seventh-day Adventists.

This did not happen overnight. Indeed, initially the unmarried Ellen Harmon was only one among a number of radical adventist visionaries attempting to make sense of what had occurred. While by the late 1840s or early 1850s she may have been the only active adventist visionary, sabbath-keeping or sabbatarian adventists had reached no consensus regarding the significance of her visions. [26] Her visions were, in fact, so troubling to many that in 1851 her husband, James White, editor of a widely distributed sabbatarian adventist paper, decided to suspend printing his wife's visions to avoid arousing further controversy (see Chapter 1). It was not until 1855, at a general meeting of the sabbatarian leadership, that James White was replaced by a new editor and Ellen White's visions were again featured in the paper. The move to a new editor signaled a more general acceptance by sabbatarian adventists of the authority of Ellen White's visions and of her status as a prophet of the movement. Those who granted her this status and thus viewed her visions as authoritative began the process of forming the Seventh-day Adventist Church under her visionary leadership six years later.[27]

While the official writings of Ellen G. White and other early sources uncovered by Adventist historians portray the process of "prophet-making" rather differently, both acknowledge the challenge that mesmerism presented to that process. The many volumes of the writings of Ellen G. White published by the Review and Herald Publishing Association, Pacific Press, and Southern Publishing Association, although historically useful, are documents of the church. These documents, including White's narratives of her life experience and her visions, were all edited to a greater or lesser extent by Ellen and James and after James's death by Ellen alone. They reflect their faith that she was called by God as a prophet to the faithful remnant in the wake of the Great Disappointment, challenged by Satan in the guise of mesmerism, and confronted by the opposition of nominal adventists on the one hand and fanatics on the other. Other historical sources discovered by Adventist historians in the last twenty years provide a view of the young Ellen Harmon only hinted at in the official writings. These sources indicate that she was one among a number of adventist visionaries who surfaced in Maine in early 1845 and that she participated fully in the "fanaticism" from which she would later want to distance herself.[28] Taken together, they illustrate how early Seventh-day Adventists "made" a prophetess by demonizing mesmerism. In doing so, Seventh-day Adventists both neutralized mesmerism and inscribed it at the heart of the Seventh-day Adventist cosmos.

Visionaries

Visionaries were common in Maine both before and after October 22. Referring to the earlier period, M. F. Whittier, a non-adventist observer and the brother of John Greenleaf Whittier, wrote that among Portland's "children of light…nothing was more common than visions." He described a teenage girl at one adventist meeting in Portland prior to the Great Disappointment who "descanted upon a sort of vision she had had the night before in which she had seen the awful scenes of the judgment enacted." In fact, Portland's adventists were notorious in Millerite circles for what Joshua Himes described as their "*continual* introduction of *visionary nonsense.*" Combing through secular newspapers published after 1844, Adventist historian Frederick Hoyt identified at least five radical adventist visionaries, in addition to Ellen Harmon, active at the time: William Foy, Emily Clemons, Dorinda Baker, Phoebe Knapp, and Mary Hamlin. According to historian Ingemar Lindén, "women served in leading positions as 'exhorteresses,' teachers and visionaries" in the informal shut-door "bands."[29]

New sources documenting the events of this period suggest that the radical adventists borrowed from the Methodist organizational structure, adopting small groups (bands) as their basic structure with visionaries traveling from group to group to convey their visionary insights regarding October 22. Although these new sources proved disconcerting for many Seventh-day Adventists, they do not so much undercut a careful reading of White's most detailed accounts of this period as heighten our understanding of the crisis of authority radical adventists faced at this time. The most startling new document is a reporter's transcript of the trial of a radical adventist from Atkinson, Maine, named Israel Dammon. Ellen White discussed this incident in the 1860 edition of her *Experience and Views,* indicating that she was present at the meeting, and indeed speaking, when "Elder Damman" [sic] was arrested. Not only was her depiction of Elder Dammon sympathetic, but the story she told about his arrest was cast in the idiom of the shout tradition. When two officers broke into the meeting, she said, "the Spirit of the Lord rested upon him [Dammon], and his strength was taken away, and he fell to the floor helpless." "The power of God," she continued, "was in that room, and the servants of God with their countenances lighted up with his glory, made no resistance." Nonetheless, the officers could neither lift the prostrate Dammon nor "endure the power of God" present in the room. Miraculously, Elder Dammon was "held by the power of God about forty minutes," such that, even with ten additional officers present, they were unable to move him.[30]

What Adventists find troublesome in the newspaper account are details that White left out or glossed over. These details do not so much contradict what White said as force modern Adventists to read her writings differently. Thus, for example, while it is clear from White's description of Dammon's arrest that she viewed him sympathetically, the fact that Dammon is understood by Adventists as one of the more extreme "fanatics" has led them to downplay White's positive assessment of him in her 1860 account. White's elimination of references to Dammon in later versions of her *Experience and Views* assisted in this process. The transcript of the trial, however, undercuts any effort to distance the young Ellen Harmon from Israel Dammon and clearly establishes that when Ellen Harmon spoke at the meeting in Atkinson, it was not to condemn Dammon as a fanatic.[31]

Both White's *Experience and Views* and the trial transcript indicate that Ellen Harmon was traveling from band to band throughout the region in order to relate her December vision. Ellen White's later attempts to distance herself from fanaticism and her negative comments in later writings about "shouting and hallooing" and "noisy" meetings led Adventists to imagine the young Ellen Harmon calmly entering "into vision" at such meetings surrounded by respectful listeners. If any hints of fanaticism were to surface, modern Adventists typically expect that she would have condemned them, given her later outspoken opposition to such things. Adventists also have tended to discount the fact that "nominal Adventists," by White's own account, reckoned her not only as a fanatic, but as the leader of the fanatics. The trial transcript, however, makes clear that the meeting in Atkinson was "noisy," owing to singing and shouting, and involved a number of practices—re-baptizing, hugging, kissing, and crawling on the floor—which most modern Adventists would imagine Ellen White condemning as fanaticism. Probably most shocking to Adventist sensibilities, all who testified, both for the prosecution and for the defense, depict Ellen Harmon lying on the floor in a trance, with James White at times holding her head in his lap.[32]

Finally, and perhaps most significant, White's *Experience and Views* was written in such a way as to give the impression that she alone was having visions. While she made numerous references in her account of her travels to the "impressions and burdens" of fanatics, modern Adventist readers typically have not interpreted these as references to the visions of other radical adventists. The trial transcript is, thus, startling in its references to the *two* "vision women"—Sister Dorinda Baker of Orrington and Sister Ellen Harmon of Portland—who spent much of the meeting in trance. According to the testimony at the trial, the witnesses all agreed that the two women spent much of the meeting lying on their backs on the floor "in a trance." One witness, Isley Osborn, described the vision women as "los[ing] their strength and fall[ing] on the floor."[33] William Crosby described Harmon "occasionally arous[ing] up and tell[ing] a vision which she said was revealed to her." Jacob Mason described her as "in a vision, part of the time insensible." According to Joel Doore, "the vision woman would lay looking up when she came out of her trance—she would point to some one, and tell them their cases, which she said was from the Lord." Numerous witnesses testified to their belief in the authenticity of both women's visions. As Joel Doore said: "We believe her (Miss Baker's) visions genuine. We believe Miss Harmon's genuine—t'was our understanding that their visions were from God."[34]

What the witnesses referred to as "revealing" or "describing out their cases" is reminiscent of a young Methodist woman, who just a year earlier had been correctly perceiving "the characters of different persons who enter[ed] the room, and...address[ing] them in reproofs, or exhortation to prayer and praise" while in trance.[35] In the adventist band, the witnesses indicated that what was revealed to the women in their visions had to do with the "cases" of band-members, that is with their faith and practice. Harmon apparently informed two young women that if they were not rebaptized they would go to hell. They were rebaptized later that evening. George Woodbury said he "believe[d] in Miss Harmon's visions, because she told my wife's feelings correctly." Harmon, according to Woodbury, told his wife and daughters that "if they did not do as she said, they would go to hell."[36] Sister Baker, according to Loton Lambert, said that Joel Doore "had doubted, and would not be baptized again—she said Br. Doore don't go to hell." Joel Doore testified that she gave him the message that he had "thought hard of her," which he acknowledged was the case. Both Lambert and Doore indicate that Doore confessed his error and that Baker and Doore "kissed each other with the holy kiss."[37]

If we read Ellen G. White's later account of her visits to the various advent bands in Maine and New Hampshire in light of this contemporary account, the presence of conflict between competing visionaries and within groups becomes evident. In Exeter, for example, "a heavy burden" rested on her until she related what she had been "shown concerning some fanatical persons present, who were exalted by the spirit of Satan." While she did not go into detail with respect to the beliefs or practices of these "fanatical persons," she did say that "they trusted every impression, and laid aside reason and judgment."[38] She also indicated that there was "fanaticism" present in the band that met at her parents' house in Portland. Two rival visionaries followed "impressions and burdens, which led to corruption, instead of purity and holiness." A "fanatic" named Joseph Turner, she reported, "labored with some success to turn my friends, and even my relatives, against me...[b]ecause I had faithfully related what was shown me respecting his unchristian course."[39]

Adventists and Mesmerism

It was in this context that charges of mesmerism started to be bandied about. As White explained in her later writings, "if the Spirit of the Lord rested upon a brother or sister in meeting, and they glorified God by praising him, some raised the cry of mesmerism. And if it pleased the Lord to give me a vision in a meeting, some would say, '[i]t is excitement and mesmerism.'"[40] Adventists in Maine probably knew of mesmerism by word-of-mouth and through notices and discussions of mesmeric lectures in the newspapers. Phineas P. Quimby, who later gained recognition for his cure of Mary Baker Eddy, was one of the better known mesmerizers performing "public experiments" in Maine during this period. He grew up in the town of Belfast, a few miles south of Bangor, and learned of mesmerism from the Frenchman Charles Poyen when he lectured there in 1838. After some searching he found a sensitive subject, Lucius Berkmar, who readily assumed the role of clairvoyant somnambule. Together they traveled throughout Maine and New Brunswick from 1843 to 1847. In 1847, Berkmar left Quimby to accompany Universalist minister John Bovee Dods on the lecture circuit.[41]

In 1845, Ellen Harmon was confronted directly by "a physician who was a celebrated mesmerizer." He told her "that [her] views were mesmerism, that [she] was a very easy subject, and that he could mesmerize [her] and give [her] a vision." She responded by telling him "that the Lord ha[d] shown [her] in a vision that mesmerism was from the devil, from the bottomless pit, and that it would soon go there, with those who continued to use it." Although the physician proved unable to induce a vision, people continued to ascribe her visions to "excitement and mesmerism." Despondent in the face of such charges, she went off to pray alone. There, too, she found that "JESUS seemed very near" and "the sweet light of heaven" would shine around her and she would enter into a trance. When she pointed out that she had solitary visions, people told her that "[she] mesmerized [her]self, and that those who lived the nearest to God were most liable to be deceived by Satan." She argued that "according to this teaching, our only safety from delusion was to remain quite a distance from God." These charges of mesmerism, she recounted, "wounded [her] spirit, and wrung [her] soul in keen anguish, well nigh to despair." Critics, she said, "would have [her] believe that there was no Holy Spirit, and that all the exercises that holy men of God have experienced, were only mesmerism or the deception of Satan."[42]

While struggling with these doubts, she continued to receive visions spelling out the errors of other radical adventists. When she passed the messages on to God's "erring children" as instructed, many of them "wholly rejected the message" and charged her with "conforming to the world." While White positioned herself in her later accounts as an opponent of fanaticism, she indicates that the moderates, whom she referred to as "nominal Adventists," charged *her* with fanaticism. Some, she says, even "falsely...represented [her] as being the leader of the fanaticism that

[she] was laboring to do away." The editor of the leading moderate newspaper, the *Advent Herald,* was, she said, among those who believed her visions "to be 'the result of mesmeric operations.' "[43]

It was in this "confusion," as she called it, that she was "sometimes tempted to doubt [her] own experience." The crisis came to a head one morning at family worship as "the power of God began to rest upon [her]." When "the thought rushed into [her] mind that it was mesmerism," she was immediately "struck dumb." Like John Wesley, who concluded he had sinned in attributing bodily exercises to animal spirits, so too Ellen White saw her "sin in doubting the power of God." When, as she predicted, her tongue was "loosed" less than twenty-four hours later, she "shout[ed] the high praises of God."[44] Both John Wesley and Ellen White rejected secular explanations of their experiences and continued to attribute them to the "power of God." Knowing full well that many believed them deluded, both Wesley and White continued to find God's presence in or through involuntary experiences.

The gap between the trial transcript and the *Experience and Views* of Ellen White reveals something of the process through which Ellen Harmon, initially one of several radical adventist visionaries, became Ellen G. White, the prophet of Seventh-day Adventism. The trial transcript helps us see more clearly the crisis of authority generated by the radical adventists' reliance on visionary solutions to the Great Disappointment. Although many of the radicals agreed that something momentous had occurred on October 22 and that the door of salvation had been shut to those who did not believe, they depended on visionaries for details of what had occurred. Without the interpretive limits and powers of enforcement typically vested in ecclesiastical institutions, visionary solutions rapidly resulted in competition and conflict. While some radicals backtracked once they experienced the hermeneutical chaos, those who were to found the Seventh-day Adventist Church forged ahead. Having opened the door to visions early on, they solved the problem of multiple solutions by granting one of the many visionaries the status of prophet and interpreting her prophetic visions, not as new revelation, but an authoritative guide to scripture.[45] In retrospect, we can see the synergistic relationship between the formation of the denomination, given its early commitment to visionary experience, and the emergence of a prophet, that is, an authoritative visionary.

This is not the only way it could have gone. Instead of creating an authoritative visionary or prophet, the sabbatarian adventists could have created an authoritative *set* of visions, that is a canon, generated by more than one visionary. Had they chosen the latter route, it would suggest, as in the case of early Christianity, that no one (visionary) interpretation was sufficient or otherwise strong enough to win out over its competitors. The fact that an authoritative visionary did emerge suggests that Ellen White brought something more to the task than her competitors. Two factors come immediately to mind, both speculative, given the current state of the historical research. First, I think it is likely that White's visions spoke more consistently to the needs of the movement both in terms of content and timing than did those of her competitors. Second, and at least as important, the "symbiotic relationship" between Ellen and James White, to borrow Jonathan Butler's phrase, provided Ellen White and her visions with a forceful promoter that the other visionaries lacked.[46] It was James's belief in his wife's visions that made the early 1850s such a crucial period of transition. By keeping Ellen's visions out of his paper, he in effect pulled back, allowing other sabbatarian adventists an opportunity to decide whether they wanted to proceed with or without a prophet. Their assent was crucial, for without it Ellen and James could not have cofounded a church.

"Fanaticism" and "mesmerism" came to symbolize the two primary threats Ellen Harmon White faced as she made the passage from adventist visionary to Adventist prophetess. "Fanaticism" represented the threat of competing visionaries and "mesmerism" the threat of secular explanations of visionary experience. In his introduction to the first published edition of his wife's *Experience and Views*, James White confronted these two primary threats directly. In 1851, three years after the first spirits "rapped" in upstate New York, James White wrote:

> We are well aware that many honest seekers after truth and Bible holiness are prejudiced against visions. Two great causes have created this prejudice. First, fanaticism, accompanied by false visions and exercises, [and] [s]econdly, the exhibition of mesmerism, and what is commonly called the "mysterious rapping."

Fanaticism with its counterfeits, he argued, was always with us, while mesmerism, he correctly implied, was a newer phenomenon. With respect to the latter, he said, "we," presumably referring to himself and Ellen, "have ever considered it dangerous [and] therefore have had nothing to do with it." To distance themselves further, he added, "We never even saw a person in mesmeric sleep and know nothing of the art by experience." The subtext here was clear. Unlike some of their Methodist contemporaries who had experimented with mesmerism, James and Ellen White insisted that they had *not*. The reader was to understand, without it having to be said, that James was not a mesmerist and Ellen was not a clairvoyant somnambule.[47]

The historical newness of mesmerism did not detract from its cosmic significance. Indeed, like the Methodists who believed the disciples must have shouted at Pentecost, Ellen White believed that opponents of adventism would have accused even Jesus of fanaticism and mesmerism. Referring to the dispute over the disciples praising God "with a loud voice" as Jesus entered into Jerusalem (a key passage in the shout tradition), Ellen White commented:

> A large portion of those who profess to be looking for Christ would be as forward as the Pharisees were to have the disciples silenced, and they would doubtless raise the cry, "Fanaticism! Mesmerism! Mesmerism!" And the disciples, spreading their garments and branches of palm trees in the way, would be thought extravagant and wild. But God will have a people on the earth who will not be so cold and dead but that they can praise and glorify Him.[48]

While adventists, like the disciples, were falsely accused, "true" fanatics and mesmerizers were demonized. Just as fanatics were "exalted by the spirit of Satan" and those who did not heed her visions were destined for hell, so it was revealed to her in a vision that "mesmerism was from the devil" and that those who used it would be damned. White expanded on these views in her first extended statement on psychology, published in the *Review and Herald* in 1862. There she described the way that Satan was using "the science of the human mind" to make "the miracles and works of Christ" look as if they were "the result of human skill and power." "The sciences of phrenology, psychology, and mesmerism are the channel," she said, "through which he [Satan] comes more directly to this generation and works with that power which is to characterize his efforts near the close of probation." Imperceptibly, Satan was gaining access to human minds through these sciences, and eventually would "destroy faith in Christ's being the Messiah, the Son of God."[49] While not a particularly sophisticated attack on either fanaticism or mesmerism, demonization effectively neutralized both threats for those willing to accept White's prophetic authority.

NOTES

1. For the song, see *The Chorus*, compiled by A. S. Jenks and D. S. Gilkey (Philadelphia, 1860), #241, quoted in Winthrop S. Hudson, "Shouting Methodists," *Encounter* 29 (1968): 73. For a discussion of the shout tradition, see Ann Taves, *Fits, Trances, and Visions: Experiencing Religion and Explaining Experience* (Princeton, NJ: Princeton University Press, 1999), 76–117, from which much of this chapter was taken.

2. Joseph A. Conforti, *Jonathan Edwards, Religious Tradition, and American Culture* (Chapel Hill: University of North Carolina Press, 1995), 17, 22.

3. On the early history of mesmerism in America, see Adam Crabtree, *From Mesmer to Freud: Magnetic Sleep and the Roots of Psychological Healing* (New Haven: Yale University Press, 1993), 213–18; and Chapter 11 of this volume.

4. Ronald Graybill, "Methodist Roots of the Adventist Tradition," unpublished paper, Loma Linda University, Department of Archives and Special Collections.

5. I use "adventists" in lower case as a synonym for followers of William Miller prior to 1844 and as a general way to encompass both moderates and radicals after 1844. I modify adventist with terms such as moderate, radical, or "shut-door" when referring to various subgroups within the movement after 1844. I capitalize Adventist only when used to refer to members of an adventist denomination (i.e., the Advent Christian Church or the Seventh-day Adventist Church).

6. Rev. Stephen Allen and Rev. W. H. Pilsbury, *History of Methodism in Maine, 1793–1886* (Augusta: Charles E. Nash, 1887), 118, 121–22; Graybill, "Methodist Roots," 5. On the connection between adventism and revivalism, see Milton Perry, "The Role of the Camp Meeting in Millerite Revivalism, 1842–1844" (Ph.D. dissertation, Baylor University, 1994), 2.

7. Perry, "Role of the Camp Meeting," 20–22. Using the affiliation of 174 adventist lecturers in 1843–1844, Everett N. Dick estimated the percentage of Methodists at 44%, Baptists 27%, Congregationalists 9%, Christians 8%, Presbyterians 7%; see Everett N. Dick, "The Millerite Movement, 1830–1845," in *Adventism in America*, ed. Gary Land (Grand Rapids, MI: Eerdmans, 1986), 1.

8. Perry, "Role of the Camp Meeting," 170–77, 207–8, 213–17, 236–66; Ruth Alden Doan, "Millerism and Evangelical Culture," in *The Disappointed: Millerism and Millenarianism in the Nineteenth Century*, ed. Ronald L. Numbers and Jonathan M. Butler (Bloomington: Indiana University Press, 1987), 118–32, esp. 118–22.

9. "Never Part," in John G. McCurry, *Social Harp* (1855; reprint ed., Athens: University of Georgia Press, 1973), 94.

10. Formal "prayer tents" started to appear at Methodist camp-meetings during the 1820s, perhaps replacing the more informal prayer circles and tent gatherings that had preceded them.

11. *Louisville Morning Courier*, Oct. 1, 1844, quoted in Perry, "Role of the Camp Meeting," 256.

12. *New York Herald Extra*, 7, quoted in Perry, "Role of the Camp Meeting," 262.

13. Undated manuscript fragment attributed to Hiram Edson, published in Numbers and Butler, *The Disappointed*, 214–15.

14. Perry, "Role of the Camp Meeting," 258.

15. Doan, "Millerism and Evangelical Culture," 119–38.

16. Ruth Alden Doan, *The Miller Heresy: Millennialism, and American Culture* (Philadelphia: Temple University Press, 1987), 214. Doan emphasizes what she refers to as the "radical supernaturalism" of the Millerites.

17. The classic scholarly study of Ellen G. White is Ronald L. Numbers, *Prophetess of Health: A Study of Ellen G. White*, 3rd ed. (Grand Rapids, MI: William B. Eerdmans, 2008). In an afterword, Ronald and Janet Numbers discuss the question of White's mental health, concluding that "from youth onward she suffered from recurrent episodes of depression and anxiety to which she responded with somatizing defenses and a histrionic personality style" (203).

18. Ellen G. White, *Spiritual Gifts*, 4 vols. (Battle Creek, MI: James White, 1858–64), 2: 17–18 (1860).

19. Ibid., 2: 19.

20. Ellen G. White, "Experience and Views" (August 1851) in *Early Writings of Ellen G. White* (Washington, DC: Review and Herald Publishing Assn., 1882), 12; White, *Spiritual Gifts*, 2: 20.

21. White, *Spiritual Gifts*, 2: 21–22.

22. Ibid., 2: 26–28.

23. Malcolm Bull and Keith Lockhart, *Seeking a Sanctuary: Seventh-day Adventism and the American Dream* (San Francisco: Harper & Row, 1989), 20.

24. David L. Rowe, *Thunder and Trumpets: The Millerite Movement and Dissenting Religion in Upstate New York, 1800–1850* (Chico, CA: Scholars Press, 1985), 141–50.

25. Ibid., 155; "Proceedings of the Mutual Conference of Adventists held in the City of Albany, the 29th and 30th of April, and 1st of May 1845," (New York, 1845), 30, quoted in Ingemar Lindén, *1844 and the Shut Door Problem* (Uppsala: Almqvist and Wiksell, 1982), 8.

26. I am using the terms "sabbath-keeping" and "sabbatarian" to designate those adventists who regarded Saturday rather than Sunday as the sabbath. This was to become a distinctive feature of the Seventh-day Adventists.

27. Numbers, *Prophetess of Health*, 27–30; Jonathan M. Butler, "Prophecy, Gender, and Culture: Ellen Gould Harmon (White) and the Roots of Seventh-day Adventism," *Religion and American Culture* 1 (1991): 3–29, esp. 19–23.

28. "Trial of Elder I. Dammon," *Piscataquis Farmer*, March 7, 1845, reprinted in Frederick Hoyt, "Trial of Elder I. Dammon Reported for the *Piscataquis Farmer*," *Spectrum: Journal of the Association of Adventist Forums* 17, no. 5 (1987): 29–36,

hereafter referred to as *Spectrum*; Numbers and Butler, eds., *The Disappointed*, 2nd ed. (Knoxville: University of Tennessee Press, 1993), 227–40; Bruce Weaver, "Incident in Atkinson: The Arrest and Trial of Israel Dammon," *Adventist Currents* (April 1988): 16–36. For discussions of the charges of mesmerism, see Butler, "Prophecy, Gender, and Culture," 13, 16; and Numbers, *Prophetess of Health*, 22–24.

29. *Portland Transcript*, Nov. 1, 1945 [sic], quoted in Frederick Hoyt, "We Lift Up Our Voices Like a Trumpet: Millerites in Portland, Maine," *Spectrum* 17, no.5 (1987): 19–20; Rennie B. Schoepflin, ed., "Scandal or Rite of Passage: Historians on the Dammon Trial," *Spectrum* 17 (No. 5, 1987): 39; Butler, "Prophecy, Gender, and Culture," 9; Lindén, *1844*, 34, note 40. "Bands" were small groups of devout adventists, who likely were meeting in order to purify their souls in preparation for the second coming.

30. White, *Spiritual Gifts*, 2: 40–41.

31. Lindén, *1844*, 50–51.

32. Numbers and Butler, eds., *The Disappointed*, 2nd ed., 233.

33. Isley Osborn testimony in Hoyt, "Trial," 234.

34. Joel Doore testimony in Hoyt, "Trial," 235.

35. Taves, *Fits, Trances, and Visions*, 145.

36. Testimony of Isley Osborn and George S. Woodbury in Hoyt, "Trial," 234–35.

37. Testimony of Loton Lambert and Joel Doore in Hoyt, "Trial," 230, 235. According to Lindén, the early EGW letters from the forties typically "include visions and direct 'messages' to various individuals" (Lindén, *1844*, 49).

38. White, *Spiritual Gifts*, 2: 39, 45.

39. Ibid., 2: 50–51.

40. Ibid., 2: 57.

41. Horatio W. Dresser, *The Quimby Manuscripts* (New Hyde Park, NY: University Books, 1969), 30–47.

42. White, "Experience," 21–22; White, *Spiritual Gifts*, 2: 57–58, 62–63; Numbers, *Prophetess of Health*, 22–24. Numbers notes that White "distanced herself from other trance mediums not on the basis of physical evidence, but spiritual content" (214).

43. White, "Experience," 22–23; White, *Spiritual Gifts*, 2:58.

44. White, *Spiritual Gifts*, 2: 59.

45. Trustees of the Ellen G. White Estate, "Historical Prologue" (1963) in Ellen G. White, *Early Writings* (Washington, DC: Review and Herald Publishing Assn., 1882, 1945), xxiii–xxiv.

46. Jonathan Butler makes this argument in Schoepflin, "Scandal," 45.

47. James White, "Preface" (1851), in Ellen G. White, *Early Writings*, vi. For a discussion of a Methodist minister and his wife who did experiment with mesmerism, see Taves, *Fits, Trances, and Visions*, 143–44.

48. *Advent Review and Sabbath Herald*, 3 (June 10, 1852), hereafter referred to as *Review and Herald*, in Ellen G. White, *Early Writings*, 109. I am grateful to Michael Zbaraschuk for locating this reference.

49. *Review and Herald* 12 (1862), in Ellen G. White, *Testimonies for the Church*, 9 vols. (Mountain View, CA: Pacific Press, 1948), 1: 290–91 (Testimony No. 7, 1862).

3

Testimonies

Graeme Sharrock

ON THURSDAY, OCTOBER 8, 1857, James and Ellen White traveled by wagon from Caledonia, Michigan, south to the village of Monterey for a preaching appointment. Arriving at the schoolhouse where local Adventists were gathering, the Whites were unsure what theme to speak on, so they encouraged the believers to fill the time by singing and praying, and waited for inspiration.

Then, unexpectedly, because her husband usually preached first, Ellen, not yet thirty years old, stood to speak and soon the meeting was "filled with the Spirit of the Lord." The feelings of the faithful quickly intensified; some were joyful, others wept. When seated again, Ellen continued to pray aloud, "higher and higher in perfect triumph in the Lord, till her voice changed, and the deep, clear shouts of Glory! Hallelujah! thrilled every heart." Ellen was in vision.

In her audience sat Victor Jones, a poor farmer and heavy drinker trying to reform his life and better care for his wife and young son. As James wrote for the church paper a few days later, Ellen delivered a "most touching and encouraging message." The man "raised his head that very evening, and he and his good wife are again happy in hope. Monterey church will never forget that evening. At least they never should."[1]

Yet Ellen did not disclose all of her vision in the meeting. Next morning she walked a mile to the nearby home of Brother Rumery, a local church leader and community pioneer present the previous evening, hoping to "speak plainly" to him. Nearing the house, she stopped and instead returned and wrote him a letter. Confident she had kept the vision confidential, she concluded with the following paragraph and sent the letter off:

Dear Brother Rumery, I came to your house purposely to tell you the vision but my heart sank within me. I knew my weakness and knew I should feel the deepest distress for you while relating it to you, and I was afraid I should not have the strength to do it, and should mar the work. Now brother, I am afflicted and distressed for you, and when at your house was *so burdened* I could not stay. I send this communication to you with much trembling. I fear from what I have seen that your efforts will be too weak. You will make no change. Oh, will you get ready for Jesus' coming? *I kept the vision from every one*, even my husband, but I must speak plainly to you. You must have a thorough work done for you or you will fail of heaven. Said the angel, "It is easier for a camel to go through a needle's eye, than for a rich man to enter the kingdom of God." Luke 18:25.[2]

Starting in the late 1840s, Ellen—or "Mrs. E. G. White" as readers came to know her—wrote hundreds of such personal letters, known as "testimonies," to individuals, families, and churches. From these intimate epistles, she forged an extraordinary career as a religious leader and writer of pamphlets, periodical articles, and books on topics ranging from biblical interpretation to health care, organizational development, and Christian spirituality. Although few expected to ever receive one, her testimony letters helped mold the fragmented Millerite movement into a new American religion denomination. The testimony letter remains Ellen White's distinctive literary signature.

Modern readers encounter these letters in nine red or black hard-bound volumes known as *Testimonies for the Church*—elegant cloth editions with corrected spelling, improved grammar, and the identities of the original recipients disguised by editors. Largely stripped of places and dates of writing, they have been read for 150 years in a deepening social and historical void. Some readers project special religious powers upon them while others have denigrated them as relics of an outmoded worldview. Clearly, the testimonies are no ordinary letters, but what are they?[3] Fortunately, more than a hundred of White's antebellum letters and manuscripts have been preserved, along with a few printed editions, accommodating research into their origins and role in early Adventism.[4]

Testimonies: Evangelical, Millerite, Adventist

In her testimony letters, Ellen White adapted a literary and rhetorical standby familiar to the Anglo-American legal and religious traditions and rich in cultural resonances. As discourses presenting an eyewitness viewpoint, secular and religious testimonies emerged after the American Revolution as important tools of public persuasion. Whether delivered as "exhortations" in a Methodist social meeting or proclaimed in a court of law, they were customarily transcribed from oral discourses and verified by the signature of the speaker or other witnesses. Religious examples reflected the Puritan emphasis on individual experience—personal narratives, confessions of faith, signs of divine workings in the soul—linking their authority to that of the Spirit through visions, voices, dreams, and providences. Whether published as broadsides or pamphlets or in denominational periodicals, the testimonies of emerging spiritual leaders harmonized their life experience with the core narratives of Christianity.[5]

Among the Millerites of the 1840s, *testimony* carried the common evangelical meanings, along with expressions of confidence in the imminent Second Coming of Christ. Even finer theological nuances arose among those who followed the revisions of Millerism advocated by James and Ellen White and their circle, known as Bridegroom and later Sabbatarian Adventists (see Chapter 9). Their solution to the problem of the "Great Disappointment" (the failed prediction of the Second Coming of Christ, on October 22, 1844) proposed that Miller was right as to the date, but wrong regarding the event. The fateful day instead marked the start of Judgment Day—a complex event centered not on earth but in heaven. With a dramatic cast of adjudicating Father, advocating Son, accusing Satan, and angelic clerks writing names and deeds in a book, this apocalyptic scene provided an ordering framework for all aspects of human life, especially for the faithful. The very first rule for reading the Bible, claimed a writer in the church paper, was "NEVER open the Book of God, without remembering that you must be tried by it at the judgment seat of Christ." Separated from unbelieving society and formed into small "bands" as they waited for the End of the World, they "carefully examined every thought and emotion" while experiencing deep raptures of hope and love—a scene that crystallized the ideals of community found in her subsequent testimonies. With the grand audit or "cleansing" of the heavenly realm already under way, White's early testimonies reported on the progress of "cases" in the proceedings and outlined the purification of heart and life expected of earthly believers.[6]

Within a few weeks of the Great Disappointment, White experienced her first "holy vision" in which she visited heaven, talked with Jesus, and saw "events all in the future" before returning to the earth (see Chapter 2). At meetings throughout New England, she fell into trances and analyzed the spiritual condition of individuals, seeming to read into their very souls. The visions offered consolations to those stymied by the failure of Miller's predictions, conveying divine sympathy for their plight and compensating for the scorn of newspapers and neighbors. White mentioned her visions in letters to friends and family and published a few in Millerite periodicals or as broadsides with local printers.[7]

Falling into trance, having a vision, and writing it out was arduous work for a young, illness-prone, and barely educated woman such as Ellen Harmon. The process of writing gave expression to her acute moral and social sensitivities, relieving her "burdens" or intense religious feelings. "It was not until I began to have visions that I could write so anyone could read it," she wrote in a later autobiographical manuscript. "One day the impression came to me as strong as if some one had spoken it, 'Write, write your experiences.' I took up a pen, and found my hand perfectly steady, and from that day to this it has never failed me." By the time the printed version came off the press, however, the "impression" had become an angel's voice, the "experiences" specified as visions, and taking up the pen was in response to a divine command. In this way, White reified her spiritual experiences to produce a lifetime of testimonies and other writings while remaining true to her inner world of images and voices.[8]

How to Recognize a Testimony when You See One

Each year, Ellen White wrote dozens of testimonies and hundreds of pages expressing her convictions and persuading Adventists to change their attitudes and habits. Not all of her letters were testimonies, however, so how would a recipient know? Growing out of White's regular familial correspondence, the testimony letter developed over a decade into a distinguishable document with a definable structure, standard sentence types, stock arguments, and repeated rhetorical strategies. Although shorter testimonies might lack or truncate portions, the letter usually followed this order (most of the following examples are from the letter to Brother Rumery):

Date, place of writing, and salutation. Most addressees are readily identifiable, including those stated as "Dear Brother...," "Dear Sister...," or "Friend." Occasionally, she played with a name, displaying satire or irony such as "Victory Jones" or "Sir Emory Fisk." These formal features become standardized early in her life and rarely changed over the years.

Occasion of writing. The opening sentence or two linked the letter to a recent vision and announced the subject of the testimony. Reading this sentence was the recipient's first clue that he or she had received a testimony letter. "You remember the vision given last Thurs. evening," she wrote to Brother Rumery. "In that vision I saw the case of Brother Victor Jones...."

Announcement of theme. In a few sentences, White summarized the general topic of the testimony and identified its principal persons. She often expressed the theme as a general complaint, or as a failure to exhibit certain traits or perform certain actions. For example, "I saw that the Lord loved him [Jones] but he had reasons for discouragement...," she announced in the same letter. "He looked for and expected to find the same disposition in his brethren but was disappointed. They said by their profession we are pilgrims and strangers, yet their heart and treasure were here." From this summary, the remainder of the letter expanded on the themes of discouragement/encouragement, wealth/poverty, and profession/practice.

Analysis of case(s). Using moral language mixed with religious images and ideas, White compared her subject's behavior or spiritual condition, as she saw it, with her own moral and social ideals. "Brother Rumery, you could have in many little acts have eased Brother Jones' burden, and never felt it," she opened her analysis of Rumery's case, "but for years you have loved money better than religion, better than God." Viewing current problems as continuous with the past, she referenced her subjects' life histories in the longer testimonies. Fully developed testimonies contained extended discussion of several linked "cases" and ran ten or twenty written pages.

Call to action. The testimony followed analytical with prescriptive language, usually a required response mixed with the language of appeal. Most often, White used imperative forms from biblical passages—"earnestly seek the Lord," "do not become discouraged," "cleanse your heart," and so forth, but also borrowed contemporary idioms. "You must cut loose, cut loose from the world," she insisted to Brother Rumery.

Warrants and principles. In order to reinforce her analysis and call to action, White called upon a half-dozen commonplace beliefs. As we have seen, her readers assumed the Adventist worldview with its apocalyptic images: Judgment scenes, an omniscient deity, record-keeping angels, and the shortness of time available to humans. If she referenced a person's sins or secrets, readers could assume that she was accessing in her visions the life histories kept by "recording angels." She also relied on moral and social ciphers accepted by most American evangelicals, such as the ban on "worldliness"—a term whose meaning varied from group to group, but which typically prohibited amusements, frivolity, and preoccupation with material matters. "Reform," on the other hand, was code for earnest concern with personal and social change. She was steeped in the language of sentimental theology that proposed shared feelings between the human and divine realms, and salvation through transformation of the affections. In these instances, she described the feelings and facial expressions of Jesus, trusting such imagery would evoke sympathy and self-reflection in her readers.

Appeal. Toward the end of each testimony, White made appeals to her readers to embrace the changes she had outlined. The mature testimony frequently appealed to particular emotions: fear, hope, anxiety, love, and sympathy. The spiritual outcome most feared was to "be left to themselves," "in darkness," or "unaware" that the Spirit had left a person or church. In her most eloquent appeals, White invoked the popular evangelical trope of the sufferings of Christ in his betrayal and death on the cross, asking believers to measure their meager inconveniences against the infinite sacrifice of Christ their "Example." Accustomed to the rhetorical strategies of sentimentalist writers such as Harriett Beecher Stowe, readers viewed such appeals as encouragement to face awkward feelings or espouse unpopular causes.[9]

Personal note. Sometimes White added a short note of greeting, an expression of love to family members, a request for her correspondent to make a copy and return the original, or instructions regarding the reading of the letter to others. The final paragraph of her testimony to Brother Rumery explained her intense "distress" and failure to arrive at his home that morning.

Sign-off. The concluding phrase White commonly used in all her correspondence echoed the urgent sense of time and the supreme social value expressed in the Millerite and Adventist communities. Although sometimes abbreviated, it rarely changed over the years: "In haste and love, Ellen G. White." But to Brother Rumery she signed off, "In trial, E. G. White."

Audiences: Individuals, Families, Churches

Adventists lived in a transparent universe. Angels scrutinized every act and word; the gaze of believing and unbelieving neighbors was continuously on church members. "I was shown, Mary, that many idle words have fallen from your lips," White wrote to her close friend Mary Loughborough. "If the recording angel should place them before you, it would astonish, distress, and alarm you." Messages tailored to individuals were needed because humans, unable to perceive the heavenly realm—or peer into their own souls or interpret the actions of others—were oblivious to the causes and consequences of their actions. "Brother and Sister Wright...could have seen and understood the spirit of Sister Booth, from observation," White wrote to friends, "and if they had stood free in God could have discerned the spirit, acts, and words, and the character developed. But they failed to see." The testimonies met this deficit by mediating knowledge from hidden sources, but she expected her readers to develop the self-insight to view and correct themselves.[10]

While White wrote most often to individuals, the best of her analyses emerge in her letters to families. As young parents, James and Ellen White traveled and visited homes in New England, observing the piety, parenting styles, and domestic practices of their hosts. "I saw that our keeping house has discovered selfishness in your families," she wrote to one family in the summer of 1851, "and I saw that there has not been true faith in the visions." The two families were joined by an emotional "link" that should be "broken" because it produced collusion rather than mutual strengthening and growth in grace. Each family needed to stand more "separate" and direct their love to Jesus, if they wanted to have "vital godliness and heart holiness."[11]

Like a modern family therapist, White used her powers of moral discernment and social observation—including critical attention to stories and snippets of conversation—along with her growing experience as a parent, to craft prescriptions for a happier and holier life. When young women wrote for advice on family matters, she answered using notes from her visits and visions. Certain types and motifs appear regularly in the testimonies: the garrulous wife undermining her husband's authority; the impulsive socialite whose unthinking actions bring bewilderment to others; the hypocrisy of religiosity that covers an underlying lack of genuine spiritual experience; overly sympathetic parents who fail to discipline their children; the unkempt and slovenly housewife; the minister who competes with or openly disrespects his fellow ministers; the elderly church leader who resists passing the baton to younger leadership. Just as middle-class mothers relied on Catherine Beecher's rules for cleanliness and amusements in her *Treatise on Domestic Economy*, the testimonies became the official source of rules and practices of domesticity for Adventist families.[12]

White's concern with character and influence expanded from individuals to larger units of believers, where the increased social and spiritual effect—either positive or negative—counted for or against the credibility of Adventism, especially in small rural towns where most believers lived. Testimonies for the church as a whole, usually addressing the spiritual health of the widespread body, were usually read at conferences and quickly printed in the church paper. She adapted and focused the testimony to the needs of the Adventist community, mediating between divine expectations and human capabilities while protecting the church's reputation.

Writing: Composition, Circulation, Reception

When Ellen White went into vision during a public meeting, associates such as James White or Hiram Edson often took notes of her utterances, which she later used to reconstruct her memory and write out her interpretation of the vision. She then addressed a letter to the subjects of the vision—a page or two up to twenty or more—describing their role in it and urging them to follow its prescriptions. A single vision, if it concerned several people or families, could generate five or ten letters, which were "circulated" to an even wider readership.

After writing, White visited the subject and read it aloud in their presence—if an individual, at his or her home; if a church or conference, before the assembly. If the recipient was not local, she mailed the letter to the named person or an associate, with instructions to pass it along to any other persons mentioned in the letter or to read it before a church gathering. Occasionally, as in a letter to the Kellogg family of Battle Creek, she waited a year or more after a vision before sending a testimony.[13]

Once the testimony was delivered, White "anxiously watched the result, and if the individual reproved rose up against it, and afterwards opposed the truth, these queries would arise in my mind. Did I deliver the message just as I should?" She sometimes met with and observed the person and her family, looking for signs of improvement. As she told Angelina Andrews, "I read over the testimony frequently for you and sister Mary...and inquire in my own mind, Are they living up to the testimony?" White then inquired of others to discover what Angelina had been doing about it before she calculated and sent her response.[14]

In return for the letter, she hoped for the original back, along with an acknowledgment of the accuracy of the visions and a "confession" of all wrongs. Others wrote back asking for clarification, or expressed gratitude and regret while promising to reform. Many of the surviving responses seem to follow a prescribed outline: I received your letter, I thank God that he notices me, I acknowledge my errors, I will try to do better.[15]

Readers: Believers, Resisters, Defenders

No one, it seems, expected to receive a testimony letter from White. Its arrival might throw its subject into a moral crisis—a person might "break in pieces" and engage in a "thorough work" by confessing wrong attitudes and surrendering to "present truth." White expected that through constant reform or "cleansing," recipients would "overcome" wrong feelings and behaviors—or expect another confrontation. Phoebe Lamson read James' and Ellen's letter to John Andrews (a young scholar and minister mentored by James White) and it "deeply affected" her. "My eyes opened to our sad state...how unworthy and unprofitable we have been in the service of the Lord." Andrews, for his part, admitted that he had "expressed opinions...in some matters" that "seemed to open the door for the prince of darkness to step in," and promised to "keep in my proper sphere"—in submission to the Whites. The testimonies became indispensable to those committed to improving themselves while maintaining social relations with the Whites.[16]

Questions about the visions arose in the reading and reception of the testimonies and became a central issue in the growing Adventist community, generating defenders and detractors. By the time the denomination was organized, many churches read White's testimonies in meeting and called for comment. Brother Carpenter read aloud and then bore his own testimony "in regard to the truthfulness of the visions respecting myself." This was followed by question time, during which Brother Breyer spoke of things "freely acknowledged by the church," and of "the faith which he had in the visions." Some were less convinced. Brother Young was "more backward" in speaking of past meetings and deferred to Carpenter to "say a few words" regarding what he knew. Carpenter completed his endorsement with confidence: "I believe," he said of the testimony, "it is true."[17]

Others, however, reacted defensively to the testimonies. More than one breakaway group cited the testimonies as evidence of Ellen White's mistaken belief in her gifts. Some organized active opposition to the Whites, citing three grounds: the visions on which the testimonies depended were spurious; the testimonies were inaccurate or false; belief in the testimonies should not be made a test of fellowship. White responded that some who "professed perfect confidence in the vision" nevertheless "found fault with the instrument" or "the manner in which the vision was delivered. They took the position that a part of it was correct and part of it was a mistake, that I had been told circumstances and thought that the Lord had shown them to me in vision." Some serial testimonies chart the Whites' efforts to maintain influence with those doubting Ellen's visions, especially those who sympathized with rival movements such as spiritualism. Most detractors, however, resisted her diagnoses of their souls, not her theology, making the widely distributed testimonies occasions of conflict as well as conciliation among local Adventists.[18]

Publication: Editing and Compiling Inspiration

White's testimony letters first found their mark in the souls of her private correspondents and in the networks of local churches that read them. Starting in the mid-1850s, however, they found new readers. When James and Ellen White's conception of a community in the last days extended beyond the surviving Millerites, they enlarged their readership by publishing for a more general audience. After the installation of a hand press at Battle Creek, the Whites printed a broadside and then a sixteen-page, tract-style pamphlet (3 ½" by 5 ½" pages) based on recent visions, titled *Testimony for the Church*. Following a reading before church members in

Battle Creek, "on whose minds it apparently made a deep impression," the Whites included endorsements by ministers—a common boost to women writers of the period.[19]

About once per year, James printed another pamphlet edited from a selection of testimonies the Whites believed would be of general interest to members. Aware that a series was in the making and each new issue could be had for the postage, readers made their own compilations. Sister M. E. Devereaux, who stitched books for the Battle Creek press, offered a female friend "all Sister White's visions.... bound in morocco." In late 1857, for the fourth pamphlet, James increased the size to thirty-six pages and the print run to 1500; he placed a note in the *Review and Herald* urging they be "circulated immediately." As a sample, the *Review* excerpted nine pages from the pamphlet, entitled "He Went Away Sorrowful for He Had Many Possessions," based on Ellen's vision at Monterey, October 8, 1857.[20]

In a few short years, the testimonies became *Testimonies for the Church*. Ellen continued to write out new visions in her handwriting as before, but the edited pamphlets lacked the intimacy of the personal letter. Names and places were deleted to give the impression of a more general message. In several printed testimonies, for example, we come across initials for persons, although it is unlikely that readers would not know who "J.N.A." and "J.N.L." were (well-known Adventist authors). To read of the spiritual weaknesses of church leaders in this way must have given lay readers the impression they shared an angelic viewpoint. When demand after the Civil War required that James republish the pamphlets from the 1850s, he saw in them only "matters of a local and personal character, which do not have a direct bearing on our time," but praised their "high-toned spirit of scriptural piety." His bound edition of 1871 became the standard text for following generations. Some omitted testimonies were never seen in print again, but early testimonies—or at least paragraphs from them—showed up in later testimonies, articles, and books, as Ellen reworked and enlarged them for wider audiences. [21]

The regular publication of the testimonies increased but complicated their status among Adventists, adding an aura of inspiration difficult for the Whites to control. There is no evidence from Ellen or James White in this period, however, that the testimony letter was considered an inspired document, in the sense that evangelicals considered the Bible inspired. Certainly there was no phenomenon like the "automatic writing" exhibited by Shakers and Spiritualists in the writing of some of their testimonies. Her testimonies were literary traces of full-bodied and socially embedded revelatory experiences, not merely the recordings of a spiritual channel. Her ideas came to her mediated through images, narratives, emotions, bodily sensations, memories, and social encounters. Ellen's widely circulated letters and manuscripts contained scratchings, rewriting, and spelling and grammatical errors incompatible with any idea of verbal inspiration. James and others early resisted the idea that the visions in any way constituted an authority rivaling the Bible and refused for a number of years to publish them in the church paper. The locus of controversy, however, was the visions—and by extension Mrs. White herself—not her writings *per se*.[22]

Despite any flaws in the mechanics of her writing and the strong editing hand of her husband James and others, Ellen insisted on an essential role for the Spirit in the production of her writings. Her clearest statement from the antebellum period, summarizing fifteen years as a visionary, came in a letter to John Andrews in 1860. Her visions are "either of God or the devil," she insisted. "There is no half-way position to be taken in the matter." After a vision, she explained, "I do not at once remember all that I have seen, and the matter is not so clear before me until I write, then the scene rises before me as presented in vision, and I can write freely...." Apparently, trance experience depleted her mental capacities for a period, but the very act of writing helped stimulate her memory and efficiently led to inspiration (see Chapter 4). By the late 1850s, Adventist lecturers freely distributed printed testimonies along with Bibles and "truth-filled" books that they sold for modest profit. Many had not only read a testimony but had also seen Ellen White in vision, witnessed her miraculous recoveries, and heard her speak. Along with the church paper and familial letters, the testimony letters played a special part in the "communicative network" spreading among Adventist from New England and New York to the Midwestern states and into eastern Canada. All this had a sacralizing effect, giving the testimonies special religious authority somewhere above the *Review and Herald* but below the Bible.

Case Study: Testimony to Brother Rumery

We return finally to Monterey, Michigan, and the testimony letter Mrs. White wrote and mailed to Brother Rumery because, overcome with feelings, she could not deliver it in person. This section examines the testimony in its historical and social context and considers how the testimony written in Monterey, Michigan, contributed to the life of the wider Adventist community.[23]

In the first half of the nineteenth century, as thousands of New Englanders, New Yorkers, and European immigrants pushed westward in the Great Lakes area, the Miami and Pottawatomie peoples of southern Michigan were removed from their traditional lands by a long series of treaties and forced marches. After the land to be known as Allegan County was surveyed and indexed in 1837, early purchasers (known as patentees) chose the best and highest lands with the best soils and stands of oak trees for $1.25 per acre. Within the county, Township No. 3 North, Range 13 West, located north of Allegan, attracted many farmers because of its rolling hills, well-drained and rich soils, and abundant stands of oak, beech, elm, basswood, walnut, and ash. Young adults from the township families quickly intermarried and began raising a new generation. In 1847, area pioneers called a meeting to organize and name a new civil township within Allegan County. The winning suggestion, offered by pioneer Sylsbre Rumery, was "Monterey," after a recent victory in the Mexican-American War.[24]

By 1856 a church was organized at "the center of a large farming community of Seventh-day Adventists." From the church-paper subscriptions list and other references, we know the names and occupations of many Adventist families, including Wilcox, Day, Lay, Clarke, Kenyon, Pierce, Russ, Wilson, Patterson, Howard, Jones, and Rumery. Before their conversion to Adventism township pioneers such as George T. Lay, Leonard Ross, Frederick S. Day, Harvey Kenyon, and Sylsbre Rumery achieved leadership positions in the new township as supervisor, clerk, treasurer, justice of the peace, and constable. Lay, the largest landowner in Monterey, with high and fertile lands, had donated the land on which the schoolhouse was built and in which Ellen White had her October 8, 1857 vision. As members pledged support for Adventist causes such as a new press for the church's printing business and the Whites' push for denominational organization, the church in Monterey quickly developed a reputation for wealth and generosity. If an exemplary Adventist community could be found anywhere, it would be the church in Monterey.[25]

Brother Sylsbre Rumery, known as "Syb," was a farmer with a growing family living in the southeastern portion of Monterey Township. Born in 1820 and raised in Lockport, New York, he moved to Allegan County in 1839, was converted to the Methodist Episcopal faith in 1840, and emerged during the next decade as an energetic community leader. In 1841, he married

Nancy Maria Lay, a sister of George T. Lay, and in 1843 purchased eighty acres of densely forested land adjacent to Lay's in Section 26, where they raised three children. Unfortunately, Nancy died (December 25, 1847), but she had a younger sister Betsy Jane, aged twenty-two, who agreed to marry Sylsbre within a year (April 1, 1848). Younger brother Solomon came in the spring of 1847, was converted at a local meeting of German Methodists (although understanding no German), and stayed on with Sylsbre for a couple of years before marrying Julia A. Elliott and building a home nearby. Sylsbre Rumery held the position of township treasurer in 1856, the same year that Lay served as supervisor, and was a charter member of the Monterey Grange, the guild encouraging farmers and their families. The Rumery brothers became prosperous during the 1850s boom, converting to Adventism just a few months before the Whites' October 1857 visit.[26]

The morning after her vision in the schoolhouse, Ellen White walked over a mile west and uphill to the Rumery farmhouse, viewing the choice property in late harvest and its extensive views to the south and east. The long walk and her mounting anxiety over Rumery's case, however, were too much for her. She returned to the Lay home, where the Whites customarily stayed, to write several pages and an apology. The surviving manuscript, 1,164 words in length, was not penned by White but copied from her hand, as was her custom, by one of her assistants or a Rumery family member. At some point later, she added the words "Vision to Brother Rumery given in Monterey" to the handwritten copy and the whole was typed up "as grammatically corrected" in 1964, the first page of which is reproduced here (Figure 3.1). Except for a few excerpts, it has never been published. Like a typical testimony letter, however, it references a vision, "last Thursday eve." "In that vision," Ellen declared, "I saw the case of Victor Jones." He was the man whom Ellen had encouraged with her message the night before, but who was he?

Victor Jones lived in a small home with his wife Elizabeth and son Frank near the large Lay farm, but with few possessions, at least in comparison to wealthier Adventists. Born and raised in New York State, like so many other Michigan settlers, he had first lived in Pennsylvania, where his son was born, before the family moved west. Rumery and Jones were each in their thirties and married, but the Rumery brothers owned sixty times the property of Jones. As Elizabeth Jones had recently published a letter in the church paper, the family was not unknown to the Whites.[27]

To supplement their income, poorer men such as Victor Jones worked as day laborers for wealthier landowners or merchants. The distinction

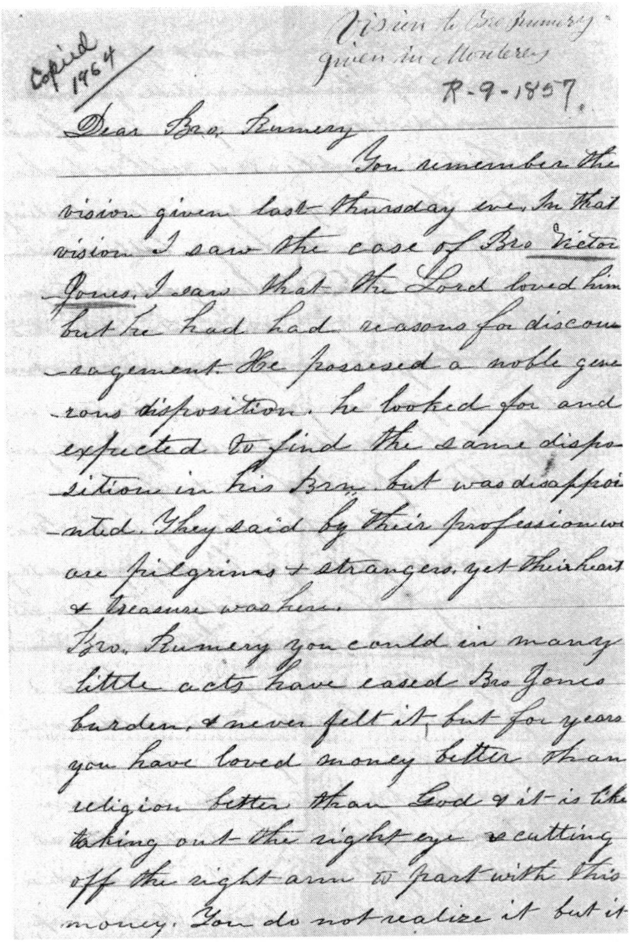

FIGURE 3.1 This Ellen White testimony letter, which is discussed in this chapter, is not in Ellen White's handwriting. It was probably copied from the original by the Rumery family and then sent to Ellen White. Before her correspondence was aided by typewriters, White routinely asked letter recipients to write out copies of testimonies and return them to her (courtesy of the Ellen G. White Estate, Inc.).

between farmers and laborers in settler culture was so clear that, almost without exception, sons of farmers were always farmers, even if they labored for their fathers and owned no land. Whether they worked on the family farm or on another, sons and brothers were increasing their stakes in the family fortune, which was rarely true for laborers such as Victor Jones. In this patrimony system, therefore, "love of the world" meant the attendant rights of property ownership such as family security and civic leadership. The sale of such property for causes such as Adventism threatened diminishment of the family's future, especially for young men such as Sylsbre Rumery's three minor sons. Young Frank Jones, as the son of a poor man, however, might receive almost nothing from his laboring father.[28]

In the written testimony Ellen reported "that the Lord loved [Jones] but he had had reasons for discouragement." He possessed "a noble, generous disposition" and expected to find the same in his fellow believers but was "disappointed." He had seen wealthy church members profess they were "pilgrims and strangers, yet their heart and treasure were here." Compared to the typical testimony, which directly addressed the subject of the vision, Ellen here used a foil. Having announced her diverting subject and her complaint in general terms, she opened the next paragraph in the second person: "Brother Rumery, you could in many little acts have eased Brother Jones' burden, and never felt it; but for years you have loved money better than religion. . . ." Rumery's problem was his "love of money" and attachment to his large property. "It is like taking out the right eye, cutting off the right arm, to part with this money. You do not realize it, but it is your god." He was blind to "the worth of the soul" and to be faulted for his "close dealing" with poorer church members such as Victor Jones, "making a little something out of them, taking advantage of them when you can." "God hates such things," she warned, "and every single instance wherein you are guilty is written in the book," and would "stand against" him unless he reformed.

Yet the testimony's main concern was the relationship between Rumery and Jones. "I saw that instead of inquiring into Brother Jones' wants, feeling a kindly sympathy for him," White charged, "you have coldly shut up the bowels of compassion toward him." When Rumery "embraced the present truth," Jones expected a "reformation" in a wealthy man known for taking advantage, but was instead "disappointed." In the vision, Jones' hands were "weakened and fell without strength by his side. He felt and said, 'It is no use. It is no use. I can't live religion. I can't keep the truth.'" Stumbling over Rumery's selfishness, Victor Jones had sunk deeper into his despair and his drink, and it was Brother Rumery's fault.

In White's vision, an angel had said to Rumery, "Thou art thy brother's keeper and in a degree responsible for his soul." Instead of neglecting and exploiting his fellow believers such as Jones, Ellen implored, Rumery should be a "brother's keeper," to "bind to your heart with strong Christian cords an erring, burdened brother," even "give your life for a brother" and love him. This would require "noble-hearted" and generous feelings from Rumery—remember her characterization of Jones as "noble" and "generous" in the opening sentences—and "every noble, generous act" would be "written in the book." This "truth" would "purge" away love of the world, or else the love of money would "crowd out all the noble principles of the soul." Reversing their relation of owner/laborer, White was implying that Jones possessed nobleness of soul that Rumery lacked. Riches were deceitful because they blind the possessor to the needs of others and to "the cause," and made it more difficult to hear "the voice of Jesus" when he called for money. God, "at present," did not call for people to sell their homes, but the time would soon come.

In her closing appeal, White acknowledged it would be hard for Brother Rumery to "deny self and take an upright, generous, noble course." He should do so, in part, because others looked for "a reformation...wrought in you by the truth." She employed a naval idiom often found among religionists of the period: "cut loose, cut loose from this world" or he would lose "heaven and its treasure." "The time has come for you to choose," she insisted.

White's subsequent feelings, not just the vision, were a key part of the testimony and of her rhetorical strategy. Near the start of the letter, she had accused Brother Rumery of a lack of sympathy; "Dear brother," she implored half-way through the letter, "in the vision God gave me as it has unfolded to my mind I have felt distressed, distressed." In the concluding personal note, she poured out her feelings, hoping to evoke his capacity to feel for others: "...my heart sank within me. I knew my weakness and knew I should feel the deepest distress for you while relating it to you, and I was afraid I should not have enough strength to do it...." "Afflicted...distressed...burdened...trembling," she "could not stay" and deliver her message: a "thorough work" was needed "or you will fail of heaven" because "it is easier for a camel to go through a needle's eye than for a rich man to enter the kingdom of heaven. Luke 18:25." White's explanation, that her irregular behavior that morning was a result of her emotional state, was exceeded only by the disclosure that she had "kept the vision from everyone, including my husband"—a statement appearing in no other letter.

In testimonies such as the one to Brother Rumery Ellen White seemed to chafe at the prosperity achieved by families who then passed it down to their sons, who in turn raised their families and took care of their aged parents—the accepted patrimony system. Holding wealth and investing in the family implicitly denied Adventism's central belief—was this world their home, or were they bound for another? If wealth was achieved at the expense of a poorer Christian brother such as Victor Jones, she had double reason for concern. Ellen also believed that suffering and sacrifice were essential to salvation; wealth not sacrificed would become an obstacle because it closes the heart and divides person from person. The failure of a distinguished convert and pillar of the Monterey community such as Sylsbre Rumery to exhibit compassion thereby risked his salvation threatened the social values and influence of Adventism.

Conclusion

Ellen White's testimony letters wielded an extraordinary spiritual power among antebellum Adventists. Based on her visions, which no one else saw and no one but she interpreted, their source was inaccessible and mysterious; they could only be admitted or ignored. For 150 years, whenever Adventists said "Mrs. White says..." they were probably quoting from one of her testimonies. Today we read them in their historical and social context and appreciate a unique religious accomplishment: the redemption of the Millerite movement's victims and their transformation into a growing community able to function in a world without end.

The testimonies are best viewed as religious texts mediating the many conflicting spiritual and social forces active in the lives of their readers. At first glance, a testimony letter in a few pages challenged its reader to examine and "cleanse" his or her life—and life records—while waiting for divine examination in the Judgment. Whether read in person, mailed through the post, sent to church leaders for congregational reading, dispersed as pamphlets, or published through the church paper, the testimonies persuaded thousands to reach for a spirituality that saw human life transparently and with feeling. As mirrors for personal reflection, they nurtured aspects of Adventist piety from Sabbath-keeping to child rearing and promoted the integration of belief and practice. In their largest range, as paradigms of community and church policy, they informed and reflected Adventism's spiritual ideals, resolved conflicting viewpoints within the church, and resisted centrifugal forces. As the Whites itinerated, they encountered local tensions such as exploitation between the wealthy and the poor in the farming town of Monterey. In response, a testimony letter advocating "systematic benevolence" or the concept of the "worthy poor" could mediate acceptable standards of Christian community and the realities of human self-interest under patrimony culture and the emerging market economy.

The moral ideal urged by the testimonies was the serious, self-controlled, sympathetic, self-aware believer whose ordered life balanced faith and feeling, conviction and compassion, improvement and sacrifice, and reflected positively on the Adventist cause—a view of Christian perfection eminently social yet advocating self-responsibility. The community of Adventism reading the testimonies was the knitted product of believing parents and children, the aged and the young, the wealthy and the deserving poor. Families receiving White's approval practiced the headship of the husband and the supportive role of the wife, suppressed their children's passions, and shaped decorous behavior and promoted respect between younger and older generations. Similarly, the ideal church successfully negotiated the space between cold formalism and heated fanaticism, established members and new arrivals from the East, and wealthy property owners and laborers. The testimonies expressed the community's difference from the larger world in personal appearance and avoidance of social fads and entertainments. In other words, in a reversal of the powerlessness of the earlier Millerites, the terms of engagement were to be set by the church, not the world.

The testimonies simultaneously addressed both the interior self (or conscience) and the social self and placed a higher value on emotion than on argument. After all, the community of the redeemed did not merely agree—they *felt* themselves to be one. What may surprise modern readers is the degree to which White relied on sentimental appeals—even sympathy for herself and her husband. In difficult cases, such as those of the Monterey church, she reached for unifying metaphors such as growth, melting, and soul education in order to transcend conflicts between loyalty and purity, wealthy and poor, the saving of the soul and the reputation of the church.

NOTES

1. See James White's report in *Advent Review and Sabbath Herald*, 10 (Oct 22, 1857): 219, hereafter referred to as *Review and Herald*.
2. Ellen G. White to S. Rumery, n. d. Emphasis by underlining in original. Unless otherwise indicated, White letters and manuscripts are from transcriptions on file at the Center for Adventist Research, Andrews University, Michigan, hereafter referred to as CAR.

3. Ellen G. White, *Testimonies for the Church*, 9 vols. (Mountain View, CA: Pacific Press, 1948).

4. This chapter reviews handwritten, transcribed, and published letters and manuscripts from 1845 to approximately the start of the Civil War.

5. The new *Webster's Dictionary* of 1828 gave a dozen literary, religious, and legal examples to suggest a broad definition for *testimony*: "A solemn declaration or affirmation made for the purpose of establishing or proving some fact." See examples in Diane Sasson, *The Shaker Spiritual Narrative* (Knoxville: University of Tennessee Press, 1983), 67–83; Jean McMahon Humez, *Gifts of Power: The Writings of Rebecca Jackson, Black Visionary, Shaker Eldress* (Amherst: University of Massachusetts Press, 1981); Thomas D. Hamm, *The Quakers in America*, Columbia Contemporary American Religion Series (New York: Columbia University Press, 2003); Alexander Struk, "The Hermeneutics of Testimony: Ricoeur and an LDS Perspective," *Aporia* 19:1 (2009): 45–56.

6. Merlin D. Burt, "The Historical Background, Interconnected Development, and Integration of the Doctrines of the Heavenly Sanctuary, the Sabbath, and Ellen G. White's Role in Sabbatarian Adventism from 1844–1849" (Ph.D. Diss., Andrews University, 2002); "Rules for Reading Scriptures," *Review and Herald* 9 (Apr. 16, 1857): 191; *Christian Experience and Teachings of Ellen G. White* (1922):, 40–49.

7. See "The Trial of Israel Dammon," *Piscataquis Farmer* 3, no. 31 (Dover, Maine), March 7, 1845; Ellen G. Harmon, "To the Little Remnant Scattered Abroad," Broadside, April 6, 1846; "A Vision of the Future," Testimony for the Church, No. 4 (Battle Creek: Steam Press, 1857), printed in Ellen G. White, *Spiritual Gifts*, Vol. 1, (Battle Creek: Steam Press, 1858), 185.

8. Compare "Life Sketches Manuscript," (1915), 8. http://text.egwwritings.org/, search LSMS; and *Life Sketches, Ancestry, Early Life, Christian Experience, and Extensive Labors of Elder James White and His Wife, Mrs. Ellen G. White* (Battle Creek, MI: Steam Press of the Seventh-day Adventist Publishing Assn., 1880), 90.

9. See Harriet Beecher Stowe's portrayal of slavery through the trope of the sufferings of Christ in *Uncle Tom's Cabin; or, Life Among the Lowly*, ed. Ann Douglas (1852; repr., New York: Penguin, 1981).

10. Ellen G. White to Mary Lyon, Jan 13, 1862; Ellen G. White to Friends at Marshall, Michigan, n. d.

11. Ellen G. White to Brother J. N. Andrews and Sister H. N. Smith," n. d. (June, 1851?) [MS 9, 1851].

12. See Catherine E. Beecher, *A Treatise on Domestic Economy: For Use of Young Ladies at Home*, rev. ed. (1842: New York: Schocken Books, 1977).

13. Ellen G. White to Bro. and Sr. Kellogg, n. d., (ca. 1862–1864) [Letter 10, 1862 and Letter 17, 1864] A more succinct version also exists [Letter 17a, 1864].

14. Ellen G. White to Angeline Andrews, n. d. (ca. 1865). See also Ellen G. White to John N. Andrews, Aug. 26, 1855; and Ellen G. White to John N. Andrews, June 11, 1860.

15. S. W. Rhodes to Ellen G. White, Mar. 18, 1855.

16. Phebe M. Lamson to James S. White, March 17, 1863; John N. Andrews to James S. White, Nov. 3, 1862.

17. William Carpenter to Ellen G. White, March 21, 1863.

18. Ellen G. White to John Andrews, June 11, 1860.

19. Ellen G. White, "To the Saints Scattered Abroad," *Testimony for the Church*, No. 1 (Battle Creek, MI: Advent Review Office, 1855), 31 (Burlington copy). The editions inspected for this essay came from the libraries of M. B. Miller of Burlington, Michigan, and John N. Andrews, both courtesy of CAR.

20. White, *Testimony for the Church*, No. 1 (16 pp.); Ellen G. White, *Testimony for the Church*, No. 2 (Battle Creek, MI: Advent Review Office, 1856), 16 pp.; Ellen G. White, *Testimony for the Church*, No. 3 (Battle Creek, MI: Advent Review Office, 1857), 16 pp.; Ellen G. White, *Testimony for the Church*, No. 4 (Battle Creek, MI: Steam Press of the Seventh-day Adventist Publishing Assn., 1857), 39 pp.; Ellen G. White, *Testimony for the Church*, No. 5 (Battle Creek. MI: Steam Press of the Seventh-day Adventist Publishing Assn., 1859), 32 pp.; Ellen G. White, *Testimony for the Church*, No. 6 (Battle Creek, MI: Steam Press of the Seventh-day Adventist Publishing Assn., 1861), 64 pp.; *Advent Review and Sabbath Herald* 11 (1857): 18 (hereafter referred to as *Review and Herald*); M. E. Deveraux to Sister Below, Nov. 9, 1856 (dated Nov. 4).

21. See James White, ed., *Testimonies for the Church*, Nos. 1–10 (Battle Creek, MI: Steam Press of the Seventh-day Adventist Publishing Assn., 1871).

22. Ellen G. White to John N. Andrews, June 11, 1860.

23. Ellen G. White to Rumery, n. d.

24. Crisfield Johnson, *History of Allegan and Barry Counties, Michigan, with Illustrations and Biographical Sketches of Their Prominent Men and Pioneers* (Philadelphia: D. W. Ensign & Co., 1880), 282–92; after the Battle of Monterrey (Mexico) of 1846, although the spelling follows the Battle of Monterey (California), also 1846.

25. Bert Van Horn, "Early History of the Church at Monterey, Mich.," *Review and Herald* 96, no. 4 (1919): 22–24; Members of the Day family held positions of supervisor, clerk, and treasurer in the 1840s and 1850s. George T. Lay was Monterey supervisor and S. Rumery was treasurer in 1856. S. H Wilcox held both clerk and treasurer positions. See Johnson, *History of Allegan County*, 282–292; and "Pledges for Power Press," *Review and Herald* 24 (1857): 192.

26. See 1850 Federal Census, 1860 Federal Census, and 1864 Michigan Agricultural Census for Monterey Township. According to the 1860 Census, two Rumery brothers with their families lived adjacent: Sylsbre (40), worth $4,000, living with Betsey (33), John (15), Andrew (12), Maria (10), Horatio (8) and Lee (3); and

Soloman (listed as "Silas") Rumery (33), worth $2,000, living with his wife Julia (32), Joshua (7), and Alice (1).

27. According to the 1860 Census, Victor Jones (34) lived with Elizabeth (27) and Frank (9), with property of $100. See Elizabeth L. Jones to Editor, May 31, 1857, *Review and Herald* 7 (1857): 54–55.

28. David E. Schob, *Hired Hands and Ploughboys: Farm Labor in the Midwest, 1815–1860* (Urbana: University of Illinois Press, 1975), 37–40.

4

Prophet

Ronald Graybill

FOR ELLEN HARMON, personal, physical, and social factors all combined to create a prophet—a person who perceived herself to be a messenger for God who received special revelations from Him. Naturally there were others who perceived her as a "wonderful fanatic and trance medium," a victim of mesmerism or demonic possession, or one who merely experienced "religious reveries, in which her imagination runs without control" and whose sentiments were obtained from "previous teaching, or study."[1]

Prophetic Identity

Ellen White never called herself a "prophet." "I have not stood before the people claiming this title," she said, "I am God's messenger." She may not have used the terms "prophet" or "prophetess," but she clearly believed that she had the gift of prophecy, that she was what other people would call a prophet, that she received, directly from God, revelations containing specific content, and that it was her calling and duty to convey these messages to others in "testimonies" and counsels. Once this conviction became a fixed part of her identity, she was essentially unable to recognize or acknowledge any evidence that might be at odds with it.

As a child her "ambition to become a scholar had been very great," doubtless an indication of success in the limited formal education she did receive before her childhood accident.[2] With that ambition thwarted, she discovered a new calling as she eagerly anticipated the literal second coming of Christ in 1844. "I arranged meetings with my young friends.... Others thought me beside myself to be so persistent in my efforts."[3] Undaunted, she continued her efforts until every one of them was converted.

Thus her identity shifted from scholar to soul-winner, an identity she never lost, even after she acquired her prophetic role. About the same time that she was converting her friends she found herself troubled by thoughts of unworthiness, despairing of her acceptance with God. Then she had some puzzling dreams. Her mother encouraged her to counsel with Levi Stockman, an aged Methodist minister who had adopted Millerite views. On hearing her story, Stockman "placed his hand affectionately upon my head, saying with tears in his eyes: 'Ellen, you are only a child. Yours is a most singular experience for one of your tender age. Jesus must be preparing you for some special work.'"[4] To this young woman it must have been a virtual ordination. It was, after all, a laying on of hands, a confirmation of a special identity. Now she had a positive, powerful identity: she was a successful soul-winner being prepared by Jesus for a special work.

Her mother was also supportive. Having seen her share of Methodist camp-meeting worshippers prostrated under religious fervor, she was not alarmed when Ellen experienced prostration. When onlookers wanted to call a doctor, her mother "bade them let me alone." For the mother, it was "the wondrous power of God" that had prostrated her daughter.[5]

She and her brother Robert, two years older, felt keenly the disapproval of the other Methodists in their class meeting when they testified about their faith in Jesus' soon return. The two decided to stop attending.[6] This was a serious decision. Failure to attend meetings was a breach of discipline that, along with other factors, led to their being put out of the Methodist church in 1843.[7]

Of the eight Harmon children, two became active Seventh-day Adventists: Ellen and Sarah, five years older, who chaperoned her when she began travelling around Maine to relate her visions (Figure 4.1). Both of Ellen White's parents (Figure 4.2) believed in her prophetic gift and died Seventh-day Adventists. Her brother Robert died a little more than ten years before the Adventist church officially organized in 1863, but he apparently accepted Ellen's gifts as genuine. Mary, six years older than Ellen (Figure 4.3), considered herself a Seventh-day Adventist, although there is no record of her formally joining the church. Her remaining three sisters, including her twin, Elizabeth, (Figures 4.4 and 4.5) and older brother, John, never joined her church and doubtless remained ambivalent about her claims. Ellen White, nevertheless, maintained close relationships with

FIGURE 4.1 This is believed to be a photo of Sarah Harmon Belden, older sister of Ellen White (1823–1868) (Courtesy of the Ellen G. White Estate, Inc.).

these siblings, corresponding and visiting with them, and sending them copies of her books and subscriptions to Adventist journals.

Ellen Harmon's first vision occurred in December 1844. In 1845 James White brought her to public notice when, in the *Day Star* journal, he shared the highlights of the vision. In doing so, he used many of the same phrases Ellen White echoed in her own later account. "I think the Bible warrants us in looking for visions," he wrote.[8]

A central question is why Ellen White's followers believed her to be a true prophet. The Whites' friend Otis Nichols provided early evidence. He testified to her good character and was impressed that although Ellen was so sickly that her voice could hardly be heard, she was miraculously strengthened and able to speak in a loud voice for nearly two hours. Nichols contended that she occasionally healed others through prayer. (Soon thereafter she abandoned her healing ministry and this claim disappeared from the apologetic accounts.) Nichols also noted that her ministry

FIGURE 4.2 Robert Harmon, father of Ellen White (1784–1866) (Courtesy of the Ellen G. White Estate, Inc.).

"fed, comforted, [and] strengthened" the believers and that at times she possessed superhuman strength.[9]

Naming the Prophet

At Israel Dammon's trial in early 1845 (see Chapter 2) witnesses identified Ellen Harmon as "Imitation of Christ." Over a century earlier John Wesley had translated Thomas à Kempis's famous devotional book of that same name. It was the first book published by the Methodist Book Concern in America in 1789.[10] The book includes a passage where Kempis offers to God "gladness of all devout hearts, their ardent affection, their mental raptures, their supernatural illuminations and heavenly visions." Any erstwhile Methodist familiar with that passage might easily have seen White's visions as an example.

"Imitation of Christ" never caught on as a nickname for White. In other early accounts of her prophetic role, believers simply referred to "the

FIGURE 4.3 Mary Harmon Foss, older sister of Ellen White (1821–1912) (Courtesy of the Ellen G. White Estate, Inc.).

visions" or "the gifts." The latter term often appeared in arguments for the "perpetuity" of spiritual gifts, which contended that they had not disappeared after New Testament times, as most orthodox Protestants believed. In 1862 a Seventh-day Adventist minister, M. E. Cornell, published a book titled *Miraculous Powers: The Scripture Testimony on the Perpetuity of Spiritual Gifts*.[11] A subtitle explained that it comprised "Narratives of Incidents and Sentiments Carefully Compiled from the Eminently Pious and Learned of Various Denominations." With James White's endorsement, Cornell cited various instances of divine visions, miracles, and prophecies. Such arguments did not, however, become a lasting part of the Adventist understanding of the gift of prophecy. Subsequent apologists for the visions never pointed to any other genuine post-biblical prophets.

The later names ascribed to Ellen White were reflected in the progression of titles of her books. At first, her visions were often referred to as "views." So her first book was titled *A Sketch of the Christian Experience and Views of Ellen G. White*. Later, she published four volumes titled *Spiritual*

FIGURE 4.4 Ellen Harmon White and her oldest sister Caroline Harmon Clough (1811–1883), 1872 (Courtesy of the Ellen G. White Estate, Inc.).

Gifts and still later another multi-volume set called *Spirit of Prophecy.*[12] The name "Spirit of Prophecy," which applied to both her writings and to Ellen White herself, arose as Sabbath-keeping Adventists came to see themselves as the "remnant" of God's true church, a people against whom the "dragon" of Revelation 12:17 went to make war. Characteristic of this remnant, according to that text, was that they "keep the commandments of God and have the testimony of Jesus Christ." Revelation 19:10 identifies this "testimony of Jesus" as the "spirit of prophecy." Because Seventh-day Adventists were among the few Christians who kept the "command-ments of God" by observing the seventh-day Sabbath of the fourth com-mandment, and because they had a prophet among them—the "spirit of prophecy"—they claimed that these two phenomena identified God's true "remnant church." Even today new Adventists, as part of their baptismal vows, are asked: "Do you accept the biblical teaching of spiritual gifts and believe that the gift of prophecy is one of the identifying marks of the remnant church?"[13] Although Adventists sometimes called Ellen White

FIGURE 4.5 Ellen Harmon White with her twin, Elizabeth Harmon Bangs (1827–1891), ca. 1878 (Courtesy of the Ellen G. White Estate, Inc.).

herself the "Spirit of Prophecy," in less formal settings they referred to her simply as "Sister White."

Another evocative title applied to Ellen White was "weakest of the weak." In the early 1890s Adventist historian J. N. Loughborough claimed that, before God chose Ellen Harmon as his messenger, he had called two other former Millerites: Hazen Foss (1818–1893) and William Foy (1818–1893). Foss—a brother-in-law of Ellen's older sister Mary—is said to have received visions but refused to relate them. In 1890 Ellen White recalled that his refusal had had dreadful consequences. She alleged that he told her he was a "lost man" because of his refusal, and warned her not to do the same.[14] Foy, an African-American Free Will Baptist and Millerite preacher, published his vision as *The Christian Experience of William E. Foy*. He is said to have received another vision, which he did not understand; so he ceased preaching. Soon afterward, according to Loughborough, he "sickened and died." In fact, Foy lived and continued as a preacher-farmer until his death in 1893.[15] Some of the language he used in describing his visions appeared again in Ellen White's descriptions of her own revelations.

After Foss and Foy refused the prophetic gift, God turned to Ellen Harmon, described by Loughborough as the "weakest of the weak."[16] This image became a trope in the Adventist narrative about White. It helps to explain why her prophetic gift never translated into any belief that women in general might be fitted for leadership roles in the church and why to this day the central church leadership has refused to approve the ordination of women to the gospel ministry.

Very early, the containment of charisma came into play, eliminating other possible recipients of the prophetic mantle. Although Adventists argued for the perpetuity of spiritual gifts, they acknowledged only one genuine manifestation of the gift in a person called to prophetic office since New Testament times: Ellen Harmon White. This contrasted with the experience of Mormons in the Church of Jesus Christ of Latter-Day Saints, who more literally believed in the perpetuity of spiritual gifts. For them, not only was Joseph Smith, their founder, a prophet, but so were all the succeeding presidents of their church.[17]

Miracles

Early followers of Ellen Harmon White attached considerable importance to what they believed were the genuine miracles that attended her ministry. Otis Nichols, one of her first converts, mentioned earlier, displayed a special fondness for miracle stories. He claimed, for example, that during a vision in his home Ellen had held a large Bible aloft above her head, pointing to particular texts and quoting them correctly even though she could not see the passages to which she was pointing. Such miraculous claims became a staple of the church's defense of Ellen White's prophetic gift. They reached their apogee with J. N. Loughborough's book *Rise and Progress of the Seventh-day Adventists*, published in 1892, but continued to echo through many other apologetic works, especially those written for children and youth.[18]

Most of the arguments for physical miracles date from the early part of Ellen White's life, when she was experiencing her dramatic day-time, ecstatic visions. These visions subsequently decreased in frequency as all forms of enthusiastic worship declined among Adventists, before dying out entirely in the 1870s.[19] After that, vivid dreams, often called "visions of the night," became her main revelatory experience. But though the visions and miracles ceased, the stories about them did not. Two proved especially popular: her apparent lack of breathing during visions and her ability to hold the 18½-pound Harmon family Bible on her outstretched hand for half an hour.

The apparent suppression of her normal respiration during her visions first attracted mention in 1848, when James White observed that Ellen had been in vision for an hour and a half during which time she "did not breathe at all." A few observers expressed concern about such spells, but "experienced Christians," such as Ellen's mother, knew that she would recover. Her mother probably also knew that William Foy, the Millerite visionary mentioned earlier, had reportedly exhibited "no appearance of life, except around his heart" during his visions.[20]

In 1866 John Loughborough made the extravagant claim that even while she was not breathing, she uttered audible words. In the same article he mentioned for the first time that others had tested her by holding a mirror in front of her nose and mouth to see if it would gather moisture. Two years later, in *Life Incidents*, James White told of witnesses pressing on his wife's chest and covering her mouth and nostrils to determine whether she was breathing during visions. For his 1892 book Loughborough collected several testimonials from eyewitnesses about Ellen White's failure to breathe during visions.[21]

Ellen White recommended a different physical test for the genuineness of visions. Confronted by a young woman she believed was having a "false vision," she recommended getting "a pitcher of cold water, good cold water" and throwing "it right in her face," which White predicted, would "bring her out of it the quickest of anything you can do." Before anyone could bring the water, however, the visionary snapped out of her trance.[22] Apparently no one ever applied this test to Ellen herself.

Shortly after her first vision, another divine revelation impressed on her a duty to travel and relate what she had seen. At first she resisted; then, during yet a third vision, she seemed to be struck by a "ball of fire." Half a century later Loughborough recast this "ball of fire" vision as the setting for an amazing feat of strength on the part of the thin, frail, seventeen-year-old Ellen. Her father had purchased an enormous Bible, one of three thousand printed by Joseph Teal in Boston in 1822. During this vision, as the story goes, she picked it up and held it open on her outstretched left hand at right angles to her body for half an hour.[23]

The actual Harmon family Bible, now called simply the "Big Bible," remains on display in the offices of the Ellen White Estate at church headquarters near Washington, D.C. It is eleven inches wide, eighteen inches tall, four inches thick, and weighs 18½ pounds. Just to hold it at one's shoulder like a waiter carrying a tray would cause severe strain. Holding it on an extended arm would create such tremendous torque as to render it impossible for a mere mortal to do so for more than two or three minutes. For a sickly, five-foot, two-inch teenage girl to hold it on her outstretched arm for half an hour defies all the laws of physics and physiology. Ellen White and her supporters made many other claims of miraculous powers, but the questionable origin and growth of the story of the Big Bible is the most dramatic example of how her visions were moved, over time, from a context of communal enthusiasm to one of physical miracle.[24]

Ellen White never mentioned the Big Bible in her published or unpublished writings. James White did mention it—the Harmon family Bible—in *Life Incidents*, but he made no reference to her having held it during vision. He says only that he and Ellen had inherited it as a precious family heirloom. The story seems to have surfaced orally in the late 1880s and then finally in print in 1892, in Loughborough's *Rise and Progress of the Seventh-day Adventists*. Loughborough was more hagiographer than historian, and often proved unreliable in the latter role.[25]

Prophecy and Family

Although James did much to establish Ellen's initial role as a prophet, as time went on he grew sensitive to criticism that he and his fellow Sabbath-keeping Adventists were making the visions a test of fellowship and an authority for doctrine outside of the Bible itself. Around 1850 he virtually stopped printing Ellen's messages in his newly minted *Advent Review and Sabbath Herald*, and for the next five years he and other church leaders made little publicly of her gift. The symbiotic relationship between the prophet and her followers is graphically illustrated by the fact that Ellen White noticed that her visions had grown less and less frequent during this period when they were neglected. She had all but concluded that her work "in God's cause was done."[26]

After a five-year delay, other church leaders acted to restore the "gifts" to the church. They confessed they had not appreciated the "the glorious privilege of claiming the gifts" and affirmed that they now believed the messages emanated "from the divine mind." In response, the prophet promised that God "would graciously and mercifully revive the gifts again."

Chastened, James resumed being Ellen's major supporter and promoter. Unfortunately, a series of strokes in the late 1870s rendered him more and more difficult. In a peevish moment, he once admonished her not to lecture him on matters of mere opinion, but he never lost confidence in her prophetic gift.[27]

Ellen White's dual role as mother and prophet also became complicated at times. She and James had four sons: Henry, Edson, Willie, and John Herbert. The youngest, John Herbert, died in infancy; the oldest, Henry, died at age 16. So it was Edson and Willie whose beliefs, actions, and influence had the greatest relevance to Ellen White's prophetic career. When her calling as a prophet conflicted with her responsibilities as a mother, she almost always opted to honor the former. While traveling extensively as a young mother, she left her children in the care of others. Edson, a problem child and teenager, was a constant source of concern and object of criticism for his mother. As an adult he earned a reputation for financial irresponsibility and for a period virtually left the church. After experiencing a reconversion in the early 1890s, he built a riverboat, *The Morning Star*, and sailed to Mississippi, where he founded Adventist churches and schools for African Americans. He frequently invoked his mother's prophetic writings to support his work and fundraising efforts; he also published her appeals for work among African Americans in a little book titled *The Southern Work*. After he left Mississippi and went into the religious publishing business in Nashville, Tennessee, his old reputation for financial irresponsibility returned, which led to frequent conflicts with church leaders in Battle Creek. When, in defense, he quoted selected passages from his mother's earlier letters endorsing his work, she rebuked him and warned him that such a practice undermined her influence. At times Edson felt that his brother, Willie, was influencing his mother against him. The mere fact that he believed she could be influenced by other humans shows that he was not altogether persuaded that every counsel she issued was divine.

Willie, in contrast, became the model son—capable, sensible, and always supportive of his mother. After the death of his father, he served as her counselor, confidant, business agent, editor, and representative on numerous church committees and boards.[28] On at least one occasion he even decided whether one of her testimonies should be delivered to its addressee. This sort of thing led inevitably to charges, even from his older brother, that he manipulated her writings. But by and large the arrangement with Willie proved advantageous to Mrs. White; in the public eye, a son could much more comfortably play a subordinate role than a husband could.

James's and Willie's contributions to Ellen White's career show her prophetic office to have been virtually a family business, a unique arrangement among the major American prophets. Joseph Smith's first wife, Emma, was "ordained under his hand to expound Scriptures, and to exhort the church." But hers was always an assigned role, as when she edited the first Mormon hymnal and was placed in charge of the Female Relief Society.[29] Similarly, the three husbands of Mary Baker Eddy, the founder of Christian Science, kept a low profile in her movement and did little to promote her career.[30]

Although Ellen White held no formal office or title in the organizational structure of her church, both her husband and son occupied very prominent positions, a fact that gave her continuous and significant involvement in organizational affairs. Prior to the formal organization of the Seventh-day Adventist Church in 1863, James White's publications served as the chief organizational instrument of the emerging denomination. These church papers served as a forum for doctrinal articles, provided news of meetings and conferences, issued financial reports, and carried members' letters and testimonials. These were the "social media" of the day, and James's service as editor during four separate stints put him, along with Ellen, at the nerve center of the church. James also served as president of the General Conference of Seventh-day Adventists, as president of the Review and Herald Publishing Association, which brought out all of his wife's early books, and as "Editor and Proprietor" of what became the Pacific Press Publishing Association in Oakland, California.

In addition to her husband and sons, numerous other helpers made up a virtual extended family. Called "copyists" by Willie, they were essentially editors, assisting in transmitting Ellen White's prophetic messages to the public (see Chapter 5). Although these literary assistants polished her prose for publication, they were forbidden to alter Ellen White's concepts or add their own ideas. After editing her drafts, they sent them back to her for her approval. Sometimes she added brief comments but in the main she did not pore over these transcripts as a professional author might do. She did not make line-by-line emendations or revisions; so these helpers played a vital role in the pipeline through which she delivered her testimonies to her public.

Critics and Other Observers

Criticisms of Ellen White's prophetic claims emerged soon after she began her ministry in the mid-1840s. By the 1860s they were circulating so widely that Uriah Smith, editor of the *Review and Herald*, felt compelled to rebut them in *The Visions of Mrs. E. G. White: Manifestation of Spiritual Gifts according to the Scriptures*. Two years after leaving the Seventh-day Adventist church in 1887, Dudley M. Canright, a former minister, evangelist, and member of the General Conference Committee, published a 156-page book, *Seventh-day Adventism Renounced*, in which he brought together all the major accusations of previous critics. Again Uriah Smith came to Ellen White's defense. In a special supplement to the *Review and Herald* he discounted each of Canright's more than thirty charges.[31]

Over the years, the criticisms were so often couched in sarcasm and ridicule that believers tended to dismiss them as unchristian and probably dishonest as well. On one occasion the *Review and Herald,* instead of responding to a critic's attack, merely published a list of his nasty rhetorical flourishes, such as references to Adventists as "illiterate dupes" and to Ellen White's "blasphemous pretensions" and "tyrannical and unreasoning domination."[32] Adventists, who felt themselves blessed and encouraged by her preaching and writing, would hardly have been swayed by such diatribes.

The average nineteenth-century lay Adventist was apparently respectful, even admiring, of Ellen White as a prophet, generally confident that she exercised a divine gift. But most of what was written came from church leaders. Not surprising, not all of her instructions met with universal compliance. When one of the leaders of the Women's Christian Temperance Union, Mrs. S.M.I. Henry, joined the Adventist church, she expressed puzzlement over finding "professed belief" in the authority of White's *Testimonies* coupled with a "practical disbelief...especially in the matter of health principles."[33] Even today, only about fifty percent of Adventists hold to her vegetarian diet counsel. Despite some ambivalence about what White told them to do, most lay Adventists seem to have felt comfortable in the prophet's presence. Indeed, Mrs. White often stayed in members' homes while traveling and frequently had her picture taken while sitting among them. The surviving photographs suggest that she engendered greater honor and respect among her American followers than among the early Adventist believers in Europe; in American group pictures she is always placed front and center, while in Europe she typically appears as just one of the crowd.[34]

Prophecies of the Prophet

Some modern commentators have pointed out that prophecy is often "forthtelling" the message of God rather than "foretelling" the future. Yet Ellen White's apologists were not loath to cite instances of predictions they believed had been fulfilled. Today it is her as-yet-unfulfilled prophecies, particularly her predictions of events that she said would immediately precede the Second Coming of Christ, that most strongly influence the world view of Adventists.[35]

Adventists' acceptance of the Saturday Sabbath of the fourth commandment as still binding on Christians has always been a source of tension between them and most other denominations, the more so in the nineteenth century, when Protestants and Catholics supported Sunday blue laws to protect what they believed to be the proper day of worship. In 1895, Adventists in Tennessee, convicted of violating local Sunday ordinances by working in their own yards on Sunday, were even placed in chain gangs (see Chapter 12).[36]

Seeing ominous times ahead, Ellen White predicted "All nations and tongues and peoples will be commanded to worship this spurious Sabbath.... The decree enforcing the worship of this day is to go forth to all the world." Ellen White even prophesied that Adventists would be threatened with death in the last days. Although she never used the phrase "death decree" herself, it became a staple in Adventist writings about last-day events and has been inserted frequently as a heading or chapter title in compilations of her eschatological prophecies. She ensured that Adventists would largely oppose any ecumenical gestures by American Protestants to improve relations with the Roman Catholic Church.[37]

The Seventh-day Adventist church, approximately 18 million strong in 2014, is growing fastest among ethnic minorities and in countries outside the United States and Western Europe. Ellen White's books have been translated into more than 165 languages.[38] Officially the church is still fully committed to the relevance and accuracy of her predictions, all of which were brought together in the book *Last Day Events* in 1992. In 2007 the popular Adventist author Herbert Douglass published *Dramatic Prophecies of Ellen White: Stories of World Events Divinely Foretold*.[39] For many devout Adventists the predictive prophecies of Ellen White are still powerfully relevant.

NOTES

1. Isaac C. Wellcome, *History of the Second Advent Message* (Yarmouth, ME: Isaac C. Wellcome, 1874), 402; James White, *A Word to the Little Flock* (Brunswick, ME: James White, 1847), 22.

2. James and Ellen White, *Life Sketches* (Battle Creek, MI: Steam Press of the Seventh-day Adventist Publishing Assn., 1880), 135.

3. Ibid., 163.

4. Ibid., 158.

5. Ibid., 160.

6. Ibid., 164–65.

7. Arthur L. White, *Ellen G. White*, 6 vols. (Washington, DC, Review and Herald Publishing Assn., 1981–1986), 1: 43.

8. James White, "Letter from Bro. White," *The Day Star* 7 (Sept. 6, 1845): 17.

9. Otis Nichols to William Miller, April 20, 1846, quoted in Arthur L. White, *Ellen G. White* 1:75–76.

10. Frederick G. Hoyt, "Trial of Elder I. Dammon, Reported for the *Piscataquis Farmer*," *Spectrum: The Journal of the Association of Adventist Forums* 17 (August 1987): 29–86, hereafter cited as *Spectrum*; Thomas à Kempis, *The Christian's Pattern; or, A Treatise of the Imitation of Christ*, trans. John Wesley (London: C. Byington, 1735).

11. Merritt E. Cornell, *Miraculous Powers: The Scripture Testimony on the Perpetuity of Spiritual Gifts* (Battle Creek, MI: Steam Press of the Seventh-day Adventist Publishing Assn., 1862).

12. Ellen G. White, *A Sketch of the Christian Experience and Views of Ellen G. White* (Saratoga Springs, NY: James White, 1851); Ellen G. White, *Spiritual Gifts*, vol. 2 (Battle Creek, MI: Seventh-day Adventist Publishing Assn., 1860); Ellen G. White, *The Spirit of Prophecy* (Battle Creek, MI: Seventh-day Adventist Publishing Assn., 1870).

13. General Conference of Seventh-day Adventists, *Church Manual*, 18th ed. (Hagerstown, MD; Review and Herald Publishing Assn., 2010), 47.

14. Ellen G. White to Mary Foss, Dec. 22, 1890, Letter 37, 1890, quoted in T. Housel Jemison, *A Prophet Among You* (Mountain View, CA: Pacific Press, 1955), 487–89.

15. Delbert W. Baker, *The Unknown Prophet* (Hagerstown, MD: Review and Herald Publishing Assn., 1987).

16. J. N. Loughborough, *Rise and Progress of the Seventh-day Adventists* (Battle Creek, MI: General Conference Assn., 1892), 73.

17. Danny L. Jorgenson, "Dissent and Schism in the Early Church: Explaining Mormon Fissiparousness," *Dialogue: A Journal of Mormon Thought* 28 (June 1, 1995): 25.

18. Ellen White quotes Otis Nichols' account of this incident in *Spiritual Gifts*, 2: 78, in 1860. The actual handwritten copy of Otis Nichols' statement is displayed

on the White Estate website: www.whiteestate.org/vault/otis_text.asp. See also Loughborough, *Rise and Progress*, 118.

19. Ronald D. Graybill, "The Power of Prophecy: Ellen G. White and the Women Religious Founders of the Nineteenth Century" (Ph.D. diss., Johns Hopkins University, 1983), 94.

20. Ellen G. White, *Christian Experience and Teachings of Ellen G. White* (Mountain View, CA: Pacific Press, 1940), 120, cites James White to Dear Brother and Sister, Aug. 26, 1848. Regarding Foy, see Tim Poirier, "Black Forerunner to Ellen White: William E. Foy," *Spectrum* 17 (August 1987): 23–28; Frederick Hoyt, " 'We Lifted Up Our Voices Like a Trumpet': Millerites in Portland, Maine," *Spectrum* 17 (August 1987): 16; and Baker, *Unknown Prophet*.

21. J. N. Loughborough, "Remarkable Fulfillments of the Visions," *Advent Review and Sabbath Herald* 29 (Dec. 25, 1866): 30, hereafter cited as *Review and Herald*; James White, *Life Incidents: In Connection with the Great Advent Movement* (Battle Creek, MI: Steam Press of the Seventh-day Adventist Publishing Assn., 1868), 272; Loughborough, *Rise and Progress*, 96; J. N. Loughborough, *The Great Second Advent Movement: Its Rise and Progress* (Nashville, TN: Southern Publishing Assn., 1905), pp. 205–10. A later writer claimed that while in vision she spoke to a large number of people for four hours while not breathing; see F. C. Gilbert, *Divine Predictions of Mrs. Ellen G. White Fulfilled* (South Lancaster, MA: Good Tidings Press, 1922), 109.

22. Ellen White interview, ca. 1906, 5, Document File 733-c, Ellen G. White Estate, Silver Spring, MD.

23. White, *Spiritual Gifts*, 2: 37; Loughborough, *Rise and Progress*, 103–4. See also *The Columbian Family and Pulpit Bible: Being a Corrected and Improved American Edition* (Boston: Joseph Teal, 1822).

24. The story of the "Big Bible" is often confused, even today, with the story Ellen White did tell of holding a Bible and quoting texts from it in Randolph, Mass.; see White, *Spiritual Gifts*, 2: 78. The Bible she held in Randolph was a "quarto" Bible, the Big Bible a "folio," sometimes called an "elephant folio."

25. W. C. White to Sarah Peck, April 2, 1919, Ellen G. White Estate Document File 732a. In statements published after Ellen White's death, her son Willie White attributed the Big Bible story to his parents.

26. James White, "A Test," *Review and Herald* 7 (1855): 61; Ellen G. White, "Communication from Sister White," *Review and Herald* 7 (1856): 118.

27. Ellen White quoted James White's words in a letter to Lucinda Hall, May 16, 1876, Letter H-066, Ellen G. White Estate.

28. Jerry Allen Moon, *W. C. White and Ellen G. White: The Relationship between the Prophet and Her Son* (Berrien Springs, MI: Andrews University Press, 1993), 439–50.

29. Richard Bushman, *Joseph Smith: Rough Stone Rolling* (New York: Alfred A. Knopf, 2005), 119.

30. Robert Peel, *Mary Baker Eddy: The Years of Discovery* (New York: Holt, Rinehart and Winston, 1966), 278.

31. Uriah Smith, *The Visions of Mrs. E. G. White: Manifestation of Spiritual Gifts according to the Scriptures* (Battle Creek, MI: Steam Press of the Seventh-day Adventist Publishing Assn., 1868); D. M. Canright, *Seventh-day Adventism Renounced after an Experience of Twenty-Eight Years by a Prominent Minister and Writer of That Faith* (Kalamazoo, MI: Kalamazoo Publishing Co., 1888). For later defenses of Ellen White, see W. H. Branson, *In Defense of the Faith: A Reply to Canright* (Washington, DC: Review and Herald Publishing Assn., 1933); and Francis David Nichol, *Ellen G. White and Her Critics: An Answer to the Major Charges that Critics Have Brought against Mrs. Ellen G. White* (Washington, DC: Review and Herald Publishing Assn., 1951).

32. George W. Amadon, "A Few of the Epithets which Eld. McLearn Applies to Sr. White and Her Work," *Review and Herald* 60 (1883): 53.

33. S.M.I. Henry, "My Telescope," *Gospel of Health* 2 (January 1898): 26–27.

34. This could, of course, merely indicate that European photographers were inclined to favor more candid, less formal scenes than their American counterparts.

35. Steven L. McKenzie, *How to Read the Bible: History, Prophecy, Literature— Why Modern Readers Need to Know the Difference and What It Means for Faith Today* (New York: Oxford University Press, 2009), esp. chap. 2, "Forthtelling not Foretelling." See, e.g., Gilbert, *Divine Predictions of Mrs. Ellen G. White Fulfilled.*

36. Jonathan Butler, "The World of Ellen White and the End of the World," *Spectrum* 10 (Number 2, 1979): 2–13; Ron Graybill, "Tales of a Tennessee Chain Gang," *Liberty* 68 (Jan. –Feb. 1973): 2–5.

37. Ellen G. White, "God's Care for His Children," *Signs of the Times* 23 (May 6, 1897): 5 (decree); Ellen G. White, MS 6, 1889, Nov. 4, 1889, published in Ellen G. White, *Selected Messages*, 3 vols. (Washington, DC: Review and Herald Publishing Assn., 1957, 1980), 3: 397 (imprisoned); Ellen G. White, *Early Writings of Ellen G. White* (Washington, DC: Review and Herald Publishing Assn., 1882, 1945), 282–83 (writing).

38. Office of Archives and Statistics, *148th Annual Statistical Report—2010* (Silver Spring, MD: General Conference of Seventh-day Adventists, 2010). The number of languages into which her books have been translated was given in a communication to the author from Tim Poirier, Ellen G. White Estate, Oct. 6, 2011.

39. Ellen G. White, Last Day Events (Boise, ID: Pacific Press, 1992); Herbert Douglass, *Dramatic Prophecies of Ellen White: Stories of World Events Divinely Foretold* (Boise, ID: Pacific Press, 2007).

5

Author

Arthur Patrick

DURING HER LIFETIME, Ellen White wrote some 26 books, 200 tracts and pamphlets, and 5,000 periodical articles. At her death the typing of her assorted manuscripts, letters, and diaries remained incomplete; when fully typed, these materials amounted to well over 70,000 pages.[1] Her literary heirs drew on these sources to assemble scores of additional titles. Although White recycled much of her prose and borrowed extensively, writing occupied more of her time and effort than any other activity. And nothing she did generated more accolades or greater controversy than her claims of authorship.

Ellen Harmon's publishing career began inadvertently in 1846, when a fellow Millerite, Enoch Jacobs, took the liberty of printing her description of her first "vision." Her future husband, James White, republished the account as a broadside, launching his career as her publisher. Until 1884, when the Seventh-day Adventist Pacific Press brought out an attractively bound edition of *The Great Controversy between Christ and Satan* for the non-Adventist public, Ellen White generally aimed her writings at fellow Adventists. Her only book initially published by a non-Adventist publisher, *Steps to Christ* (Fleming H. Revell, 1892) became her all-time best-seller, eventually circulating in over 100 million copies in more than 165 languages.

Methods

Ellen White always wrote in longhand, but later in her career shorthand enabled her assistants to record her oral presentations, which often became articles and chapters. During the early period, her writing served as an adjunct to her larger role as an itinerant speaker among scattered Millerites who were becoming Sabbatarians and seeking a new identity. After her marriage in 1846 she took on various wifely duties and, between 1847 and 1860, she became the mother of four sons. So often was she absent from her family that one of her sons reflected, "I had lots of mothers and they were all good ones."[2] Between 1868 and 1909, White complained of "head troubles" that at times limited her writing to half a day: "some of the time my head troubles me and then I have to rest, lie down, stop thinking, and take my time for writing when I can do so comfortably."[3] Two decades later, when resident in her much-loved Sunnyside in Australia, White wrote most frequently while others slept, occasionally from 11:30 p.m., but more often between 3 a.m. and breakfast at 7 a.m. After her Australasian sojourn she hurried back to the United States in 1900, eager to confront emerging heresies. During her seventies and eighties, White and her staff brought to completion literary tasks that had long been on her mind, but without the flourish of the previous decade. Her hopes for Elmshaven, in California's Napa Valley, as a sanctuary for reflective writing went largely unrealized because she increasingly turned her attention to protecting her educational, medical, and theological ideas.

White repeatedly expressed a profound sense of inadequacy, even to the point of feeling "less than nothing." She often described herself as "prostrated with sickness" or "sorely afflicted" by illness that brought her "very near death's door." This was especially true during the early years of Adventism, when she experienced a number of episodes from which she was miraculously restored by prayer. With only three or four years of formal schooling she acutely felt her academic limitation. Even after becoming well established as an author, she lamented being neither a "scholar" nor a "grammarian." During the 1890s, the most fruitful decade of her literary career, she confessed: "I am but a poor writer, and cannot with pen or voice express the great and deep mysteries of God."[4]

White long cherished the editorial and publishing assistance of her husband, James White (1821-1881), the principal founder of Adventist publishing and frequent editor of its flagship periodical, *Second Advent Review and Sabbath Herald*, widely known simply as the *Review*. When her son Henry was three, Ellen White mentioned that she was "denied the privilege" of his company "as our house is all employed in writing and folding and wrapping papers." After the Whites acquired their first hand press in 1852, their house doubled for three years as the office of the

Review. By 1854 the *Review* was providing "almost the only visible cohesion" for Sabbatarian Adventism, and the Whites' Rochester (New York) home was at once "editorial office, printshop, bindery, and staff boarding house" for a group of fifteen to twenty persons. Later, according to memories recorded by the Whites' third son, William (Willie, 1854-1937), Ellen would read manuscripts aloud to James, and "if he discovered weaknesses in the composition, such as faulty tenses of verbs, or disagreement among subject, noun, and verb, he would suggest grammatical corrections" that she would incorporate into the manuscript before continuing to read.[5] Understandably, Ellen felt "inexpressibly sad" on the occasions when James fell too ill to fulfil his role as "helper and counsellor." "I cannot prepare my own writings for the press," she lamented. "Until I can do this I shall write no more. It is not my duty to tax others with my manuscript."[6] Fortunately, such desperate feelings did not usually last long. Late in 1877 James reported: "Her books now in print amount to not less than five thousand pages, besides thousands of pages of epistolary matter addressed to churches and individuals."[7]

Even before James's death in 1881 Ellen began turning to her favorite son, Willie, for assistance. After his father's death, Willie increasingly became his mother's travelling companion, confidant, editor, counsellor, staff manager, representative, and custodian. At first he shrank from the criticism that he knew "would come to any person who assisted mother in her literary work."[8] But his mother convinced him that it was God's commission that he should help prepare her writings for publication. When Willie became so "overwhelmed with responsibilities" that he did not have "time to read any articles of any description," she experienced an acute sense of bereavement.[9]

Others also assisted. In 1907, for example, one of White's secretaries, Clarence C. Crisler (1877-1936), solicited the help of William W. Prescott (1855-1944) in preparing for publication a series of articles by White on Old Testament history.[10] A graduate of Dartmouth College, Prescott had built an impressive reputation within Adventism. At thirty years of age, he had accepted the presidency of Battle Creek College; thereafter, his long and very public service involved administering and founding educational institutions, editing the *Review,* traveling, teaching, writing, and engaging in various aspects of church leadership, including close association with six General Conference presidents. Ellen White and her associates valued Prescott's erudition. During the final revision of *The Great Controversy* (1911), Willie White and others urged Prescott to check the manuscript.

Prescott suggested over a hundred changes that he thought would improve the book and make it more accurate.

Initiatives to engage the expertise of individuals such as Prescott dovetailed with White's own pattern of relying on the skills of individuals whom she deemed reliable. White frequently entrusted manuscripts to ministers, administrators, editors, and others for advice. Once after placing copy in the hands of a senior minister, she recorded her disappointment: "He just did a miserable job. He did not change anything or improve it at all."[11] By contrast at the time, White especially prized the literary assistance of her niece, Mary Clough, an experienced journalist who worked for her aunt in 1876 and 1877. Although she never converted to Adventism, Clough worked "tremendously," at times "driving to the uttermost" until midnight or later. The quality of her work prompted White to describe her as "the best copyist for me, I can ever have."[12]

In preparing her main volume on the "Life of Christ" for publication in the 1890s, a project on which White spent three thousand dollars of her own money for literary "workers," she relied most heavily on her long-time "bookmaker," Marian Davis, who served as her trusted friend and assistant from 1879 to 1904 (Figure 5.1a).[13] White began writing about Christ as early as 1858, in a manuscript published as the first volume of *Spiritual Gifts*. Later, in the 1870s, she expanded her treatment of Christ's life from 50 to 640 pages for her *Spirit of Prophecy* volumes; and in the 1890s her writings on Christ culminated in a plethora of articles and four volumes: *Steps to Christ* (1892), *Thoughts from the Mount of Blessing* (1896), *The Desire of Ages* (1898), and *Christ's Object Lessons* (1900). To keep the production moving forward while travelling in New Zealand during much of 1893, White delegated to Davis, a former school teacher and proofreader, the task of assembling her materials on the life of Christ. Writing from Melbourne, Australia, Davis explained "the necessity of having the matter from articles and scrapbooks, that might be available for use in the life of Christ, copied, so as to be convenient for reference." "Perhaps," she continued, "you can imagine the difficulty of trying to bring together points relating to any subject when these must be gleaned from thirty scrapbooks, a half-dozen bound volumes, and fifty manuscripts, all covering thousands of pages."[14]

In 1900, Ellen White described Davis's bookmaking role to the General Conference president, G. A. Irwin. Davis, she explained, took "my articles which are published in the papers" and pasted them into blank books. As Davis prepared a book chapter, White explained, "Marian remembers that I have written something on that special point, which may make the matter more forcible. She begins to search for this, and if when she finds it, she sees that it will make the chapter more clear, she adds it." When White was travelling, Davis at times wrote to her employer suggesting "improvements to be made in articles" or chapters; White implemented some suggestions and declined others. In addition to combing through and selecting snippets from a wealth of written material in scrapbooks and other sources, Davis occasionally gleaned additional insights from attending lectures on subjects related to White's themes.

Davis played a large role in the production of *The Desire of Ages,* working "for a better opening to the chapters" so the book would seem less like a diary, trying to begin both chapters and paragraphs with short sentences, simplifying where possible, dropping out "every needless word," and making the book "more compact and vigorous." In a letter to Willie White Davis wrote: "I never realized the power of simplicity and compactness, as since I began this work." Keeping her mind on "the many thousands who will read the book," she wanted "just as little human imperfection as possible to mar its divine beauty." Davis repeatedly urged individuals such as H. Camden Lacey (1871-1950), the brother of Willie White's second wife and a teacher of Scripture and Greek, to assist with editing the manuscript. Reflecting on his knowledge of Davis's role, Lacey noted that the title page or preface should clearly state "that *The Desire of Ages* was written by Mrs. E. G. White, and edited by Miss Marian Davis."[15] On the occasion of Davis's death from tuberculosis in 1904, White wrote: "Of Sister Davis it can be truly said, 'She hath done what she could.' All the energies of her being were freely given to the work that she loved. Her quick appreciation of truth, and her sympathy for the seeker after truth, enabled her to work enthusiastically in preparing for the press the matter which the Lord had given me for his people."[16]

From such examples, Ellen White's method of writing becomes apparent. White wrote letters—always in longhand—on a host of topics addressed to people in different parts of the world. She also kept a diary and notes on her reading; she travelled frequently, spoke often, and wrote articles and books on multiple themes. Rarely a solitary author, White customarily led a team of valued associates who helped her produce her prophetic writings. Davis and other secretaries typed and retyped developing manuscripts as they were readied for printing. Although White hoped and attempted to read all the copy to ensure that the final product accorded with her views, on many occasions she simply had to trust others to complete the editing processes.

In addition to being a highly collaborative author, White drew freely from religious tracts, magazines, and books that related to her subjects. For decades she had access to the range of magazines that came to the *Review* office, exchanged with other publishers. In addition, White often requested her associates to seek, secure, or send reference materials to her:

> You need not send Walks and Homes of Jesus when you send the books I laid out.[17]
>
> Send books, red-covered Jewish Antiquities and the Bible Dictionary. Is Night Scenes of the Bible there? If so, send it.[18]
>
> Tell Mary to find me some histories of the Bible that would give me the order of events.[19]

White's staff took an active role in finding and recommending books that might be valuable in their group Bible study or in "the preparation of articles on Bible subjects."[20] Her personal and office libraries at the time of her death comprised some 1,400 volumes.

Often White's development of a particular idea or theme can be followed from its first expression in a letter or a diary entry, through its form as a periodical article, to its appearance in a book chapter. Her description of the Protestant Reformation, for example, evolved from five tiny pages in *Spiritual Gifts* in 1858 to more than a hundred pages in the 1884 edition of *The Great Controversy* to almost 200 pages in the 1911 edition.

White's treatment of the Czech reformer John Hus (ca. 1369-1415) is of particular interest, owing to the fact that, atypically, her initial handwritten manuscript has survived. Hus does not appear in White's 1858 account of the Reformation, but he attracts 540 words in the 1884 edition of *The Great Controversy* and about 4,800 words in the 1888 edition. As historian Donald R. McAdams has shown, White selectively abridged and adapted the sources that she used. At times she followed one earlier historian "page after page, leaving out much material, but using their sequence, some of their ideas, and often their words." McAdams "found no historical fact in her text that is not in their text." She included both "historical errors and moral exhortations." His study "revealed that Mrs. White's literary assistant at the time, Miss Marian Davis, not only improved Mrs. White's English but also played a very significant role in deleting a large amount of original material dealing with the spiritual significance of events and adding additional material from [James A.] Wylie," a well-known historian of Protestantism.[21]

At times White took precautions to avoid being influenced by the thoughts of others. On one occasion she explained, "I have not been in the habit of reading any doctrinal articles in the paper [*Review and Herald*], that my mind should not have any understanding of anyone's ideas and views, and that not a hold of any man's theories should have any connection with that which I write."[22] Willie believed that although his mother received heaven-sent messages, she remained free to borrow the expressions of others. As he explained:

> In the early days of her work, Mother was promised wisdom [from the Holy Spirit] in the selection from the writings of others, that would enable her to select the gems of truth from the rubbish of error. We have seen this fulfilled, and yet when she told me of this, she admonished me not to tell it to others. Why this restriction I never knew, but am now inclined to believe that she saw how this might lead some of her brethren to claim too much for her writings as a standard with which to correct historians.[23]

The above depiction of White's authorial methods would seem unexceptional except for two factors: her explicit claims of divine agency and her copious, unacknowledged use of sources written by others. As a teenager Ellen Harmon opened her first written communication of its type with the bold claim, "God has shown me in holy vision." The four-volume Index to her writings lists more than a hundred references by White to herself as in some way the "Lord's special messenger."[24] The tone of her first "testimony" matches countless remarks made during a lifetime of writing. "Sister White," she wrote later in life, "is not the originator of these books. They contain the instruction that during her life-work God has been giving her. They contain the precious, comforting light that God has graciously given His servant to be given to the world."[25]

Concerns

Typical of Ellen White's literary borrowing is the following example:

> The greatest want of the world is the want of men–men who will not be bought or sold, men who in their inmost souls are true and honest, men who do not fear to call sin by its right name, men

whose conscience is as true to duty as the needle to the pole, men who will stand for the right though the heavens fall.[26]

White's sentence has been quoted often by Adventist authors, memorized by devout believers, and cited on plaques that adorn the walls of Adventist homes. However, it was not original with her. A common aphorism in nineteenth-century North America, versions of it even appeared in the *Review:*

> The great want of this age is men. Men who are not for sale. Men who are honest, sound from center to circumference, true to the heart's core—men who will condemn wrong in a friend or foe, in themselves as well as others. Men whose consciences are as steady as the needle to the pole. Men who will stand for the right if the heavens totter and the earth reels.[27]

White did not limit her copying to nicely phrased passages and historical facts. Occasionally, the words of others found their way into descriptions of visionary experiences. In 1890, for example, she recorded in her diary what she had seen in a recent vision, in which her "guide" said:

> The whys and wherefores are often concealed from you, yet speak the words I shall give you, however painful it may be to you. The ways in which God leads his people are generally mysterious.... God knows better than you do what is good and essential for his children. He never leads them otherwise than they would wish to be led if they were able to see as clearly as He does what they must do to establish characters that will fit them for the heavenly courts.

The latter part of this passage was subsequently recycled in *The Desire of Ages* as "God never leads his children otherwise than they would choose to be led, if they could see the end from the beginning." Decades earlier, in a work published in English in 1836, the German author Frederick W. Krummacher had penned the following in his *Elijah the Tishbite:*

> The whys and wherefores are concealed from us.... The ways God leads us are generally mysterious.... God... knows exactly and much better than we do what is good and necessary for His children; and, in truth, He never leads them otherwise than they would

wish Him to lead them, if they were able to see as clearly into their hearts and necessities as He does.[28]

The issue of White's use of sources, mooted as early as the 1840s, increasingly became a focus of debate between her defenders and detractors. During the 1860s, her early treatises on health, which displayed a striking similarity to the writings of other health reformers, prompted skeptics to charge her with copying. In response she insisted that her "views were written independent of books or the opinion of others." She explained in the *Review* that although she was as "dependent upon the Spirit of the Lord in writing my views as I am in receiving them, yet the words I employ in describing what I have seen are my own, unless they be those spoken to me by an angel, which I always enclose in marks of quotation."[29] For her critics, her strong denials of copying from or even being influenced by earthly sources compounded the problem.

Among White's colleagues one of the most troubled was Dudley M. Canright (1840–1919), a minister who served two years as one of the three-member General Conference committee. By the 1880s, after ruminating on the problem for two decades, Canright began openly expressing his doubts. In 1889, after leaving the church, he published *Seventh-day Adventism Renounced*, which explicitly charged White with plagiarism, most notably in her *Sketches from the Life of Paul* (1883) and in the fourth volume of *Spirit of Prophecy* (1884). That year the *Healdsburg Enterprise* reported at length on the growing controversy. Some non-Adventist clergy in the northern California town, where Adventists had established an academy, imported Canright from Michigan to help them address the issue "Is Mrs. White a Plagiarist?"

Would not any literate critic judging from the quotations adduced and a comparison of the passages indicated, conclude that Mrs. White in writing her "Great Controversy" Vol. IV had before her the open books and from them took both ideas and words. We ask the candid reader if we have sustained our position. Does she not stand convicted of "introducing passages from another man's writings and putting them off as her own." If so, we have proved the point in issue, and, according to Webster, Mrs. White is a plagiarist, a literary thief.[30]

Henceforth Canright's expose would provide the normative arsenal for many subsequent critics of White and Adventism.

As the furor over her writings loomed, White commissioned her editorial staff to identify previously uncited quotations and append sources. She relied on them to advise her about literary conventions and to do the hack work that made the disputed text of the 1884 edition of *The Great Controversy* more publicly acceptable. The Canright controversy provides essential background for understanding the "Author's Preface" added to the 1888 and subsequent editions of the book, which contains White's most detailed statement about the use she made of the writings of other authors:

> In some cases where a historian has so grouped together events as to afford, in brief, a comprehensive view of the subject, or has summarized details in a convenient manner, his words have been quoted; but except in a few instances no specific credit has been given, since they are not quoted for the purpose of citing that writer as authority, but because his statement affords a ready and forcible presentation of the subject. In narrating the experience and views of those carrying forward the work of reform in our own time, similar use has occasionally been made of their published works.[31]

The year before this preface appeared, Ellen White had hired an additional literary assistant, Fannie Bolton, who served White for almost a decade (Figure 5.1b). A skilled writer and poet who had previously worked as a correspondent for the *Chicago Daily Inter Ocean,* Bolton at times accomplished twice the work of others, but she felt unable to remain silent about the processes she observed. She complained that her work (and that of such other literary assistants as Marian Davis) went unacknowledged, as did White's use of the writings of other authors. Bolton's allegations made her both a "traitor" and an "Adversary," in White's terms. White's "testimonies" addressed to Bolton, and Bolton's confessions, multiple dismissals, reinstatements, and psychiatric problems reveal a talented but troubled woman. (Whether legend or fact, Canright's claim that, near the end of her life, Marian Davis also grew distressed by the plagiarism issue, persists among those who believe White's critics more than her apologists.)[32]

The evidence of extensive literary borrowing unsettled even some of White's most loyal supporters. In 1883 Uriah Smith, long-time editor of the *Review* and author of an 1868 defense of White, outlined in a letter to Canright "present difficulties" for which he saw no solution:

FIGURE 5.1 Two of Ellen White's editors: Marian Davis (a) worked for her during 1879–1904; Fanny Bolton (b) began assisting her in 1887 and continued for nearly a decade (Courtesy of the Ellen G. White Estate, Inc.).

> The idea has been studiously instilled into the minds of the people that to question the visions in the least is to become at once a hopeless apostate and rebel, and too many, I am sorry to say, have not strength of character enough to shake off such a conception, hence the moment anything is done to shake them on the visions, they lose faith in everything and go to destruction. I believe this state of things never would have occurred had the position of our people on this manifestation of the gifts been correct.[33]

Smith felt that many individuals, "too doggedly bigoted and stubborn," would prevent Adventists from coming "together and calmly, candidly, kindly and freely" to find a consistent position.

Other church leaders made similar observations. On one occasion Prescott expressed his concerns to Willie White:

> The way your mother's writings have been handled and the false impression concerning them which is still fostered among the people have brought great perplexity and trial to me. It seems to me that what amounts to deception, though probably not intentional, has been practiced in making some of her books, and that no serious effort has been made to disabuse the minds of the people of what

was known to be their wrong view concerning her writings. But it is no use to go into these matters. I have talked with you for years about them, but it brings no change. I think however that we are drifting toward a crisis which will come sooner or later and perhaps sooner.[34]

Arthur G. Daniells, Adventism's longest-serving General Conference president and one who knew Mrs. White's consultative and editing processes firsthand, bluntly advised Willie White:

I think that you and Sister White should make a clean, clear statement with reference to the question of plagiarism. Give the exact reason why there was a failure to give proper credit to the authors quoted. I presume we all must admit that it would have been better to have given quotation marks or some other kind of credit than to have put the matter out as it was.[35]

Neither Willie nor his mother responded to Daniells' request.

By the first decade of the new century concerns about White's writing habits had grown to such an extent that on March 30, 1906, White wrote that she was "directed by the Lord to request" John Harvey Kellogg "and any others who have perplexities and grievous things in their minds regarding the testimonies that I have borne, to specify what their objections and criticisms are. The Lord will help me answer these objections, and to make plain that which seems to be intricate."[36] In response, Dr. Charles Stewart, a medical colleague of Kellogg's at the Battle Creek Sanitarium, wrote three letters to White, one of which was published as *A Response to an Urgent Testimony from Mrs. Ellen G. White Concerning Contradictions, Inconsistencies and Other Errors in Her Writings.* (The blue cover of this 89-page work caused it to become infamously known as *The Blue Book.*) In it Stewart stated:

The foregoing refers entirely to your testimonies, but there is one other point upon which I would like some information, and that is with reference to your books. I have been told that several of your works contain material very similar to that of other authors, and it has been stated by those who have worked with you and others familiar with your work that you consulted these freely in the preparation of your books, and have felt free to appropriate many of their sayings and ideas without giving credit for the same. This, of course, gives one the impression that you are the author of all. Are your books, such as "Great Controversy," "Desire of Ages," and the "Life of Paul," entirely original matter, and are they, as is always claimed so far as I know, what God has revealed to you?

Stewart illustrated his concerns, showing, for example, that careful comparison of an 1855 work, *The Life and Epistles of St. Paul* by William John Conybeare and John Saul Howson, with White's volume on the same topic (1883) disclosed "over two hundred places in your book which correspond very closely to passages in the book by Conybeare and Howson." In parallel columns Stewart quoted six passages from each volume. He then pointed out that similar parallels could be found by comparing White's *Great Controversy* with Wylie's *History of the Waldenses* and J. H. Merle d'Aubigne's five-volume *History of the Great Reformation of the Sixteenth Century*, published in an American edition between 1846 and 1853. Stewart alluded to various arguments that White's defenders employed "to explain the great similarity between some of your books and those of other authors which antedated yours several years," dismissing the possibility that proofreaders had failed in their responsibility before pressing the question: "Is that special light you claim to have from God revealed to you, at least to some extent through your reading the various commentaries and other books treating of religious subjects?" White never acknowledged Stewart's letters but reportedly commented that God had instructed her not to respond to her critics.

White and Her Publishers

Soon after James White initiated the publication of periodicals for the scattered Advent believers in 1848, it became evident that the community needed its own printing facilities. In the summer of 1851, Ellen White gathered some of the periodical, broadside, and pamphlet accounts of her early visions into a booklet of 64 pages, entitled *A Sketch of the Christian Experience and Views of Ellen G. White*. For this first book of hers, the Whites contracted out the printing, but the very next year they acquired their own hand press, which the itinerants took with them from town to town in New York and New England. Finally, in 1855 they and their press settled permanently in Battle Creek. There they established the Seventh-day Adventist (later Review and Herald) Publishing Association, which was joined in 1875 by the Pacific Press Publishing Association in Oakland, California. During White's lifetime one or the other of these two presses published most of her books.

James White managed most of his wife's publishing until his death in 1881; thereafter, until his mother's death in 1915, Willie assumed that role. The logistics of publishing often burdened James, as did the editing of Ellen's manuscripts. In 1857 James began to raise funds for the steam press, which the next year published Ellen's *Spiritual Gifts: The Great Controversy between Christ and His Angels, and Satan and His Angels*. In 1884 Ellen White and her son accepted the idea of using door-to-door canvassers or colporteurs to sell the then-enlarged *Great Controversy* to the general public. This arrangement proved so successful that when White was preparing *Steps to Christ* for publication, some of her associates discussed the possibility of selecting a non-Adventist publisher in order to distribute the volume more widely. George B. Starr, a minister close to White who had worked with Dwight L. Moody in Chicago before his conversion to Adventism, suggested Moody's brother-in-law, Fleming H. Revell, as a possible publisher. By the early 1890s Revell had become one of the most successful Christian publishers in the United States. In 1891 (just two years after publishing Canright's *Seventh-day Adventism Renounced*) he wrote to an Adventist representative stating that he "greatly enjoyed the manuscript" of *Steps to Christ* and that he "should be very glad to bring it out." He explained that "Our usual terms are 10 per cent royalty after the first 1,000, but we shall be quite willing to give 5 per cent royalty on the first 1,000, with 10 per cent on all subsequent issues."[37] Assisted by Marian Davis, who gathered and arranged material from White's letters and manuscripts, as well as from other sources, White completed the manuscript in short order. The 160-page clothbound book, which retailed at 75 cents, underwent seven printings in its first year. Within five years, one hundred thousand copies had been sold. Such sales greatly cheered Ellen White. "Some felt very much dissatisfaction that Steps to Christ was given to Revell," she observed in 1897. "I have received quite a sum of money, more than has come to me from some books; and I think more would come to me if he had more of my books to handle... there is an advantage in doing this, because they get the truth before a class that we will not reach."[38] A short time later the Review and Herald purchased the copyright from Revell, and in 1900 White herself acquired the copyright. By 1935 *Steps to Christ* had been translated into more than fifty languages; a half-century later the number had grown to 122.

White's relations with the Review and Herald Publishing Association and the Pacific Press were not always so amicable, a fact illustrated by tensions over publication priorities, marketing issues, and royalties. When her Adventist publishers held back the distribution of her books until other stock was sold, she became irked to the point where she invoked her prophetic authority to break the logjam. James White had always watched out for his wife's (and his own) financial interests, but after his death Ellen experienced periods of deep dissatisfaction with the meager royalties granted to her. Moreover, the church's publishing arm at times served as a conduit for the transfer of funds from the United States to Australia; when the system failed to meet White's expectations, she expressed her frustrations in graphic terms. The physical appearance of her books, especially their illustrations and bindings, also on occasion became a source of friction.[39]

White's dissatisfaction with her publishers and her determination to ensure that her writings would "speak as long as time shall last" prompted her late in life to borrow heavily to buy back plates and rights to her books and lock them safely away in her Elmshaven vault. At the time of her death in 1915 she owed her debtors some $96,000—so much that publication of her work had to be temporarily suspended. The trust she created to manage her estate called for legal independence from the church. However, because her liabilities exceeded her assets, to avoid embarrassment and protect the debt holders, her beneficiaries, sons Edson and Willie, and the latter's heirs, agreed to transfer the estate to the General Conference. Thus White's wishes as expressed in her will were not all implemented. Further, it soon became clear that the General Conference officers did not want Willie White and the Elmshaven office to exercise control over the literary materials in the estate. At the end of a protracted period of negotiation the General Conference took ownership of the estate and paid off all the liabilities. The surviving entity, known as the Ellen G. White Estate, Inc., has remained in the hands of the General Conference.[40]

Aftermath

Even after Ellen White's death, controversy continued to swirl around her career as a writer. A significant event for White's contemporaries occurred in 1919, when church administrators and Bible and history teachers met in the first Adventist conference of its type (see Chapter 17). Leaders such as Daniells, Prescott, and Lacey, who had known White firsthand and had participated in her publishing initiatives, shared their insights frankly and constructively, raising questions about White's authority in history and other areas. Stenographers recorded most of the discussions, but for a half-century the transcriptions remained inaccessible.[41] Instead of fostering a more realistic understanding of White, the conference provoked an aggressive pamphlet war that may have cost Daniells the presidency of the General Conference in 1922.[42] A fundamentalist trend in Adventism led to a rebuttal of Canright's charges in 1933 and a consummate defense of Ellen White in 1951.[43]

In the 1970s, however, a group of young university-trained Adventist scholars launched a reassessment of the historical Ellen White. In response to their troubling studies and the specific charges of plagiarism levelled by Walter Rea, the General Conference in 1980 commissioned a seven-year research project under the leadership of Fred Veltman, a New Testament textual analyst, to identify the sources White had used in *The Desire of Ages (DA)*. Restricting himself to just fifteen of the 87 chapters in White's tome, Veltman scanned about 500 volumes on which White might have relied. He discovered that White had drawn on more than twenty authors and "that 31.4 percent of the *DA* text is dependent to some extent on literary sources." He described the text as "largely an edited compilation of text portions written by Ellen White in earlier documents, including letters, articles, manuscripts, and to a small extent her diary notations." In the end he concluded that Ellen White's "literary dependency" was a "serious problem" that "strikes at the heart of her honesty, her integrity, and therefore her trustworthiness."[44]

In recent years the developing field of Adventist Studies, along with its subset Ellen White Studies, has exploded with the availability of online data and interpretation.[45] Even though the White Estate has joined in identifying White's literary sources, some detractors and defenders are as far apart as ever. Walter Rea, a leader in exposing White's dependency, has claimed that "far more than 80% of the material enclosed within the covers" of some of White's volumes "was taken from others"; White's apologists have sought to reduce even Veltman's cautious statistics. Seventh-day Adventism and its prophet, like Christianity itself, remain caught up in "a constant process of struggle and rebirth."[46]

NOTES

1. This chapter relies heavily on typescripts of Ellen White's manuscripts, letters, and diaries that are available at Ellen G. White Estate, Inc., Silver Spring, Maryland and at Ellen G. White/Seventh-day Adventist Research Centers around the world. All other sources cited are in original, microfilm, microfiche, or photocopied form in the Ellen G. White/Seventh-day Adventist Research Center at Avondale College, Cooranbong, Australia.
2. Cited by Jerry Allen Moon, *W. C. White and Ellen G. White: The Relationship between the Prophet and Her Son* (Berrien Springs, MI: Andrews University Press, 1993), 3.
3. Ellen G. White to James S. White, April 25, 1876.
4. Ellen G. White to Harriet Stevens, March 10, 1854; Ellen G. White Diary, January 1873; Ellen G. White to William W. and Sarah Prescott, January 18, 1894.
5. Moon, *W. C. White and Ellen G. White*, 2, 62.
6. Ellen G. White Diary, 10 January 1873.
7. J. W. [James White], "Half a Century," *Signs of the Times* 3 (1877), 372.
8. Moon, *W.C. White and Ellen G. White*, 61.
9. Ellen G. White to O. A. Olsen, [Letter 55, 1894, 5]. See also Ellen G. White to "Dear Brethren," October 10, 1894.
10. Gilbert M. Valentine, "The Church 'Drifting toward a Crisis': Prescott's 1915 Letter to William White," *Catalyst* 2 (November 2007), 32–96, available at www.sdanet.org/atissue/white/valentine-drifting.htm.
11. Ellen G. White to Lucinda Hall, April 8, 1876.
12. Ellen G. White to James S. White, April 18, 1876; Ellen G. White to William C. White and Mary K. White, October 26, 1876.
13. Ellen G. White to Mrs. Wessels, July 16, 1896.
14. Marian Davis to William C. White, March 29, 1893, available in Document File 393, Ellen G. White/Seventh-day Adventist Research Centers.
15. Marian Davis to William C. White, April 11, 1897; H. Camden Lacey to D. E. Robinson, August 17, 1931; both cited by Robert W. Olson and Ron Graybill, "How *The Desire of Ages* Was Written," Ellen G. White Estate, 33, 45.
16. Mrs. E. G. White, "Notes of Travel—No. 3," *Review and Herald*, 82 (February 16, 1905), 8.
17. *Ellen G. White to Mary K. White*, circa May 22, 1876.

18. Ellen G. White to Mary K. White, December 8, 1878.

19. Ellen G. White to James Edson and William C. White, December 22–23, 1885.

20. William C. White to B. L.Whitney, January 16, 1887, cited by Olson and Graybill, *"How The Desire of Ages Was Written,"* 21.

21. Donald R. McAdams, "Ellen G. White and the Protestant Historians: The Evidence from an Unpublished Manuscript on John Hus" (unpublished manuscript, 1974; updated 1978), located in the Document Files of the church's Research Centers; Donald R. McAdams, "Shifting Views of Inspiration: Ellen G. White Studies in the 1970s," *Spectrum: The Journal of the Association of Adventist Forums* 10 (March 1980), 34, hereafter referred to as *Spectrum*.

22. Ellen G. White to Ellet J. Waggoner and Alonzo T. Jones, February 18, 1887, cited in Ellen G. White, *Selected Messages,* 3 vols. (Washington, D.C.: Review and Herald Publishing Assn., 1958–1980), 3:64 (1980).

23. Robert W. Olson, "Ellen G. White's Use of Historical References in *The Great Controversy,*" *Adventist Review* 161 (February 23, 1984), 3–5.

24. Board of Trustees of the Ellen G. White Estate, *Comprehensive Index to the Writings of Ellen G. White,* 4 vols. (Mountain View, CA: Pacific Press, 1962–1963), 1992.

25. Ellen G. White to "Dear Brethren and Sisters: An Open Letter From Mrs. E.G. White to All Who Love the Blessed Hope," *Review and Herald* 80 (January 20, 1903), 14–15.

26. Ellen G. White, *Education* (Mountain View, CA: Pacific Press, 1903), 57.

27. "Men Wanted," *Review and Herald* 37 (1871), 47.

28. See Ellen G. White Diary, November 20–24, 1890; Ellen G. White, *The Desire of Ages* (Mountain View, CA: Pacific Press, 1898), 324; Frederick Krummacher, *Elijah the Tishbite* (New York: American Tract Society, 1836), 20–21. For further discussion, see Ron Graybill, "The 'I Saw' Parallels in Ellen White's Writings," *Adventist Review* 159 (1982), 716–18.

29. Ellen G. White, "Questions and Answers," *Review and Herald* 30 (1867), 260.

30. For historical data, see Ron Graybill, "D. M. Canright in Healdsburg, 1889: The Genesis of the Plagiarism Charge," *Insight,* October 21, 1980, 7–10.

31. Ellen G. White, "Introduction," *The Great Controversy* (Mountain View, CA: Pacific Press, 1888), 7–14.

32. "The Fannie Bolton Story–A Collection of Source Documents," Ellen G. White Estate, 1982, is available on the Internet. See also Alice Elizabeth Gregg, "The Unfinished Story of Fannie Bolton and Marian Davis," *Adventist Currents* 1 (October 1983): 24–27, 34–35; 1 (February 1984): 23–25, 29.

33. Uriah Smith to Dudley M. Canright, April 6, 1883.

34. Valentine, "The Church 'Drifting toward a Crisis' " quotes the entire letter.

35. A. G. Daniells to W. C. White, June 24, 1907.

36. Ellen G. White to "Those Who Are Perplexed Regarding the Testimonies," March 30, 1906.

37. Fleming H. Revell to "My dear Mr. Chadwick," October 17, 1891.

38. Ellen G. White, MS 80, July 4, 1897.

39. The complex relationships between White and her publishers is well explored by Gilbert M. Valentine, *The Prophet and the Presidents* (Nampa, ID: Pacific Press, 2011), 103, 148–49, 167, 317–27.

40. Gilbert M. Valentine, *The Struggle for the Prophetic Heritage: Issues in the Conflict for Control of the Ellen G. White Publications, 1930–1939* (Muak Lek, Thailand, Institute Press, 2006).

41. Michael W. Campbell, "The 1919 Bible Conference and Its Significance for Seventh-day Adventist History and Theology" (Ph.D. diss., Andrews University, 2008).

42. Mollerus Couperus, "The Bible Conference of 1919," *Spectrum* 10 (May 1979): 23–57.

43. William H. Branson, *Reply to Canright: The Truth about Seventh-day Adventists* (Washington, DC: Review and Herald Publishing Assn., 1933); Francis D. Nichol, *Ellen G. White and Her Critics* (Washington, DC: Review and Herald Publishing Assn., 1951).

44. Fred Veltman, "Full Report of the Life of Christ Research Project" (November 1988). For succinct summaries, see Fred Veltman, "*The Desire of Ages Project: The Data,*" *Ministry* 63 (October 1990): 4–7; Fred Veltman, "*The Desire of Ages Project:* The Conclusions," *Ministry* 63 (December 1990): 11–15. http://dedication.www3.50megs.com/David/index.html.

45. See my website for illustrative resources: adventiststudies.wordpress.com.

46. Regarding Rea, see Walter T. Rea, *The White Lie* (Turlock, CA: M & R Publications, 1982) and Rea's letter to the editor of *Spectrum* 14 (October 1983): 63–64. See also Arthur Patrick, "Contextualising Recent Tensions in Seventh-day Adventism," *Journal of Religious History* 34 (September 2010): 272–88.

6

Speaker

Terrie Dopp Aamodt

IT WAS 1842, and the world was supposed to end soon. Ellen Harmon, a teenaged girl in Portland, Maine, wrestled with her awakening religious experience. Not yet fifteen, self-conscious about her facial injury, and reticent, she resisted an impression to pray in public. After weeks of agonizing spiritual isolation, her private prayers led her to join a group worshiping in her uncle's home. "I consented to go with my mother to a little prayer meeting, to please her," she recalled. "I knelt on my knees, and my mouth was opened. No sooner did I begin to speak than The power of God gave voice that reached a mile, and There I dedicated myself to God....from that day the cloud burst." When she achieved this victory over her reluctance to pray aloud, she later recalled,

> I held it with a grip that never would let it go. I went from house to house, and I did not go to greet the people. I went right to my companions, and I talked with them all night long, and I would pray with them until they gave their hearts to God.[1]

Many years later, in August 1876, Ellen Harmon White encountered a setting far removed from her adolescent world of 1842. At the Groveland camp meeting site near Haverhill, Massachusetts, train after train emptied passengers onto the grounds until an estimated 15,000 to 20,000 listeners awaited her temperance sermon. The next evening a thousand of the "finest and most select of the city" packed an auditorium in Haverhill to hear her again. "The Queen of England could not have been more honored," she wrote to her family.[2] Her spiritual messages and speaking practices had placed her firmly in the public sphere.[3]

How did this religious woman evolve from the ecstatic shouts of 1842 to the sober cadences of her 1876 lecture at Groveland, and how did public speaking shape her historical role? Ellen Harmon White's movement from spontaneous public physical behaviors to formalized oral and written discourse traced the route of her own spiritual experience. Likewise her Adventist flock, drawn initially by her public visions, came to rely on the apparently more objective world of her transcribed sermons and written words. Ellen White's physical, charismatic discourse—her bodily texts—faded into the background, while her written discourse became canonical. Her public speaking, from the early shouted ecstasies to the eventual full-text published transcriptions, bridged the two discourses. The trajectory of Ellen White's speaking career traces several chronological phases: reliance on the visions in small gatherings during the 1840s and 1850s; creation of a dynamic with James in the 1860s, initially featuring visions but evolving into a dual sermon approach; development of an independent speaking voice during the mid-1870s as James's illnesses separated their labors; and expansion of her solo career after James's death in 1881, increasing contact with the general public.[4] Although Ellen White never claimed the title of "prophet" and never was voted into a church office, her words carried more weight than any other leader of her denomination. Throughout her seventy-year career, public speaking renewed her own confidence in her message, established and reinforced her authoritative voice, and supported her institution-building role.

In the United States, women speaking in public were at best curiosities when Ellen Harmon began to be heard. The American public sphere in her lifetime scarcely heard a female voice, let alone one like hers. Those who wished to speak presented contexts and qualifications: the egalitarian Quakerism of Lucretia Mott, Susan B. Anthony, and Angelina Grimké, the reformism of Lucy Stone, the didacticism of Catherine Beecher, the politics of Anna Dickinson, or the literary world of Harriet Beecher Stowe. These worlds were not open to Ellen Harmon in the 1840s. She shared the role of charismatic female prophet with a handful of all-but-unknown women such as Dorinda Baker and Phoebe Knapp.[5] Although the Millerite preaching of Sojourner Truth, Zilpha Elaw, and Harriet Livermore had familiarized some early Adventists with the sound of female voices raised in public discourse, most Millerite preachers were men, as were almost all Adventist preachers.[6] The avenue of communication open to charismatic religious women had more in common with early Quakers and Shakers than with social reformers or conventionally published authors. The mode was more Mother Ann Lee than Elizabeth Cady Stanton. It was the avenue used by religious enthusiasts bursting with spiritual intensity but lacking formal education and conventional social clout, and it comprised public physical manifestations of personal religious experience. It was a familiar context for Ellen Harmon's fellow Methodists.

In spite of her initial awkwardness, painful shyness, and physical infirmities, Ellen White found the speaking role manageable; it did not require mediation by unpredictable visions or insistent editors. Skilled publicists framed her messages to best advantage in their own accounts of her speaking appointments, but she welcomed the scrutiny of newspaper reporters who found their way onto camp meeting grounds and into Methodist churches and public buildings for her talks. These news reports provide a valuable perspective beyond her circle of believers.

Ellen Harmon would not have gained a consistent audience or confidence in her own voice without a physical requisite: a reliable speaking instrument. An ironic legacy of her childhood accident was a quality shared with only a few men and even fewer women—a resonant voice that carried across distances and was distinctly audible indoors or out. She described the quality of her voice as a compensation for her childhood injury: After the accident "I began to talk down lower. In time, by using the abdominal muscles in talking, I could extend my voice to almost any company."[7] An individual who witnessed many of Ellen White's sermons recalled that she had two voices: a mezzo soprano for conversation or visiting and her speaking voice, which she called her " 'stomach' voice. It was a deep contralto with a wonderful carrying power. It was not a monotonous voice but a constant voice. She never raised her voice in an effort to be heard."[8] Although at times Ellen White talked herself hoarse, she spoke up to 150 times a year for decades and kept a regular speaking schedule well into her eighties. Knowing that her voice could be heard, she repeatedly found that speaking in public made her feel stronger. In June 1865, she described a series of tent meetings in Wisconsin: "I took my position with much trembling, knowing my exhausted condition of body, but the Lord strengthened me."[9]

An aspiring public speaker has to establish authority; a credible voice gains an audience. For early Adventists, Ellen Harmon's frail body in vision provided evidence of her spiritual authenticity (see Chapter 4). Her early travels, aided by James White and sometimes Joseph Bates, sifted the disparate remnants of Millerites into supportive and antagonistic groups. "Most of our meetings were held in private houses," she recalled. "Our congregations were small. It was seldom that any came into our meetings excepting Adventists, unless they were attracted by curiosity to hear a woman speak."[10] Curiosity to see a woman in vision was also a factor. The public aspect of the spectacle invited viewers to test her body themselves. In 1845, during a vision at the Thayer home in Randolph, Massachusetts, the host decided to establish her veracity by placing a large Bible on her as she reclined against the wall in a corner of the room.[11] When Ellen went into vision while she and James were making presentations together, James would invite people from the audience, including physicians, to evaluate whether she was breathing. Onlookers' curiosity about Ellen White's female body in vision, their willingness to touch her with apparent freedom, and James White's encouragement that they do so seem incongruous in the setting of a religious meeting. The experiences of other women speakers in the nineteenth century, however, provide a context. In 1858 an Indiana audience goaded Sojourner Truth into baring her breast to prove she was a woman.[12] Unconventional speakers seeking a hearing were in some cases willing to be tested.

Ellen Harmon's marriage to James White in 1846 created a speaking alliance that endured for decades. Early in their marriage they traveled to meetings in homes and then in barns as Adventist groups, still without churches of their own, grew larger. During their joint speaking engagements in the 1850s and 1860s, James and Ellen White's public speaking developed a pattern: James would preach a closely reasoned, text-based message during the morning sermon hour, and Ellen would conduct a more emotive service in the afternoon, reflecting on her own experience and sharing her vision-related testimonies about other individuals. Often such sessions were followed by a "social meeting," when members of the congregation gave their personal testimonies. The number of testimonies at these social meetings became an index to the success of their joint efforts. James's and Ellen's approaches complemented each other. As Ellen noted, "My husband would give a doctrinal discourse, then I would follow with an exhortation of considerable length, melting my way into the feelings of the congregation. Thus my husband sowed and I watered the seed of truth, and God did give the increase."[13]

When Ellen experienced public visions, James reminded audiences that the visions occurred spontaneously and that Mrs. White dreaded having them. In the aftermath of her December 1865 vision on health reform, which led to several thousand pages of written testimonies, James reported that "Mrs. W. has said, more than twenty times...if she could have her choice, to go into the grave or have another vision, she should choose the grave."[14] The visions exhausted her because the real work began after the vision ended. A conventional sermon, in contrast, concluded when she was finished speaking, and this fact may have affected her reliance on sermons as time went on.

After Seventh-day Adventists formed a denomination in Battle Creek, Michigan, in 1863, its membership continued to expand outside the context of New England religion. At the same time, Ellen White spoke more frequently to audiences who were not Adventists. These guest sermons followed traditional discourse modes and did not include visions. At these appointments she carefully avoided offending the congregations with sectarian messages, and she refrained from the pointed testimonies she frequently aimed at her fellow church members. While traveling through Michigan with James in the spring of 1868 she was invited to speak in the Tuscola Methodist church. She spoke for about an hour and a half on themes of salvation to a standing-room-only congregation. After her sermon she was surprised to learn that she had used the same text employed by the Methodist minister that morning. She noted with satisfaction that one of the "wealthiest and most influential men in town" stated that she "carried it much higher than our minister."[15] Ellen White welcomed the opportunity these speaking forays presented to dissipate prejudice against Adventists. A prominent feature of her 1878 and 1880 trips to the Northwest were multiple public-speaking engagements. After a sermon at a large Methodist church in Salem, Oregon, Ellen reported to James that "one of the Methodist ministers said to Brother Levitt that he regretted Mrs. White was not a staunch Methodist for they would make her a bishop at once."[16] Her reputation continued to extend beyond her own denomination.

As Ellen's speaking career increased in the 1870s, James's health became more precarious. Constitutionally unable to stop hurling himself into every challenge, he kept up a stiff work regimen even after a series of paralytic strokes debilitated him physically and emotionally. He became depressed and querulous when his body gave out under his demands and when his closest colleagues, including his wife, would not bend to his will. James White's biographer Gerald Wheeler discusses the strains James's condition placed on the Whites' marriage.[17] Ellen was torn between her desires to tend to James's needs and to keep pushing "the work" forward.

For James, the 1870s involved significant travel, periods of enforced rest, and attempts to restore his health, first at their new home in California and later back at Battle Creek. For Ellen, the 1870s involved a decision: If "the work" beckoned, and if James remained unable to participate, she would go on alone.

In response to James's erratic health, Ellen began to surround herself with younger assistants, in addition to her son W. C. (Willie) White. In 1875 she engaged her niece Mary Clough as an editorial assistant (see Chapter 5). Mary was bright, well trained in writing and editing, and a congenial companion for Ellen. Although her primary responsibility was editorial assistance, she soon proved to be an outstanding publicist for Ellen White's speaking engagements. By the summer of 1875 Mary was doing advance work along the camp-meeting circuit, sending news releases to nearby newspapers and arranging interviews with journalists on the camp-meeting grounds. Mary dove enthusiastically into her publicity work. She hired up to six copyists to make transcripts of news releases and copies of White's remarks for eventual publication. Ellen noted that even when both she and Mary lost their appetite for the appalling food served at camp meetings, Mary did not complain.[18] Ellen and Mary, sometimes accompanied by James, swept through the Midwest and the East Coast during the summers of 1875, 1876, and 1877.

Near the beginning of the 1875 camp-meeting season, Ellen and James traveled to Gallatin, Missouri. Delayed from their onward travels by rain, they decided to preach at a Christian church in the evening. James delivered a sermon on Adventist doctrine and then announced that Ellen would speak at the same church on Sunday morning, at a time that would not interfere with the services of other churches. According to a newspaper account, the pastor of the church "stated that, as there was a positive command in the Bible against women teaching, she would not have the use of their church." Instead of speaking at the church on Sunday morning, Ellen spoke on Sunday afternoon at the court-house. "The court room was crowded," reported the newspaper. "She delivered a very interesting and instructive discourse concerning the duties of parents in the proper training of their children, both physically and morally. No one could object to the sentiment she proclaimed, and we doubt not many will be benefitted by having heard her. She is a pleasant, forcible speaker, and the audience, after having listened attentively an hour, were not weary."[19]

With Mary Clough's help, the accomplishments of Ellen White came to the attention of a large public. As curiosity seekers were drawn in larger numbers onto Adventist campgrounds, White offered more sermons and lectures on health and temperance. This activity peaked in 1876 during the camp meeting at Groveland, Massachusetts. Swelling the audience of 500 campers, crowds of non-Adventists flocked to the site on special trains dedicated to the event, undoubtedly encouraged by Mary Clough's glowing press releases. By Sunday, August 27, Clough later reported, trains from nearby towns, filled with "intelligent [in other words, well-educated] people," arrived for the morning meeting and heard James White preach. As the trains continued to roll in, Ellen White prepared to take her turn at the podium to deliver a sermon on temperance. She later noted that an estimated 20,000 gathered on the grounds that day, calling it "the most solemn sight I ever beheld."[20]

To top it off, the Temperance Reform Club from nearby Haverhill invited her to address an audience of 1,000 at the city hall on Monday evening. Ellen and James were escorted to a large platform fifteen or twenty feet above the audience, which included "the first men of Haverhill," Ellen wrote to Edson and Emma. Although she had had a severe headache for several days and was "nervous," she recalled, "the Lord helped me speak. I was never more clear....I was stopped several times with clapping of hands and stomping of feet. I never had a more signal victory."[21]

A Haverhill journalist who followed Ellen White that day reported: "The railroads were taxed beyond the utmost capacity of all their preparations for the occasion, and large numbers were prevented from attendance" by lack of transportation. He described how thousands waited at the railroad station in Lawrence while sixteen full cars left for the camp. Steam yachts plied the Merrimac River, arriving hourly, and many visitors traveled by horse and carriage. The reporter noted that doctrinal sermons were nearly continuous that day, interspersed with two temperance lectures by Ellen White. The site, he said, was destined to be a permanent meeting spot for the Adventists' annual camp meetings, and it could be "thus occupied till the time shall arrive which is fixed in the dream which we think constitutes their faith; if so, it may be a very long time, the duration of which the B. and M. Railroad will not object to. It always was the desire and delight of the race to occasionally assemble in great numbers, and in order to do so they must have a central idea to rally round, and that of this sect may as well be one of those ideas as anything else."[22] When Uriah Smith published this article in the *Review and Herald*, he retained the skeptically condescending final paragraph, perhaps to reinforce the veracity of the crowd-size estimate earlier in the article.

Ellen White's development as a public speaker faltered when James died in 1881, a few days after contracting malarial fever. Two days after sharing the pulpit in the Battle Creek Tabernacle on July 30, they both were hospitalized with the malady. Ellen rallied just enough to be at James's bedside when he died on Sabbath afternoon, August 6. She was devastated. "The shock of my husband's death—so sudden, so unexpected—fell upon me with crushing weight," she recalled. "In my feeble condition I had summoned strength to remain at his bedside to the last, but [then]...exhausted nature gave way, and I was completely prostrated."[23] At midnight that evening Ellen thought she was dying. Her pulse became imperceptible, and Dr. John Harvey Kellogg stimulated her heartbeat with an electrical shock. Nurses sponged her spine with hot and cold water for three hours until her pulse improved. Her life remained in the balance for several more days.

One week after James's death, on August 13, his funeral was conducted in the church where he had preached two weeks earlier. Ellen was transported to the service in a wheelchair and sat on a couch near the front of the sanctuary. Although she had been bedridden for nearly two weeks, she felt it was her "duty" to testify to the congregation why a bereaved spouse would feel hope in the Resurrection. She was assisted to the pulpit. "I shall be alone, and yet not alone, for my Saviour will be with me," she told the congregation. "My heart can feel to its very depths, and yet I can tell you I have no tears to shed for the dead. My tears are for the living. And I lay away my beloved treasure to rest,—to rest until the morning of the resurrection, when the Lifegiver shall call the captives from the prison-house to a glorious immortality."[24] Even though she and James had often worked separately in the 1870s, she was not sure she could survive alone. She later recalled, "For one year after his death, I felt my loss keenly, until the Lord, when I was at the gates of death, healed me instantly. This was...about a year after my husband's death."[25]

Ellen White returned to California after James's funeral and attended a Sacramento camp meeting in October 1881. Newspaper accounts noted that she was still recovering from a recent illness and from the death of her husband. During the camp meeting she was able to rekindle some of her usual fervor against one of her favorite villains, tobacco, the "most enslaving" of the vices. "The Tree of Life has no branches that bear tobacco," she warned her audience.[26] Her speaking engagements for the next year, though, were few and far between. In late August 1882 she was felled by another serious bout of fever while in Oakland. Willie and his wife transported her to Healdsburg in September, fearing she would die before they arrived. In early October she asked Willie to take her to the local camp meeting, and once again public speaking rallied her. After the Sabbath afternoon sermon, Ellen asked Willie and an assistant to help her to the pulpit so she could speak. "For five minutes I stood there," she said, trying to speak, and thinking it was "the last speech I should ever make—my farewell message." She steadied herself against the pulpit. "All at once I felt a power come upon me, like a shock of electricity. It passed through my body and up to my head. The people said that they plainly saw the blood mounting to my lips, my ears, my cheeks, my forehead." She recalled feeling healed both physically and emotionally. Uriah Smith, who was present, said she spoke six times during the camp meeting "with her ordinary strength of voice and clearness of thought." Arthur L. White identified this event as a turning point in Ellen White's physical condition.[27] She would spend several more decades speaking in public.

Ellen White's nine-year sojourn in Australia during the 1890s was in many ways a retreat from the demands of the American church that allowed her to focus on the production of some of her most important books. In spite of an eleven-month struggle with inflammatory rheumatism and periodic flare-ups of malarial fever, she maintained a vigorous schedule of public speaking and camp-meeting appointments. Relying on letters and articles to communicate with believers in the United States, she missed the face-to-face public communication she had depended on there to underscore her writing. As she wrote to her fellow female Adventist speaker, the temperance activist S.M.I. Henry, in 1899, "I would much prefer to meet the people in America face to face than to send them written communications." She complained that the brethren who knew her best did not understand her, which prompted her to labor even harder over her letters.[28]

During the nineteenth century Ellen White had played a significant role in developing the Seventh-day Adventist faith, but her most far-reaching influence on its institutional structure came in the twentieth century, in her old age. Her spoken words proved crucial; it is unlikely that her written discourse would have had the same effect if she had remained in Australia. She returned to the United States in time to make a significant impact on the 1901 General Conference session in Battle Creek, the denominational governance meeting that at that time convened biennially. When the sitting General Conference president, George A. Irwin, gaveled the meeting to order on April 3, he called the roll, made his opening remarks, and asked if there was any new business. Ellen White walked to the podium and delivered what was essentially the event's keynote address. Although that moment was not photographed, there is an image of her speaking to the same gathering several days later, with some of the same platform participants (see Figure 6.1). She said the denomination had outgrown its original rudimentary organization. She took church leaders to task for not following her advice on the matter ten years earlier: "What we want now is a reorganization;" she stated.

> We want to begin at the foundation, and to build upon a different principle....Greater strength must be brought into the managing force of the conference. But this will not be done by intrusting [*sic*] responsibilities to men who have had light poured upon them year after year for the last ten or fifteen years, and yet have not heeded the light that God has given them....God wants them to be removed.[29]

She called for a new church structure as well as new leadership. After her remarks, President Irwin stated that he accepted her testimony and

FIGURE 6.1 Ellen White addresses the 1901 General Conference Session in Battle Creek, Michigan. The General Conference president, G. A. Irwin, who was replaced during the session by A. G. Daniells, is seated behind her to her right (courtesy of the Ellen G. White Estate, Inc.).

asked for suggestions. Elder A. G. Daniells, an Ellen White protégé and the president of the Australasian Union Conference, stood and brought a recommendation that had been worked out the previous day by a group of church leaders with Ellen White present. During the ensuing sessions, the church body put the organizational changes in place, creating an intricately designed church structure intended to bind the growing church together. Daniells was installed as head of the General Conference and served as its president until 1922.

White was seventy-three years old at the time of the 1901 General Conference, but her speaking engagements continued. She became more selective, though, in her acceptance of appointments and more careful about the way her words were used. Adventists in the United States, cut off from direct access to her for nearly a decade, thronged to her for counsel. At subsequent speaking appointments she refused to have private conversations with anyone, not wanting to lend credence to rumors that people had put ideas into her head that became part of her public messages. She complained that people were distorting her words. When she spoke in public, she decided to write out all her remarks ahead of time to document exactly what she had said, so that "when my enemies or friends shall unadvisedly report falsely what I say I can produce the original." When she was past 80, she noticed that her private conversations were more physically taxing than speaking to large congregations, because "I could use my abdominal muscles and throw out my words without taxing my throat and my lungs."[30] Even at this late stage of her life, public speaking provided relief from other stresses.

Ellen White also played a significant role in the General Conference session of 1909 at Takoma Park, Maryland. At this session she returned to her religious roots: the imminent end of the world. Her convictions about this topic propelled her, at age 81, into her final nationwide speaking tour. "We can not afford to lose any more time" became her theme as she urged her audiences toward spiritual revival.[31] From her home in northern California she traveled to Union College in Lincoln, Nebraska, delivering a Sabbath sermon to 2000 people. Then she embarked on one of the most challenging portions of her itinerary, touring the South during a time of racial turmoil and violence, speaking to both black and white congregations in Tennessee, Alabama, and North Carolina. She viewed the South as "one of the barren places of the earth to be worked" because of its endemic racial prejudice.[32] She proceeded to Oakwood School in Huntsville, Alabama, which had been established in 1896 to serve black students. "If we will do justice...the Lord Himself will be our Keeper," she assured her audience there. "I want to meet you each in the kingdom of God." At a black church in Haywood, North Carolina, she preached on John 15, lingering after the service to shake hands with the members, a courageous public statement in the local context (see also Chapter 14).[33] White then moved on to the General Conference session at Washington Missionary College in Takoma Park, Maryland, where she addressed the gathering eleven times. And her speaking plans did not end there.

One of her motives for traveling eastward was to visit her old hometown again. "I expect to visit some of the places where I labored in my early youth during the 1844 movement," she told a congregation in Takoma Park. "I should like to visit Portland, Maine, once more, where in my childhood, as it were, The Lord gave me a message that bore everything before it." No doubt her own mortality was on her mind as she read news accounts of religious persecution and international strife: "I was instructed only a few weeks ago that Portland must be given this last message to the world," she told her Takoma Park audience, noting that she felt drawn to her roots in Maine.[34] "We can not afford in the few days that we have here on earth to spend our time in trifling and nothingness," she told one Adventist gathering, hoping to enlist their help in evangelizing the large cities of the East. "When I think of the great work there is to be done...I feel that I must get right out as I did in my younger days. Then I labored when I was no stronger than I am now, and I saw the power of God revealed in a remarkable manner."[35] As Ellen White headed north to New England, the infirmities of age caught up with her, and once again she drew energy from standing in front of a crowd. When she left South Lancaster, Massachusetts, to take the train to Portland, she was too tired to sit in the seat and instead lay down in the crowded car. "But after I got [to Portland]," she reported, "that weakness passed away, because I had work to do."[36]

The visit to Portland took Ellen White deep into her memory. "You see," she told a congregation that summer,

The difficulty was here: A stone was thrown that broke my nose. Everybody said I would die, but the very ones that pronounced that I should die have heard me, in the city of Portland, stand before the people years ago. I did not think she could live [some of them said], but I can understand every word she says. Why did the Lord Jesus choose me? He wanted to go to somebody that could not understand a great many words so that they should have the very simplest words to communicate His will.[37]

As she looked back to the beginning of her career in New England, she referred to it as her "childhood," when "The Lord gave me a message that bore everything before it. In those days it was not the testimony of a young girl that had a telling effect; it was the power of the Holy Spirit accompanying the message, that touched hearts."[38] On her way home to California, speaking in Massachusetts, New York, Michigan, Iowa, Kansas, and Colorado, she asked the believers she met to contribute funds for a church building for the small congregation in Portland.[39] Clearly, the city where she began her speaking career was on her mind as she neared the end of her life.

Ellen White stayed closer to her northern California home after 1909, although she traveled around the state for several more years. She spoke at her last camp meeting in 1911, and she paid several visits to Loma Linda, where the medical school she had envisioned and defined was taking shape. After her fall and broken hip in February 1915 initiated a fatal decline, church officials notified newspapers that Ellen White did not have long to live. Her assistant, Clarence C. Crisler, prepared a lengthy obituary to distribute to church periodicals and newspapers when the end came. He mentioned that in her role as an evangelist "she often preached to thousands, her voice having resonance and carrying power." After her death on July 16, newspapers drew on the news release and added their own analysis. The *Toledo Blade* commented, "Besides unusual talents as preacher, she had organization and administrative powers." Ellen White would have been startled by the conclusion that "had she lived in an earlier period of the career of Christianity and escaped the bigots and the fire she would most surely have been canonized. She was of the flesh of which saints are made." In August *The Independent* noted that the United States had recently lost its two prophetesses: Mary Baker Eddy (1910) and Ellen G. (Harmon) White. "Many of Mrs. Eddy's disciples believed she would never die," noted the author, "and Mrs. White hoped to be one of those who would be taken up alive to meet the Lord in the air. But the Lord delayed His coming, and she entered into rest, just as others do," in her eighty-eighth year.[40]

For Ellen White, public speaking supplied a measure of confidence and energy. The congregants who streamed to the front during her altar calls were a measure of her success. Her speaking role defined her authoritative voice within the church and among the thousands who heard her temperance lectures. The drinkers who abandoned their whiskey bottles, the church members who swallowed hard and accepted her testimonies, and the seasoned church officials who recast the denomination according to her counsel in various ways acknowledged her authority. The denominational structure she rebuilt, and the accredited higher education system that grew out of her vision for a full-fledged medical school, owe their genesis to her spoken words. Although no audio recordings of her sermons are known to exist, her spoken words continue to reverberate in Adventist history.

NOTES

I would like to thank the Walla Walla University Faculty Research Grants committee for support for this project; Jon Solis, David Mack, Dustin Kelley, and Ian Field for research assistance; and Christy Scott and Meghan Williams of the Walla Walla University Peterson Memorial Library staff for obtaining microfilm newspapers.

1. Ellen White, MS-125 1909, Three Rivers, MI, July 24, 1909, Sabbath Sermon by Mrs. E. G. White (Ellen G. White Estate, Silver Spring, MD). Except where attributed to another collection, all White manuscripts are in the White Estate. This sermon was delivered just after Ellen White had preached in Portland, Maine, 67 years after the events described previously.

2. Ellen White to J. E. and Emma White, Aug. 30, 1876. See also "Grand Rally in New England," *Advent Review and Sabbath Herald* 48 (September 7, 1876): 84 (hereafter referred to as *Review and Herald*), which includes an excerpt from the August 29, 1876, issue of the *Haverhill Publisher*.

3. For discussion of nineteenth-century emphasis on distinction between the domestic (private, women's) and public (men's) spheres, see Barbara Welter, "The Cult of True Womanhood: 1820–1860," *American Quarterly* 18 (1966): 151–174; Barbara Welter, *Dimity Convictions: The American Woman in the Nineteenth Century* (Athens: Ohio University Press, 1977); and Ellen Carol Dubois and Lynn Dumenil, *Through Women's Eyes: An American History with Documents*, 3rd ed. (Boston: Bedford/St. Martin's, 2012).

4. More than a half-century ago Horace John Shaw wrote a dissertation on Ellen White's rhetoric: "A Historical Analysis of the Speaking of Mrs. Ellen G. White a Pioneer Leader and Spokeswoman of the Seventh-day Adventist Church" (Ph.D. diss., Department of Speech, Michigan State University, 1959). The present study seeks to describe Ellen White's speaking practices, identify

major events in her public-speaking career, and evaluate their impact on her historical role.

5. Historians Frederick Hoyt and Ronald Graybill have identified several female prophets in nineteenth-century New England in addition to Ellen Harmon: Emily Clemons, Dorinda Baker, Phoebe Knapp, and Mary Hamlin. See Rennie Schoepflin, ed., "Scandal or Rite of Passage? Historians on the Dammon Trial," *Spectrum: Journal of the Association of Adventist Forums*, 17 (August 1987), 39, hereafter referred to as *Spectrum*.

6. Nell Irvin Painter, in *Sojourner Truth: A Life, A Symbol* (New York: W. W. Norton, 1996), 79–87, describes Sojourner Truth's preaching career with the Millerites in 1843.

7. Ellen White, "Sermon Thoughts on Deuteronomy 4," July 3, 1909, MS-120. Childhood friends, however, recalled that she had a distinctive voice before the accident; one early friend recognized her on a train as an adult by the sound of her voice. She said that when Ellen read the students' lessons aloud, "we could understand them better when you read them than when anyone else did." Document File (DF) 733c, quoted in Arthur L. White, *Ellen G. White*, 6 vols. (Washington, D C: Review and Herald Publishing Assn., 1981–1986), 1: 25.

8. P. S. Sanford to Arthur L. White, December 15, 1957.

9. Ellen White to J. E. White and W. C. White, June 13, 1865.

10. Ellen White, *Testimonies for the Church*, 9 vols. (Mountain View, CA: Pacific Press, 1948), 1:75 (Biographical Sketch).

11. Ellen White included a portion of the text of Otis Nichols' description of this event in *Life Sketches of James and Ellen White* (Battle Creek, MI: Seventh-day Adventist Publishing Assn., 1880), 232–234. Arthur L. White in *Ellen G. White*, 1:103–105, quoted the entire account, noting that it was written down in 1859 or 1860.

12. Painter, *Sojourner Truth*, 158–160.

13. White, *Testimonies*, 1:75; *Life Sketches* (1880), 127.

14. James White, "Monterey and Battle Creek," *Review and Herald* 31 (1868): 409.

15. Ellen White to J. E. White, March 2, 1869.

16. Ellen White to J. S. White, June 23, 1880. During this Northwest trip, Ellen White and Steven Haskell also divided speaking duties in the Hall Street Methodist Episcopal Church in Portland. See Portland *Morning Standard*, June 6, 1880, 3.

17. Gerald Wheeler, *James White: Innovator and Overcomer* (Hagerstown, MD: Review and Herald Publishing Assn., 2003), 218–223. Arthur L. White, in a lengthy chapter on James's and Ellen's relationship in the 1870s, describes the effects of the aftermath of James's strokes on their correspondence: *Ellen G. White*, 2: 442–443.

18. Ellen White to W. C. and Mary White, June 27, 1875.

19. *The North Missourian*, quoted by James White, "In the Field," *Review and Herald* 25 (1875): 196. James reported that in 12 days while traveling 1300 miles, Ellen gave 14 sermons, and he spoke 12 times.

20. Mary Clough, *Signs of the Times*, Sept. 16, 1876, Periodical Articles, Ellen G. White Writings CD-ROM.

21. Ellen White to Edson and Emma White, August 30, 1876; "Social Meeting," *General Conference Bulletin*, 1909, 15: 226.

22. "The Advent Camp," *Haverhill Publisher*, Aug. 29, 1876, quoted by Uriah Smith in "Grand Rally in New England," *Review and Herald* 11 (1876): 84.

23. White, *Testimonies* 1: 110.

24. Ellen G. White, "A Sketch of Experience," in *In Memoriam: A Sketch of the Last Sickness and Death of Elder James White* (Battle Creek, MI: Review and Herald Press, 1881), 41.

25. Ellen White, Letter 396, 1906, as quoted in Ellen G. White, *The Retirement Years* (Hagerstown, MD: Review and Herald Publishing Assn., 1990), 165.

26. See the *Sacramento Record-Union*, October 24, 1881.

27. Arthur L. White, *Ellen G. White*, 3: 203–205.

28. Ellen White to S. M. I. Henry, June 21, 1899.

29. *General Conference Bulletin*, 1901, 4: 25–26.

30. Ellen White, "The Work in Portland, Maine, and the East," July 3, 1909, MS-113-1909.

31. Sermon on May 17, "A Call to Service," *General Conference Bulletin*, 1909, 4: 56.

32. MS 24, 1891, 15–16 (Diary, January 1–30, 1891), in Ellen G. White, *Manuscript Releases*, 4: 1.3.

33. MS 17, 1909, 2, sermon delivered April 25, 1909, in the Nashville colored church, Ellen G. White, *Manuscript Releases*, 4: 33.3; MS 27, 1909, 1–5, "Words of Encouragement," talk given at the Oakwood School, Huntsville, Alabama, April 29, 1909, 2: 85.1. Arthur White documents the Haywood sermon in *Ellen G. White*, 6: 192.

34. Sermon on May 27, "Let Us Publish Salvation," *General Conference Bulletin*, 1909, 15: 225.

35. Ellen G. White, Sermon on May 29, "Get Ready!" *General Conference Bulletin*, 1909, 20: 345.

36. Ellen G. White, "Sermon Thoughts on Isaiah 56," July 7, 1909, Portland, ME, MS-122-1909.

37. Ellen G. White, "Sermon Thoughts on Isaiah 55," July 18, 1909, Buffalo, NY, MS-124-1909.

38. "Proclaiming the Third Angel's Message in Cities at Home and Abroad," talk by Mrs. E. G. White before the General Conference Committee, June 11, 1909, Washington, DC.

39. Ellen White, "An Address to the Workers Assembled at the Pacific Union Conference, Mountain View, CA, Jan. 28, 1910," MS-025, 1910.

40. "A Modern Prophetess," *Toledo Blade*, July 19, 1915; "An American Prophetess," *The Independent*, August 23, 1915, 249.

7

Builder

Floyd Greenleaf and Jerry Moon

"AN INSTITUTION IS the lengthened shadow of one man," wrote Ralph Waldo Emerson in an 1841 essay celebrating the genius of the individual. Historically, however, a founder has usually needed the support of a diverse team to create a viable institution. Ellen White arguably exerted a greater influence on the development of Seventh-day Adventist institutions than any other one person, but she did not act alone. Much of her work was that of a consultant, sometimes initiating new directions, often evaluating and refining the suggestions of others, but always acting as part of a team. She never held an elective or administrative office in the denomination. She often served as an adviser to such boards, because, in the words of one Adventist historian, she "generally had a more expansive view of the possibilities for the denomination than did its voted leaders."[1] Her role as an institution builder began to emerge in 1848, about four years after her first vision.

Publishing

The first institution that Ellen White co-founded, a publishing house, started from almost nothing. "I have a message for you," she said to her husband, James, after a vision in December 1848. "You must begin to print a little paper and send it out to the people. Let it be small at first; but as the people read, they will send you means with which to print, and it will be a success from the first. From this small beginning it was shown to me to be like streams of light that went clear round the world."[2]

In July 1849, James located a printer who was willing to print a paper on credit and wait for payment until readers could send donations. The Whites mailed *The Present Truth*, postage due, to all the Adventists they knew in Maine, New Hampshire, Vermont, Massachusetts, Connecticut, New York, and Eastern Canada. By September 3, the printer had been paid.[3]

After James had published ten issues of *Present Truth*, his wife reported another vision, in which she was instructed to "take the testimonies that the leading Adventists published in [18]44 and republish them and make them ashamed" of abandoning their earlier faith.[4] Because this paper would primarily reprint the writings of the Millerite Adventists, James called it the *Advent Review*. He soon merged the two papers, *Present Truth* and *Advent Review* into one, *Advent Review and Sabbath Herald*, which later became *Review and Herald* and is now published as *Adventist Review*.

Despite the apparent success of the paper, Joseph Bates, the elder statesman among sabbatarian Adventists, opposed it. To him, publishing a periodical looked like imitating other religious movements that had lost their initial fire and settled into conventional religion. Bates's attitude so "discouraged" James White that he vowed to give up publishing journals "forever." But that night Ellen White had a vision that "God did not want James to stop yet; but he must write, write, write, write, and speed the message and let it go." Hearing this, James wrote to a friend, "I do not doubt for a moment Brother Bates' good will and kindness toward us; still he does not see everything correctly at one glance. I shall write to him this vision, which will, no doubt, make him see a little differently in some things."[5]

Believing that publishing the message in a paper was "as necessary" as preaching it, Ellen admonished Bates for not supporting James and the paper. She warned her husband not to feel "jealous" of his older colleague. She urged them both to "press together" to keep the fledgling movement intact. The disagreement took thirteen months to resolve. From December 1849 to January 1851, Bates refused to write for the paper. His opposition, combined with James White's physical exhaustion, so discouraged James that in January 1851 he wrote a note for the paper that he would "publish no more." But the next morning his wife had a vision in which she saw "that my husband must not give up the paper, for such a step was just what Satan was trying to drive him to take. I was shown," she went on, "that he must continue to publish, and that the Lord would sustain him." Meanwhile, her strong words eventually got through to Bates. Realizing his mistake, Bates reversed himself and became a wholehearted supporter of the *Review*, writing for it, soliciting subscriptions, and raising funds to buy a press on which to print it.[6]

In 1860 the need to protect the growing assets of the publishing work prodded the reluctant Adventists to form their first legal corporation—the Seventh-day Adventist Publishing Association in Battle Creek, Michigan. This was the first official use of the name Seventh-day Adventist.[7] By the time of Ellen White's death in 1915, three Adventist publishing associations covered North America: the Review and Herald in Takoma Park, Maryland; the Pacific Press in Mountain View, California; and the Southern Publishing Association in Nashville, Tennessee.

Organizing a Denomination

Adventist leaders recognized the need for an organization as early as 1849; by 1853 it had become a public campaign, and in 1863 the goal was reached with the creation of the General Conference of Seventh-day Adventists. Ellen White's role in building a membership base and confirming a doctrinal core for the emerging denomination was so challenging that it consumed her energy for more than a decade, as it did for Joseph Bates and James White. All three of them were heavily involved in traveling, preaching, teaching, evangelizing, and writing. Bates, the eldest (1792–1872), was the foremost evangelist among the three, the leader in integrating the concepts of Sabbath and Sanctuary with the end-time prophecies of the book of Revelation. He did so by authoring small books and by taking strategic trips to engage with other leaders.[8]

James White possessed gifts for writing, editing, and administration. He started several new periodicals (*Present Truth*, 1849; *Advent Review and Sabbath Herald*, 1850; *Youth's Instructor*, 1852; and *Signs of the Times*, 1874), and from 1869 to 1873 his editorial skills and good judgment rescued the *Health Reformer* from almost certain demise. With the possible exception of his protégé John Harvey Kellogg, his ability to organize institutions was unsurpassed among his Adventist contemporaries.[9] Ellen White's distinguishing contribution was her visions, which often provided specific, focused guidance to her colleagues and followers.

James White seems to have been the first to notice the need for organization. In September 1849, he urged the necessity of financial support for ministers and asserted congregational authority to expel misbehaving members. In March 1850, he argued the need for "gospel order" in credentialing ministers. His wife's first mention of the subject came in December 1850. Her endorsement helped convince the scattered Adventists that uniting was according to God's will.[10]

During the 1850s Ellen White maintained a lower profile than did the other two founders, in part because James for years refused to publish her writings in the *Review and Herald*. Throughout her life her role was advisory rather than executive. It could be added that each of the three founders had a period of dominance. Bates had exercised the decisive leadership during the period of doctrinal formation (1846–1849), with collaboration from James and confirmation from the visions of Ellen. During the organizational phase (1850–1863) and for almost twenty years afterward, James White had led the charge, with Ellen as counselor and advisor. His death in 1881 would divide his wife's career almost exactly in two. For thirty-five years her life had been "so interwoven" with his that she thought it might be "impossible for [her] to be of any great account without him."[11] But she would continue her ministry for another thirty-four years, during which she would produce more than half of the books and articles she published during her lifetime. Thus for seventy years after the crisis of 1844, the last of the founders would exert a steadying influence on the movement.

Developing the Western Health Reform Institute

On June 5, 1863, just ten days after the organization of the General Conference, a two-and-a-half-hour vision revealed to Ellen White that the laws of health were just as much God's laws as were the Ten Commandments. Care for personal health was, therefore, a religious obligation. Although numerous health-related articles had already appeared in denominational magazines, this health reform vision symbolizes the beginning of the special Adventist emphasis on health (see Chapter 11).[12] By August 1864 Ellen White had completed the fourth volume of *Spiritual Gifts*, which included an article on "Health" summing up her 1863 vision. Immediately on sending the book to press, she and James White led five other ailing Adventists on a three-week visit to James Caleb Jackson's "Home on the Hillside," a prominent water cure in Dansville, New York. They came away favorably impressed and began to spread through the churches what they were learning about drugless healing. "Our people are generally waking up to the subject of health," wrote James White, "and they should have publications on the subject to meet their present wants, at prices within reach of the poorest." Already available were books on health reform by Sylvester Graham, William Alcott, James C. Jackson, Russell T. Trall, Joel Shew, and Larkin B. Coles, a Millerite physician. But many of these books were too large, too technical, or too expensive for the average lay person. So the Whites prepared a series of six pamphlets collectively titled *Health: or, How to Live* (1865), with content drawn from "personal experience, from the word of God, and from the writings of able and experienced health reformers."[13]

This flurry of activity took place against the background of the American Civil War and James White's already excessive workload. In August 1865, he suffered a paralyzing stroke. After Ellen had cared for him at home for five weeks without discernible improvement, they decided to go back to Dansville. This time they stayed for almost three months, gathering "many things of value" from those more experienced in health reform. But the Dansville physicians advocated entire rest—complete physical and mental inactivity—for James White.[14] They also believed that because his breakdown had resulted from overwork in religious lines, recovery would require a complete break from religious exertion, even prayer. Contrary to the physicians, Ellen White reasoned that for her husband, who was "naturally a man of great activity, both of body and mind," to "sink down in aimless inactivity" would hinder rather than help his recovery. As she saw him declining mentally, she determined to take him away from Dansville to nearby Rochester, New York, where he had friends. There, on Christmas Eve 1865, among a group praying for James's recovery, Ellen received another vision. On the basis of this vision, she laid before the next General Conference session in May 1866 a proposal for an Adventist-owned health care institution.[15]

Ellen White pointed out that the work of health reform among Adventists had barely begun, and that for God to hear their prayers for healing, they needed to change their way of living. She appreciated Jackson's pioneering work in drugless therapies. But she also maintained that maximum therapeutic benefit required hope, optimism, and faith. Because of the dissonance between the Adventist faith and the popular amusements at Our Home, she believed that Adventists could not "receive that benefit from the popular health institutions of the day that others of a different faith can. They [Adventists] have to carry along with them at all times the gospel sieve and sift everything they hear, that they may choose the good and refuse the bad." Therefore, she concluded, "Our people should have an institution of their own, under their own control, for the benefit of the diseased and suffering among us, who wish to have health and strength that they may glorify God in their bodies and spirits which are His."[16]

She did not have to belabor the need. Five leading Adventist ministers had been virtually disabled from ill health, another had died, and for months the three-member executive committees of both the General Conference and the Michigan Conference had been unable to conduct business for lack of a quorum.[17] By the time she finished her presentation, the delegates were ready to approve the proposal.

The rapidity of the church's response suggests that the need for health reform was both obvious and acute. Four weeks later the *Review* carried a "prospectus" for a new journal, *The Health Reformer*, to be edited by Horatio S. Lay, an apprentice-trained Adventist physician who had spent time in Dansville.[18] Despite James White's illness, Adventists organized a fundraising campaign that brought in almost $11,000, allowing them to purchase a five-acre site in Battle Creek with two usable buildings. By September the Western Health Reform Institute had opened for business with Lay and Phoebe Lamson—who had graduated from Trall's hydropathic degree mill in New Jersey—in charge.

Ellen White's role in founding the water cure, as hydropathic institutions were commonly called, included not only the vision and the imperative call to the church; she continued for many years as a consultant to the institution, warning against both therapeutic and financial extremes, as she saw them, and advising on human resources and staffing. In the first flush of success, the managers wanted to enlarge the capacity by adding an entirely new building. James and Ellen White were away on a farm where, through physical labor, James was recovering his health. When they read of the drive for immediate expansion, Ellen White expressed alarm. Believing that too rapid expansion could lead to collapse, she pointed out that the plans for a new building were based on three unproved assumptions: continued influx of patients, continued generous financial support, and continued health of the two physicians. Many of the early patients were Adventist church members, of whom there was a limited supply. Raising the initial $11,000 had virtually drained the small denomination's available resources. The tiny medical staff already had its hands full. For these reasons, she urged that it was premature to think of enlarging the facility.[19]

A few months later, Trall, a well-known non-Adventist hydropath, began to promote in the *Health Reformer* what Ellen White (though not James) regarded as extreme views—such as complete abstinence from salt, sugar, and milk—which pushed its subscription base into a nosedive. As James White's physical and mental health gradually improved, he took over the editorship of the *Health Reformer*. During the next four years (1869–1873) he was able to build the circulation to over 10,000 and eventually set the Western Health Reform Institute on the path to solvency.[20]

The most critical limitation remained the lack of qualified staff. In November 1872, the Whites sent twenty-year-old John Harvey Kellogg and four others (including the Whites' two sons, Edson and Willie) to Trall's Hygeo-Therapeutic College in Florence Heights, New Jersey. For four months they studied such subjects as osteology, phrenology, and chemistry, returning to Battle Creek in April 1873 with diplomas inscribed on sheepskin, "conferring the 'Degree of Doctor of Medicine,' with the 'rights, privileges, and immunities pertaining to the legalized practice of medicine.'"[21]

By this time James White was wary of both Trall and his four-month medical degrees. "Our institute buildings are already larger than our doctors," he wrote a few months later. Remedying that deficiency required sending students to the University of Michigan (Kate Lindsay) and to Bellevue Hospital Medical School in New York City (John Harvey Kellogg) for credible training. In 1876, Kellogg became medical superintendent of the Health Reform Institute, which he renamed the Battle Creek Medical and Surgical Sanitarium and turned into a nationally famous hospital with branches scattered across the country.[22]

Educating

Beginning in 1872 and continuing nearly to her death in 1915, Ellen White was also the primary voice shaping the philosophy of Seventh-day Adventist education. The story of denominational schools does not, however, begin with her at the center. Adventists typically attribute the beginning of their educational enterprises to Goodloe Harper Bell, who started what he called a "select school" in Battle Creek, Michigan, in 1868. When the General Conference of Seventh-day Adventists adopted it four years later, this small venture became the first official Adventist school. Both James and Ellen White encouraged this change of ownership. Under denominational direction, Bell's school developed successively into Battle Creek College (1874–1901), Emmanuel Missionary College (1901–1959), and Andrews University (1959–present).[23]

In July 1872, two months after the transfer of Bell's school, Ellen White wrote "Proper Education," her first statement in the relatively large body of literature she produced about education during the next forty-plus years. In this essay White emphasized health issues as they relate to education and advised practical education for women, in contrast to the more socially oriented training that female seminaries offered. Many of her ideas bore an unmistakable similarity to those of Horace Mann, one of the most influential architects of nineteenth-century American education. Although she did not mention him at this time, James had already reprinted a short piece by Mann in the *Advent Review and Sabbath Herald*, and much later in her career Ellen indicated that she read Mann and owned some of his books.[24]

In his many writings Mann stressed the intimate relationship between health and education. In 1840, while serving as secretary of the Massachusetts State Board of Education, he warned that to require young students to "sit both dumb and motionless, for three successive hours" with only brief interruptions violated "every law the Creator has impressed upon both body and mind." Two years later he issued a plea for the study of physiology in order to improve public health. He blamed most deaths on "sheer ignorance" of the laws of health, deeming "a knowledge of algebra, of ancient mythology or history, or of all the Grecian and Latin lore" worthless in comparison to a knowledge of "laws upon which the Creator of the body has made its health and vigor depend." In his view, the common schools were the only means to diffuse knowledge about the laws of health. As the first president of newly founded Antioch College, a Christian Connexion institution in Ohio, Mann continued to advocate hygienic living, muscular effort, and the teaching of agriculture and the mechanical arts—all themes that Ellen White also endorsed. In one of her most oft-quoted statements she described education as "the harmonious development of the physical, the mental, and the spiritual powers."[25]

Although the efforts of Horace Mann and many other nineteenth-century reformers to strike a balance between intellectual effort and manual labor frequently foundered, Ellen White made this concept a cardinal point of Adventist education. Within two decades following the appearance of "Proper Education" five major Adventist schools were operating in the United States: the aforementioned Battle Creek College; Healdsburg College in Northern California, 1882 (now Pacific Union College); South Lancaster Academy, Massachusetts, 1882 (the now-defunct Atlantic

Union College); Union College, Nebraska, 1891; and Walla Walla College, Washington, 1892 (now Walla Walla University).

The lack of well-developed manual-labor departments on these campuses greatly disappointed Ellen White. Her references to a work program emphasized that physical labor would balance mental exertion and bring equilibrium to students' lives. The failure to found Battle Creek College on sufficient acreage to support training in agriculture had brought her to tears. Work opportunities later materialized at Battle Creek, but labor superintendents struggled to carry out her recommendations. Their major complaint was the financial risk of student labor. Speaking at a Battle Creek College stockholders' meeting in the 1880s, she urged college administrators to redouble their efforts to strengthen the manual-training department.[26]

White remained dissatisfied with the progress of Adventist educational reform until the founding of Avondale School for Christian Workers (now Avondale College of Higher Education) in Australia. When she embarked for the South Pacific in 1891, she went with the understanding that establishing a school would be one of her major tasks. In Cooranbong, New South Wales, a short drive from Sydney, she helped direct students and other workers as they hacked this campus out of the wilderness. Shortly after the institution opened in 1897, White confided to her son Willie, "No breezes from Battle Creek are to be wafted in. I see I must watch before and behind and on every side to permit nothing to find entrance that has been presented before me as injuring our schools in America." For Ellen White, the Australian school represented the best "in every respect that we have ever seen, outside our people, or among Seventh-day Adventists."[27]

At Avondale students arose early and went to bed early. They devoted their mornings to study and most of the afternoon to labor in shops, agriculture, and institutional services such as the cafeteria. Female as well as male students fulfilled labor assignments. Distributed throughout the day were slots for private time and devotions. This daily schedule resembled the work-study experiments that American schools had previously conducted, most notably Oberlin College.[28]

After her return to the United States in 1900, White seemed resigned to the prospect that Adventist schools in America probably would not fulfill the ideal of balanced education as she envisioned it. "For many years," she said to Adventist teachers, "I have kept before our people the need, in the education of the youth, of an equal taxation of the physical and mental powers. But for those who have never proved the value of the instruction given to combine manual training with the study of books, it is hard to understand and carry out the directions given."[29]

Although White viewed Adventist schools in the United States as less than ideal, her support for them remained strong. She consistently expressed her belief that they had providential origins and were accomplishing spiritual purposes. As important as manual labor was to White, she stated repeatedly that the primary need on Adventist campuses was a deeper spirituality; she appealed for greater spiritual commitment by teachers and more Scripture study and dedication to church work by students.[30]

White's support for Adventist education assumed a new dimension following the financial crisis in the United States in the 1890s. Church revenues plummeted 14 percent between 1893 and 1895, and "irresponsible" management pushed many Adventist institutions into staggering indebtedness. School managers had not yet discovered annual budgets or parsed the distinction between capital and operating funds, and they too often compounded their problems by functioning day to day on borrowed money. Alarmed by the mounting debts at Adventist schools, White did not spare her candor. If "managers of a school find that it is not meeting running expenses," she wrote, "and debts are heaping up, they should act like levelheaded businessmen and change their methods and plans." By 1900 the combined debt of Adventist schools approximated $350,000. To settle the arrears and avoid an impending catastrophe, White donated the profits from the sale of *Christ's Object Lessons*, her recent book about the parables of Jesus. By 1903 the debt had diminished by about $200,000. Her generosity had been a major factor in reducing the debt, but school finances did not improve until managers followed her advice and changed their methods.[31]

Nowhere did White enunciate her philosophy of education more clearly than in *Education*, a book she began in Australia and published in 1903, three years after her return to the United States. During her sojourn in the South Pacific her thoughts about reforming education had crystallized. Her defining statement about Adventist education declares her belief that the perfect world that nineteenth-century millennialists hoped for would result from redemption, not human effort, although education had a supportive role to play. "To restore in man the image of his Maker," she explained, "to bring him back to the perfection in which he was created, to promote the development of body, mind, and soul, that the divine purpose in his creation might be realized,—this was to be the work of redemption. This is the object of education, the great object of life." But while she saw a spiritual purpose defining the meaning of education, she did not lessen her commitment to intellectual achievement. In one of her most widely quoted passages about education, she asserted that true education would "train the youth to be thinkers, and not mere reflectors of other men's thought."[32]

During the forty-three years Ellen White lived after writing "Proper Education," she did not veer from her basic view of reformed education. However, she did alter some details if she saw that conditions warranted change. An example is the meaning of her statement in 1872 that small children should run as "free as lambs" and that until they reached the age of eight or ten their parents should be their only teachers. Many Adventists understood her statement to be a general rule of educational readiness, and when denominational elementary schools became common in the 1890s, students typically could not enroll until they were ten.

Even though Adventists accepted White's advice as divinely inspired, questions cropped up about this topic. In the Adventist community surrounding St. Helena Sanitarium in Napa Valley, California, the board of a newly established elementary school divided on the matter of the minimum age for school entry. In 1904 board members convened at White's nearby home to thrash out the issue. The seventy-six-year-old White explained that conditions had changed since 1872. Referring to the growing kindergarten movement in which teachers planned a curriculum with activity, she said the problem of immobilizing children at their desks had been resolved. In such circumstances, five-year-old youngsters were educable. Apparently, the school board in St. Helena had not noticed that in 1888 White had suggested that the Adventist community in nearby Oakland should start a kindergarten.[33]

Ellen White's personal favorite among Adventist educational institutions in the United States was a privately owned institution that operated outside of denominational controls. On the banks of the Cumberland River north of Nashville, Tennessee, Percy T. Magan and E. A. Sutherland founded the Nashville Agricultural and Normal Institute (later Madison College) in 1904. These experienced educators shared White's passion for a program combining formal study and manual training. White led in the selection of the institute's location; she also served as a member of its board, the only official position she ever held, and she maintained close ties with its key administrators, documented in a photograph taken there during her nationwide tour in 1909 (see Figure 7.1). Over the years the

FIGURE 7.1 Ellen White and her entourage in 1909 with staff members of the Nashville Agricultural Normal Institute, founded in 1904 as an innovative, self-supporting institution independent of denominational control. Accredited in 1928 and 1933, it became Madison College in 1937. Standing: C. C. Crisler, P. T. Magan, Minnie Hawkins, Nellie Druillard, E. A. Sutherland, Sara McEnterfer. Seated: W. C. White, Ellen White, Emma White, J. Edson White (courtesy of the Ellen G. White Estate, Inc.).

Madison school begat smaller high-school replicas throughout the South. In 1915 P. P. Claxton, United States Commissioner of Education, commended the Madison network for bettering a region still suffering the impact of the Civil War.[34]

While spurring on Magan and Sutherland, White ventured more aggressively into the fields of health and medical education. Turning westward, she urged church and sanitarium leaders to establish health care centers in California. Specifically pointing to the Redlands-Riverside area, she explained that this location had "been presented" to her as the site for a medical center that should also become an educational hub. Pursuing opportunities they regarded as miraculous, by mid-1905 church leaders had bought a resort hotel in Loma Linda that answered to White's description. Under the name of the College of Evangelists, a teaching faculty assembled in 1906. At first, the new college concentrated on preparing nurses who would be "gospel medical missionaries" engaging in public health ministry. But in 1910, equipped with a new state charter, a changed name, and White's blessing, the school added a physicians' course and began a new existence as the College of Medical Evangelists (CME). As the name suggested, its primary mission remained to train gospel medical missionaries.[35]

Despite Ellen White's support, the new institution nearly foundered under the financial burden of equipping a medical school that would meet American Medical Association (AMA) standards, first issued in 1905. In the wake of warnings and near-threats from the AMA, Adventists debated how to proceed, with White arguing that Adventist youth should "not be compelled to go to medical schools conducted by men not of our faith." CME, she insisted, should offer "a medical education that will enable them [students] to pass the examinations required by law of all those who practice as regularly qualified physicians."[36] She visited Loma Linda frequently during the final years of her life, guiding the college's development and speaking there in 1906 when the school opened (see Figure 7.2).

FIGURE 7.2 In 1905 Ellen White led the denomination to purchase a resort property in Loma Linda, California. Here she speaks to an audience at the site in 1906, when the College of Evangelists opened. In 1910, with her blessing, it offered physicians' training and became the College of Medical Evangelists; in 1961 it became Loma Linda University (courtesy of the Ellen G. White Estate, Inc.).

This counsel proved to be a seminal statement that profoundly influenced Seventh-day Adventist education far beyond White's lifetime. During the 1920s and 1930s the growing power of regional and professional accrediting organizations spawned sometimes rancorous debate among many denominational educators and church leaders about how Adventist schools would preserve their identity. Some feared that accreditation was a process that would prevent religious bodies from controlling their own schools. In 1936, after more than a decade and a half of hard exchanges, Adventist leaders finally concluded that Ellen White's advice to CME applied to all education, and accreditation became an official reality on Adventist campuses.[37] Later, when the AMA and the Association of American Medical Colleges jointly formed the Liaison Committee on Medical Education to accredit medical schools in 1942, the leaders of CME, like those of other medical schools, sought accreditation. White similarly modified her views regarding the training of ministers. She appeared to move from an emphasis on short programs that educated workers for the field as soon as possible to an interest in deeper professional preparation. In 1881 she warned faculty at Battle Creek College not to encourage ministerial students to spend years in study "to obtain an education." However, as the 1880s progressed she saw the need to improve education for pastors and eventually suggested that some might attend "higher colleges" to broaden their study.[38]

Most of the medical, educational, publishing, and other institutions of the Seventh-day Adventist church are traceable directly or indirectly to the counsels of Ellen White. In retrospect she recognized that her "life work" had been "closely intermingled" with the history of Adventist "enterprises" and "institutions," for which both she and her husband had "labored with pen and voice." Today, almost a century after White's death, her institutional shadow embraces about 18 million adult members in over 200 countries, with 7,806 schools, 173 hospitals and sanitariums, and 63 publishing houses.[39]

NOTES

1. R. W. Emerson, "Self-Reliance." In *Essays; First Series*, new ed. (Boston: James Munroe, 1850), first published in 1841; Warren S. Ashworth, "Edward A. Sutherland: Reformer," in *Early Adventist Educators*, ed. George R. Knight (Berrien Springs, MI: Andrews University Press, 1983), 179.
2. Ellen G. White, *Life Sketches of Ellen G. White* (Mountain View, CA: Pacific Press, 1915), 125.

3. *Present Truth* 1 (July 1849): 1; facsimile reprint in *Earliest Seventh-day Adventist Periodicals*, ed. George R. Knight (Berrien Springs, MI: Andrews University Press, 2005); Arthur L. White, *Ellen G. White: A Biography*, 6 vols. (Washington, DC: Review and Herald Publishing Assn., 1981–1986), 1: 164, 168.

4. Ellen G. White to Arabella Hastings, August 4, 1850; in Ellen G. White, *Manuscript Releases*, 21 vols. (Hagerstown, MD: Review and Herald Publishing Assn., 1981–1993), 19: 129.

5. James White to L. Hastings, January 10, 1850, Center for Adventist Research (CAR), Andrews University, Berrien Springs, MI. Hereafter referred to as CAR.

6. Ellen G. White, "Dear Brethren and Sisters," *Present Truth* 1 (Nov. 1850): 86–87; E. G. White, "Need for Unity Among Spiritual Shepherds," MS 14, 1850, in White, *Manuscript Releases*, 12: 246, 250–252; *Life Sketches: Ancestry, Early Life, Christian Experience, and Extensive Labors of Elder James White and His Wife Mrs. Ellen G. White* (Battle Creek, MI: Seventh-day Adventist Publishing Assn., 1880), 281; George R. Knight, *Joseph Bates: The Real Founder of Seventh-day Adventism* (Hagerstown, MD: Review and Herald Publishing Assn., 2004), 166.

7. Incorporation of the publishing house was begun in 1860 and completed in 1861. The General Conference of Seventh-day Adventists was organized in 1863.

8. George R. Knight, *Organizing to Beat the Devil: The Development of Adventist Church Structure* (Hagerstown, MD: Review and Herald Publishing Assn., 2001), 33–38, 48–66; Joseph Bates, *Autobiography of Joseph Bates* (Battle Creek, MI: Seventh-day Adventist Publishing Assn., 1868); James White, *Life Incidents: In Connection with the Great Advent Movement* (Battle Creek, MI: Seventh-day Adventist Publishing Assn., 1868); Knight, *Joseph Bates*, 80, 96–101.

9. Jerry Moon, "Historical Introduction," to James White, *Life Incidents* (Berrien Springs, MI: Andrews University Press, 2003), viii–ix.

10. James White to Brother and Sister Collins, Sept. 8, 1849, CAR; Knight, *Organizing*, 34. See also Ronald Graybill, "The Power of Prophecy: Ellen G. White and the Women Religious Founders of the Nineteenth Century (Ph.D. diss., Johns Hopkins University, 1983), 140–144; A. G. Mustard, *James White and SDA Organization: Historical Development, 1844–1881* (Berrien Springs, MI: Andrews University Press, 1987), 191–192, n. 4.

11. See Mustard, 128, 191–192; and Barry D. Oliver, *SDA Organizational Structure: Past, Present, and Future* (Berrien Springs, MI: Andrews University Press, 1989), 55–57; E. G. White to W. C. White, Sept. 12, 1881, CAR.

12. Dores Eugene Robinson, *The Story of Our Health Message*, 3rd ed. (Nashville, TN: Southern Publishing Assn., 1965), 76, 77; Herbert E. Douglass, *Messenger of the Lord: The Prophetic Ministry of Ellen G. White* (Nampa, ID: Pacific Press, 1998), 278, 281–342. Ronald L. Numbers, *Prophetess of Health: A Study of Ellen G. White*, 3rd ed. (Grand Rapids, MI: William B. Eerdmans, 2008), chapter 5, gives a more detailed history of the Western Health Reform Institute.

13. Ellen G. White, *Spiritual Gifts*, 4 vols. (Battle Creek, MI: Seventh-day Adventist Publishing Assn., 1864), 4: 120–154; Robinson, *Health Message*, 99–103; E. G. White, *Testimonies for the Church*, 9 vols. (Mountain View, CA: Pacific Press, 1948), 1:490–491 (Testimony No. 11, 1867); James White, "The Health Reform," *Advent Review and Sabbath Herald* 3 (1864): 20–21. Hereafter referred to as *Review and Herald*.

14. Ellen G. White, "Our Health Message," MS release 333, *Manuscript Releases* 5: 390–391.

15. Robinson, *Health Message*, 135.

16. Ibid., 141; White, *Testimonies*, 1:489–492 (Testimony No. 11, 1867).

17. Robinson, *Health Message*, 146.

18. Ibid., 148–154.

19. Ibid., 175–176, 180–181.

20. Virgil E. Robinson, *James White* (Washington, DC: Review and Herald Publishing Assn., 1976), 194; cf. Robinson, *Health Message*, 195–200.

21. Robinson, *James White*, 240–241, 143; A. L. White, *Ellen G. White*, 2: 380; James White to Edson and Willie White, Dec. 30, 1872, DF 718a, CAR. Despite the pretentious phrase, "legalized practice of medicine," it is doubtful that either New Jersey or Michigan required a license to practice medicine in 1872. See Samuel L. Baker, "Physician Licensure Laws in the United States, 1865–1915," *Journal of the History of Medicine and Allied Sciences* 39 (1984):173–197. See also Ronald L. Numbers, "Health Reform on the Delaware," *New Jersey History* 92 (Spring 1974): 5–12, which describes the visit.

22. James White to G. I. Butler, July 13, 1874, 6, microfilm, CAR; Robinson, *Health Message*, 210–213; *General Conference Bulletin*, July 1897, 116; Richard W. Schwarz, *John Harvey Kellogg, M.D.* (Nashville, TN: Southern Publishing Assn., 1970), 66–67.

23. Emmet K. Vande Vere, *The Wisdom Seekers: The Intriguing Story of the Men and Women Who Made the First Institution for Higher Learning among Seventh-day Adventists* (Nashville, TN: Southern Publishing Assn., 1972), 18.

24. Ellen G. White, "Proper Education," first published in 1872, subsequently appeared in White, *Testimonies* 3: 131–160. It also came out in serial form in *The Health Reformer*, beginning with 7 (September 1872): 284–286, and continuing in the April, May, June, July, and September issues of 1873. Two decades later she compiled her articles on education in *Christian Education* (1893), which in turn furnished much of the substance for her book *Education* (1903). In 1968 the Ellen G. White Estate assembled her statements about education from all testimonies under a separate title, *Counsels on Education*. See also Horace Mann, "Manners and Morals," *Review and Herald* 34 (1869): 190; and Ellen G. White to Edson and Emma White, June 5, 1899, *Manuscript Releases*, 14:281.

25. Horace Mann, "Report for 1840," in *Life and Works of Horace Mann*, ed. Mary Mann, 5 vols. (Boston: Lee and Shepard, 1891), 3: 54; Horace Mann, "The Study of

Physiology in the Schools–Dissertation upon the Subject: Report for 1842," ibid., 3: 131–144, 177; Horace Mann, *Demands of the Age on Colleges* (New York: Fowler and Wells, 1857), 22–23; Ellen G. White, *Education* (Mountain View, CA: Pacific Press, 1903), 13.

26. Vande Vere, *Wisdom Seekers*, 22; "Educational Society Proceedings," *SDA Yearbook*, 1884, 55–58; *SDA Yearbook*, 1885, 52–55; *SDA Yearbook*, 1888, 78–82; White, *Testimonies*, 6: 176–180.

27. Arthur L. White, *Ellen G. White*, 4: 215–227, 287–303, 322; Milton Hook, "Avondale College" in *Seventh-day Adventists in the South Pacific, 1885–1985*, ed. Noel Clapham (Warburton, Victoria: Signs Publishing Co., 1985), 146–151; Ellen G. White to W. C. White, June 10, 1897, White, *Manuscript Releases*, 20: 215.

28. C. B. Hughes, "Avondale School," *Union Conference Record*, 5 (May 1898), 63, 64; Hook, "Avondale College," 150–154. To compare with Oberlin, see James H. Fairchild, *Oberlin: The Colony and the College, 1833–1883* (Oberlin, OH: E. J. Goodrich, 1883), 187–195.

29. White, *Testimonies*, 7: 267.

30. On a Bible-centered curriculum and spiritual issues in education, see White's testimonies published from 1880 to 1904.

31. H. E. Rogers, comp., *Seventh-day Adventist Conferences, Missions, and Institutions: The Fifty-sixth Annual Statistical Report Year Ending December 31, 1918* (Washington, D.C: General Conference of Seventh-day Adventists, 1919), 15; Arthur L. White, *Ellen G. White*, 5: 198-99; White, *Testimonies*, 6: 210; *General Conference Bulletin*, 1903, no. 2, 19.

32. White, *Education*, 15–17.

33. Vande Vere, *Wisdom Seekers*, 86; Ashworth, "Edward A. Sutherland," 165–66; Ellen G. White, "Counsel on Age of School Entrance: Report of an Interview," *Manuscript Releases*, vol. 6, no. 405; E. M. Cadwallader, *A History of Seventh-day Adventist Education* (Lincoln, NE: Union College Press, 1958), 288–89.

34. Ira Gish and Harry Christman, *Madison, God's Beautiful Farm: The E. A. Sutherland Story* (Mountain View, CA: Pacific Press, 1979), 142; Louis A. Hansen, *From So Small a Dream* (Nashville, TN: Southern Publishing Assn., 1968), 182–190. Madison College closed in 1964.

35. Arthur L. White, *Ellen G. White*, 6: 11–21. During the first decade of the twentieth century Ellen G. White devoted hundreds of pages of published *Testimonies for the Church* to the health work; see White, *Testimonies*, 6: 219–53; ibid., 7: 51–137; ibid., 8: 123–212; ibid., 9: 153–98. See also Ellen G. White, *Loma Linda Messages*, abridged by Lindsay A. Semmens (Loma Linda, CA: Privately printed, 1935). The story of the acquisition of the Loma Linda property and its formative years is documented in Richard A. Schaefer, *The Glory of the Vision: Book One* (Hagerstown, MD: Review and Herald Publishing Assn., 2010), 9–28.

36. W. A. Ruble, "A Medical School at Loma Linda," *Review and Herald* 87 (May 19, 1910): 17–18; White, *Loma Linda Messages*, 383.

37. W. E. Howell, "Educational Report to General Conference," *Review and Herald* 107 (1930), 57–60; Floyd Greenleaf, *In Passion for the World: A History of Seventh-day Adventist Education* (Nampa, ID: Pacific Press, 2005), 299–323.

38. White, *Testimonies*, 5: 583–84.

39. White, *Life Sketches* (1915), 196; Jerry Moon, *W. C. White and Ellen G. White: The Relationship between the Prophet and Her Son* (Berrien Springs, MI: Andrews University Press, 1993), 211–213. These statistics, the latest available, reflect the state of the denomination at the end of 2012. They are available at www.adventist.org/world-church/facts-and-figures/index.html.

8

Theology

Fritz Guy

IT IS IMPOSSIBLE to discuss Ellen White and theology without paradox. On the one hand, if one thinks of "theology" in its broad etymological sense— Greek *theos* (god or God) + *logos* (thought, speech, message) = "God talk"— Ellen Harmon White produced a great deal of it in her seventy years and millions of words of prophetic thinking, speaking, and writing. On the other hand, if one thinks of "theology" in its more specific formal sense as "faith seeking understanding" or "the interpretation of faith," she produced very little theology. In that context it is more accurate to discuss "some theological implications of Ellen White's thinking," and that is the intention of this chapter. For her, theology was always incidental to her primary vocation as a "messenger of the Lord" whose mission was to call "the remnant church" to prepare for and facilitate the imminent Second Advent of Jesus the Messiah. To the extent that her thinking was theological, it was intuitive rather than deliberate, informal rather than structured, practical and occasional rather than theoretical and systematic.[1]

Strictly speaking, very seldom did Ellen White "do theology." That is, she did not ordinarily do what professional theologians typically do. She did not produce a book of or about theology. She did not think, speak, and write in theological language. She did not expound detailed arguments. She did not outline a comprehensive conceptual system. She did not analyze and critique traditional or technical theological terms. She did not compare and contrast various views of Scripture, God, human nature, salvation, and eternal life. She did not elaborate a particular doctrine of the Trinity, atonement, God and time, or free will. She did not explain the precise meaning and broader implications of her own language and ideas, nor did she always use her theological vocabulary consistently. She did not endeavor to explain verbal or conceptual inconsistencies—either those of Scripture or her own—or to reduce the tensions inherent in her overall theological understanding.

Perhaps the most striking exception to this generalization is her vigorous response in 1904 to the alleged pantheistic views of John Harvey Kellogg, the physician-entrepreneur who had joined the Western Health Reform Institute in 1876 and by the end of the century had developed it into the world-famous Battle Creek Sanitarium and affiliated American Medical Missionary College. To address the controversy—which she described four years later as involving "new theories" and "sciences of satanic origin," and which editors forty years later described as precipitating "the greatest crisis the Seventh-day Adventist Church has ever faced"— she wrote eighty-one pages on the "The Essential Knowledge," including discussions of "A Personal God," "Danger in Speculative Knowledge," and "The Knowledge Received Through God's Word." But even this theological enterprise was motivated by practical concerns; it concluded with a description of "Our Great Need," referring to the experiences of Enoch and John the Baptist and citing God's promises.[2]

An equally influential involvement in Adventist theological conversation was her affirmation of traditional Christology, when, in opposition to the practice of some Adventists to speak of Christ as the first created being rather than eternally pre-existent, she asserted unequivocally that "in Christ is life, original, unborrowed, underived." Earlier she had said that the Son and the Father "were of one substance, possessing the same attributes," and later she explained that "Christ was God essentially, and in the highest sense."[3]

White did not have a high opinion of the traditional discipline of theology and its practitioners. Although she did mention "true theology" on a couple of occasions, many of her references to "theology" and "theologians" appear in negative or (at best) neutral contexts, as in her observations that "the errors of popular theology have driven many a soul to skepticism, who might otherwise have been a believer in the Scriptures," and that "Theology is valueless unless it is saturated with the love of Christ." Indeed, she was convinced that "To a large degree, theology, as studied and taught, is but a record of human speculation, serving only to darken 'counsel by words without knowledge' [Job 38:2]."[4]

She did, however, maintain a continuing interest in what might be called "practical theology"—careful reading of the Bible and accurate

understanding of its teachings as vital ingredients in personal and eccle-
sial spiritual health (see Chapter 9). Her theological ideas emerged in
letters, articles, and manuscripts addressing spiritual issues, church matters, and Scripture. Some of her most important theological ideas were
expressed succinctly and powerfully in her devotional classic, *Steps to
Christ*, intended to encourage and facilitate a mature Christian spirituality. An example is her explanation of the spiritual dynamic of prayer,
which "does not bring God down to us, but brings us up to him." This suggested that the proper objective of prayer is not to persuade God to fulfill
one's desires, however well-motivated, but to align one's own will with the
divine will. Always, her thinking was thoroughly "Advent-ist," motivated
by her continuing expectation of the imminent "coming of the Lord."[5]

Cultural and Personal Context

Ellen Harmon White was very much American in her thinking, speaking, and writing; and in spite of travels in Europe (1885–1887) and a pro-
longed stay in Australia (1891–1900) she remained thoroughly American
in her thinking throughout her life. She revealed a typical national
self-consciousness in interpreting the Scriptural prophecies in the biblical book of Revelation in terms of a decisive American contribution to the
historical future of the world (see Chapter 12). Her view of the American
future, however, differed significantly from the optimistic idea of "mani-
fest destiny" propounded to justify the controversial Mexican-American
War (1846–1848) and the continent-wide expansion of the United States;
she envisioned the United States going radically wrong religiously and
politically, to the extent of harassing and persecuting "the people of God."
This pessimistic outlook contrasted also with the postmillennialism of
many Protestants, according to which the Second Advent would occur
after rather than before a thousand years of peace and prosperity.[6]

White lived in a Protestant America of widespread anti-Catholic sentiment, with much nervousness about Catholic immigration and its resulting influence. "To Protestants, Catholics threatened American civilization
at two points: temperance and Sabbath [i.e., Sunday] observance," writes
Jonathan Butler. "Hard-drinking Catholic laborers were suddenly invading
American city life, with their more permissive continental Sabbath unset-
tling Protestants reared on the idea of American Sabbath-keeping." To
combat this and other tendencies toward a lax view of Sunday sacredness,

in 1888 and 1889 Senator H. W. Blair introduced in the United States Congress national legislation mandating the observance of Sunday as a day of worship. Seventh-day Adventists helped to defeat the effort, but the threat was regarded as real.[7]

Her culturally inherited literalistic understanding of Scripture was reinforced by the prophetic interpretations expounded by ex-army officer, ex-deist, and reconverted Baptist farmer William Miller (1782–1849). A crucial instance was the "day-year principle," which, applied to the "two thousand three hundred days" of Daniel 8:14, led to the calculation of a 2,300-year period beginning in 457 BCE and ending in 1844 CE (since there was no year 0), when the "sanctuary" (understood as symbolizing the Earth) would be "cleansed" by the climactic events of the Second Advent.

Being a woman also made a difference in White's theological thinking. It helps to explain, for example, her continuing relational emphases on divine love and human community, as well her preference for the term "messenger" rather than "prophet" to describe her own role in Adventist Christianity. Her gender may well have been a factor also in her attention to practical and pastoral concerns—illustrated by her books on education and health as well as spirituality—and her comparative lack of theoretical interests (see Chapter 15).[8]

Basic Principles

Although Ellen White was not a theologian in any formal sense, she did articulate clear convictions about philosophical and theological matters that have often been addressed under the headings of "philosophy of religion," "philosophical theology," or "theological prolegomena." These include the relation of faith, evidence, and reason; the nature of biblical revelation; the relation of science and Scripture; and the progressive understanding of truth.

She directly addressed the relation of faith, evidence, and reason in at least nine statements published over a period of nearly forty years, from 1864 to 1903.[9] The most familiar—and also the most comprehensive—is a paragraph from 1892:

> God never asks us to believe, without giving sufficient evidence upon which to base our faith. His existence, His character, the truthfulness of His Word, are all established by testimony that

appeals to our reason; and this testimony is abundant. Yet God has never removed the possibility of doubt. Your faith must rest upon evidence, not demonstration. Those who wish to doubt will have opportunity; while those who really desire to know the truth, will find plenty of evidence on which to rest their faith.[10]

Her reasoning here was clear and succinct: (1) faith is properly based on available evidence, which (2) "appeals" to "reason" and (3) is abundant, but (4) is not rationally coercive, so that doubt is always possible, with the result that (5) faith is a rationally responsible but free choice, and unbelief is also a rational (although decisively mistaken) option.

White insisted on the theological and spiritual priority of Scripture over secular knowledge and personal experience. Although there is no evidence that she ever used the Protestant Reformation slogan *sola Scriptura,* or advocated the idea in any absolute sense (as if no other sources of information about the character and activity of God were valid), she certainly did advocate the Bible in the sense of *prima Scriptura,* as the preeminent, supremely authoritative source of religiously relevant knowledge:

> The Bible, and the Bible alone, is to be our creed, the sole bond of union; all who bow to this holy word will be in harmony. Our own views and ideas must not control our efforts. Man is fallible, but God's word is infallible. Instead of wrangling with one another, let men exalt the Lord. Let us meet all opposition as did our Master, saying, "It is written." Let us lift up the banner on which is inscribed, The Bible our rule of faith and discipline.[11]

Convinced that the Bible teaches the whole will of God concerning human life, she habitually thought, spoke, and wrote in the language of Scripture. She devoted four of the five books of the "Conflict of the Ages" series—known informally as *Patriarchs and Prophets, Prophets and Kings, The Desire of Ages,* and *The Acts of the Apostles*—to elaboration and interpretation of the biblical narrative. In addition, *Christ's Object Lessons* is a series of expositions of the parables of Jesus, and *Thoughts from the Mount of Blessing* is an exposition of the Sermon on the Mount. *Education* also relies significantly on Scripture.[12]

In short, White advocated what *sola Scriptura* had meant in the Reformation—namely, not only that one does not need the church or its clergy to interpret Scripture, but also that it is the privilege and responsibility of every believer to read the Bible for oneself: "Jesus said to all, Search for yourselves. Allow no one to be brains for you, allow no one to do your thinking, your investigating, and your praying."[13]

Although the explicit message here was to encourage personal diligence in the study of Scripture, the clear implication was that with "painstaking effort" and "diligent searching" one can indeed "understand the treasures of the word of God." It was indicative as well as dramatic that in 1909, at the end of her last address to a session of the church's General Conference, she "spoke a few words of good cheer and farewell, and then turned to the pulpit, where lay a Bible. She opened the book, and held it with hands that trembled with age. And she said, 'Brethren and sisters, I commend unto you this book.' Without another word she closed the book, and walked away from the platform."[14]

At the same time that she was convinced of the divine origin and authority of Scripture as "God's Word," she insisted that it is not God's *words*. Responding to those "who think they find something to criticize" in the Bible, she replied, "I take the Bible just as it is, as the Inspired Word. I believe its utterances in an entire Bible." But she recognized that "the writers of the Bible had to express their ideas in human language" rather than "in grand superhuman language," and that "everything that is human is imperfect." As she explained:

> The Bible is written by inspired men, but it is not God's mode of thought and expression. It is that of humanity. God, as a writer, is not represented....The writers of the Bible were God's penmen, not His pen....It is not the words of the Bible that are inspired, but the men that were inspired....The divine mind and will is combined with the human mind and will; thus the utterances of the man are the word of God. [15]

The most basic reason for the perceived and sometimes troubling diversities in Scripture, she insisted, is the inherent impossibility of adequately formulating infinite truth in finite language.

Another, related, dimension of White's view of Scripture is reflected in her understanding of the conditional nature of prophetic predictions. When this became an issue in regard to her own expectation of an imminent Advent and her claim in 1851 (at the age of 24) that "time cannot last but a very little longer," she replied, "How is it with the testimonies of Christ and His disciples? Were they deceived?" Then, after

FIGURE 8.1 Ellen White at the Reno, Nevada, camp meeting in 1888, the year she allied with advocates of righteousness by faith (see Chapter 1). Her long-time colleague J. L. Loughborough is seated to her left (courtesy of the Ellen G. White Estate, Inc.).

citing the New Testament expectation of an imminent return of Jesus, she concluded:

> The angels of God in their messages to men represent time as very short. Thus it has always been presented to me. It is true that time has continued longer than we expected in the early days of this message. Our Saviour did not appear as soon as we hoped. But has the word of the Lord failed? Never! It should be remembered that the promises and threatenings of God are alike conditional.[16]

Regarding the progressive understanding of truth, Ellen White insisted that the Adventist idea of "present truth" was a historic characteristic of Christianity and a permanent characteristic of authentic Adventist Christianity. In 1889, in the aftermath of the traumatic Adventist controversy over the spiritual dynamics of salvation (the relation of faith and works, grace and obedience; see Figure 8.1)—an Adventist replay of Christian controversies in the first and sixteenth centuries—she addressed the issue at length:

> The fact that there is no controversy or agitation among God's people should not be regarded as conclusive evidence that they are holding fast to sound doctrine. When no new questions are started by investigation of the Scriptures, when no difference of opinion

arises which will set men to searching the Bible for themselves, to make sure that they have the truth, there will be many now, as in ancient times, who will hold to tradition, and worship they know not what.... The present attitude of the church is not pleasing to God. There has come in a self-confidence that has led them to feel no necessity for more truth and greater light.... God wills that a voice shall be heard arousing His people to action.[17]

In years to come her comments about the progressive nature of revelation remained emphatic. Indeed, White taught that progress in understanding divine truth would continue into the eternal future: "The years of eternity, as they roll, will bring richer and still more glorious revelations of God and of Christ. As knowledge is progressive, so will love, reverence, and happiness increase."[18]

The Metanarrative

A theological construction of Ellen White's thinking can plausibly take the form of a theology of cosmic history, expressed as a grand metanarrative of the "great controversy," the cosmic "conflict of the ages," more than a century before the idea of narrative theology came into scholarly vogue. The term "great controversy" was evidently suggested by the title of a book self-published in 1858 by H. L. Hastings, *The Great Controversy between God and Man,* and noted briefly but positively in James White's *Advent Review and Sabbath Herald* in April of that year. But Ellen, perhaps in collaboration with James, revised the language to *The Great Controversy between Christ and His Angels and Satan and His Angels,* giving the controversy an extraterrestrial dimension and avoiding the implication that God and humanity are enemies.[19]

Drawing on passages from both the Old and New Testaments, White began to articulate her understanding of "the great controversy" in 1858, beginning with the figure of Satan, who "wished to be consulted concerning the creation of man," and who was "filled with envy, jealousy and hatred" of Christ. He aspired, indeed, "to be the highest in heaven, next to God." Extraterrestrial in origin, the controversy was cosmic in scope; so was its resolution in what she regularly called "the plan of redemption," which, she maintained, "had a yet broader and deeper purpose than the salvation of man. It was not for this alone that Christ came to the earth; it was not merely that the inhabitants of this little world might regard the law of God as it should be regarded; but it was to vindicate the character of God before the universe."[20]

As White described it, the "great controversy" comprises three principal elements. The central issue is the character of God—that is, the moral nature of Ultimate Reality—as expressed in divine law, or the way God exercises authority in relation to created reality. This, she emphasized, is a matter of love rather than coercion. Her *magnum opus,* the five-volume mega-narrative of "the conflict of the ages" began with the words "God is love," and immediately explained, "His nature, his law is love. It ever has been, it ever will be." More than 3,500 pages of text later, the narrative ended on the same note and with the same words:

> The great controversy is ended. Sin and sinners are no more. The entire universe is clean. One pulse of harmony and gladness beats through the vast creation. From Him who created all, flow life and light and gladness, throughout the realms of illimitable space. From the minutest atom to the greatest world, all things, animate and inanimate, in their unshadowed beauty and perfect joy, declare that God is love. [21]

Another principal element in White's metanarrative is the imminence of the Second Advent of Christ, the beginning of the end of the "great controversy." For her, the eschaton was not simply a "far-off divine event to which the whole creation moves"; it was the literal, visible return of Jesus, which had been anticipated and described in the New Testament, and which, though it had not occurred in 1844, she anticipated would yet occur within the lifetimes of her contemporaries.[22]

Before that event could occur, she believed, Christ would carry out an "investigative judgment"—a review of the "books of heaven" to determine, or at least to reveal, the identity of those who, during the whole of human history, have responded positively to God's infinite love and have participated in the process of salvation. The completion of this process would mark "the close of probation," irrevocably sealing for eternity the individual destiny of all humanity. White received this view of eschatological judgment from the community of Adventists who responded to the "great disappointment" of 1844 by maintaining the calculated date but reinterpreting the eschatological "cleansing of the sanctuary" as a purely celestial rather than terrestrial event. The anticipated earthly development was a religio-political crisis symbolized by the imposition of "the mark of the beast," for which, she was convinced, the critical issue would be observance of the seventh-day Sabbath as a recognition of, and demonstration of obedience to, the love-motivated authority of God.[23]

A third element of her metanarrative was her vision of the role of the "remnant church." Like other sabbatarian Adventists, she derived this self-designation from the apocalyptic prediction: "The dragon was wroth with the woman and went off to make war with the remnant of her seed, which keep the commandments of God, and have the testimony of Jesus Christ" (Rev. 12:17 King James Version). She understood the mission of this "remnant church" as communicating the Christian gospel, including the "perpetuity of the law" and the significance of the seventh-day Sabbath, to "all the world." The unique, divinely ordained mission of the "remnant church" in preparation for the Second Advent was to involve the effective communication of salvation by faith as symbolized by the faithful experience of the Sabbath.[24]

As prerequisites to the return of Christ and the end of history, the combination of these two related developments offered, she believed, the possibility of "hastening" the eschaton: "Christ is waiting with longing desire for the manifestation of Himself in His church. When the character of Christ shall be perfectly reproduced in His people, then He will come to claim them as His own." Thus "It is the privilege of every Christian not only to look for but to hasten the coming of our Lord Jesus Christ" (2 Peter 3:12). Yet she harbored no illusions about the ambiguous moral and spiritual status of the church: "Enfeebled and defective as it may appear, the church is the one object upon which God bestows in a special sense His supreme regard."[25]

Related Theological Convictions

In the context of the "great controversy" over the preeminence of love in the character, actions, and requirements of God, Ellen White's pervasive pastoral concern centered on the dynamics of salvation. Reading the King James Version of Romans and Galatians in the light of Reformation theology, she understood "justification" as "imputed righteousness" and primarily a matter of penal substitution. "In dying upon the cross," she observed, Christ "transferred the guilt from the person of the transgressor to that of the divine Substitute, through faith in Him as his personal Redeemer. The sins of a guilty world...were imputed to the divine Surety." Perhaps she intended "justification" and "imputed righteousness" to convey the divine forgiveness that is God's fundamental attitude toward humanity; but she did not explicate her meaning. As was her practice, she simply used the available language.[26]

Although she seemed to favor the language of penal substitution, she casually used the language of other, sometimes conflicting and competing, atonement theories as well:

> ...The divine Son of God was the only sacrifice of sufficient value to fully satisfy the claims of God's perfect law.

> Christ has purchased the world by making a ransom for it.

> The cross of Calvary challenges, and will finally vanquish every earthly and hellish power....This sacrifice was offered for the purpose of restoring man to his original perfection;...it was offered to give him an entire transformation of character....

Thus, intentionally or not, she used the language of various theories of atonement—perhaps regarding them as complementary, like the atonement language of Scripture itself. Perhaps she was intuitively aware that no one theory captures the total theological significance of divine atonement and that multiple linguistic formulations are essential to express its richness and depth.[27]

Yet White emphasized that there was more to human salvation than the "justification" of "imputed righteousness"; there was also the "sanctification" of "imparted righteousness" that was to characterize the true people of God individually and collectively at the end of time. This she understood not as absolute moral perfection, but as "the completeness of Christian character," which she believed was "attained when the impulse to help and bless others springs constantly from within—when the sunshine of heaven fills the heart and is revealed in the countenance." This is presumably what she had in mind when she referred to "the character of Christ" being "perfectly reproduced in His people." Then they can "stand in the sight of a holy God without a mediator....While the investigative judgment is going forward in heaven, while the sins of penitent believers are being removed from the sanctuary, there is to be a special work of purification, of putting away sin, among God's people on earth."[28]

So concerned was she about the moral and ethical dimensions of salvation, along with the importance of serious effort, that, reflecting the

New Testament letter of James, she referred repeatedly to "faith" and "works" as "two oars which we must use equally if we press our way up the stream against the current of unbelief." Simply put, "Many will be lost while hoping and desiring to be Christians.... They do not now *choose* to be Christians." Clearly, she was no universalist; for her, salvation was a gracious divine gift that must be received, appropriated, and actualized in obedience to God's will.[29]

Accordingly, once she was convinced in 1846 (thanks largely to the efforts of Joseph Bates) of the continuing meaning and spiritual validity of the seventh-day Sabbath, it occupied a major place in her thinking. Her understanding of the Sabbath was based largely on literal readings of the account of creation in Genesis and of the Fourth Commandment in Exodus. She was especially interested in its role in spiritual formation, devoting a brief chapter to it in *Education*, and she was especially interested in its symbolic significance as she understood the apocalyptic messages of Daniel and the Revelation. She was convinced that observance of the Sabbath would become a decisive, world-wide eschatological issue. She referred to the Sabbath throughout *The Great Controversy*.[30]

Theological Characteristics

Ellen White's most obvious—but not most important—theological characteristics were the inevitable consequences of her historical, cultural, and biographical context. Like all prophets in all ages, she was a child of her times. From a twenty-first century perspective, nearly a hundred years after her death, the most prominent characteristic of all was her direct King James Version literalism. She had no recourse to the original languages in which Scripture was composed and made little use of more recent versions based on the best ancient manuscripts. Although she recognized the possibility of errors in the transmission and translation of the biblical text, her own use of the text does not reflect a significant concern about this issue. Her occasional use of revised versions may well have been the work of her editors or editorial assistants.

She endorsed the traditional authorship of biblical materials—the Mosaic authorship of the Torah and the Pauline authorship of the Letter to Hebrews, traditional assumptions affirmed not by the biblical text but by the titles of the respective documents in the KJV. She endorsed also the Petrine authorship of the Second Letter of Peter and the apostolic authorship of the Book of Revelation, now almost unanimously regarded by biblical scholars as highly unlikely. She recognized chronological and theological discrepancies among the Gospels but did not discuss the complexities of these relationships or their implications for an understanding of the biblical message. Although she was aware of text-critical issues, she did not address any of them specifically.

She was not perfectly consistent (there are minor discrepancies in her interpretations of Scripture), and she was sometimes theologically imprecise. In regard to the divine Trinity, for example, she referred to "three living persons of the heavenly trio," possibly approaching tritheism, a doctrine rejected by most Christians. Concerning Jesus' words on the cross, "It is finished," she explained: "When Christ spoke these words, He addressed His Father. . . . With clasped hands they entered into the solemn pledge that Christ would become the substitute and surety for the human race if they were overcome by Satan's sophistry." In saying that "faith and works are the two oars which we must use equally" (cited earlier), she seemed almost to advocate a synergistic understanding of salvation.[31]

Interpretive Summary

Ellen Harmon White was more interested in exhorting and encouraging the faithful than explaining and interpreting the faith. So the paradox of Ellen White and theology remains. But it now has an added dimension: her pastoral, Advent-oriented thinking was obviously "conservative" in some ways and just as obviously "progressive" in others.

Nearly a century after her death in 1915, three "conservative"—almost "fundamentalist"—characteristics remain particularly prominent. First, in her use of Scripture she depended on the King James Version and interpreted it literally and concretely. Second, except for distinctively Adventist doctrines, she affirmed much traditional and popular Protestant thinking regarding the Trinity and atonement. Third, she was deeply and continually concerned about Christian behavior in anticipation of and preparation for the Second Advent. She was convinced that one's diet, dress, and recreational activities all carried inherent and profound spiritual implications.

At the same time, she was "progressive" in important ways. At least in principle, she remained open to new understandings of Scripture and opposed to what she regarded as a conservative attitude in relation to truth and procedures. She insisted on "sufficient evidence" as the basis for religious belief, while recognizing that the evidence is rarely coercive. She emphasized love as the fundamental character of God and the principal motivation for moral behavior. She addressed social issues—opposing slavery and advocating temperance and environmental concern. She insisted on individual responsibility for studying Scripture and thinking theologically. And except when she believed the integrity of her church was threatened, she was more interested in practical spirituality than theoretical sophistication. Even in her concern about behavior, she defined spiritual maturity more in terms of relational graciousness than in terms of religious fastidiousness or theological correctness.

Throughout the seventy years of her prophetic ministry, Ellen Harmon White was always more a prophet than a theologian, but on occasion she expressed significant theological insights.

NOTES

1. Fritz Guy, *Thinking Theologically: Adventist Christianity and the Interpretation of Faith* (Berrien Springs, MI: Andrews University Press, 1999), 4–5.

2. Ellen G. White, "Circulate the Publications—No. 1," *Advent Review and Sabbath Herald* 85 (Aug. 6, 1908): 8 (hereafter referred to as *Review and Herald*); Ellen G. White, *Testimonies for the Church*, 9 vols. (Mountain View, CA: Pacific Press, n.d.) 8: 5, 255–335.

3. Ellen G. White, *The Desire of Ages: The Conflict of the Ages as Illustrated in the Life of Christ* (Mountain View, CA: Pacific Press, 1898), 521; Ellen G. White, "The True Sheep Respond to the Voice of the Shepherd," *Signs of the Times* 19 (Nov. 27, 1893): 54; Ellen G. White, "The Word Made Flesh," *Review and Herald*, 83 (Apr. 5, 1906): 8.

4. Ellen G. White, "The First Blow of the Reformation," *Signs of the Times* 9 (June 28, 1883): 290 (true theology); Ellen G. White, *The Great Controversy between Christ and Satan: The Conflict of the Ages in the Christian Dispensation* (Battle Creek, MI: Review and Herald Publishing Assn., 1888), 525 (errors); Ellen G. White, Letter to the Editor, *Gospel Herald* (Jan. 1, 1901): 4 (valueless); Ellen G. White, *The Ministry of Healing* (Mountain View, CA: Pacific Press, 1905), 442 (speculation).

5. Ellen G. White, *Steps to Christ* (New York: Fleming H. Revell, 1892), 93.

6. See White, *Great Controversy*, 439–43, 579–80, 615–16.

7. Jonathan Butler, "The World of E. G. White and the End of the World," *Spectrum: Journal of the Association of Adventist Forums* 10 (Aug. 1979): 6. Hereafter referred to as *Spectrum*. See also Chapter 10 of this volume.

8. See Ellen G. White, *Education* (Mountain View, CA: Pacific Press, 1903).

9. Chronologically the statements range from Ellen G. White, *Spiritual Gifts: Important Facts of Faith, In Connection with the History of Holy Men of Old* (Battle Creek, MI: Seventh-day Adventist Publishing Assn., 1864), 94; to White, *Education*, 169.

10. White, *Steps to Christ*, 105.

11. Ellen G. White, "A Missionary Appeal," *Review and Herald* 62 (1885): 769.

12. Ellen G. White, *The Story of Patriarchs and Prophets: The Conflict of the Ages Illustrated in the Lives of Holy Men of Old* (Mountain View, CA: Pacific Press, 1890); Ellen G. White, *The Story of Prophets and Kings as Illustrated in the Captivity and Restoration of Israel* (Mountain View, CA: Pacific Press, 1917); White, *Desire of Ages;* Ellen G. White, *The Acts of the Apostles in the Proclamation of the Gospel of Jesus Christ* (Mountain View, CA: Pacific Press, 1911); Ellen G. White, *Christ's Object Lessons* (Washington, DC: Review and Herald Publishing Assn., 1900); Ellen G. White, *Thoughts from the Mount of Blessing* (Mountain View, CA: Pacific Press, 1900); White, *Education*, 20–22, 33–44, 45–50, 51–70, 73–96, 123–92.

13. Ellen G. White, "Study the Bible for Yourselves," *Review and Herald* 71 (1894): 577.

14. William A. Spicer, *The Spirit of Prophecy in the Advent Movement: A Gift That Builds Up* (Washington, DC: Review and Herald Publishing Assn., 1937), 30, reporting a personal memory.

15. Ellen G. White, *Selected Messages from the Writings of Ellen G. White*, 3 vols. (Washington, DC: Review and Herald Publishing Assn., 1958), 1: 21, from a document originally written in 1886.

16. Ellen G. White, *A Sketch of the Christian Experience and Views of Ellen G. White* (Saratoga Springs, NY: James White, 1851), 46.

17. Ellen G. White, "The Mysteries of the Bible a Proof of Its Inspiration," *Testimonies for the Church*, 5:706–709 (Testimony 33, 1889).

18. Ellen G. White, "Open the Heart to Light," *Review and Herald* 67 (1890): 177; White, *Great Controversy*, 677–78.

19. Ellen G. White, *Spiritual Gifts: The Great Controversy between Christ and His Angels and Satan and His Angels* (Battle Creek, MI: James White, 1858); H[orace] L[orenzo] Hastings, *The Great Controversy between Christ and Satan: Its Origin, Progress, and End* (Rochester, NY: H. L. Hastings, 1858); Book Notice, *Review and Herald* 11 (1858): 144.

20. White, *Spiritual Gifts* (1858), 17. See also White, *Patriarchs and Prophets*, 68–69.

21. White, *The Great Controversy*, 678. White reiterated this emphasis in her *Steps to Christ*.

22. The phrase "far-off divine event" appears in Alfred, Lord Tennyson, "In Memoriam A. H. H.," epilogue, stanza 36 (1849).

23. White repeatedly discussed the "investigative judgment" and related events in *Great Controversy*.

24. For an early reference to the "remnant," see Ellen G. Harmon, "To the Little Remnant Scattered Abroad," a broadside published by James White on April 6, 1846.

25. White, *Christ Object Lessons*, 69; White, *Acts of the Apostles*, 12.

26. White, *The Desire of Ages*, 667; Ellen G. White, MS 84a, 1897, quoted in *Seventh-day Adventist Bible Commentary*, ed. Francis D. Nichol, 7 vols. (Washington, DC: Review and Herald Publishing Assn., 1953–1957), 7: 462; Ellen G. White, MS 35, 1895, ibid., 463.

27. Ellen G. White, *The Spirit of Prophecy*, 4 vols. (Mountain View, CA: Pacific Press, 1870–1884), 2: 9–10; *Seventh-day Adventist Bible Commentary*, 7: 460, 6: 1113.

28. White, *Christ Object Lessons*, 69, 384; Ellen G. White, "Gifts and Offerings," *Review and Herald*, 84 (Jan. 17, 1907): 8. See also White, *Great Controversy*, 425.

29. Ellen G. White, "Laborers Together with God," *Review and Herald* 78 (1901): 371.

30. See White, *Great Controversy*, 250–52. See also, George R. Knight, *A Search for Identity: The Development of Seventh-day Adventist Beliefs* (Hagerstown, MD: Review and Herald Publishing Assn., 2000), 66–71.

31. Ellen G. White, MS 111, 1897, quoted in *Seventh-day Adventist Bible Commentary*, 5: 1149.

9

Practical Theology

Bert Haloviak

ELLEN HARMON WHITE's community understood her role in the Seventh-day Adventist Church as a contemporary manifestation of the New Testament "gift of prophecy" (Rom. 12:6; 1 Cor. 14:1; Eph. 4:11). Functionally her role was that of a practical theologian, undergirded and reinforced in her community by the authority attributed to her divinely endowed charisma. White's ministry was clearly consistent with the branch of theology called *practical* theology. Distinct from the role and function of a biblical or systematic theologian, her vision-based expressions were the practical application of a theological system already largely embraced by her church community. While the roles of practical and biblical theology worked closely together within early Seventh-day Adventism, the evidence suggests that White's function was not to resolve theological issues as an authoritative "biblical theologian" (see Chapter 8). Rather, she consistently urged lay church theologians to resolve disputed issues of theology through their own careful scriptural analysis.

Ellen White did not introduce distinctively new doctrinal insights to Seventh-day Adventists; neither did she directly correct even the erroneous theological teachings of others, as one might reasonably expect an authority on biblical interpretation to do. On those few occasions when White considered that she had resolved points of theological conflict using the authority of her charisma, she maintained unity by deemphasizing the supposed importance of the theological issues that were being contested. She brought a measure of unity to the church by emphasizing its core theological positions and focusing her fellow believers on mission and the daily task of forming a Christian character that would make them ready for the Second Coming of Jesus.

Ellen White's emphasis on practical theology presupposed the presence of other approaches to "doing theology" in the Seventh-day Adventist community, evident in the work of colleagues such as her husband, James, John Nevins Andrews, Joseph Bates, and Uriah Smith. Her approach also presupposed a broadly agreed on theological framework of understanding. This overarching theological system had been framed during the Second Great Awakening and later became known as the "restorationist movement" because of its effort to return to early Christian practices and beliefs. Shaping White's role as a practical theologian was the intense eschatology introduced by William Miller. In the years following 1844, White's visionary experiences enabled her community to discern the practical implications of this theological system, inherited primarily from the Christian Connexion faith as it was shaped by the Millerite Adventist experience.

The Christian Connexion

Not long after Ellen Harmon began to experience visions, she gained the acquaintance of former Christian Connexion minister and staunch Millerite believer James White. Ellen had earlier known something of this Connexion faith through her attendance at the Casco Street Connexion church in her hometown of Portland, Maine, where her family at times worshipped after their dismissal from the Methodist Church. At the Christian church on several occasions Ellen had listened to William Miller expound on the soon return of Jesus. The Christian Connexion faith, the first indigenous Christian movement in America, thus became a major influence during the earliest history of what became the Seventh-day Adventist church. Its distinctive theological features—such as its belief in a minimal organizational structure, as well as its involvement in the anti-slavery movement, advocacy of religious freedom, temperance, health reform, manual labor, and women in leadership—all had a pervasive impact on Seventh-day Adventism through much of the nineteenth century; some of its teachings survive to this day.[1]

The Christian Connexion had developed simultaneously at the conclusion of the eighteenth century in three separate geographical areas and out of three separate faith traditions in the United States: Virginia (from

Methodism), Kentucky (from Presbyterianism), and New England (from the Baptist tradition). Initially, none of the groups knew of the existence of the others. In seeking a broad unity based on the premise "when the scripture is silent, we are silent," the believers preferred using only biblical names and phrases for their beliefs and structure and hence rejected such terms as "trinity," "deity of Christ," and "imputation" and took the name "Christian." Their sole basis for church fellowship was Christian character.

Challenging the orthodoxy of Christian Connexion believers, Presbyterian theologian Gilbert McMaster provided a list of their "errors," which included (1) denial of the Trinity, relegating Christ to a created being; (2) denial of the Holy Spirit as a distinct person; (3) conditional immortality; (4) emphasis on achieving human obedience to God's requirements rather than admitting humanity's fallen nature; (5) denial of imputationist views of the atonement; (6) teaching annihilation instead of everlasting punishment of the lost; and (7) belief that women could be public teachers of religion.[2] James White's use of a sermon chart emphasizing the law of God (Figure 9.1) reflects his careful emphasis on Christian obedience. This listing is useful for our purposes because these ideas are all found not only within Christian Connexionism but also in the earliest Seventh-day Adventist theological system inherited by Ellen White. She especially integrated into her understanding of ministry the stress on the overwhelming importance of Christian character. When she married James White, an ordained Christian Connexion minister, she moved into the orbit of Christian Connexion theology.

The newly wed Ellen Harmon White received a vision in April 1847 that her husband, James, printed later that year as *A Word to the Little Flock*. This vision stressed the importance of observing the seventh-day Sabbath as the day of worship. White's understanding came not from her biblical exegesis but from such biblical theologians as Joseph Bates and James White and from her own visionary insight when she saw a "halo of glory" surrounding the fourth commandment. Through this vision White "saw that the holy Sabbath currently was, and will be, the separating wall between the true Israel of God and unbelievers; that the Sabbath was the great question, to unite the hearts of God's dear waiting saints." Not only were God's people to evangelize the former Adventists concerning the Sabbath; they were to do so with the knowledge that such evangelization would generate persecution from the existing churches, as well as from "nominal Adventists," and usher in the end. Reflecting an emphasis on

FIGURE 9.1 James White displays his chart depicting the Ten Commandments, ca. 1864. In the 1870s and 1880s James and Ellen White developed graphic images for home display depicting the role of the Law of God in Adventist theology, as discussed in Chapter 13 (courtesy of the Ellen G. White Estate, Inc.).

adherence to God's commands, inherited from the Christian Connexion, the vision reported that obedience to the neglected commandment of God gave Sabbath-keepers a *"right* to the tree of life" (Rev. 22:14).[3]

The initial body of Sabbath-keeping Adventists originated sometime in 1844 or early 1845 from a Christian Connexion group that had coalesced in Washington, New Hampshire, in the 1830s. These Christians had become Adventists in 1842 through the ministry of Millerite evangelist Joshua Goodwin and sabbatarians when William Farnsworth, an influential

Christian Connexion believer, stood during a service and informed the congregation that his study of Scripture had convinced him that the seventh day was the day to be observed as Sabbath. Before long a group of at least 15 worshiped in his father's house.[4]

These members of the Christian Connexion tended to a very literal reading of scripture, as did Ellen Harmon. This approach affected Farnsworth's Sabbath observance in several ways. He concluded that Revelation 11:19 applied to the last days: "God's temple in heaven was opened, and the ark of his covenant was seen within his temple." Since the ark contained the Ten Commandments, the seventh-day Sabbath continued to be relevant. Farnsworth carefully studied the creation week in the beginning of Genesis and concluded that the Sabbath began when the sun went down on Friday evening. He inferred from Exodus 20 that the fourth commandment demanded not only observance of the seventh-day Sabbath, but also that "six days shalt thou labor." As the Washington Sabbath-keepers continued to grow, they so outnumbered the Christians that the latter voted in 1862 to donate their church building to the Seventh-day Adventists, who for the past eighteen years had been meeting in private homes.

By 1867 the Whites had held meetings in Washington on at least four occasions. In that year, one of Farnsworth's sons, Eugene, noticed that his father had very discreetly relapsed in his usage of chewing tobacco. He decided to test Ellen White's ability to uncover this practical issue. If she could reveal his father's secret, Eugene would consider her visionary gift genuine. White in due time received a vision, which led her publicly to castigate William Farnsworth for telling the community that he had disavowed chewing tobacco. William accepted the public reprimand and gained life-long confidence in her gift. He also helped vindicate White's role within the Washington community. As she wrote: "We pleaded earnestly with the children, until thirteen arose and expressed a desire to be Christians."[5] Several of the children were William Farnsworth's, including Eugene, who was among the youth baptized after the meeting with the Whites. He ministered for many years for the Seventh-day Adventist church and planned the Elmshaven funeral of Ellen White in 1915.

Shut-Door Ministry

Another aspect of Ellen White's earliest ministry involved retaining the confidence of her followers that the Lord had guided the Adventists in the past and continued to do so. Her group was frequently identified with the term "shut door," a phrase that arose from Jesus' parable of the ten virgins—five wise and five foolish—who attended a wedding, recounted in Matthew 25:1–13. Just before the bridegroom arrived, the five foolish virgins discovered that their lamps had gone out for lack of oil. When they went to buy more oil, the groom arrived—"and the door was shut." The message: "Watch therefore, for ye know neither the day nor the hour wherein the Son of man cometh."

Reflecting on this parable, most sabbatarian Adventists concluded that salvation was available solely to those who had accepted Miller's teaching that Jesus would return in 1844, a belief that estranged them from the larger Christian community. About the time of his marriage and acceptance of the seventh-day Sabbath in late August of 1846, James White described to a friend his intention to preach a funeral sermon for a fellow believer, moaning that he would be in a community of "hard, ugly Congregationalist and Methodist" believers. He had already become convinced of the futility of trying to convert them to the Advent faith for, he quipped, "It's too late." In another situation he considered it not too late to "give a reason of our hope...even to swine."[6] After visiting a group of Adventists in Portland, Maine, in April 1845, Joshua V. Himes noted that the shut-door teaching prevented those believers from "exercis[ing] benevolent feelings toward sinners, with a view to save them, so that that most essential element of the spirit of Christ, and of Christian character, is annihilated. Under such circumstances, the wonder with us is, not that there have been some extravagances, but that there have not been more."[7]

A shut-door ministry demanded a practical theologian. As James White was beginning to lead the sabbatarian group toward a more organized structure in the early 1860s, he reflected on the nature of the group's ministry during its shut door-period of late 1844 to 1852, when members believed that "our work for the world was finished." Back then they considered that the world and "fallen churches" had been given their last opportunity to receive the everlasting gospel message and been called out of "Babylon" or the fallen Protestant churches:

> As individuals would go scores and even hundreds of miles to present the truth to one or two who had been believers in the first message, so would the laborers go long distances to visit, to comfort, and to strengthen the scattered ones who had embraced the faith. In all cases where difficulties existed they were untiring in their

efforts to give aid, traveling far, holding meetings sometimes all
night, enduring toils and trials sufficient to exhaust the energies of
any class of men.[8]

The experience of Samuel Rhodes, "one of the most faithful, and
self-sacrificing lecturers on the Second Advent," illustrates the commitment to the shut-door teaching. After the Great Disappointment he
became discouraged and isolated himself "in an uninhabited part of
New York State." Encouraged by Ellen White, who had seen Rhodes in
vision, Hiram Edson and a "Bro Ralph" traveled over 1,000 miles over a
period of months to persuade Rhodes to rejoin his Adventist colleagues.
In vision White had seen "that Brn Edson and Ralph should make him
believe there was hope and mercy for him, and tear him away, then he
would come among the flock; and that Angels would attend them on their
journey. I heard an Angel say 'Can ye not see the worth of the soul?'"
White also "saw that in Bro Rhodes' mouth there had been no guile in
speaking against the present truth," that is, "the Sabbath, and Shut Door."[9]
   Ellen White's visionary experiences validated the community's understanding of shut-door theology. On at least seven occasions she invoked
visions endorsing the shut door. In 1850 she was instructed during a vision
to urge her husband to publish the shut-door statements that Millerite
Adventist leaders had made in 1844. Given the pre-disappointment theological perspective of that time, those statements exhibit the most extreme
interpretations of shut-door theology. In addition, in 1850 Ellen White
received a vision about the Adventist preacher Joseph Baker, a former
member of the Christian Connexion: "I saw that Brother Baker must not
sink down, that God had a work for him to do, not to feed the dogs, but
the starving sheep, feed the sheep, feed the sheep, said my accompanying
angel. It was melting weeping time when I related the vision."[10]

The Third Angel and the Sabbath

Seventh-day Adventists during 1848 convened six separate "Sabbath
Conferences" designed to solidify the community on the importance of
obedience to the seventh-day Sabbath, which they considered to be the
message of the Third Angel of Revelation 14. An August 1848 conference
at Volney, New York, typified White's role at these gatherings. As James
White described it: "One of the number was not on the Sabbath but was

humble and good. Ellen rose up in vision, took the large Bible, held it up before the Lord, talked from it, then carried it to this humble brother who was not on the Sabbath and put it in his arms." Here again she performed no explicit exegetical role; instead, according to James White, she remained in vision for one and a half hours without breathing. In his letter James gave the rationale for the present truth held by Seventh-day Adventists: "So the Shut door and Sabbath is the present truth. These truths will form and keep up the same mark of distinction between us and unbelievers as God made in 1844."[11]

James White made a similar linkage in his next letter, on October 2, 1848: "The principal points on which we dwell as present truth are the 7th day Sabbath and Shut Door. In this we wish to honor God's most holy institution and also acknowledge the work of God in our Second Advent experience."[12] White and Joseph Bates, the first Adventist evangelist of the seventh-day Sabbath, coordinated their travels in proclaiming that message, and for several years the two former Christian Connexion believers were the sole sabbatarian Adventists proclaiming the Third Angel's Message regarding the seventh-day Sabbath.

Joseph Bates witnessed Ellen White in vision a number of times, taking notes from her spoken words both during and after these experiences. In his tract *A Seal of the Living God* he quoted her remarks after coming out of a couple of visions in November 1848 during meetings in Dorchester, Massachusetts: "Who has relaxed that fourth commandment?... Stand out from him entirely.... I saw that he rolled, and turned on his bed, to see how he could get round this law of God.... Who was this you saw? Answer J B Cook."[13] Cook was a former Second Adventist minister who had initially espoused the seventh-day Sabbath but had recently given it up. In a vision in January 1849 Ellen White continued to emphasize the practical importance of obedience to the fourth commandment while the saints eagerly awaited the Second Advent. Referring to a company she had seen "howling in agony," she explained that they had lost out on salvation because they had once kept the Sabbath but had given it up. Here again, without biblical explication, White stressed her understanding of the practical results from disobedience to the Sabbath.[14]

As White reflected on the context of the Third Angel's message in Revelation 14, she identified the Sabbath as a final testing truth that would pit the obedient children of God against those who instead followed the "beast," interpreted as a prophetic representation of the papacy. She saw in vision that some would be lost through their failures to dispense means that would support the "messengers" giving the final truth of the Sabbath. The soon-to-occur final events would destroy their possessions. According to the vision, "The angel said, can such enter heaven? Another answered, No never! never! never!" An angel also informed White that not all those going forth as so-called messengers were truly called. Some took it upon themselves to waste money in travels that prevented God's true messengers from giving the truth to souls that were starving. Every dollar spent in useless traveling would have to be accounted for in the soon-coming judgment. "I saw that the judgments were just upon us, and that the trouble would soon be to this land, and that blood would flow in streams."[15]

James White soon wrote his close friend Leonard Hastings, whose wife had recently died, with some details that illustrate how Ellen functioned nonexegetically: "As God has revealed some things relative to your wife's death to Ellen in vision we felt that our first duty was to communicate it to you....Ellen is writing a cutting message for Brother [E.L.H.] Chamberlain, that God has never called him to travel." James believed that Chamberlain possessed the gift of tongues, a gift displayed at an 1848 Sabbath conference, which seemed to confirm to the believers that the true time for the Sabbath to begin was 6 p.m. Friday night. "It is true that God may occasionally call on those who have *other gifts*, but they are not the messengers. 'A messenger has a message,' said Ellen in vision."[16]

Ellen White also wrote to Hastings about this vision. She informed him that Joseph Bates had recently had a dream

which if he had followed he would have been with you in your wife's distress and if Brother Chamberlain had not been with him he [Bates] would have gone to God alone and he would have seen by the dream and by the drawings of the Spirit, that he must come directly to your house, when Satan had got your wife in his grasp, and by faith in God would have wrenched her from the power of the enemy, but he leaned upon Brother Chamberlain some for duty and followed his impressions instead of the light God gave him in the dream.

Ellen assured Hastings that his wife "would come up at the voice of God" and that those criticizing him for having his wife's funeral on the Sabbath were wrong to do so.[17]

Although there were just several hundred Sabbatarian Adventists in the early 1850s, White's confidence in the sabbatarian message of the

Third Angel led her to announce that they were witnessing the birth of a movement that would fulfill God's purpose at the end time: "I asked the angel if Zion should languish. Said the angel, She is rising never to fall again. God has stretched out his hand the second time to recover the remnant of his people." White sought to unify a group of believers on one central truth, the message of the Third Angel. So crucial was this issue that White reported a vision of August 10, 1851, that reflected the regnant system of theology: "we had a perfect right in the city for we had kept the commandments of God."[18]

The first sabbatarian Adventist, William Farnsworth, had concluded from Scripture that the Sabbath began at sundown Friday evening. In contrast, Joseph Bates believed that it began at 6 p.m. In 1848 the ecstatic experience of E.L.H. Chamberlain convinced the majority, including James White, that the 6 p.m. time was correct. According to James, "the Holy Ghost came down," filling Chamberlain with the gift of tongues after which the group concluded that the Sabbath began at 6 p.m. "Here is where the Sabbath begins at 6 p.m.," said James. "Satan would get us from this time. But let us stand fast in the Sabbath as God has given it to us and Brother Bates. God has raised up Brother Bates to give this truth." The controversy continued, however, and sundown remained a minority position that surfaced from time to time. James White eventually commissioned various biblical theologians to study the sundown position. Finally, in 1855, John N. Andrews reexamined the subject and concluded that the Sabbath began at sundown. James White now affirmed that he had "never been fully satisfied with the testimony presented in favor of six o'clock."[19]

James White later reflected on the entire experience in a *Review and Herald* article. Sensitive about accusations that Ellen White had endorsed the 6 p.m. time through her visionary experience, he discussed her 1847 vision at Topsham, Maine, when Ellen had heard an angel affirm, "From even unto even shall ye celebrate your Sabbath." Interestingly, Joseph Bates, present at the meeting where the vision occurred, "succeeded in satisfying all present [including Ellen White] that "even" was six o'clock. Far from resolving the issue through her own biblical analysis, Ellen White, as she seems to have consistently done, deferred to the conclusion of the biblical theologians in whom she maintained confidence. James affirmed that Ellen's vision in the aftermath of the Andrews study in 1855, which argued that the "sunset time was correct," brought unity to that conclusion and even convinced Bates.[20]

Christian Character

Joseph Bates had introduced the seventh-day Sabbath message to believers in Jackson, Michigan, in 1849, but the church soon disunited and James and Ellen White felt constrained to visit it to offer counsel. Their doing so provides a telling example of the tenet of Christian character as a central test of church fellowship and of the practical ministry of Ellen White. She had seen in vision that certain of the ministers who served as itinerant evangelists in that area "lorded it over God's heritage," through their severe requirements demanding sacrifice of property by the believers.

> I saw an oppressive spirit exercised by some of the brethren toward others. Bro [J. A.] Bowles has partaken largely of this oppressive exalted spirit. So, also, had Brn [H. S.] Case and [C. P.] Russell, drinked deeply of it. Some others have been affected with it. The little leaven has almost leavened the whole lump, and in order for sweet union and harmony to be in the church this unholy leaven must be entirely purged from it.

She also saw that other ministers within the church should have perceived this negative influence and "stood in a place to correct these errors, and exerted a good influence in the church." "Those [chosen] to be teachers," she advised, "should be patterns of piety, meekness and great humility, possessing a loving, kind spirit winning souls to Jesus, and the truth of the Bible." Instead, the Jackson church had become a hugely negative influence within the community.[21]

This pioneer Midwestern church had splintered over an incident involving the wife of Dan Palmer, one of the earliest believers in Jackson. On one occasion Mrs. Palmer had placed her washing on the clothes line; when it had almost dried, her upstairs neighbor, a non-Adventist, had thrown water over the ledge, which splattered in the mud and dirtied the clothes. The daughter of minister Case, in reporting the incident to her father, heard Palmer call the woman a "bitch." Palmer denied using that word. Case and his ministering partner, Russell, demanded strong church discipline for Mrs. Palmer. It was within that setting that Ellen White experienced visions emphasizing Mrs. Palmer's error in losing self-control—but subsequently revealed that Mrs. Palmer had not used the word of which she was accused, but rather one that sounded like it. Mrs. Palmer then confessed her error and admitted that she had used the word "witch." As a result of the controversy, Case and Russell, who had initially acknowledged White's visions to be from God, bolted from sabbatarian Adventism and formed the first splinter group to spring from the community. Reflecting on this experience, Ellen White explained her role within the sabbatarian community as it had developed in the Jackson incident. Late in June 1853 she informed the Jackson church that *God* had pled "with you face to face" through the "weak clay" of her ministry. She urged the believers there to "acknowledge the teaching of God" through her. They should not ignore "the means God had taken" to set them in the right.[22]

Perhaps the most dramatic example of a practical application springing from Ellen White's early theological world is evidenced in her assessment through vision of the family and person of Elon Everts, Seventh-day Adventist minister, writer, and originator of the term "investigative judgment." Following their abandonment of the shut-door theological system, Seventh-day Adventists had embarked on a major evangelistic thrust centering on spreading the Third Angel's Message to midwestern America. In the mid-1850s the Review office had moved to Battle Creek, Michigan, prompting a number of ministers, including Everts, to transfer to the Midwest, where they intended to engage in evangelism. As early as 1855 Ellen White had been "shown the danger of those brethren who moved from the East to the West of becoming worldly minded, and warnings were given me for them." The ministers making the move should be supreme exemplars of sabbatarian Adventism in their daily living; "They must live out their faith, and show that they regard the present truth above everything else." Ellen White exhibited an understanding of her role when she wrote the following: "If those moving from the East to the West had regarded these warnings, and had stood in the *counsel of God*, he would have wrought through them to the salvation of many souls." Unfortunately, a number who made the move became bogged down in non-evangelistic matters and "their works have shown that their object in settling West was for gain, and not to save souls. The special frown of God has rested upon those who have taken this course, especially upon some the Lord had called into the gospel field."[23]

Ellen White specifically applied this view to the Everts family, which included Elon, his wife, and their daughter. In 1856 White reported that God had intervened and "removed" Everts' wife through death: "Three times she was reproved by vision, and the third time I was shown if she did not stand out of her husband's way, that he might be free to teach perishing souls the truth, God would move her out of the way. It is even so; she sickened and died. Her passage to the tomb was dark." Later White described the experience more fully for the entire church. Instead of sell-ing off some of their massive farm property to advance the "last warning message," she explained in the *Review and Herald,* the Everts family had "plainly declare[d] by their works, that this world was their home, that here was their treasure." Elon's wife, White learned through a vision, "must unfasten her grasp" on her husband since "she was holding him back, and was unwilling that he should sell and give alms," and was also "unwill-ing that he should go out to talk the truth to others." White informed the church, "I was shown in vision that God had taken the mother away in anger, and unless the father and daughter submitted to God, unless they cut loose from this world and had their affections weaned from it, God would step over the threshold again in judgment." In the late 1850s White saw that Elon, now influenced by his daughter, was continuing his downward course. "The next news I heard was, that he was dead, and had left his large property to his daughter," White reported. "Nothing was bestowed upon the cause of God."[24]

Legacy

In the 1880s Seventh-day Adventists came to face a theological crisis of leadership and ministry over justification by faith, the doctrine that salva-tion was a gift from God, not a reward for keeping his law. Ellen White again responded as a practical theologian.

Early Seventh-day Adventists believed that the gospel brought Christians to where Adam was prior to the fall, while final salvation depended on obedience to God's law. John Nevins Andrews concluded his 1851 tract, *Thoughts on the Sabbath and the Perpetuity of the Law of God,* with a poetic rendition of this doctrine:

> *The law reveals and makes us know*
> *What duties to our God we owe;*
> *But 'tis the Gospel must reveal*
> *Where lies our strength to do his will.*

Andrews also expressed the idea in prose: "By faith in the atonement of the Saviour our hearts are cleansed from sin, and we receive the 'renew-ing of the Holy Ghost.' Then with that perfect love to God restored to us, which Adam lost at his fall, we are prepared to render acceptable obedi-ence to God, and thus to fulfill 'the righteousness of the law.' "[25] All early

Seventh-day Adventist biblical theologians agreed with this view, often citing in its support Revelation 22:14: "Blessed are they that *DO* his commandments, that they may have *RIGHT* to the tree of life."

As late as 1868 James White, reflecting his Christian Connexion background, was still emphasizing the imperative of personal obedience to gain right to the tree of life. He saw only two categories of human beings: those that obeyed the commandments and those who broke them. "The great design of the sacred Scriptures was to give man a perfect rule of faith and practice," he concluded. "God purposed that his people should follow this rule and *by it* develop characters perfect before him." However, by the time of his death in 1881 he was reconsidering his emphasis on the law. He and Ellen had resolved earlier that year to retire from their constant speaking assignments and together prepare studies on "the glorious subject of redemption that should long ago have been more fully presented to the people." In informing the church of their intention to refocus the message, James stated, "We feel that we have a testimony for our people at this time, relative to the exalted character of Christ, and His willingness and power to save."[26]

A month after the death of her husband Ellen White recounted a significant dream following a time of "pleading with the Lord for light in regard to duty." She had dreamed of riding in her horse-drawn carriage with her husband driving next to her. When she inquired whether James had been resurrected because *"half of me was gone,"* her deceased husband said it was not so. In the dream James continued, "Oh, those precious subjects the Lord would have had me bring before the people, precious jewels of light." He urged Ellen to continue her mission, for "There is important matter which the people need."[27]

By the late 1870s and 1880s Ellen White had become convinced that the Adventists' low spiritual condition had resulted from the failure of their theology. At a General Conference session in Minneapolis in 1888 she endorsed the views of second-generation Seventh-day Adventist biblical scholars Alonzo Jones and E. J. Waggoner on justification by faith. Near the conclusion of the session she announced her intention of taking the new message to grassroots Adventists, for "if the ministers will not receive the light, I want to give the people a chance."[28]

Afterward she took the lead in weaning Adventists away from their legalistic Christian Connexion theology. Although she had not originated the new initiative, she eagerly embraced the view of Jones and Waggoner and helped create a positive atmosphere for its reception. No longer would Seventh-day Adventists receive a *right* to the tree of life by keeping the commandments but rather through the righteousness of Christ. This new emphasis also led to the most *open door* ever perceived by Seventh-day Adventists up to that time: "God has children, many of them, in the Protestant churches, and a large number in the Catholic churches, who are more true to obey the light and do to the very best of their knowledge than a large number among Sabbath-keeping Adventists."[29]

After the Minneapolis session Ellen White considered it her mission to point out Adventism's past erroneous message and to promote the new view. Believing that "the understanding of the people of God has been blinded," she offered an alternative: "We have precious light to present before the people, and we rejoice that we have a message for this time which is present truth. The tidings that Christ is our righteousness has brought relief to many, many souls, and God says to His people, 'Go forward.'" White believed that the Lord had given her a message that she, "with pen and voice," intended to proclaim until the old legalism had been expelled. Those who had bound themselves to their "legal religion" must "see the better things provided for them—Christ and His righteousness."[30]

Ellen White, alone in Adventism, saw the reconciling possibilities between the past message that centered on the law and the new message that centered on the gospel. She told the ministers at an 1890 Bible school of her travels throughout the camp-meeting circuit after Minneapolis, "where the message of the righteousness of Christ was preached." She felt privileged to stand beside Jones and Waggoner to give her support for "the message for the time" as the trio "pointed men to the Lamb of God that taketh away the sin of the world." The focus on the "righteousness of Christ" was "special light" that God had for His people during the past two years. "We want the past message and the fresh message," she pleaded.[31]

At a Rome, New York, camp meeting in June of 1889 Ellen White confessed that Seventh-day Adventists, in the past, "have not been instructed as they should have been, that Christ is unto them both salvation and righteousness." At that same camp meeting she identified the new hope for the future of the Church: "The present message—justification by faith—is a message from God. . . . The thought that the righteousness of Christ is imputed to us, not because of any merit on our part, but as a free gift from God, seemed a precious thought." The next year she expressed her hope that one theme would dominate Seventh-day Adventists: "One interest will prevail, one subject will swallow up every other,—Christ our righteousness."[32] This would be her legacy to the Seventh-day Adventist church.

NOTES

1. Although the church name, "Seventh-day Adventist," was not generally accepted until 1860, I use the term anachronistically beginning after October 1844 to avoid confusion.

2. Gilbert McMaster, *An Essay, In Defence of Some Fundamental Doctrines of Christianity: Including a Review of the Writings of Elias Smith* (Schenectady, NY: Riggs and Stevens, 1815).

3. Ellen G. White to Joseph Bates in *A Word to the Little Flock* (Gorham, ME: James White, 1847) 19, emphasis added.

4. *Constitution of the First Christian Society in Washington, New Hampshire, April 4, 1832,* 16.

5. Ellen G. White, "Further Labors," *Testimonies for the Church*, 9 vols. (Washington, DC: Review and Herald Publishing Assn., 1948) 1: 661.

6. James White to "Bro" Collins, Aug. 26, 1846; James White to Stockbridge Howland, March 14, 1847. Unless otherwise noted, all unpublished correspondence can be found in the Ellen G. White Estate, Silver Spring, MD.

7. Joshua V. Himes, "Editorial Correspondence: Visit to Portland with Bro. Miller—A Good Hearing, State of the Cause—Duty of Adventists," *Morning Watch* (June 12, 1845): 192.

8. James White, "Conference Address," *Advent Review and Sabbath Herald* 18 (June 11, 1861), 21, hereafter referred to as *Review and Herald*.

9. Ellen G. White, "Article," *Present Truth* 1 (Dec. 1849): 35.

10. Ellen G. White, "Vision at Paris, Maine," Dec. 25, 1850 (re: James); Ellen G. White to Stockbridge and Frances Howland, Nov. 12, 1851 (Baker). See also Ellen G. White to Arabella Hastings, Aug. 4, 1850; Ellen G. White to Stockbridge and Frances Howland, Aug. 15, 1850; Ellen G. White, "A Vision the Lord Gave Me at Brother [William] Harris," Aug. 24, 1850. For thorough treatments of the shut-door issue, see Ingemar Lindén, *1844 and the Shut Door Problem* (Uppsala: Almquist & Wiksell, 1982); and Douglas Hackleman, "Picking the Shut-Door Lock," *Adventist Currents* 1 (July, 1984): 10–18, 41.

11. James White to Arabella and William Hastings, Aug. 26, 1848.

12. James White to Brother and Sister Hastings, Oct. 2, 1848.

13. Joseph Bates, *A Seal of the Living God: A Hundred Forty-Four Thousand of the Servants of God Being Sealed in 1849* (New Bedford, CT: Press of Benjamin Lindsey, 1849), 31–32.

14. Ellen G. White, Letter dated Jan. 17, 1849, in *To Those Who Are Receiving the Seal of the Living God*, a broadside published Jan. 31, 1849.

15. James White, "A Copy of Ellen White's Vision, Which She Had at Oswego, NY," Jan. 26, 1850.

16. James White to Leonard Hastings, March 18, 1850.

17. Ellen G. White to Leonard Hastings, March 18, 1850.

18. Ellen G. White, "A Vision the Lord Gave Me at Oswego," July 29, 1850; Ellen G. White, to "Sister" Harriet, Aug. 11, 1851, reporting on a vision of the previous day.

19. James White to "My Dear Brother [Stockbridge Howland]," July 2, 1848; James White, "Time of the Sabbath," *Review and Herald* 7 (1855): 76–78.

20. James White, "Time to Commence the Sabbath," *Review and Herald* 31 (1868): 168.

21. Ellen G. White, "Vision Given at Jackson, Michigan," June 2, 1853, MS 1-1853.

22. Ibid.; James and Ellen White, *Life Sketches of James White and Ellen G. White* (Battle Creek, MI: Review and Herald Publishing Assn., 1888), 328–29; Ellen G. White to the Church in Jackson, June 29, 1853. See also Arthur L. White, *Ellen G. White*, 6 vols. (Hagerstown, MD: Review and Herald Publishing Assn., 1981–1986), 1: 276–77.

23. The details in this paragraph are from Ellen G. White, *Spiritual Gifts*, 4 vols. (Battle Creek: James White, 1858–64), 2: 213–15 (1860); and Ellen G. White, "A Warning," *Review and Herald* 11 (1858): 174.

24. White, "A Warning."

25. J. N. Andrews, *Thoughts on the Sabbath and the Perpetuity of the Law of God* (Paris, ME: James White, 1851), 9; J. N. Andrews, "The Perpetuity of the Law of God," *Review and Herald* 1 (January 1851): 34.

26. James White, *Life Incidents in Connection with the Great Advent Movement as Illustrated by The Three Angels of Revelation XIV*, vol. 1 (Battle Creek, MI: Steam Press of the Seventh-day Adventist Publication Assn., 1868), 321, 327; Ellen G. White, "A Sketch of Experience," in *In Memoriam: A Sketch of the Last Sickness and Death of Elder James White* (Battle Creek, MI: Review and Herald Press, 1881), 54; James White, "Eastern Tour," *Review and Herald* 57 (1881): 88.

27. Ellen G. White to W. C. White, September 12, 1881, emphasis supplied.

28. Ellen G. White, "Morning Talk at Minneapolis," October 24, 1888, MS 9–1888.

29. Ellen G. White, "Repentance the Gift of God," *Review and Herald* 67 (1890): 193.

30. Ellen G. White, "Camp-Meeting at Ottawa, Kansas," *Review and Herald* 66 (1889): 465–66; Ellen G. White, "Looking Back at Minneapolis," MS 24–1888.

31. Ellen G. White, "The Present Message," Morning Talk at Ministers' School, February 4, 1890, *Review and Herald* 67 (1890): 161–62.

32. Ellen G. White, "Camp-Meeting at Rome, New York," *Review and Herald* 66 (1889): 545–46; Ellen G. White, "Be Zealous and Repent," *Review and Herald*

Extra, December 28, 1890. A. T. Jones had made this precise point in his initial righteousness sermon at Ottawa, Kansas, a month earlier, when he stated that Seventh-day Adventists had previously understood John 3:16 as meaning free salvation, but that they had not perceived of righteousness as likewise being a gift.

10

Second Coming

Jonathan M. Butler

IN 1856 ELLEN White delivered what came to be known as her "Food for Worms" sermon. Speaking to sabbatarian Adventists at a conference in Battle Creek, Michigan, she electrified them with a prediction: "I was shown the company present at the Conference. Said the angel: 'Some food for worms, some subjects of the seven last plagues, some will be alive and remain upon the earth to be translated at the coming of Jesus.'"[1] As the Adventist prophet, who kept company with angels by way of visions and quoted them verbatim, White preached in the sobering language of immediacy, for each of her listeners now lived in the "last generation" of earth's history.

But with just sixty-seven believers in her audience, she also spoke with a compelling sense of intimacy. This was God's "remnant people." And for them, the end of the world would be an altogether personal matter. In the "last hour" of earth's history, these sixty-seven Adventists would each represent roughly a minute on the ticking end-time clock, with perhaps only a few minutes to spare. Every death among them and every life transformed by the crucible of tribulation would push the hands on the clock a minute closer to Christ's coming.

White's Battle Creek sermon therefore allowed these Adventists to cast their eyes from pew to pew that day and take heart at seeing teenagers and even infant children in the meetinghouse. There was, thankfully, still time remaining. There had to be time before some of them were "food for worms," and, judging by the inattentive children among them, some time to prepare for their translation, too. But how much time? To the children her sermon no doubt seemed to last forever. In contrast, the aging saints could wonder how many more sermons had life allotted them.

If they needed time to prepare for death or deliverance, they could nonetheless be encouraged that the "*last* generation" was also the "last *generation.*" The prophet who preached the sermon was herself still frail enough to be of concern regarding her own longevity. But two of her children, James Edson and Willie, were turning just seven and two that year, and John Harvey Kellogg fidgeted in his seat as a four-year-old. Even if a generation equaled a nineteenth-century lifespan, however, none of them could be sure when his or her life would end. Sister Clarissa Bonfoey said she felt fine that day but was nevertheless deeply impressed that she would become "food for worms" before Christ's coming. And within three days she was gone.[2]

The End of Her Millerism

The twenty-eight-year-old prophet who delivered the "Food for Worms" sermon was more than a decade removed from the teenage girl who, through Millerism, had converted to a soon-coming Jesus. Though she remained the spiritual child of Father Miller, in many respects she had also grown up and left home. Like many Adventists at that Battle Creek conference, White had once been a Millerite who measured the end time in a few short years, then months, and finally a single, fateful day, as depicted in William Matthew Prior's Millerite prophetic chart (Figure 10.1). But it was *two months after* the Great Disappointment of October 22, 1844, that she had received her first vision. Its contents made clear that Ellen Harmon had been called as a prophet less to proclaim Christ's imminent coming than to explain His delay.[3]

Her publication of the vision, more than a year after receiving it, was exit literature from Millerism. In the dark, troubled waters that engulfed the grief-stricken Adventists after the bitterest of disappointments (they had "wept and wept until the day dawned" on October 23), Harmon's vision provided a life raft to rescue them from the sensational highs and the incredible lows of their turbulent Millerite experience. But immediately following the Millerite debacle, her apocalyptic timetable still remained short enough that she could be almost persuaded by specific predictions of the end, for example on the first anniversary of the Great Disappointment (1845) and on the seventh (1851). In this period, she still

FIGURE 10.1 William Matthew Prior, *A Chronological Chart of the Prophecies of Daniel and Revelation*, 1843. This image depicts explications of the 1260-day and 2300-day prophecies, along with the arithmetic that determined the end of the world in 1843 as initially predicted by William Miller. (Private Collection, New York. Courtesy of Fenimore Art Museum, Cooperstown, New York.)

felt certain that there would be no time to marry, to bear children, to pursue a career, to seek converts around the world, much less to enjoy a long and prosperous life. She saw such plans as a denial of her faith in an imminent end to the world.[4]

By 1856, however, much had changed for the prophet and her people. In the ten years since her marriage to James White she had co-founded with him and their mentor, a former New England sea captain named Joseph Bates, a flourishing new movement whose nearly 2,000 members exceeded all her earlier expectations. Drawing on the pamphlets of Bates, Adventism's "first theologian," Ellen White had fostered the transformation of a single-minded, short-term apocalyptic revival into a complex, durable church that measured time not in days but in a generation that would, she came to believe, see death before seeing heaven.[5]

White's interpretations of the "third angel's message" in Revelation 14:9–11 not only distanced her from other churches but from William Miller himself, for the third angel called for true Christians to observe the seventh day, not the first, as the Sabbath. The "beast" was Roman Catholicism; the "image of the beast," the fraudulent Sunday worship introduced by the papacy. Bates had convinced the newly wedded James and Ellen White of the correctness of seventh-day Sabbath observance, and Ellen had confirmed the all-important biblical view of Bates in vision. She saw into "the most holy place" of the heavenly sanctuary, where the original Ten Commandments lay carved in stone within the Holy Ark. The fourth commandment—hallowing the seventh-day Sabbath—occupied a vaunted place within the Decalogue. Indeed, the visionary saw "a brighter light shining upon it than upon the other nine, and a halo of glory all around it." For White, seventh-day sabbatarianism had become the ultimate shibboleth. Only through keeping the true Sabbath could the faithful reach heaven.[6]

Not only her belief in sabbatarianism on earth but also her understanding of the sanctuary in heaven distinguished Ellen White from William Miller. Miller had seen the biblical sanctuary of the ancient Hebrews as a symbol of the earth about to be cleansed by Christ's Second Coming. Following the Great Disappointment, however, White radically revised Miller's view of the biblical sanctuary. Drawing on a Millerite lecturer and editor, O.R.L. Crozier, by way of Bates and a Methodist-turned-Adventist, Hiram Edson, White came to account for Christ's delayed Advent by locating the biblical sanctuary in heaven, not on earth as Miller had done. By way of the sanctuary doctrine, the prophet "spiritualized" the Second

Coming; and, more important, she reinterpreted it as a non-falsifiable event. In 1844, Christ had not gone from heaven to earth to cleanse it cataclysmically of all sin and establish forever the kingdom of God. Instead, He had stayed in the sanctuary in heaven—an archetype of the sanctuary of the Jewish people—and had then as "our High Priest" moved from the "holy" to the "most holy place." If the history of the world amounted to a single Jewish year, 1844 marked the beginning of the Jewish "Day of Atonement." Humanity had entered, in effect, the highest and holiest of days on a figurative Jewish calendar: *Yom Kippur.*[7]

For several years the visionary viewed humankind as largely a lost cause post-1844, as most would be judged and found wanting. Only those who had been Millerite Adventists, and who remained faithful despite the disappointments of 1844, had a chance to be saved. But theirs was only a slim chance, as slim as the ascending path in her first vision. God had shown her what her fellow Adventists had seen for themselves by December of 1844. Many had "rashly denied the light," Harmon complained. For some once-ardent Adventists, who trekked upward toward heaven, "the light behind them went out, leaving their feet in perfect darkness, and they stumbled and lost sight of the mark and of Jesus, and fell off the path down into the dark and wicked world below." Those Adventists who kept the faith, however, had to traverse the upward path warily, for this was a solemn, morally demanding time. They must keep their robes "spotless." During their "Day of Atonement"—which, in time, would seem less like a day than an era—they must prepare for the end, for the Lord would cease his duties as High Priest and then return to the earth as Judge and Redeemer. The prophet warned Adventists of just how high the moral bar had been set. In Oswego, New York, in 1850, she "saw that many do not realize what they must be in order to live in the sight of the Lord without a high priest in the sanctuary through the time of trouble."[8]

The prophetic timetable that ended for Miller "about 1843" stretched into the future for White and her sabbatarian Adventist following. With the Second Coming an intangible, spiritual reality for them, their small company of stalwart fellow believers pressed on in their Adventist belief. They remained believers in the Advent because they experienced the outpouring of the Spirit—the numerous visionaries and healers, tongues-speakers, and exorcists—and these visible expressions of the Spirit demonstrated to them that their belief had not been "a cunningly devised fable."[9] But the passage of time had allowed the movement to outgrow such youthful enthusiasms, which Miller's colleague Joshua V. Himes had dubbed "visionary nonsense" and White herself came to denounce as "fanaticism." The Adventist prophet instead encouraged a more stable "Gospel order" and eventually shunned any outbreaks of enthusiasm in her community as a Satan-provoked counterfeit of her prophetic ministry. The Holy Spirit would be channeled through White as the single prophetic figure. Indeed, by 1846, only *her* prophetic gift provided an unprecedented and compelling evidence of God's Spirit in the Advent movement. Only *she* personified the "Spirit of prophecy."[10]

In passing from instability to order, sabbatarian Adventists and their prophet mirrored the shift from a transitory pre-Victorian ferment to a more stable, durable Victorian culture. Such a pervasive religious and social transformation provided time for the prophet's immediate family to grow and for her church to expand as well. Though at first Harmon had shut the door to salvation on all but the post-disappointment Adventists, by the early 1850s she saw that door was now open to a wider world of potential converts.[11] There was now time for White to immerse herself in travel, writing, and publishing. There was time for her and her husband to relocate the movement's headquarters from New England to western New York and then to Michigan. And in a generation, there was time for accomplishments that not even the prophet could have earlier imagined.

The extension of time allowed Adventists to launch a publishing enterprise, organize a church, create an impressive network of sanitariums and hospitals, and establish a huge system of elementary and secondary schools, colleges and universities (see Chapter 7). There was also time for them to make their mark in this world. No wonder American religious historians Winthrop Hudson and Edwin Gaustad could agree that while "Seventh-day Adventists were expecting a kingdom of God from the heavens," as Hudson put it, "they worked diligently for one on earth." Their prophet allowed Adventists time to experience a kind of "realized eschatology."[12]

The hyphenated name adopted in 1860—*Seventh-day Adventism*—reflected the variegated identity by which the movement abandoned its millenarian enthusiasm for a new kind of community. Ellen White's *Adventism* acknowledged on a daily basis the absence of Christ. A *coming* Lord was not yet here but delayed. Her *seventh-day sabbatarianism* established a new rule, a new morality by which her community experienced, on a weekly basis, Christ's presence among them. On every seventh-day of the week White called on Adventists in their meetinghouses to remember earth's creation and long for earth's re-creation in the palpable presence

of Christ. The ache of Christ's absence was relieved weekly when the sabbatarian church itself served as a sacrament of His presence. The Second
Coming had eluded expectant Adventists, but the seventh-day Sabbath
had not.[13]

Touring the eastern United States with her husband in 1857, the year
after her "Food for Worms" sermon, the prophet preached Sabbath-keeping
Adventism, not Millerism. "I saw that this message would not accomplish
its work in a few short months," she told a new generation of Adventists.
"It is designed to arouse the people of God, to discover them their backsliding, to lead them to zealous repentance, that they may be favored in
the presence of Jesus, and be filled with the loud cry of the third angel [that
is, proper Sabbath observance]." She added, "If the message had been of
as short duration as many of us supposed, there would have been no time
for them to develop character." In these demanding cadences, the prophet
had moved from apocalyptic pronouncement to prophetic jeremiad. In
identifying her church as Laodicea, she had shifted her focus from an
immediate eschatological deliverance into another world in favor of the
indefinite timetable and the manifold expectations of a spiritual life in this
world. Taking this for the moment as the extent of her eschatology, White
had here abandoned the apocalyptic telescope, trained on cosmic events in
politics, society, religion, and astronomy, which had captivated Millerites.
Instead, she now placed her people under a spiritual microscope and
looked to their moral development as the means to the Second Coming.[14]

The End of Her World

Nothing more clearly indicates how immersed Ellen White had become
in her own world than an examination of how she expected it to end. For
this it is necessary to turn from the spiritual interiors of her eschatology
as a jeremiad addressed to her people and focus on the exterior world
that she saw coming to an eschatological end. William Miller had dramatized the historicist interpretation of Daniel and Revelation by deciphering
its prophecies as an actual historical timeline ending in 1844. Late in the
"70 weeks" and the "2,300 days" of Daniel's prophecies, events such as
the Lisbon earthquake (1755), the "wounding" of the papacy (1798), New
England's "dark day" (1780), the "star showers" (1833), and the "fall" of the
Ottoman Empire (1841) all served as signs of *his* times that the world was
about to end.[15] For White, these signs were still recent and vivid enough

to remain valid and potent as signs of *her* times. But she fully understood the first rule of prophetic interpretation that an apocalyptic perspective must continually regenerate itself. The end of the world could not be near unless Daniel and Revelation proved especially applicable to her own times. However idiosyncratic her slant on the world and how it would end, it is fully apparent when reading her that she wrote in the context of her own world, not Miller's. Catholic immigrants flooded into the United States. Protestants capitulated to Catholics in regard to papal Sunday worship, with the ominous threat of a national "blue law" that could persecute a sabbatarian Adventist minority. Spiritualism became a popular influence on liberal religion. The labor-capitalist conflict subsequently erupted in a series of social "earthquakes." Intemperance became a cancer that metastasized in American society. All this marked for the prophet a decline in America's republican and Protestant values that spelled doom for *her* world.[16]

White stubbornly stuck to Miller's historicist approach to the end-time prophecies even as she emphatically abandoned his ill-conceived time setting. And her adherence to historicism ensured that her Seventh-day Adventist followers would remain in an American backwater of prophetic interpretation for generations to come, while the British-based John Nelson Darby popularized dispensationalism as a total departure from the discredited historicist approach. The Darby view, which came to define American evangelicalism, divided history into long, chronologically successive periods or dispensations in which God related to humanity in different ways according to different biblical covenants. Unlike the historicist White, Darby promoted a futurist biblical hermeneutic that bracketed contemporary history as mostly irrelevant to prophetic fulfillments. White and Darby, therefore, saw the world through the same lens of biblical apocalyptic but in notably contrasting ways. The Anglo-Irish Darby assigned no prophetic significance to American history, but the American White believed that she was witnessing the American story uncannily play itself out in Bible prophecy. Moreover, modern Jews were fundamentally important to Darby's eschatology as the latter-day Israel would occupy Palestine and provoke the final events of earth's history. White, in contrast, identified the Seventh-day Adventists themselves as the latter-day, spiritual "Israel" that would prove integral to the last-day scenario.[17]

White in effect embraced the sacrosanct doctrine of *sola scriptura*, but she arrived at her own unique interpretations of the Bible, especially the books of Daniel and Revelation. To use James West Davidson's analogy, the

186   ELLEN HARMON WHITE: AMERICAN PROPHET

images in these books served as Rorschach inkblots that, when scrutinized by an apocalypticist such as White, revealed less about the Scriptures than the interpreter herself. Because the apocalyptic Scriptures by themselves were opaque, they invited a prophet's imagination to interpret them. For example, White based her prophetic scheme on two miniscule but critical proof texts in Numbers 14:34 and Ezekiel 4:6—upholding a "day" in prophecy as a "year." White's contributions to apocalyptic interpretation, however, proved useless as biblical exegesis for anyone outside the tight circle of her faith community. Indeed, biblical exegetes have found her less interesting than cultural historians have. Even Adventists, who looked to her writings for their understanding of end-time events, did not follow the Bible as much as they adopted what *she saw* in the Bible.[18] Reading Ellen White's writings on Daniel or Revelation caused the scales to fall from Seventh-day Adventist eyes. Her visions of the end did not so much provide Adventists with a crystal ball that revealed events in the distant future as they gave a new understanding of the past, present, and the immediate future. White's self-proclaimed predictions of the future were, in fact, more like projections on a screen that only enlarged and dramatized the scenes of her contemporary world.

For White, America would reprise Europe's dark past. A once promising nation would assume the "power to wage war against God's holy people," because for her, America was the "second beast" in Revelation 13:11–17, "coming out of the earth." Its origins in the "earth" meant America had materialized in an unpopulated area (Native Americans did not count here) rather than the "sea" of densely populated Europe. America had "two horns like a lamb, but it spoke like a dragon." The two horns represented America's high-minded claims of Protestantism and republicanism. Its dragon speech meant that it recanted those principles for Catholic totalitarianism and intolerance. Catholics, Protestants, and Spiritualists (the "unclean spirits like three frogs") would join in a conspiratorial triad that would carry out a medieval inquisition in modern America. It would do so by first denying commerce to seventh-day Sabbath-keepers. They could not "buy or sell" unless they had the "mark of the beast" tattooed on their "foreheads" or "right hands," as would all Sunday keepers. Ultimately, an American-triggered Apocalypse would spread to a worldwide pogrom, as capital punishment would be imposed on Seventh-day Adventists everywhere.[19]

White believed that the American "two-horned beast" exposed its true colors as a dragonic nation during the Civil War. America's organized churches, both Catholic and Protestant, had fallen. American slavery, and the complicity of the American churches in slavery, had made obvious a decaying nation and, ultimately, a dying world (see also Chapter 14). In a chapter on "The Sins of Babylon" in *Spiritual Gifts* (1858) White could have been channeling William Lloyd Garrison or Harriet Beecher Stowe in writing:

> All heaven beholds with indignation human beings, the workmanship of God, reduced by their fellow men to the lowest depths of degradation and placed on a level with brute creation. Professed followers of that dear Saviour whose compassion was ever moved at the sight of human woe, heartily engage in this enormous and grievous sin, and deal in slaves and souls of men. God will restrain His angels but little longer. His wrath burns against this nation and especially the religious bodies that have themselves engaged in it....

The cries of the oppressed have reached unto heaven, and angels stand amazed at the untold, agonizing sufferings which man, formed in the image of his Maker, causes his fellow man. Said the angel, "The names of the oppressors are written in blood, crossed with stripes, and flooded with agonizing, burning tears of suffering. God's anger will not cease until He has caused this land of light to drink the dregs of the cup of His fury, until He has rewarded unto Babylon double."[20]

White's political jeremiad on the state of the Union blended apocalypticism with Radical Republicanism. Like Abraham Lincoln, she saw Union setbacks at the First Battle of Bull Run and elsewhere as divine judgments. Unlike the Lincoln prior to emancipation, however, she felt sure of the reason. "God is punishing this nation," she declared in a testimony to the church in 1862, "for the high crime of slavery. He has the destiny of the nation in His hands. He will punish the South for the sin of slavery, and the North for so long suffering its overreaching and overbearing influence."[21]

By the 1880s, however, America's political and social landscape had fundamentally changed, and a remarkably malleable prophet had adapted her eschatological message accordingly. Radical Republicanism had receded into an unhappy memory, and the prophet had mostly forgotten her dire predictions that the American Civil War had lit the fuse of a world-sized Armageddon. The Republican Party had realigned itself around new issues that included contemporary attitudes on Rum and Romanism. In the new context, White shifted her focus from the American slaves that she had once believed would be in shackles at Christ's return to the American Adventists who would suffer an even worse fate at the hands of a failed Republic. Again she saw the end in terms of a delayed end. Though still not enamored of the social and political order, White nevertheless envisioned a less imminent collapse of the Republic. If in the 1860s her eschatology had reflected President Lincoln's world, in the 1880s she resonated with Protestant clergyman Josiah Strong's more parochial American nationalism. In so many respects, she hoped to save Strong's America, at least for a short time. Here she departed from her earlier, fatalistic interpretation of the two-horned beast in Revelation 13 and wrote that America *still* brandished the lamblike horns of civil and religious tolerance and only *eventually* would become a dragon. For the eyes that could see what she had been shown, however, a dark cloud of conspiratorial forces gathered, threatening to smother the republic.[22]

White saw the American "crisis" along the lines that Strong did in his widely read *Our Country*, but she rejected his optimism in the face of it. She also translated his supremacist evangelicalism into her own sectarian dialect. For White, the variegated elements of contemporary religion, politics, and society had polarized, as in any Apocalypse, but her world had divided seventh-day sabbatarians from Sunday-keepers as well as the temperate from the intemperate, labor from management, and country-dwellers from urbanites. Her Seventh-day Adventists were either caught in the middle of or forced to take sides in this "great controversy" between good and evil, but finally they would be victimized by it. Catholic, Protestant, and occult Spiritualist—virtually everyone in White's purview—would form a malevolent alliance against the Adventist "Remnant," as Sunday-keepers would oppose seventh-day sabbatarians in a spirit of religious intolerance. In the long counter tradition of the "suffering church," White expected the abuse of an Adventist minority—not a slave minority—to prove the undoing of American republicanism. Eschatologically, the oppression of an American minority remained central, but the particular minority proved transferable.[23]

"When Protestantism shall stretch her hand across the gulf to grasp the hand of the Roman power," White wrote in a testimony given in 1885, "when she shall reach over the abyss to clasp hands with spiritualism, when, under the influence of this threefold union, our country shall repudiate every principle of its Constitution as a Protestant and republican government, and shall make provision for the propagation of papal false-hoods and delusions, then we may know that the time has come for the marvelous working of Satan and that the end is near." Certainly, there was no question here as to *whether* the American Apocalypse would occur but *when* was a different matter. "*When*" these events take place, "*then* we may know that . . . *the end is near.*" For the time being, the hands reaching across the abyss to destroy the American creation had not yet touched.[24]

In a paradox that should by now be expected of her, the prophet devoted her considerable energies to building up the church as long as time lasted (see Chapter 7). Adventists were not to wait "in idle expectancy, but in earnest work." In an address at Battle Creek College in 1883, she challenged the students with a series of questions: "What is the aim and purpose of your life? Are you ambitious that you may have a name and position in the world? Have you thoughts that you dare not express, that you may one day stand upon the summit of intellectual greatness; that you may sit in deliberative and legislative councils, and help to enact laws for the nation?" White asked. "There is nothing wrong with these aspira-tions. You may every one of you make your mark." The implications of such a statement were clear. Contrary to Uriah Smith, sometime editor of the *Review and Herald* and author of *The Prophecies of Daniel and the Revelation*, White believed that a new generation of Adventists could has-ten or retard the end.[25]

In order to save the world, Adventists needed to save America, at least temporarily. In White's view, the two vital ways that Adventists could preserve a Protestant Victorian America were by opposing Sunday legislation and backing prohibition. The prophet had turned to politics, but her political agenda remained rooted in a highly self-interested reli-gious sensibility. She did not pursue political activism in an effort to transform the political and social order but to preserve the status quo, a status quo that sheltered God's Advent people. Protestant Victorian Americans, including the Seventh-day Adventists, should retain the religious freedom to worship as they pleased. But Seventh-day sabba-tarianism meant more than a quiescent retreat from society to worship on Saturday. Adventists also must mount a political opposition to the Sunday-law movement. Temperance, too, involved more than dietary restrictions and personal sobriety to preserve the individual as a "temple of God." "The honor of God, the stability of the nation, the well-being of the community, of the home, and of the individual, demand that every possible effort be made in arousing the people to the evil of intemperance," insisted White. "Let the voice of the nation demand of its lawmakers that a stop be put to this infamous traffic."[26] To lose this land to the beast of religious intolerance or the demon of intemperance was to incite apocalyptic consequences for the world, a world that would target Adventists as a persecuted religious minority. To sustain a Protestant Victorian America, however, the prophet once again had to slow down the eschatological clock. In hoping for the end, Adventists should hope for its delay. The Second Coming must be delayed, ironically, to allow time for Adventists to prepare for and preach of that very Second Coming.

The Adventist prophet's expectation that an insidious dark conspiracy of Catholics, Protestants, and Spiritualists would soon put an end to Protestant America did not materialize. But Protestant America did end, just not in the way White predicted that it would. No Sunday-worship bill passed comparable to the one that appeared in Congress in the 1880s (owing in small part to the effectiveness of the Adventist lobby), and the prohibition movement, in the long run, fared no better than a national "blue law," as prohibition was repealed in 1933. Protestant America waned but without bringing about the end of American democracy, an Adventist pogrom, or the Second Coming. White prophesied that American Protestants would identify Seventh-day Adventists as the albatross of American and even world civilization. The Adventists manacled in Tennessee chain gangs for their Sunday violations were, in White's view, the harbinger of an American and ultimately a worldwide persecution that would turn their misdemeanors in the American South into grounds for capital punishment around the world. White's eschatology presupposed that the entire world would behave as if it were a "sacred America." A Protestant American persecution of Seventh-day Adventists would make sense to everyone, from one end of the earth to the other.[27]

As a Sunday-violating religious minority, Adventists would be "denounced as enemies of law and order, as breaking down the moral restraints of society, causing anarchy and corruption, and calling down the judgments of God upon earth." As the Protestant American worldview became the *world's view,* and the Sunday Sabbath gained universal acceptance, White prophesied that not "just Americans but all mankind would come to see the violation of the Sunday Sabbath" as bringing "calamities which will not cease until Sunday observance shall be strictly enforced." As a religious minority, Seventh-day sabbatarians would be blamed for natural catastrophes. "There are calamities on sea and land," wrote White, "and these will increase, one disaster upon another; and the little band of conscientious Sabbath-keepers will be pointed out as the ones who are bringing the wrath of God upon the world by their disregard of Sunday."[28]

At the moment of greatest peril, White predicted that Christ will appear "in the east" in "a small black cloud, about half the size of a man's hand." And the saints will be "lighted up with the glory of God" as a "never-ending blessing" is pronounced on those who have "honored God in keeping His Sabbath holy." She saw, too, "the pious slave rise in victory and triumph, [and] shake off the chains that bound him, while his wicked master was in confusion and knew not what to do." In one of her more singular contributions to eschatology, White witnessed the saints *in heaven* for the millennium while the earth lay desolate. There they reigned as "kings and priests" and judged "the wicked dead" as Christ had done in the heavenly sanctuary, "comparing their acts with the statute book, the Word of God." Here the democracy that Americans squandered on earth would be reinstated in heaven, as "Christ, in union with His people" reviewed the heavenly books to determine that justice had been done. "Deciding every case according to the deeds done in the body," the saints together with Christ "meted out to the wicked the portion which they must suffer." The woman who had deserted Calvinism's eternal punishment as a teenage girl still breathed some of its fire, for the greater the sins the longer the flames burned. "Satan's punishment," she noted with gratification, "was to be by far greater than that of those whom he had deceived."[29]

The same prophet who implanted these indelible images of the Second Coming and the New Earth in the Adventist imagination had also once preached the "Food for Worms" sermon. And Adventists had not forgotten it. It is one more testimony to her impact on them that some Adventists carried a list of the names present in her Battle Creek congregation of 1856 in the fly leaves of their Bibles, and they crossed off each name as these Adventists passed into the grave. Christ would come before the last person among those 67 believers had become "food for worms." Adventist historian John Loughborough reported that White became annoyed by this practice, however well intentioned it had been. According to Loughborough, two brethren had gone "to see Sister White to ask her if she could remember any names they had omitted." But the prophet protested their making of such a list. "Instead of working to push on the message," she complained, Adventists "will be watching the *Review* every week to see who died."[30]

Certainly White expected to be taken literally on end-time events. The national Sunday law would be the first link in a chain that would lead to Christ's coming. Adventists still living in the end would be translated to heaven. But in taking her literally, Adventists could lose the spirit of her message. Charting the timeline in her eschatology, like crossing off the names of deceased Adventists, could miss the prophet's point. It could turn the end times into mere waiting, watching. The lapsed Adventist who awaited a national Sunday law to materialize before returning to church did violence to the prophet's intentions. The disfellowshipped Adventist John Harvey Kellogg, whose health practices and natural longevity kept him alive on the "Food for Worms" list until 1943, could be especially galling as grounds for Adventist procrastination. Adventists should be preparing themselves, perfecting themselves so that Christ would come. Adventists who marked the end times by way of external events or names in the obituaries needed to look within themselves. For all prophecies of the end were conditioned on Adventists as a people. The prophet could not fail; only her people could fail. In 1900, she wrote, "Christ is waiting with longing desire for the manifestation of Himself in His church. When the character of Christ shall be perfectly reproduced in His people, then He will come to claim His own."[31] In the end then, White's eschatology turned on a tautology. Christ's coming prompted Adventists to prepare for it; if they prepared, Christ would come.

NOTES

1. Ellen G. White, *Testimonies for the Church*, 9 vols. (Mountain View, CA: Pacific Press Publishing Assn., 1948), 1:131–32 (Testimony 2, 1856).

2. Editor's note, ibid., 132. For a complete list of those present at the conference, compiled by Evelyn Lewis-Reavis in 1910, see www.truthorfables.com/Food_for_Worms.htm.

3. Ellen G. White, *A Sketch of the Christian Experience and Views of Ellen G White* (Sarasota Springs, NY: James White, 1851; rpt. in *Early Writings* in 1954 by Review and Herald Publishing Assn.), 13–20.

4. Arthur L. White, *Ellen G. White*, 6 vols. (Washington, DC: Review and Herald Publishing Assn., 1981–1986), 1:53; Ronald L. Numbers, *Prophetess of Health: A Study of Ellen G. White*, 3rd ed. (Grand Rapids, MI: William B. Eerdmans, 2008), 71; Ronald Graybill, "The Courtship of Ellen Harmon," *Insight* (January 23, 1973), 4–7.

5. Roy Branson, "Adventists between the Times: The Shift in the Church's Eschatology," *Spectrum: The Journal of the Association of Adventist Forums* 8 (September 1976): 11–26 (hereafter referred to as *Spectrum*); Jonathan M.

Butler, "The Making of a New Order: Millerism and the Origins of Seventh-day Adventism," in *The Disappointed: Millerism and Millenarianism in the Nineteenth Century*, ed. Ronald L. Numbers and Jonathan M. Butler (Bloomington: Indiana University Press, 1987), 189–208; George R. Knight, *Joseph Bates: The Real Founder of Seventh-day Adventism* (Hagerstown, MD: Review and Herald Publishing Assn., 2004), x.

6. For the first two angels' messages of Revelation 14, see White, *Early Writings*, 232–37; and "Charles Fitch" in Gary Land, *Historical Dictionary of the Seventh-day Adventists* (Lanham, MD: Scarecrow Press, 2005), 101–102; David T. Arthur "Millerism," in *The Rise of Adventism: A Commentary on the Social and Religious Ferment of Mid-Nineteenth Century America*, ed. Edwin S. Gaustad (New York: Harper & Row, 1974); White, *Early Writings*, 238.

7. White, *Early Writings*, 250–53; "Sanctuary Doctrine" in Land, *Historical Dictionary*, 260–262; Frank B. Holbrook, ed., *Doctrine of the Sanctuary: A Historical Survey, 1845–1863* (Hagerstown, MD: Review and Herald Publishing Assn., 1989).

8. White, *Early Writings*, 15, 71.

9. George R. Knight, *Millennial Fever and the End of the World: A Study of Millerite Adventism* (Boise, ID: Pacific Press Publishing Assn., 1993), 171–78; Jonathan Butler, "Prophecy, Gender and Culture," *Religion and American Culture* 1 (1991): 3–29; White, *Ellen G. White*, 1:53.

10. David L. Rowe, *Thunder and Trumpets: Millerites and Dissenting Religion in Upstate New York, 1800–1850* (Chico, CA: Scholars Press, 1985), 147; Ellen G. White, *Spiritual Gifts: My Christian Experience, Views and Labors in Connection with the Rise and Progress of the Third Angel's Message*, 4 vols., (Battle Creek: James White, 1858–1864), 2:49–52; Butler, "Prophecy, Gender and Culture," esp. 19–23; Rennie B. Schoepflin, ed., "Scandal or Rite of Passage: Historians on the Damon Trial," *Spectrum* 17, no. 5 (1987): 39–45.

11. White, *Early Writings*, 42–45; Numbers, *Prophetess of Health*, 56–57, 71–72; P. Gerard Damsteegt, *Foundations of the Seventh-day Adventist Message and Mission* (Grand Rapids, MI: William B. Eerdmans, 1977), *passim*; Ingemar Lindén, *1844 and the Shut Door Problem* (Uppsala: Almquist & Wiksell, 1982).

12. Winthrop Hudson, *Religion in America* (New York: Charles Scribner's Sons, 1965), 347; Edwin S. Gaustad, *Historical Atlas of Religion in America* (New York: Harper & Row, 1966), 115; Richard W. Schwarz and Floyd Greenleaf, *Light Bearers: A History of the Seventh-day Adventist Church*, rev. ed. (Nampa, ID: Pacific Press Publishing Assn., 2000), 69–159, 241–72; Malcolm Bull and Keith Lockhart, *Seeking a Sanctuary: Seventh-day Adventism and the American Dream*, 2nd ed. (Bloomington: Indiana University Press, 2007). For their discussion of Ellen White, see especially 21–37.

13. White, *Early Writings*, 254–258. See also White, *Testimonies for the Church*, 1:154–64, 531–33 (Testimony 4, 1857; Testimony 12, 1867); Bull and Lockhart, *Seeking a Sanctuary*, 38–51.

14. White, *Spiritual Gifts*, 2:224–225; White, *Testimonies* 1:185–195 (Testimony 5, 1859). Knight discusses the various estimates on Millerite numbers in *Millennial Fever*, 213. By White's death in 1915, Seventh-day Adventist membership had reached 136,000; see "Seventh-day Adventist Conferences, Missions, and Institutions: The Fifty-third Annual Statistical Report, Year Ending December 31, 1915" (Takoma Park, MD: General Conference of Seventh-day Adventists, 1915), 1, at www.adventistarchives.org.

15. David Rowe, *God's Strange Work: William Miller and the End of the World* (Grand Rapids, MI: William B. Eerdmans, 2008), 72–81; Paul Boyer, *When Time Shall Be No More: Prophecy Belief in Modern American Culture* (Cambridge, MA: Harvard University Press, 1992), 80–86. See also Wayne Judd, "William Miller: Disappointed Prophet," in Numbers and Butler, *The Disappointed*, 18–35.

16. An earlier discussion of White's eschatology and its nineteenth-century cultural context appears in Jonathan Butler, "The World of E. G. White and the End of the World," *Spectrum*, 10 (August 1979): 2–13.

17. Boyer, *When Time Shall Be No More*, 88; J. B. Lethbridge, "'Look Again, and Look a Little Higher': The Historical Apocalyptic in the Earlier Writings of Ellen G. White," *Millennial Thought in America: Historical and Intellectual Contexts, 1630–1860*, ed. Bernd Engler, Joerg O. Richte, Oliver Scheiding (Trier: Wissenschaftlicher Verlag Trier, 2002), 355–84. For her view of the Jews, see White, *Early Writings*, 74–76, and Ellen G. White, *The Great Controversy between Christ and Satan* (Oakland, CA: Pacific Press Publishing Assn., 1888), 457–60; and Ellen G. White, *Prophets and Kings* (Mountain View, CA: Pacific Press Publishing Assn., 1917), 703–21, esp. 713–15.

18. James West Davidson, "Searching for the Millennium: Problems for the 1790's and the 1970's," *New England Quarterly*, 45 (1972): 242–61, esp. 255. On the fact that "Revelation is a book whose literary interest has been transferred from the text to the readers," see Bernard McGinn, "Revelation," in *The Literary Guide to the Bible*, ed. Robert Alter and Frank Kermode (Cambridge, MA: Harvard University Press, 1987), 523–24.

19. White, *Testimonies*, 5:449–54; White, *Great Controversy*, 582–92.

20. White, *Early Writings*, 275.

21. White, *Testimonies*, 1:264 (Testimony 7, 1862). The next few pages are taken from my earlier study on "Adventism and the American Experience," in *Rise of Adventism*, 173–206, esp. 184–85, 193–95. Douglas Morgan explores the same terrain in *Adventism and the American Republic: The Public Involvement of a Major Apocalyptic Movement* (Knoxville: University of Tennessee Press, 2001), 15–59.

22. Butler, "Adventism and the American Experience," 192–93; Morgan, *Adventism and the American Republic*, 59, 64–65.

23. White, *Testimonies*, 5:451 (Testimony 32, 1885).

24. Ibid.; White, *Great Controversy*, 579.

25. Ellen G. White, *Fundamentals of Christian Education* (Mountain View, CA: Pacific Press Publishing Assn., 1923), 82.

26. Ellen G. White, *Spirit of Prophecy Counsels Relating to Church-State Relations in the United States* (Mountain View, CA: Pacific Press Publishing Assn., 1973), 56–65; Ellen G. White, "Temperance and the License Law," *Review and Herald*, 58 (November 8, 1881), 289–90; Morgan, *Adventism and the American Republic*, 36–38; Eric D. Syme, *A History of SDA Church-State Relations in the United States* (Mountain View, CA: Pacific Press Publishing Assn., 1973), 49–68. Ellen G. White, *The Ministry of Healing* (Mountain View, CA: Pacific Press Publishing Assn., 1905), 346.

27. Syme, *History of SDA Church-State Relations*, 28; White, *Great Controversy*, 442. For the concept of a "sacred America," see William Clebsch, *From Sacred to Profane America: The Role of Religion in American History* (New York: Harper & Row, 1968).

28. White, *Great Controversy*, 592; Ellen G. White, "A Sabbath Reform Needed," *Review and Herald* 61 (March 18, 1884), 177–78.

29. White, *Early Writings*, 286, 290–91.

30. J. N. Loughborough, "The Coming of the Lord," *Review and Herald* 101 (June 12, 1924), 4.

31. Ellen G. White, *Christ's Object Lessons* (Mountain View, CA: Pacific Press Publishing Assn., 1900), 69.

II

Science and Medicine

Ronald L. Numbers and Rennie B. Schoepflin

FOR A NINETEENTH-CENTURY woman with little formal education, Ellen White took a surprisingly active interest in science and medicine. She wrote frequently on physiology and hygiene and occasionally on astronomy, biology, and geology. She expressed strong feelings about "the sciences of phrenology, psychology, and mesmerism," denouncing them as theories of Satanic origin. As we shall see, her greatest influence on popular science and medicine lay in the fields of health reform and creationism.

Along with many other Christians Ellen White frequently adopted the metaphor of nature as a book. "Since the book of nature and the book of revelation bear the impress of the same master mind, they cannot but speak in harmony," she explained in a typical passage.

> By different methods, and in different languages, they witness to the same great truths. Science is ever discovering new wonders; but she brings from her research nothing that, rightly understood, conflicts with divine revelation. The book of nature and the written word shed light upon each other. They make us acquainted with God by teaching us something of the laws through which He works.

Since God had written both books, she never doubted that "True science and Bible religion are in perfect harmony." However, because conflict could arise when interpreters of nature or the Bible misread their sources, she repeatedly warned against "science falsely so called" (1 Timothy 6:20), characteristic of what she thought was taught in non-Adventist schools. To avoid exposing Adventist young people to "infidel" science, in 1874 she supported the founding of a denominational institution, Battle Creek College, which she hoped would show "the harmony of science and Bible religion."[1]

Despite her professed love of "true science," White consistently subordinated science to her religious community's interpretation of Scripture. "The Bible is not to be tested by men's ideas of science," she explained, "but science is to be brought to the test of the unerring standard." She warned fellow believers "to guard continually against the sophistry in regard to geology and other branches of science falsely so called, which have not one semblance of truth. The theories of great men need to be carefully sifted of the slightest trace of infidel suggestions. One tiny seed sown by teachers in our schools, if received by the students, will raise a harvest of unbelief."[2]

Ellen White attributed most of her scientific and medical knowledge to divinely inspired "visions" rather than to reading or research. Her earliest vision relating to science came about the time of her nineteenth birthday, when she was "wrapt in a vision of GOD's glory, and for the first time had a view of other planets." As her new husband, James White, proudly reported, "She was guided to the planets, Jupiter, Saturn, and I think one more. After she came out of vision, she could give a clear description of their Moons, etc. It is well known, that she knew nothing of astronomy, and could not answer one question in relation to the planets, before she had this vision." Apparently she received this revelation primarily for the benefit of another former Millerite, Joseph Bates, who harbored doubts about the validity of her visions. "A great lover of astronomy," he was so impressed by her detailed knowledge of the heavens—especially the number of moons circling Jupiter, Saturn, and Uranus and her description of the "opening heavens" in the constellation Orion—that he concluded her vision was "of the LORD" and joined her band of believers.[3]

A couple of years later, using wings provided by the Lord, she flew in vision with her unnamed angel attendant from one heavenly abode to another, occasionally stopping to chat with the local inhabitants. Coming at a time of great speculation about the possibility of life on other worlds, this vision, as one historian has noted, "provided her church with what few congregations can claim: a theology incorporating extraterrestrial beings." Again she saw "the open space in Orion, from whence came the voice of God"—and through which, she predicted, the Holy City (New Jerusalem) would eventually come.[4]

Health Reform

In the early 1830s the Presbyterian evangelist and temperance lecturer Sylvester Graham (best remembered for his namesake crackers) began warning Americans of the dire consequences of flesh foods, drugs, corsets, stimulants, and frequent sex. In 1837 he united with other health reformers to form the American Physiological Society. This organization taught "that the millennium...can never reasonably be expected to arrive, until those laws which God has implanted in the *physical* nature of man are, equally with his moral laws, universally known and obeyed." This postmillennial expression was virtually identical to the premillennial message of the Millerite preacher-physician Larkin B. Coles. Taking as his theme the proposition that "it is as truly a sin against Heaven, to violate a law of life, as to break one of the ten commandments," he developed the traditional arguments of the health reformers for fresh air and exercise, a vegetarian diet, the nonuse of stimulants, reform in dress, sexual purity, and drugless medicine.[5]

As a self-described "great sufferer from disease" and "lifelong invalid," Ellen White took more than a passing interest in health-related matters. From time to time throughout her life she complained of weakness and fainting, episodes of unconsciousness, breathing difficulties, "heart disease," pain in her lungs, "pressure of blood on the brain," intense headaches and "inflammation on the brain," dropsy, weak back, lameness, "tenderness of the stomach," nosebleeds, pleurisy, and rheumatism. On occasion she experienced dimmed eyesight, paralysis, lack of sensation, and muteness—to say nothing of repeated visions and hallucinations. She frequently suffered from depression and despondency.[6]

She dated her discovery of the health-reform movement to a vision in June 1863, during which God showed the thirty-five-year-old prophetess the evils of medicinal drugs, alcohol, tobacco, tea, coffee, meat, spices, fashionable dress, and sex and the benefits of a twice-a-day vegetarian diet, internal and external use of water, fresh air, exercise, and a generally abstemious life style. However, she had known about health reform for some time and had recently used the water cure recommended by some of its leaders to save the lives of two of her sons from diphtheria. Even before his marriage to Ellen, James had abandoned alcohol, tobacco, tea, and coffee; and their close associate Joseph Bates, who enjoyed excellent health, had embraced Grahamism in the 1830s. From time to time the *Advent Review and Sabbath Herald* had published advice on healthful living, and

Ellen herself had experienced at least two previous visions touching on health. The first came in the fall of 1848. According to James's testimony years later, she was then shown that tobacco, tea, and coffee should be put away by those looking for the Second Coming of Christ. In a private letter to a brother struggling with the tobacco habit Ellen mentioned that her "accompanying angel" had told her in the vision that the weed was not fit even for medicinal purposes. In 1854 she received a second health-related vision, reminiscent of Graham's teaching, in which she saw that Sabbath-keepers were making "a god of their bellies," that instead of eating so many rich dishes they should take "more coarse food with little grease." The next year witnessed a spurt of anti-tobacco articles in the *Review and Herald*. The early 1860s also saw a dramatic increase in such articles, as well as in articles about health generally.[7]

In the wake of her 1863 vision Ellen White first turned her attention to the subject of sex. In addition to what she had seen, she had a deeply personal reason for doing so. Her eldest son, Edson, had turned thirteen in 1863 and had begun to display some disturbing behaviors: a lack of interest in religion, a "passion" for reading story books, a fondness for girls, and irresponsibility—all characteristics that she, along with other health reformers, associated with self-abuse or masturbation. By 1864 Ellen White had acquired at least two recently published books on sex— Russell T. Trall's *Pathology of the Reproductive Organs, Embracing All Forms of Sexual Disorders* (1862), and James Caleb Jackson's *The Sexual Organism, and Its Healthful Management* (1862)—and was penning her first work on health, a plain-looking pamphlet similar in content and appearance to *Solitary Vice: An Address to Parents* (1839), printed in White's hometown of Portland and attributed to Mary Gove (Nichols). White entitled her work *An Appeal to Mothers: The Great Cause of the Physical, Mental, and Moral Ruin of Many of the Children of Our Time* (1864).[8]

Writing for an Adventist audience expecting the imminent end of the world, White warned that "solitary vice" would ruin life and health on Earth and preclude a future existence in Heaven. She told of how her angel guide had exposed her to the horrors of human depravity. "Everywhere I looked," she recalled as though describing a real event, "I saw imbecility, dwarfed forms, crippled limbs, misshapen heads, and deformity of every description"—all the result of the practice of solitary vice, so widespread that "a large share of the youth now living are worthless." Even adults had fallen victim to this satanic lure. At one point in her vision she recognized an acquaintance, "a mere wreck of humanity," who had been brought near death by this demonic habit. To drive her message home, White noted that continued masturbation would produce not only hereditary insanity and deformities but a host of diseases, including "affection of the liver and lungs, neuralgia, rheumatism, affection of the spine, diseased kidneys, and cancerous humors." Not infrequently, it led its victims "into an early grave."[9]

White believed that special care should be taken to protect the young from the contaminating influence of other children. As an adult she had come to view her crippling childhood accident, which had left her an invalid for years, as a blessing in disguise that had preserved her innocence. Self-conscious about her intimate knowledge of masturbation, she insisted (as had Mary Gove before her) that she had grown up in "blissful ignorance of the secret vices of the young" and had learned about them only after marriage, from "the private death-bed confessions of some females." To maintain the purity of her own offspring, she never permitted them to associate with "rough, rude boys" or to sleep in the same bed or room with others of their age.[10] She expressed particular concern about two neighbor boys, Samuel and Charles Daigneau, who, she saw in vision, had "gone to great lengths in this crime of self-abuse"—so great that Charles was losing his intellect and eyesight. (Somehow he survived to age 71 without going blind or insane. Samuel went on to serve two terms in the Michigan state senate and died at age 82 after enjoying a life of "remarkably good health.")[11]

Although White, unlike other health reformers, grounded her sexual advice on revelation, not reason, in her writings on sex she invoked both religious and scientific sanctions. She not only attributed her insights and advice to special revelation but sprinkled her text with Devil-talk, religious admonitions, and biblical citations. The editor of *Appeal to Mothers* (undoubtedly her husband) appended a 29-page essay on "Chastity," which cited persons "of high standing and authority in the medical world" who agreed with her: Graham, Gove, Jackson, Coles, the phrenologist O. S. Fowler, and Samuel B. Woodward, superintendent of the Worcester State Lunatic Hospital. So closely did the views of these individuals parallel those of Ellen White, the publisher (that is, James White) felt compelled to add a note denying that she had read their works before writing out what she had seen in vision. Taking her word at face value, he asserted that "she had read nothing from the authors here quoted, and had read no other works on this subject, previous to putting into our hands what she has written. She is not, therefore, a copyist, although she has stated important truths to which men who are entitled to our highest confidence, have borne testimony."[12]

Nearly five months after the appearance of *Appeal to Mothers*, Ellen White published a brief account of her 1863 vision, a 32-page sketch tucked into the fourth volume of *Spiritual Gifts*. In an essay entitled "Health," influenced heavily by Coles, she recited the established principles of health reform, attributing them to her recent vision. Willful violations of the laws of health—particularly "intemperance in eating and drinking, and the indulgence of base passions"—caused the greatest human degeneracy. Tobacco, tea, and coffee depraved the appetite, prostrated the system, and blunted the spiritual sensibilities. Meat-eating led to untold diseases; pork alone produced "scrofula [a form of tuberculosis], leprosy and cancerous humors." Living in low-lying areas exposed one to fever-producing "poisonous miasma." Following Coles virtually word for word, she declared: "It is as truly a sin to violate the laws of our being as it is to break the ten commandments."[13]

Because of the glaring similarities between her health advice and that of other reformers, some who heard or read early accounts of her vision suspected that she had borrowed from her predecessors. Her stock reply, however, was that she had not and would not read the writings of others until she had fully written out her views, "lest it should be said that I had received my light upon the subject of health from physicians, and not from the Lord." But the embarrassing questions persisted until finally she issued a formal statement in the *Review and Herald* disclaiming any familiarity with health-reform publications prior to receiving and writing out her vision. "My views," she insisted, "were written independent of books or of the opinion of others."[14]

On October 2, 1868, over five years after her first view of the world's corrupt state, Ellen White received a second major vision on sex, which left her confidence in humanity "terribly shaken." As the sordid lives of "God's professed people" passed before her, she became "sick and disgusted with the rotten-heartedness" of her fledgling church. Protected by the cloak of divine revelation, she voyeuristically reported seeing reputable Adventist brethren leaving the "most solemn, impressive discourses upon the judgment" and returning to their rooms to engage "in their favorite, bewitching, sin, polluting their own bodies." Adventist children, she learned, were "as corrupt as hell itself." Speaking to the Battle Creek Seventh-day Adventist church in March 1869, she insisted that "Right here in this church, corruption is teeming on every hand."

Privately, she estimated "that there is not one girl out of one hundred who is pure minded, and there is not one boy out of one hundred whose morals are untainted." Given the odds of any petitioner being a health-sapping masturbator, she decided to refuse future requests for prayers of healing.[15]

For years Ellen White had held physicians in low esteem. As early as 1849 she had counseled her followers not to seek medical assistance:

> If any among us are sick, let us not dishonor God by applying to earthly physicians, but apply to the God of Israel. If we follow his directions (James 5:14,15) the sick will be healed. God's promise cannot fail. Have faith in God, and trust wholly in him . . . .

Relying on prayer instead of physicians became common practice among sabbatarian Adventists in the early 1850s. Many times during her early public career White herself was blessed with the power to heal. But when the death of an Adventist sister in New York in the early 1850s was charged to the young prophetess, White had a vision condemning the Adventists who had attended the dying woman for carrying "matters to extremes" and for engaging in fanatical behavior by not calling in a doctor. In 1860 she denied having ever opposed the use of physicians, advising that "in some cases the counsel of an earthly physician is very necessary."[16]

In addition to the multitudes who were abusing themselves, there were many others, she soon learned, who were abusing their spouses. In *How to Live* (1865), a set of bound pamphlets reporting various health-related aspects of her 1863 vision along with excerpts from the writings of like-minded reformers, she had urged couples to "consider carefully the result of every privilege the marriage relation grants," but until her 1868 vision she had focused on self-abusers, not spouse-abusers. After 1868, however, she warned that even married persons were accountable to God "for the expenditure of vital energy, which weakens their hold on life and enervates the entire system." In phrenological language (discussed below) she counseled Christian wives not to "gratify the animal propensities" of their husbands, but to seek instead to divert their minds "from the gratification of lustful passions to high and spiritual themes by dwelling upon interesting spiritual subjects." Husbands who desired "excessive" sex she regarded as "worse than brutes" and "demons in human form." In 1870 her husband brought out an expanded version of *Appeal to Mothers*, covering not only self- but spousal-abuse and published under the revealing title *A Solemn Appeal Relative to Solitary Vice, and the Abuses and Excesses of the Marriage Relation.*[17]

Central to White's understanding of sexual physiology was the then-common notion of "vital force," the mysterious energy that maintained human life. As she saw it, God had endowed each person, according to sex, with "a certain amount of vital force"; when this was expended, death ensued. Since each sexual act used up an irreplenishable amount, it behooved those who coveted a long life to keep their sexual activities to a minimum. "The practice of secret habits," she wrote, "surely destroys the vital forces of the system," producing "diseases of various kinds," such as tuberculosis, and leading to premature death.[18]

Following the spate of sex-oriented testimonies in 1869 and 1870, some of which she published with the guilty identified by name, Ellen White wrote little on the subject for the rest of her life. One of the primary reasons she ceased to write about sex was that her protégé John Harvey Kellogg replaced her visionary mantle with his own cloak of scientific authority, beginning in 1877 with his *Plain Facts about Sexual Life* (1877), which in later editions became a turn-of-the-century bestseller. She remained generally antipathetic toward sex, though she always stopped short of advocating celibacy. As far as we can determine, she never wrote a positive word about sex. In her waning years she looked forward expectantly to an idyllic existence in the New Earth free from such unpleasant activities. When some members inquired in 1904 if there would be any children born in the next life, she replied sharply that Satan had inspired the question. It was he, she said, who was leading "the imagination of Jehovah's watchmen to dwell upon the possibilities of association, in the world to come, with women whom they love, and of their raising families." As for herself, she needed no such prospects.[19]

From 1863 until her death in 1915 Ellen White, with varying degrees of success and zeal, proclaimed the gospel of personal health reform (while largely ignoring the public-health reforms of the day). Although she at first reported great progress in changing the eating habits of Adventists, there soon appeared signs of "a universal backsliding on health reform." Fish and flesh reappeared on believers' tables, and even among ministers vegetarianism became the exception rather than the rule. By the mid-1870s White herself was indulging her appetite for flesh foods, to the chagrin of the few who remained true to her health-reform message. It was not until the 1890s that she finally gained a permanent victory over meat and began leading her church back into the vegetarian fold.[20] (As Laura Vance shows in Chapter 15, dress reform proved equally frustrating for White.)

During her seminal 1863 vision White learned that she was to direct the world "to God's great medicine, water." Since the 1840s, water enthusiasts, called hydropaths, had been curing the sick with an arsenal of baths, packs, and douches; and water-cure establishments had sprung up across the nation. In 1864 and again in 1865 Ellen and James White visited one of the most successful of these operations, in Dansville, New York, and returned home determined to start an Adventist water cure in Battle Creek (see Chapter 7). The Western Health Reform Institute experienced a rocky first decade. Then young Dr. John Harvey Kellogg took over and turned the ailing institute into a world-famous sanitarium (Figure 11.1). In his spare time he invented flaked cereals and other health foods, from which his brother W. K. made a fortune. (Dr. Kellogg had initially offered the rights to his wheat flakes to the Adventist church, accurately predicting that the organization could "make enough money out of it to support the entire denominational work," but White ignored his offer, and a decade later she vetoed a chance to obtain the rights to the even more successful corn flakes.)[21]

FIGURE 11.1 In 1866, Seventh-day Adventists founded a water-cure facility in Battle Creek, the Western Health Reform Institute, following advice from Ellen White, who urged the move on the authority of a vision (Courtesy of the Ellen G. White Estate, Inc.).

In the years after 1863 Ellen White wrote hundreds of pages on health-related subjects. As medical science changed, so too did her vocabulary. In her early writings, for example, she related how God had shown her that flesh-meats filled the blood "with cancerous and scrofulous humors." Within a few decades, however, scientists such as Louis Pasteur and Robert Koch convinced the world of the existence of "germs," and White revised her terminology accordingly. Thus in her most mature work on health, *The Ministry of Healing* (1905), she discarded humors for the more scientifically up-to-date "tuberculous and cancerous germs." Until his expulsion from the church in 1907 Kellogg made a point of supplying the prophetess with the latest data from his laboratories and apprising her of developments in medicine and nutrition. When visiting Battle Creek, she stopped by Kellogg's office to learn of any new scientific discoveries relating to health. At other times, she relied on his multitudinous publications or corresponded with him by mail. Whether because of his influence or not, she did late in life recommend blood transfusions, undergo an extensive series of x-ray treatments for a dark spot on her forehead, and receive a vaccination against smallpox.[22] Following her return from Australia in 1900 she vigorously encouraged the opening of a medical school and sanitariums in southern California (see Chapter 7).

Mind, Body, and Soul

In the November 1871 issue of *The Health Reformer*, Ellen White wrote that "Mental and moral power is dependent on the physical health." Decades later she asserted, even more explicitly, that "The brain is the organ and instrument of the mind, and controls the whole body. In order for the other parts of the system to be healthy, the brain must be healthy. And in order for the brain to be healthy, the blood must be pure. If by correct habits of eating and drinking the blood is kept pure, the brain will be properly nourished."[23] In seeking how she came to these conclusions and why she believed that the brain—the locus of the mind—was the sacred place for authenticating the authority of her prophetic (sacred) words, we need to go back to her experience with Millerism in the 1840s, when she suffered a crisis of faith in God because of her inability to reconcile a loving God with an eternally burning hell for the damned. Fearful for her own salvation, she became so disturbed that she later commented that "many inmates of insane asylums were brought there by experiences similar to my own."[24]

Consoled by her mother's belief that the dead remain unconscious and heartened by a Christian Connexion preacher's sermons that argued the same, Ellen rejected her earlier belief in an immaterial and immortal soul housed in a body and instead came to believe that human identity comprises only the body and its faculties (attributes and powers).

This conviction eventually led White to a new understanding of the human self with a highly relational definition of the mind and body.[25] She concluded that the minds of humans are continuously open to influences from the mind of God and the mind of Satan. The extent to which an individual human's will submits to the voice of God or Satan determines that person's mortal and eternal destinies. The relationship of humans with the natural and the supernatural, however, was not an either/or relationship, but rather a continuous, dynamic encounter among all three natures—God's, Satan's, and the person's—in a lifetime process of struggle to choose good over evil. During her ministry White taught that

> it was a person's responsibility continuously to place his or her will on the side of Christ. When you yield your will to his, he immediately takes possession of you, and works in you to will and to do of his good pleasure. Your nature is brought under the control of his Spirit. Even your thoughts are subject to him. If you cannot control your impulses, your emotions, as you may desire, you can control the will, and thus an entire change will be wrought in your life. When you yield up your will to Christ, your life is hid with Christ in God. It is allied to the power which is above all principalities and powers. You have a strength from God that holds you fast to his strength; and a new life, even the life of faith, is possible to you.[26]

The means whereby the Spirit came to possess a person were "natural." According to White, "The brain nerves which communicate to the entire system are the only medium through which Heaven can communicate to man, and affect his inmost life. Whatever disturbs the circulation of the electric currents in the nervous system, lessens the strength of the vital powers, and the result is a deadening of the sensibilities of the mind."[27]

By the same token, she argued, "All should guard the senses, lest Satan gain victory over them; for these are the avenues to the soul." According to White, it was "the special work of Satan in these last days to take possession of the minds of youth, to corrupt their thoughts, and inflame their passions, knowing that by thus doing he can lead them to moral pollution, and then all the noble faculties of the mind will become debased, and he can control them to suit his own purposes."[28]

Just as God uses visions and dreams by way of the senses to access the mind, reasoned White, so Satan and his evil angels possess the intermediary means of mesmerism, hypnotism, and spiritualism. White believed that "Angels of God will preserve his people while they walk in the path of duty; but there is no assurance of such protection for those who deliberately venture upon Satan's ground. An agent of the great deceiver will say and do anything to gain his object. It matters little whether he calls himself a spiritualist, an 'electric physician,' or a 'magnetic healer.' "[29] She often used the catchall "spiritualism" to mean all mind-healing methods and mystical teachings, which for her included mesmerism, hypnotism, Christian Science, the Emmanuel Movement, and spiritualism. "There are many," she warned, "who shrink with horror from the thought of consulting spirit mediums, but who are attracted by more pleasing forms of spiritism, such as the Emmanuel movement. Still others are led astray by the teachings of Christian Science, and by the mysticism of theosophy [an occult sect] and other Oriental religions."[30]

Mesmerism, or animal magnetism as it was popularly called, proved especially popular in helping Americans to relax nervous tensions, relieve spiritual ennui, and restore physical health. First widely publicized across New England by the public lecture tour of the Frenchman Charles Poyen in 1836, mesmerism (similar to the hypnotism of today) fascinated Americans with its mysterious manifestations of clairvoyance, somnambulism, anesthesia, and ecstatic utterance. By touching their patients with hands or by making mental suggestions, mesmerists claimed to be able to diagnose disease and sometimes effect a cure. Professor and peasant alike were attracted to the magnetic healers, spiritualists, and preachers who used mesmerism to awe, cure, or hoodwink.[31] Noting the striking similarity of White's visions to a mesmeric trance, many attributed them to mesmerism. She herself entertained the possibility on at least one occasion, and because she doubted their divine origin, God chastised her by striking her dumb for twenty-four hours. Little wonder that she made all such ethereal sciences her bête noir for the remainder of her life.[32]

By the 1850s the spirit rapping of the Fox sisters, Margaret and Kate, had mushroomed into arguably the fastest growing popular religion in America. Like mesmerists, spiritualists believed in a reality that transcended the mundane world of human sense. Mesmeric fluids and the disembodied spirits of the dead each lifted Americans to consider the grandeur of God and the limitations of human knowledge. The veracity of each could be demonstrated by the simple, empirical tests available to common men and women. Trance mediums and healing mediums abounded, each serving as a conduit to the spirit world and the untold wisdom of the ages. Claiming to diagnose disease and provide prescriptions from the beyond, many spirit mediums set up healing practices and earned comfortable incomes.[33]

Christian Science, a medico-religious movement formally founded by Mary Baker Eddy (1821–1910) in 1879, became widely noted for its radical theological affirmation of the goodness of reality, its denial of the existence of sin, sickness, and death, and the numerous physical healings that followed its practice. Threatened by the apparent success of the movement, physicians attacked the authenticity of its healings, clergy declared its teachings un-Christian, and in an effort to provide a "truly Christian" form of religious healing members of both groups even banded together to form the Emmanuel Movement, a Boston-based religious-healing ministry founded by Elwood Worcester and Samuel McComb, which blended mental-health therapy with Christianity.[34]

In White's view, these systems all required patients to submit their will to that of the healer, and only persons under the influence of Satan would put themselves under the influence of another human. She did not engage seriously with the possibility that these healers might be applying a divinely ordained process, that they might be charlatans, or that they were self-delusional. Instead, she proscribed any discussion of these systems, claiming that "I have been shown that we are not to enter into controversy over these Spiritualistic theories, because such controversy will only confuse minds." Some dabblers in spiritualism, she continued, "will depart from the faith, giving heed to seducing spirits and doctrines of devils." White often linked psychology to these systems and asserted that Satan, using such sciences of the mind, poisons the minds of thousands and leads them into infidelity.[35]

According to White, when the mind of Satan is in control, not only do persons meditate on carnal desires, but they indulge in rich and fancy foods, alcohol, tobacco, fashionable clothes, fiction and sentimental literature, popular music, dance, "bad company," and all the temptations of urban culture. When the mind of God is in control, humans choose plain food, pure water, and clean air; work and recreation in the out-of-doors; and realist and moral literature, the didactic purpose of which is to uplift morals. Such persons enjoy observing and nurturing the plants and animals of God's natural world and spending time in the company of good, upstanding friends and acquaintances. In contrast, declared White, "Satan takes control of every mind that is not decidedly under the control of the Spirit of God."[36]

Her seamlessly melded system of body, mind, and will lay at the crux of a spiritual life and seemed to be supported by empirical evidence. If one indulges a taste for rich and stimulating foods, then one "create[s] unnatural appetites"; the "system becomes fevered, the organs of diges-tion become injured, the mental faculties are beclouded, while the baser passions are excited, and predominate over the nobler faculties." Pursuing the fads of fashion and entertainment could also lead to dire results. When a woman wears a wig or hairpiece it will "heat and excite the spinal nerves centering in the brain," making it "almost impossible to arouse the moral sensibilities." According to White, "Many have lost their rea-son, and become hopelessly insane, by following this deforming fashion." Meals that follow late-evening dancing injure both physical and moral health; the stomach becomes irritated, the "finer feelings of the heart" are benumbed, and "the entire system must feel it, for this organ [stom-ach] has a controlling power upon the health of the entire body." Echoing Sylvester Graham's popular teachings on the centrality of the digestive system to human physiology and its close connection to the reproductive system, White insisted that "If the stomach is diseased, the brain nerves [which] are in strong sympathy with the stomach, and the moral powers are overruled by the baser passions. Irregularity in eating and drinking, and improper dressing, deprave the mind and corrupt the heart, and bring the noble attributes of the soul in slavery to the animal passions."[37]

To combat this terrible curse, which most seriously followed on the heels of masturbation, White stressed self-control, an abstemious diet, parental vigilance, and warnings about the loss of eternal life. She thought it important "to teach our children self-control from their very infancy, and learn them the lesson of submitting their wills to us." Like Graham before her, she regarded a bland diet as one of the best means of curbing the urge to masturbate. She proscribed all stimulating substances such as "mince pies, cakes, preserves, and highly-seasoned meats, with gravies," since they created "a feverish condition in the system, and inflame[d] the animal passions," a phrenological term for sexual arousal. In addition to guarding their children's diets, parents were to watch constantly for signs of self-abuse: absent-mindedness, irritability, forgetfulness, disobedience, ingratitude, impatience, disrespect for parental authority, lack of candor, a strong desire to be with the opposite sex, and a diminished interest in spiritual things. If apprehended in the act, the children were to be told "that indulgence in this sin will destroy self-respect, and nobleness of character; will ruin health and morals, and its foul stain will blot from the soul true love for God, and the beauty of holiness."[38]

White attributed mental illness and insanity to the over-excitation and inflammation of the brain. This could result from a variety of causes, including wig-wearing, masturbation, stimulating food and drink, excessive study, and uncontrolled guilt. But in each case the root cause lay in a person's failure to discipline and control his or her imagination, desires, and passions. Failure to abstain from evil practices or to moderate good activities, such as work or study, could result in undisciplined and disordered minds. The nervous breakdowns suffered by her husband, James, were the result, she believed, of overtaxing his brain by worrying and doing work that others in the Advent movement should have assumed; on occasion she wondered if he had become insane. Over the years she grew convinced that "Nine tenths of the diseases from which men suffer have their foundation" in "sickness of the mind," including worry, anxiety, excess remorse, and belief in false doctrines such as an "eternally burning hell and the endless torment of the wicked." Such beliefs arose from a lack of willpower "to rise above and combat disease of body and mind." Fortunately for Christians, "The religion of Christ, so far from being the cause of insanity, is one of its most effectual remedies; for it is a soother of the nerves."[39]

Among the metaphors and analogies that White drew on to illustrate this grand scheme of things were the well-balanced machine, the well-managed household, and the growth and development of plants. Horticulture formed the basis of many of her commentaries on the parables of Jesus in *Christ's Object Lessons* (1900) and earlier in "Mrs. White's Department" in *The Health Reformer* during the 1870s. Just as the cultivation of a garden requires the removal of weeds and the trimming of plants so God tends to the "human garden."[40]

The fundamental structure of this picture of reality persisted to the end of White's life. "It is the duty of every person," wrote White in *The Ministry of Healing* (1905), "for his own sake, and for the sake of humanity, to inform himself in regard to the laws of life, and conscientiously to obey them. All need to become acquainted with that most wonderful of all organisms, the human body." She went on to explain the necessity of such knowledge, declaring that the body is the only medium through which the mind and the soul are developed for the upbuilding of character. Hence it is that the adversary of souls [Satan] directs his temptations to the enfeebling and degrading of the physical powers. His success here means the surrender to evil of the whole being. The tendencies of our physical nature, unless under the dominion of a higher power, will surely work ruin and death.

For White, "The knowledge that man is to be a temple for God, a habitation for the revealing of His glory, should be the highest incentive to the care and development of our physical powers." True science, revelatory of God's laws in nature, could serve as an immense aid in the struggle against "hereditary and cultivated tendencies to evil."[41]

Along with many contemporary thinkers, White embraced a common-sense moral philosophy grounded in a "faculty psychology" of the self and located in an embodied mind.[42] Faculty psychologists believed that human nature comprised the faculties of gods, animals, and plants— the moral and rational powers, the emotional and instinctive impulses, and the mechanical reflexes. The respective strengths of the faculties in a post-Edenic world ranked inversely to their position in a hierarchy of value; the base faculties of reflex and impulse were stronger than the elevated, god-like faculties of understanding and will. Therefore, without disciplining the mind and body, carefully monitoring the senses, and developing good habits, the lower faculties would lead to the corruption of the individual self and to social chaos.

The physical location of these faculties proved more problematic for nineteenth-century Americans: the stomach, the liver, the blood, and the brain each had its champions. By mid-century this anatomico-physiological model had become pervasive. Bodily health came to be viewed as essential to the operations of psychology; the brain and its "electrical" processes became the locus of the mind and its faculties of understanding; the heart and the blood became the seat of emotion and the transport system for nutrients and feelings; and other organs, such as stomach and liver, reflexively processed the ingredients necessary to the proper function of the higher faculties.[43]

This physicalist understanding of the human self and of the mind represents the most important cultural influence on Ellen White's understanding of the self and of the place of the mind in human destiny. Phrenological teachings provided a primary source of her psychological

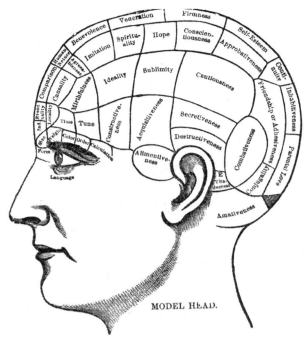

MODEL HEAD.

NUMBERING AND DEFINITION OF THE ORGANS.

FIGURE II.2 O. S. and L. N. Fowler, *The Self-Instructor in Phrenology and Physiology,* 1895. The authors reproduced this phrenological chart throughout the second half of the nineteenth century (Courtesy of the Department of Special Collections, Memorial Library, University of Wisconsin-Madison).

views. Developed by the German physician Franz Joseph Gall and popularized by two disciples, Johann Gaspar Spurzheim and George Combe, phrenology taught that the brain comprised various "organs," such as amativeness, conscientiousness, and veneration. O. S. and L. N. Fowler cataloged these qualities in a widely reproduced diagram (Figure 11.2). Through exercise, one could strengthen the mental organs responsible for positive characteristics and weaken the negative. When Spurzheim and Combe lectured in the United States during the 1830s, some Americans received the new science with great enthusiasm as further evidence of God's design. In 1864 White submitted her sons, Edson and Willie, to phrenological readings by James C. Jackson during one of their stays at his water cure in Dansville.[44]

Although a physicalist, White was neither a materialist nor a deist—she did not believe that the body, once created, ran of its own accord. "It is not as the result of a mechanism, which once set in motion continues its work, that the pulse beats, and breath follows breath," she wrote. "In God we live and move and have our being. Every breath, every throb of the heart, is a continual evidence of the power of an ever-present God."[45]

Believing that the mind controlled the body, White identified the nerves as "the messengers that transmit its orders to every part of the body, guiding the motions of the living machinery." Electricity played a central role in her neurophysiology. As she wrote in 1903,

> The influence of the mind on the body, as well as of the body on the mind, should be emphasized. The electric power of the brain, promoted by mental activity, vitalizes the whole system, and is thus an invaluable aid in resisting disease. This should be made plain. The power of the will and the importance of self-control, both in the preservation and in the recovery of health, the depressing and even ruinous effect of anger, discontent, selfishness, or impurity, and on the other hand the marvelous life-giving power to be found in cheerfulness, unselfishness, [and] gratitude should also be shown.

She suspected that "Spiritualist physicians" healed by channeling Satan's "electric currents."[46]

White even applied such beliefs to her own prophetic role. In recollecting an 1877 visionary experience in Danvers, Massachusetts, she wrote:

> Monday evening I stood in the stand at a tent meeting in progress at Danvers, Mass. A large congregation was before me. I was too weary to arrange my thoughts in connected words; I felt that I must have help, and asked [God] for it with my whole heart. I knew if any degree of success attended my labors, it would be through the strength of the Mighty One. The Spirit of the Lord rested upon me as I attempted to speak. Like a shock of electricity I felt it upon my heart, and all pain was instantly removed. I had suffered great pain in the nerves centering in the brain; this also was entirely removed. My irritated throat and sore lungs were relieved. My left arm and hand had become nearly useless in consequence of pain in my heart; but natural feeling was now restored. My mind was clear; my soul was full of the light and love of God. Angels of God seemed to be on every side, like a wall of fire.[47]

Unfortunately for her, such divine healings never lasted long.

Science Falsely So-Called

During the early decades of the nineteenth century geologists carefully constructed the so-called geological column, which reflected a history of life going back, in the opinion of the Oxford geologist William Buckland, "millions of millions of years." By the early 1840s many evangelical Christians had broken free from the notion of a 6,000-year-old Earth and a geologically significant Noachian deluge and had reinterpreted the first chapter of Genesis to accommodate the growing fossil evidence of the antiquity of life. One of the most common ways of harmonizing Genesis and geology was to interpret the Mosaic "days" as geological ages; another inserted the geological column into the alleged "gap" between the creation in "the beginning" and the much later Edenic creation.[48] Ellen White, in contrast, staunchly defended the recent appearance of life on Earth and a universal flood that had produced most of the fossils.

In her earliest account of Earth history, published in 1864, Ellen White claimed that God had taken her back in vision to witness the actual creation of the world. Pleased that the Lord had made her "his humble instrument in shedding some rays of precious light upon the past," she eagerly grasped the opportunity to flesh out the brief history given in the Bible. During her out-of-body experience she had seen "that the first week, in which God performed the work of creation in six days and rested on the seventh day, was just like every other week." She also confirmed "that the world is now only about six thousand years old."[49]

Having "been shown that without Bible history, geology can prove nothing," she condemned "the infidel supposition, that the events of the first week required seven vast, indefinite periods for their accomplishment." She especially feared anything that might weaken the argument for observing Saturday rather than Sunday as the Sabbath. From the beginning of her ministry she had stressed the importance of the fourth commandment of the Decalogue found in Exodus 20 (but never the version in Deuteronomy 5), which mandated that the seventh day be kept holy, "because in six days the Lord made heaven and earth, the sea, and all that in them is, and rested the seventh day: wherefore the Lord blessed the Sabbath day, and hallowed it." In White's opinion, "The infidel supposition, that the events of the first week required seven vast, indefinite periods for their accomplishment, strikes directly at the foundation of the Sabbath of the fourth commandment." As her husband reasoned, if the first six days of creation were indefinite stretches of time, then "the day on which Jehovah rested from his work, was another immense indefinite period." Such an idea, making the Bible seem absurd, could not be tolerated.[50]

To account for the geological record, White endorsed the by then largely discarded view of Noah's flood as a worldwide catastrophe that had buried the fossils and reshaped the earth's surface. This catastrophic event, evidence of which she noted as she traversed the Rockies and the Alps, was so terrifying that "even Satan himself, who was compelled to be amid the warring elements, feared for his own existence." After the floodwaters had subsided, exposing the rotting carcasses of antediluvian life, God had buried the organic debris, she wrote, by causing "a powerful wind to pass over the earth...in some instances carrying away the tops of mountains like mighty avalanches, forming huge hills and high mountains where there were none to be seen before, and burying the dead bodies with trees, stones, and earth." The buried forests subsequently turned into coal and oil, which God occasionally ignited to produce "earthquakes, volcanoes and fiery issues."[51]

In discussing the diversity of life at the time of the flood, Ellen White invoked the process of "amalgamation," writing that

> Every species of animals which God had created, were [sic] preserved in the ark. The confused species which God did not create, which were the result of amalgamation, were destroyed by the flood. Since the flood there has been amalgamation of man and beast, as may be seen in the almost endless varieties of species of animals, and in certain races of men.

This statement—especially the allusion to crossbreeding between humans and animals—raised questions in the minds of some of her readers. Which races of men did Mrs. White have in mind? Did she mean that some races were part animal? Critics charged her with teaching that Negroes were not members of the human race and claimed that her husband had explained to one fellow minister that Ellen "had seen that God never made the *Darkey*." Uriah Smith, editor of the *Advent Review and Sabbath Herald*, insisted in *The Visions of Mrs. E. G. White* (1869), a defense of the prophetess warmly recommended by James White, that such accusations were unfair. The mere possession of some animal blood, Smith argued, did not strip one of humanity, because organisms remained human if they had "any of the original Adamic blood in their veins." No one familiar with primitive peoples in Africa and America could reasonably doubt the validity of Mrs. White's view, Smith insisted, apparently relying for scientific authority on *Negro-Mania: An Examination of the Falsely Assumed Equality of the Various Races of Men* (1851), a book that had made its way into Mrs. White's library. "Moreover, naturalists affirm that the line of demarcation between the human and animal races is lost in confusion. It is impossible, as they affirm, to tell just where the human ends and the animal begins."[52] (For more on amalgamation, see Chapter 14.)

Years later Mrs. White extended her amalgamation theory from the zoological to the botanical world. "All tares are sown by the evil one" she wrote, referring to weeds. "Every noxious herb is of his sowing, and by his ingenious methods of amalgamation he has corrupted the earth with tares." Such views prompted one of her disciples to describe Satan as "the great primal hybridizer...the real instigator of all the mixing and crossing of the races of mankind, and also the mixer of thousands of kinds of plants and animals which God designed should remain separate."[53]

Beyond her repeated condemnations of unnamed "infidel geologists," many of whom were actually practicing Christians, Ellen White said little about developments in the natural sciences. In her published writings she never mentioned Charles Darwin by name, though by 1890 she was denouncing those who traced the origin of humans "to a line of developing germs, mollusks and quadrupeds." By the early twentieth century she was complaining that "Evolution and its kindred errors are taught in schools of every grade, from the kindergarten to the college. Thus the study of science, which should impart a knowledge of God, is so mingled with the speculations and theories of men that it tends to infidelity."[54]

During the nineteenth century no one outside the Adventist community, as far as we can tell, paid any attention to Ellen White's views regarding the creation and the flood. But in 1902 a young Canadian convert, George McCready Price, published the first of an eventual shelf full of books expounding on White's insights, *Outlines of Modern Christianity and Modern Science*. As a young man he had wrestled with the seemingly compelling evidence for geological ages. After much anguish and prayer he found the solution to his dilemma in White's "revealing word pictures of the Edenic beginning of the world, of the fall and the world apostasy, and of the flood." Her suggestion that the deluge and related events had buried the fossils, a notion no longer held by any trained geologist, particularly intrigued him. He determined to make it the centerpiece of what he called "flood geology" or "the new catastrophism." In a statement of his intellectual indebtedness, addressed to an Adventist audience in 1927, he said: "Every thinking man among us must acknowledge that our safety and immunity in this respect is due to our faith in the simple Bible narrative, supplemented by the writings of Mrs. E. G. White."⁵⁵

By that time he had become, as the editor of the journal *Science* described him, "the principal scientific authority of the Fundamentalists." Although virtually all of the leading antievolutionists in the 1920s, including William Jennings Bryan, cited his arguments against evolution, they did not abandon the popular day-age and gap interpretations of Genesis 1 for his White-inspired flood geology. It was not until the early 1960s, when the non-Adventists John C. Whitcomb, Jr., and Henry M. Morris made Price's flood geology the heart of young-earth creationism in their influential book *The Genesis Flood* (1961) that Price's (and White's) views entered the evangelical mainstream. About 1970 this view came to be known as "scientific creationism" or "creation science." There was, however, one significant difference: Unlike White and Price, who had written of inhabited worlds that antedated the Edenic creation, the leaders of the creation-science movement tended to limit the entire history of the universe to under 10,000 years.⁵⁶

Ellen White's influence on the creationist movement was almost entirely posthumous and largely accidental. While unwaveringly opposed to Satan's science of geology, she wrote relatively little on the topic; and although she may have met Price in Loma Linda during the years 1906–1912, when he worked there as a handyman and teacher, there is no evidence to suggest that she knew him or read his early attacks on evolution. She certainly never imagined launching a crusade.⁵⁷ In contrast, she devoted entire books and much energy to promoting health reform, the "right arm" of Adventism. She avidly supported the building of sanitariums, treatment rooms, and vegetarian restaurants—not for humanitarian reasons, as John Harvey Kellogg preferred, but for the "one object" of converting souls to Adventism. She may not have been the most original American health reformer, but she ranks among the most influential, especially when we factor in her impact on Kellogg. When she died at age eighty-seven, she left behind a string of thirty-three sanitariums on six continents, a medical school with campuses in Loma Linda and Los Angeles, California, and thousands of disciples eager to preach the gospel of health and creationism. Recent epidemiological studies indicate that those who have adopted her recommended lifestyle, especially the avoidance of tobacco and alcohol, live substantially longer and healthier lives.⁵⁸

NOTES

1. Ellen G. White, *Education* (Oakland, CA: Pacific Press Publishing Assn., 1903), 128; Ellen G. White to John Harvey Kellogg, May 27, 1896 (Ellen G. White Estate, courtesy of Tim Poirier), published, without identification of the recipient, in the *Seventh-day Adventist Bible Commentary*, ed. Francis D. Nichol, 7 vols. (Washington, DC: Review and Herald Publishing Assn., 1953–1957): 4:1167; E. G. White, "Science Falsely So Called," *Signs of the Times* 10 (1884): 657–58, 673–74; Ellen G. White, *Testimonies for the Church*, 9 vols. (Mountain View, CA: Pacific Press, n.d.), 4:274 (Testimony No. 28, 1879, Battle Creek College).

2. Ellen G. White, "Science and Revelation," *Signs of the Times* 10 (1884): 161 (unerring standard); Mrs. E. G. White, "True Christianity," *Review and Herald* 75 (1898): 133 (sophistry).

3. Ellen G. White, *Spiritual Gifts: My Christian Experience, Views and Labors in Connection with the Rise and Progress of the Third Angel's Message* (Battle Creek, MI: Seventh-day Adventist Publishing Assn., 1860), 83 (wrapt); James White, *A Word to the "Little Flock,"* privately published booklet dated May 30, 1847, 22; J. N. Loughborough, *Rise and Progress of the Seventh-day Adventists* (Battle Creek, MI: General Conference Association of the Seventh-day Adventists, 1892), 125–27 (lover of astronomy).

4. E. G. White, "To Those Who Are Receiving the Seal of the Living God," broadside dated January 31, 1849, Topsham, ME (wings, Orion); Michael J. Crowe, *The Extraterrestrial Life Debate, 1750–1900: The Idea of a Plurality of Worlds from Kant to Lowell* (Cambridge: Cambridge University Press, 1986), 241.

5. American Physiological Association, *Annual Report* (June, 1839), quoted in Ronald G. Walters, *American Reformers, 1815–1860*, rev. ed. (New York: Hill and Wang, 1997), 151; L. B. Coles, *Philosophy of Health: Natural Principles of Health and Cure*, rev. ed. (Boston: Ticknor, Reed, & Fields, 1853), 216. This and the following paragraphs are based in large part on Ronald L. Numbers, *Prophetess of Health: A Study of Ellen G. White*, 3rd ed. (Grand Rapids, MI: William B. Eerdmans, 2008).

6. Numbers, *Prophetess of Health*, 276. For a chronology of her physical and psychological experiences, see ibid., 291–319.

7. Numbers, *Prophetess of Health*, 84–90. In 1852 Joseph Bates had preached against "rich foods" at a meeting of Adventists in Ballston, NY; see "The Conference," *Review and Herald*, 2 (1852): 108. T. Joe Willey generously provided the data regarding the frequency of articles on tobacco and health in the *Review and Herald*.

8. [Mary Gove], *Solitary Vice: An Address to Parents and Those Who Have the Care of Children* (Portland, ME: Journal Office, 1839); Ellen G. White, *An Appeal to Mothers: The Great Cause of the Physical, Mental, and Moral Ruin of Many of the Children of Our Time* (Battle Creek, MI: Seventh-day Adventist Publishing Assn.,

1864). Regarding Edson, see Ronald D. Graybill, "The Power of Prophecy: Ellen G. White and the Women Religious Founders of the Nineteenth Century" (Ph.D. dissertation, Johns Hopkins University, 1983), 62–68. This and the following paragraphs are based in large part on Ronald L. Numbers, "Sex, Science, and Salvation: The Sexual Advice of Ellen G. White and John Harvey Kellogg," in *Right Living: An Anglo-American Tradition of Self-Help Medicine and Hygiene*, ed. Charles E. Rosenberg (Baltimore: Johns Hopkins University Press, 2003), 206–26. See also Numbers, *Prophetess of Health*, 207–18.

9. White, *Appeal to Mothers*, 17–18, 24–25, 27–28.

10. Ibid., 11–12.

11. Ellen G. White, *Special Testimony for the Battle Creek Church* (Battle Creek, MI: Seventh-day Adventist Publishing Assn., 1869), 21; "C. L. Daigneau, Old Resident of City, Dies," Benton Harbor, Mich., *News-Palladium*, February 13, 1928, 8; "Body of Late S. E. Daigneau Is Here for Burial," ibid., July 8, 1931, 3. The Daigneau family lived a couple of houses away from the Whites; son Samuel was about the same age as Edson White. When Ellen White first published what she had seen in vision about the Daigneau family, she mentioned the parents and children by name; later, when this testimony appeared in her collected *Testimonies for the Church*, 2: 404, the family members were identified solely by sequential letters of the alphabet. In *Shameless: The Visionary Life of Mary Gove Nichols* (Baltimore: Johns Hopkins University Press, 2000), 47–48, Jean L. Silver-Isenstadt notes that Gove professed to have no knowledge of female masturbation until she read about it.

12. White, *Spiritual Gifts: Important Facts of Faith, Laws of Health, and Testimonies Nos. 1-10* (Battle Creek, MI: Seventh-day Adventist Publishing Assn., 1864), 133 (physicians); White, *Appeal to Mothers*, 34.

13. Ellen G. White, "Writing Out the Light on Health Reform" (MS-7-1867, White Estate); Ellen G. White, *Spiritual Gifts* (1864), 120–51. For literary parallels between White and Coles, see Numbers, *Prophetess of Health*, 127, 134–35. As a former secretary of the Ellen G. White Estate has shown, in this essay White also lifted a passage about tobacco from John C. Gunn's popular *New Domestic Medicine* (1857); see Robert W. Olson, "Ellen White's Denials," *Ministry* 64 (February 1991): 15–18.

14. White, "Writing out the Light on Health Reform." See also Numbers, *Prophetess of Health*, 135–37.

15. White, *Testimonies for the Church*, 2: 349–50, 360, 439, 468–69; 4: 96.

16. White, "To Those Who Are Receiving the Seal of the Living God" (James 5); Numbers, *Prophetess of Health*, 76–82.

17. Ellen G. White, *Health; or, How to Live* (Battle Creek, MI: Seventh-day Adventist Publishing Assn., 1865), No. 2, 48; White, *Testimonies for the Church*, 2: 472–75; James White, ed., *A Solemn Appeal Relative to Solitary Vice, and the Abuses*

and Excesses of the Marriage Relation (Battle Creek, MI: Seventh-day Adventist Publishing Assn., 1870).

18. White, *Appeal to Mothers*, 27–28; reprinted in *Solemn Appeal*, 74. See also Ellen G. White, *Christian Temperance and Bible Hygiene* (Battle Creek, MI: Good Health Publishing Co., 1890), 64-65; and Numbers, *Prophetess of Health*, 211–15.

19. Quoted in Numbers, *Prophetess of Health*, 218. See also John Harvey Kellogg, *Plain Facts about Sexual Life* (Battle Creek, MI: Office of the Health Reformer, 1877).

20. On Ellen White and dietary reform, see Numbers, *Prophetess of Health*, 219–38.

21. Numbers, *Prophetess of Health*, 250–51.

22. White, *Testimonies to the Church*, 3: 563 (humors, first published in 1875); Ellen G. White, *The Ministry of Healing* (Mountain View, CA: Pacific Press, 1905), 313 (germs); Alonzo L. Baker, "My Years with John Harvey Kellogg," *Spectrum* 4 (Spring, 1972): 11; J. H. Kellogg to E. G. White, October 30, 1904 (White Estate); Ellen G. White, *Selected Messages: From the Writings of Ellen G. White*, 3 vols. (Washington, DC: Review and Herald Publishing Assn., 1958, 1980), 2:303 (transfusions, etc.).

23. Ellen G. White, "Words to Christian Mothers, on the Subject of Life, Health, and Happiness, No. 3," *Health Reformer* 6 (1871): 154; Ellen G. White, MS 24, 1900, in *Mind, Character, and Personality: Guidelines to Mental and Spiritual Health*, 2 vols. (Nashville, TN: Southern Publishing Assn., 1977), 1:60.

24. White, *Testimonies for the Church*, 1:25.

25. For helpful discussions of the issues raised in this section, see Catherine L. Albanese, *A Republic of Mind and Spirit: A Cultural History of American Metaphysical Religion* (New Haven: Yale University Press, 2007); Anne Harrington, *The Cure Within: A History of Mind-Body Medicine* (New York: W.W. Norton, 2008); and James C. Whorton, *Nature Cures: The History of Alternative Medicine in America* (New York: Oxford University Press, 2002).

26. Mrs. E. G. White, *Christian Temperance*, and Eld. James White, *Bible Hygiene* (Battle Creek, MI: Good Health Publishing Company, 1890), 148.

27. Ellen G. White, *Healthful Living* (Battle Creek, MI: Medical Missionary Board, 1898), 54.

28. Ibid.; White, *Appeal to Mothers*, 29.

29. Ellen G. White, "Shall We Consult Spiritualist Physicians?" *Testimonies*, 5:193.

30. Ellen G. White, "The Fall of the House of Ahab (Continued)," *Review and Herald* 91 (1914): 52–53.

31. On mesmerism, see Robert C. Fuller, *Mesmerism and the American Cure of Souls* (Philadelphia: University of Pennsylvania Press, 1982); Peter McCandless, "Mesmerism and Phrenology in Antebellum Charleston: 'Enough of the Marvellous,'" *Journal of Southern History* 58 (1992): 199–230; Alison Winter, *Mesmerized: Powers of Mind in Victorian Britain* (Chicago: University of Chicago Press, 1998).

32. Ellen G. White, *Early Writings* (Battle Creek, MI: Review and Herald Publishing Assn., 1882), 21–24.

33. On spiritualism, see R. Laurence Moore, *In Search of White Crows: Spiritualism, Parapsychology, and American Culture* (New York: Oxford University Press, 1977); and Mary Farrell Bednarowski, "Women in Occult America," in *The Occult in America: New Historical Perspectives*, ed. Howard Kerr and Charles L. Crow (Urbana: University of Illinois Press, 1983), 177–95.

34. For a history of Christian Science as a medico-religious movement, see Rennie B. Schoepflin, *Christian Science on Trial: Religious Healing in America* (Baltimore: John Hopkins University Press, 2003).

35. Ellen G. White, Letter 175, 1904, in *Mind, Character, and Personality*, 2:718 (spiritualism); 1:19 (psychology).

36. Ellen G. White, Letter 57, 1895, ibid., 1:3. See also Ellen G. White, MS 48, 1899, ibid., 2:692.

37. White, "Disease and Its Causes, Chapter II," in *Health: or, How to Live*, No. 2, 25 (foods); Ellen G. White, "Words to Christian Mothers, on the Subject of Life, Health, and Happiness, No. 2," *Health Reformer* 6 (1871): 121 (wigs and digestive system). On wigs, see also Numbers, *Prophetess of Health*, 205.

38. White, *Appeal to Mothers*, 5–10, 13, 19–20.

39. White, *Testimonies*, 3: 9–21; Ellen G. White, Letter 66, 1876, in *Daughters of God* (Hagerstown, MD: Review and Herald Publishing Assn., 1998), 269 (James); White, *Testimonies*, 5: 444 (nine tenths); Ellen G. White, "Will-Power," *Health Reformer* 5 (1871): 132–33; White, *Testimonies*, 5: 443–44 (religion of Christ).

40. Ellen G. White, *Medical Ministry* (Mountain View, CA: Pacific Press, 1932), 221 (machine); White, *Testimonies*, 7:62 (house). On horticulture, see E. G. W[hite], "Spring Has Come," *Health Reformer* 5 (1871): 196–97; "Mrs. White's Department: Beautiful May," *Health Reformer* 5 (1871): 260–61; and "Mrs. White's Department: June Has Come," *Health Reformer* 5 (1871): 292–94 (human garden).

41. White, *Ministry of Healing*, 128, 133, 271, 453.

42. The following discussion of faculty psychology draws extensively on Daniel Walker Howe, *Making the American Self: Jonathan Edwards to Abraham Lincoln* (Cambridge, MA: Harvard University Press, 1997).

43. On the seat of the emotions, see John Corrigan, *Business of the Heart: Religion and Emotion in the Nineteenth Century* (Berkeley and Los Angeles: University of California Press, 2002).

44. Ellen G. White, Letter 6, 1864, in *Manuscript Releases from the Files of the Letters and Manuscripts Written by Ellen G. White*, 21 vols. (Silver Spring, MD: Ellen G. White Estate, 1981–1993), 6:no. 346. On the history of phrenology in America, see Christopher G. White, *Unsettled Minds: Psychology and the American Search for Spiritual Assurance, 1830–1940* (Berkeley and Los Angeles: University of California Press, 2009); and John D. Davies, *Phrenology—Fad and*

Science: A 19th-Century American Crusade (New Haven: Yale University Press, 1955).

45. Ellen G. White, *Special Testimonies on Education* (no imprint, [1897]), 33.

46. Ibid.; Ellen G. White, *Education* (Mountain View, CA: Pacific Press, 1903), 197; White, "Shall We Consult Spiritualist Physicians?," 193.

47. Ellen G. White, *Life Sketches of Ellen G. White* (Mountain View, CA: Pacific Press, 1915), 226–27.

48. Nicolaas A. Rupke, "Geology and Paleontology," in *Science and Religion: A Historical Introduction*, ed. Gary B. Ferngren (Baltimore: Johns Hopkins University Press, 2002), 179–94, quoting Buckland on 181; Ronald L. Numbers, *Creation by Natural Law: Laplace's Nebular Hypothesis in American Thought* (Seattle: University of Washington Press, 1977), 105–18; Rodney Lee Stiling, "The Diminishing Deluge: Noah's Flood in Nineteenth-Century American Thought" (Ph.D. diss., University of Wisconsin-Madison, 1991). This section is based largely on Ronald L. Numbers, *Darwinism Comes to America* (Cambridge, MA: Harvard University Press, 1998), 92–110.

49. White, *Spiritual Gifts* (1864), 90–92. This seems to have been her first reference to 6,000 years, but she used that figure at least eighteen times before the end of the century. See "Ellen G. White Statements Touching on Geology" (DF 518, White Estate). White's account of the flood and her attack on geology appear in much the same form in *The Spirit of Prophecy: The Great Controversy between Christ and His Angels and Satan and His Angels* (Battle Creek, MI: Seventh-day Adventist Publishing Assn., 1870), 1:66–90; and, in somewhat different language, in *Patriarchs and Prophets; or, The Great Conflict between Good and Evil as Illustrated in the Lives of Holy Men of Old* (Oakland, CA: Pacific Press, 1890), 90–116.

50. White, *Spiritual Gifts* (1864) 91; [James White], "The First Week of Time," *Review and Herald* 55 (1880): 104–5.

51. White, *Spiritual Gifts* (1864), 70, 77–80. For personal observations of the work of the flood, see E. G. White, "Notes of Travel: A Sermon on the Cars," *Review and Herald* 62 (1885): 114; and Ellen G. White, journal for April 15, 1886 (MS 73, 1886, White Estate).

52. White, *Spiritual Gifts* (1864), 75; B. F. Snook and Wm. H. Brinkerhoff, *The Visions of E. G. White Not of God* (Cedar Rapids, IA: Cedar Valley Times Book and Job Printers, 1866), 9 (Darkey); [Uriah Smith], *The Visions of Mrs. E. G. White: A Manifestation of Spiritual Gifts According to the Scriptures* (Battle Creek, MI: Seventh-day Adventist Publishing Assn., 1868), 102–104; James White, "New and Important Work," *Review and Herald* 32 (1868): 160; John Campbell, *Negro-Mania: An Examination of the Falsely Assumed Equality of the Various Races of Men* (Philadelphia: Campbell & Power, 1851). Smith's defense of White's statement first appeared in "The Visions—Objections Answered," *Review and Herald* 28 (1866): 65–66. In *The Visions of Mrs. E. G.*

White, 74–75, Smith also appealed to contemporary science to corroborate Ellen White's statements about the immense size of humans and animals before the flood. Regarding the amalgamation issue, see also Gordon Shigley, "Amalgamation of Man and Beast: What Did Ellen White Mean?" *Spectrum* 12, no. 4 (1982): 10–19; and T. Joe Willey, *A Beast in the Garden: Who Were the Confused "Races of Men" Created by Amalgamation of Man and Beast?* (n.p.: Aegis Group, 2009). We are indebted to Willey for several of these references.

53. Ellen G. White, Manuscript 65, 1899, quoted in *Selected Messages*, 3 vols. (Washington: Review and Herald Publishing Assn., 1958, 1980) 2:288; George McCready Price to Martin Gardner, May 13, 1952, quoted in Ronald L. Numbers, *The Creationists: From Scientific Creationism to Intelligent Design*, expanded ed. (Cambridge, MA: Harvard University Press, 2006), 101.

54. White, *Spiritual Gifts* (1864), 91–92 (geologists); White, *Patriarchs and Prophets*, 45 (quadrupeds); White, *Education*, 227 (evolution). In this last work (130) she has evolutionists arguing that humans descended "from germs and mollusks and apes" as well as from "quadrupeds."

55. George McCready Price, *Genesis Vindicated* (Washington, DC: Review and Herald Publishing Assn., 1941), 299–300; George McCready Price, "Some Early Experiences with Evolutionary Geology," *Bulletin of Deluge Geology* 1 (1941): 79; George McCready Price, "The Significance of Fundamentalism," *Review and Herald* 104 (1927): 13. See also George McCready Price, *Evolutionary Geology and the New Catastrophism* (Mountain View, CA: Pacific Press, 1926). On Price, see Numbers, *Creationists*, especially Chapter 5.

56. "Letter to the Editor of Science from the Principal Scientific Authority of the Fundamentalists," *Science* 63 (1926): 259. On Price's growing influence, see Numbers, *Creationists*, 114–19, 210–13, 223–24; on the rechristening of "flood geology" as "creation science," see ibid., 268–79.

57. Numbers, *Creationists*, 95, 465.

58. Numbers, *Prophetess of Health*, 249; Gary E. Fraser, *Diet, Life Expectancy, and Chronic Disease: Studies of Seventh-day Adventists and Other Vegetarians* (New York: Oxford University Press, 2003), 45–58.

Society

Douglas Morgan

A VISIT BY "men of intemperance" in 1859 to the Seventh-day Adventist publishing office in Battle Creek, Michigan, marked a transition in Ellen White's conception of how believers in the near second advent of Christ should interact with the society around them. The visitors commended the sabbatarian Adventists now headquartered in Battle Creek for holding convictions against voting, similar to those of Quakers.

The Adventist prophet detected satanic purpose behind the visitors' "flattering manner." She approved of a consensus that the movement's leaders had just reached about using the vote "in favor of right and against wrong" rather than by inaction contributing to the electoral success of "intemperate men." She relished the hope that Satan would be "disappointed" by the Adventists thus abandoning radical separatism and taking responsibility for their influence in the public arena of "our city."

The course change led, by the 1870s, to benevolent initiatives that included selective yet fervent advocacy in the political arena. Between the Civil War and the Great War, as movements proliferated to rectify injustices created by rapid industrialization, urbanization, and immigration and to address the dilemma of emancipated slaves trapped far short of freedom, Ellen White guided Adventist responses to the nation's social problems.

Her castigation of the manipulative "men of intemperance" as earthly workers for "Satan and his evil angels" in her diary points to the religious narrative that motivated her. A vision experienced at Lovett's Grove, Ohio, the previous spring had presented to her "the great controversy of the ages between Christ and Satan," which became the central theme of her

career.[1] In White's "great controversy" narrative the American government, employing coercion like all human governments, remained essentially enemy territory. White looked instead to a radical renewal movement
within the Christian church—the "remnant church" in Adventist terminology (see Rev. 12:17)—as the decisive human instrument through which
God would resolve the controversy.

The "great controversy" narrative shaped, though not without tension
and ambiguity, her approach to public issues such as temperance and
prohibition, woman's rights, poverty and economic injustice, race relations, and religious liberty. The "great controversy" employs the Whig or
republican view of history, centering on the Protestant struggle for liberty
from the union of ecclesiastical and royal power that corrupted medieval
Catholic Christendom. In Protestant America's failure to live up to its
ideals of religious and civil liberty, Ellen White and the Adventists saw
signs of a final collapse of freedom in a soon-coming "time of trouble"
immediately prior to the return of Christ and full establishment of God's
government.[2]

From the beginning, the theme of freedom drives White's "great controversy" narrative. Since "the exercise of force is contrary to the principles
of God's government," God did not snuff out the primeval rebellion—the
fountainhead of all the evil, suffering, and death that afflicts humanity.
Redemption from Satan's domain and the full restoration of God's government on earth likewise must unfold in accordance with the principle of
freedom. Because God "takes no pleasure in forced obedience," he created
human beings as "free moral agents...with full liberty to yield or with-
hold obedience."[3]

Amidst the controversy, in this view, God's faithful witnesses struggle
against evil by deploying the principles of liberty rather than the coercive
power of government. The people of God are most authentic when they
are a suffering, dissenting minority, bearing costly, non-coercive witness
to truth and righteousness while striving against oppressive powers. This
is the human agency for cooperation with divine power through which the
"great controversy" finally reaches a happy end.[4]

Such witnesses do not invest hope in any human government or political program, however idealistic, but only in the coming reign of Christ. Yet
White also recognized a historical pattern in which the prophetic minority
exerts a transforming influence in society. In the book *Education* (1903)
she urged that the study of history center on "the great reformatory movements" and how advocates of reform based on divine principles, "though

often brought to the dungeon and the scaffold, have through these very sacrifices triumphed."[5]

Though submission to God's government comes only by way of free choice, prescribed order and content–"the law of love"–structures that government. In 1895, White referred to the beneficent tree in the dream of the ancient Babylonian king Nebuchadnezzar (see Daniel 4) as a "representation" of "the only kind of ruling acceptable to [God]—a government that protects, restores, relieves, but never savors of oppression."[6]

"The Great Controversy" and the Politics of Temperance

Ellen White never made political transformation of American society a central target of her work. Her ministry focused on holistic transformation of individuals in the contexts of family, church, and benevolent agencies connected with the church's apocalyptic mission. Yet her early formation in New England took place in an antebellum evangelical culture that drew no sharp boundaries between sins involving one or two individuals and evil embedded in the nation's political and economic system, most notably slavery.[7]

In an 1847 account of an early vision depicting dramatic events connected with the second coming of Christ, Ellen White's narrative moves seamlessly from vindication of the "little flock" persecuted for adherence to the biblical Sabbath (Saturday) to the "jubilee"—the liberation of the slaves—at least the "pious" among them (see Chapter 14).[8]

By the 1864 presidential election, many Adventists, in a shift paralleling that of abolitionist leader William Lloyd Garrison, had come to see the importance of using the ballot to resist slavery. But, as we have seen, temperance had already generated momentum in favor of voting, and after the Civil War it was the issue that drew Ellen White, along with thousands of other American women, most directly into the public arena. Indeed, her involvement closely paralleled the rise of the Woman's Christian Temperance Union (WCTU) as one of the nation's most powerful reform agencies.[9]

White assumed the role of temperance reformer in 1874, the same year the WCTU organized, and the cause remained a primary focus during the remaining four decades of her life. As she mobilized her people at churches and camp meetings and in scores of articles, she repeatedly

urged them to join forces with the WCTU. She also became a public lecturer, speaking to crowds, sometimes numbering in the thousands, in the
United States, Europe, Australia, and New Zealand (see Chapter 6). Her
public debut was orchestrated by an interdenominational committee in
Battle Creek, where she spoke to an audience of more than five hundred
at a rally held in a city park on July 14, 1874. Three years later, collaboration among the WCTU, the Battle Creek Reform Club, and the Adventists'
Battle Creek Sanitarium drew a crowd of five thousand to hear her.[10]

Initially emphasizing "gospel temperance" efforts to influence drunk-
ards and liquor sellers to repent and reform, the WCTU soon added legislation to its arsenal, endorsing state prohibition laws in 1876. Ellen White,
too, ventured this far into politics. Her temperance articles, which began
appearing in 1878, urged that governmental leaders be held accountable
not only for their laws and policies but also for their own sobriety of life. In
1881, though, she became more emphatic about the necessity of working
for prohibition laws.

An incident at the Adventists' Iowa Conference camp meeting that
year reflects the depth of her conviction on this point. After battling to be
heard over a heavy thunderstorm during a Sunday afternoon meeting, she
retired to her tent for the night. But in response to an urgent summons,
she returned to the main tent to head off a move to delete "the ballot box"
from a proposed resolution specifying the ways that Adventists should
support the temperance cause. She declared that Adventists should vote
for prohibition "to a man, everywhere," adding "perhaps I shall shock
some of you if I say, If necessary, vote on the Sabbath day for prohibition
if you cannot at any other time."[11]

In the *Review and Herald* the following November she insisted that
helping individuals change would never bring success to the temperance
cause as long as the liquor traffic enjoyed the support of law in overwhelming human weakness with the allure of drink. By licensing liquor sales
governments "sustain an evil which is sapping their very foundations" and
"causing a moral paralysis on society." Because in America "every voter has
some voice" in those laws, she reasoned, all share responsibility for them.
Lecturing in California in 1881, she ridiculed state policies that regulated
liquor sales while funding "inebriate asylums" to free individuals from
addiction. National prohibition, "rigidly enforced from ocean to ocean,"
she declared, would be "the grandest inebriate retreat ever erected."[12]

However, like many in the WCTU itself, Ellen White did not share
the conviction of Frances Willard, elected the Union's national president

in 1879, that women themselves needed the ballot as a means for exerting virtuous influence on society. White did not oppose woman suffrage as an intrinsic evil, but she seemed to regard suffragism as an unnecessary distraction from the benevolent work that she saw as the more urgent task for Adventist women (see Chapter 15). White did not follow Willard in the latter's "Do Everything" program for extending the WCTU's political work beyond prohibition to comprehensive social and economic reform. The "great controversy" marks this difference. As a type of premillennialism, White's theology of history expected destruction of the present sinful world at the return of Christ *before* the millennium, and an eternity beyond free of evil. Willard's rhetoric as WCTU president, in contrast, reflected postmillennialism—Christian reforming endeavor would lead to a millennial era in which righteousness holds sway over earthly society, *after* which Christ would establish His eternal, divine Kingdom.[13]

After the Civil War, postmillennialism lost influence as a system for understanding literal fulfillment of end-time prophecy, but it continued, for Protestant social reformers such as Willard, to generate the language of hope for progressive advance toward the perfection of society. Thus, at the 1887 national convention, the WCTU president called on her audience to "recognize Christ as the great world-force for righteousness and purity and enthrone Him king of nations in faith, as he will one day be in fact, through Christian politics and laws, no less than Christian living."[14]

Given the differences between postmillennial reformers and Adventist premillenialists, how could Ellen White urge her people to cooperate with the WCTU on behalf of prohibition laws, which she continued to do during Frances Willard's leadership? White and the Adventists, like Willard and the WCTU, believed that the church was to carry forward the work of Christ in society, which meant a ministry of healing and restoration for the poor, the suffering, and the oppressed, not just the saving of sinful souls.

In White's view, however, the outcome envisioned was not realization of the kingdom of God through national institutions, but the vindication of the faithful minority (the remnant church) and the establishment of God's eternal reign (see Chapter 10). Thus, she kept her focus firmly on the mission of the remnant church—its institutions, agencies, and interests took precedence over all else.

White's commentary on the aftermath of the San Francisco earthquake in 1906 illustrates how her premillennialism held out the possibility that prohibition could bring about social change that was meaningful but much more limited in scope and duration than that envisioned by Willard's postmillennialism. With liquor stores and saloons closed for two and a half months after the earthquake, the city had been largely free of violence and crime, despite expectations to the contrary. "Thinking men," including editors of some of the leading newspapers, thus advocated keeping the saloons closed, but the city government, with an eye on tax revenues, allowed them to re-open, leading to a dramatic upsurge in crime. On the basis of these developments, White summoned her followers to a two-fold task of apocalyptic warning and social action. First, in fulfilling biblical prophecies, "whereby we may know that Jesus will soon appear in the clouds of heaven," the events in San Francisco added urgency to proclaiming the message of apocalyptic warning. Paradoxically, though, she also pointed to the societal benefits resulting from the prohibition laws passed immediately after the earthquake as rationale for ameliorating the same social evils pointing to Jesus' soon return.

> ... How important it is that God's messengers shall call the attention of statesmen, of editors, of thinking men everywhere, to the deep significance of the drunkenness and the violence now filling the land with desolation and death! As faithful colaborers with God, we must bear a clear, decided testimony on the temperance question.
> ... O that our cities might reform!....[15]

The signs of Jesus' imminent return called for a mission both to transform individuals and improve public policy as *preparation* for the Savior's eternal reign, but not to *bring about* the kingdom of God through the reform of human institutions. Social activism could disappoint the devil but only the second coming of Christ could defeat him.

Just as mission driven by the "great controversy" involved both intense apocalyptic warning and vigorous social action, it also required Adventists, in White's view, both to adhere to their own distinctive purpose and to cooperate with interdenominational reform agencies "in benefiting and elevating humanity." She envisioned Adventists "at the head in the temperance reform," indeed "in the forefront of every true reform," but recognized how experienced activists could guide them to that goal. Thus, she recommended inviting WCTU women to Adventist camp meetings to "teach our sisters how to work."[16]

White's calls for cooperation with the WCTU became more fervent and frequent after Willard's death in 1898 and the conversion to Adventism of S.M.I. Henry, a prominent figure in the Union's national leadership. In a letter to Henry sent from Australia in December, 1898, White noted that she had been saddened that in recent years many in the WCTU were "becoming politicians," involving themselves in "questions and debates and theories that they have no need to touch."[17]

Remarkably, though, even during the late 1880s, when the WCTU was most vigorous in lobbying for national Sunday rest legislation as a means of protecting the rights and welfare of industrial workers, White continued to advocate Adventist cooperation on matters of agreement. No issue alarmed Adventists as much as Sunday legislation, which they saw as central to the drive for a "Christian America" through political coercion—the trigger for the demise of liberty and the final "time of trouble" before Christ's return. However, in remarks at the annual meeting of the American Health and Temperance Association held in Oakland in 1887, White urged Adventists not to be put off by the situation but to view it as an opportunity: "You say they are going to carry this [temperance] question right along with the Sunday movement. How are you going to help them on that point?... How are you going to let your light shine without uniting with them in this temperance question?"[18]

Although it was supremely important for White that Adventists keep their allegiances free from other power centers in society, she wanted them to do so without unnecessarily provoking conflict or creating barriers to cooperation. Thus she sought to mute criticism and avoid confrontation as much as possible. After Willard's death, the appearance of eulogistic poems and stories effusively lauding her virtues in some Adventist publications prompted a lengthy rebuke from White to A.T. Jones, co-editor of the *Review and Herald*. The prophet was incredulous that Adventists would "extol Frances Willard in so ample a manner," especially in view of her leadership in the movement to exalt the "false Sabbath" (Sunday) in defiance of God's law. White herself had never publicly criticized Willard despite points of intense disagreement, and she quickly followed up her missive to Jones with instruction that he not show it to anyone other than co-editor Uriah Smith and Dr. John Harvey Kellogg. She did not want "indiscreet" persons to "blaze this matter abroad" so that she would be seen as denouncing the late, widely beloved leader of benevolent reform. Her concern was the blurred sense of identity and mission reflected in the fawning praise, but she did not want Adventist periodicals to expound on the negatives of Willard's legacy, either. Her approach was to "leave this our sister in the many good and valuable works, with her God." [19]

The WCTU was, by far, the most influential agency for public activism in the American culture that Ellen White encountered in her role of guiding a small, new religious movement through the decades from the Civil War to the turn of the twentieth century. And the temperance issue, according to the noted economist and social gospel advocate Richard Ely, stood at the center of "the deep, wide movement for social reform" that was "spreading out in ever more inclusive circles."[20] No better gauge of White's interaction with the public realm could be found, and it shows a pattern of vigorous, whole-hearted involvement, without loss of distinct identity and purpose through absorption into the broader movement. White's approach included strategic alliances in the service of a distinctive agenda, derived from her understanding of the "great controversy." She wanted benevolent impact on American society to accompany that mission, but structural transformation of the nation's political and economic order was not her main target.

Healing Social Maladies

Though she was willing, even eager, to engage the political process as a component of the church's broader mission, White emphasized that such involvement must not become partisan. While she lived in Australia during the 1890s, some Adventist ministers and teachers, it seems, used their positions to advocate the Populist proposal for the coinage of silver, touted as a panacea for the economic woes of rural and working classes. Silver became the central issue in the election of 1896, when the Democratic and Populist parties fused to support William Jennings Bryan.[21]

White viewed "the changing of the circulating currency" as a plan deriving from the devil rather than God. The danger she saw lay not in the envisioned ideal of economic justice for the poor, but in the fact that its result would be the very opposite of its promise: "a state of things that will bring oppression to the poor, and create great distress." In this, she may have been influenced by the Republican position. Yet Bryan biographer Michael Kazin writes that the Democratic nominee never overcame the "uncomfortable reality" that the urban working class not only "had nothing concrete to gain from free silver" but would be hurt by the inflation that proponents intended as a benefit to debt-ridden farmers. White declared that the voice of the "only-begotten Son of God" gave direction on the matter: "ye will not give your voice or influence to any policy to enrich a few, to bring oppression and suffering to the poorer classes of humanity."[22]

White was adamant that the church and its funds should not be used to underwrite partisan political advocacy. Yet nothing indicates that she changed her 1883 view affirming Battle Creek College students who harbored ambitions to "sit in deliberative and legislative councils, and help to enact laws for the nation." As individuals, Adventists could succeed in the realm of government without sacrificing principles. By taking "firm hold on divine power," the prophet exhorted, they would be positioned to "stand in society to mold and fashion, rather than to be fashioned after the world's model."[23]

Even in her lengthy 1897 warning about the dangers associated with politics, Ellen White reminded readers "not to live reclusive lives" but, like Christ, to meet human needs. The admonition against bringing partisan political strife into the church was not an exemption from the battle against the social sins of economic, racial, and religious oppression.

During the Progressive era, when, as White put it, "largehearted men and women" were "anxiously considering the condition of the poor and what means can be found for their relief," she commended the instructions in the Mosaic law concerning the sabbatical and Jubilee years as the best solution for "the labor question and the relief of the poor." She issued sharp apocalyptic warnings to violators of those principles and called on Adventists to address the social crisis by proclaiming the final message of warning and extending Christ's mission of mercy to the poor and oppressed.[24]

Sabbatical and jubilee provisions to restore property and to release debtors and slaves constituted God's safeguard against the evils resulting from "the continued accumulation of wealth by one class, and the poverty and degradation of another." She even asserted that God designed these regulations "to promote social equality." Such egalitarianism would not equally distribute resources or obliterate class distinctions, however. Rich and poor would always exist; indeed she believed the different classes needed each other for mutual benefit: the poor making essential contributions to the common good—and uplifting their status—through hard work and the rich developing Christian character by fulfilling their duty to the poor. All, she wrote, are "woven together in "the great web of humanity," in which "whatever we can do to benefit and uplift others will reflect in blessing upon ourselves."[25]

In White's view, laissez-faire was clearly not the operative principle in God's provisions for the nation's "social and political economy." Implementing "principles which God has enjoined" could well "hinder the amassing of great wealth and the indulgence of unbounded luxury," but would also "prevent the consequent ignorance and degradation of tens of thousands whose ill-paid servitude is required to build up these colossal fortunes" and "bring a peaceful solution of those problems that now threaten to fill the world with anarchy and bloodshed."[26]

But Ellen White had no more sympathy for labor unions than for unfettered capitalism. Though the "principles governing the forming of these unions seem innocent," she observed in 1902, they demanded a corporate loyalty that she believed would coerce the believer to violate the law of God. White, and Adventists generally, regarded with suspicion any kind of large corporate entity or "combination" as a potential threat to the individual freedom of dissenters. Here the influence of the "great controversy" was particularly direct, for White viewed the union movement as preparatory to reception of the "mark of the beast"—the designation identifying those in rebellion against God in the final time of trouble. It was one way in which men were "binding up in bundles ready to be burned."

Such severe apocalyptic warnings brought no comfort to the capitalists, either. In this same testimony of December, 1902, White wove together imprecations of equal force against both labor unions and "gigantic monopolies" amassing wealth by oppressing the poor.

> In the world gigantic monopolies will be formed. Men will bind themselves together in unions that will wrap them in the folds of the enemy. A few men will combine to grasp all the means to be obtained in certain lines of business....
>
> ...How can men obey these words ["love thy neighbor as thyself"], and at the same time pledge themselves to support that which deprives their neighbors of freedom of action? And how can men obey these words, and form combinations that rob the poorer classes of the advantages which justly belong to them, preventing them from buying or selling, except under certain conditions![27]

Along with the apocalyptic warning message, which, if heeded, would radically change the practices of wealthy oppressors, White called for extension of Christ's ministry of healing and compassion to the victims of oppression. One of her most widely sold books, *The Ministry of Healing* (1905), drew together her conception of how Adventists should address the social ills accompanying rapid urbanization and industrialization. She focused on the individual rather than on economic re-structuring advocated by proponents of the social gospel. However, the solutions she sketched, drawn from her reading of Hebrew Scripture—including industrial education, land resettlement for tenement dwellers, and benevolent institutions—proposed not only to relieve the suffering of the poor but also to empower them in a lasting way.[28]

White challenged Adventists to take the offensive against Satan in the large cities, where they had been all but invisible until the mid-1880s, with missions that combined the gospel message with compassionate outreach to the poor and medical missionary work. John Harvey Kellogg spearheaded the initiative, even as his Battle Creek Sanitarium gained a national reputation as a center for innovative health care. He organized the Medical Missionary and Benevolent Association in 1893, and within ten years the endeavor grew to employ more people than the denomination's General Conference and state conferences combined.[29]

Kellogg particularly targeted Chicago, the second closest major city to Battle Creek (after Detroit) and a city that epitomized the era. Launched in 1893, the Chicago Medical Mission provided free medical care for the poor, child care for working mothers, a "penny lunch counter," a workingmen's home for the unemployed, and many other services. A separate but connected enterprise led by Dr. David Paulson, the Life Boat Mission, operated a "rescue home" for unwed mothers and prostitutes and published a magazine, *The Life Boat*, with a circulation in the hundreds of thousands. It addressed social problems such as juvenile delinquency, child labor, and prison conditions.[30]

As reports from the United States reached her during her nine-year sojourn in Australia, White expressed pleasure that Adventists were beginning to spread their health ministry more broadly, rather than clustering so much of their efforts and resources in Battle Creek. Soon after returning to the United States late in 1900, she wrote approvingly about work in San Francisco that featured a "hygienic restaurant" as well as a food store and "treatment rooms." She hoped such medical missionary work would expand, linking health with evangelism for "the uplifting and saving of human beings."[31]

By this time, though, White was becoming critical of the Kellogg-led work in Chicago. Too much was being invested there, she believed, at the expense of other locales. Moreover, too much emphasis was being placed on "non-sectarian" work for the most destitute classes. As her continued praise for the work of Paulson and the Life Boat Mission indicates, though, White had not abandoned her fervor for humanitarian work in the cities, but she insisted that Adventist work not be disconnected from the church's distinctive mission in the culmination of the "great controversy." Adventists could not be satisfied simply to relieve temporal suffering; their work must also confront the sin and evil at the heart of the human dilemma with the gospel that Adventism had been raised up to recover and propagate in the "last days." [32]

Ellen White's approach to the social maladies of a rapidly urbanizing, industrializing nation bore some similarities to the social gospel. Like the social gospellers, she insisted that genuine Christian faith must prioritize ministry to the poor and oppressed. However, she did not embrace the social gospel's attempted renovation of the American economic and political system.

As did the stalwarts of the Salvation Army, White made repeated, fervent appeals for authentic Christians to dedicate themselves to meeting the needs of "suffering humanity." But in a "letter to physicians" in 1904, she made clear that such work was not to define nor preoccupy the Adventist mission. Adventist humanitarian work must neither be detached from nor overshadow its evangelical proclamation of "the truth for this time." She did not want Adventists to denounce or oppose the admirable work of the Salvation Army on behalf of the "neglected, downtrodden ones," but its ways and methods did not define "the work the Lord has given us to do."[33]

Along with the foremost revivalist of the day, Dwight L. Moody, White held to the central importance of preaching and teaching the gospel message to convert sinners and advance believers along the path of holiness. Though differing in important details, the variations on premillennialism held by White and Moody both rejected the notion that American civilization was advancing toward the kingdom of God—the present order faced cataclysmic divine judgment. Unlike Moody, though, White connected soul-winning to healing the whole person. While the revivalist found that preaching the premillennial return of Christ greatly aided soul-winning, he concluded that linking charity with evangelism, as he had early in his career, did not. He observed that when he offered the Bible in one hand and a loaf of bread in the other, peoples' attention focused on the bread rather than Christ. For White, meeting human need remained the most effective way of leading another into a saving spiritual relationship with

Christ, and progressive sanctification of the Christian had to include the body and mind as well as the heart. The point here is not that White's Christian compassion surpassed Moody's, but rather that the two differed on which weapons were indispensable in the climactic struggle against Satan's forces.[34]

Principles under Pressure: Race and Religious Liberty

If Ellen White drew her positions on public issues in a relatively coherent and integrated fashion from her understanding of the "great controversy," she also freely adapted ideals to meet the demands of the church's mission in varying contexts. White's coupling of pragmatic accommodation and lofty ideals appeared in two further issues that brought her ministry into the public arena—race relations and religious liberty. The Seventh-day Adventist church included only a handful of African American members in 1891 when White, in "Our Duty to the Colored People," repudiated attempts to draw the color line in the church and called for a new initiative to reach the nation's impoverished and oppressed black population. Over the following two decades she persistently pressed church leaders to devote greater attention and resources to this endeavor. The program for the "southern work" that she developed in articles and letters during the 1890s resembled in some important ways her proposals for dealing with urban poverty (see also Chapter 14). However, the initiative coincided with a "national capitulation to racism," in which the state and local governments of the American South, with federal acquiescence, fully developed legal segregation and racial repression. White's handling of the problem of the color line in this changing context provides a striking example of how her view of the "great controversy" shaped her approach to a major public issue.[35]

As conditions worsened in the late 1890s, the only way White could envision ministering to both races in the South was to avoid confrontation. If the church were to trumpet the racial ideals of the gospel, as she had done in 1891, and provocatively defy segregation laws and deeply ingrained customs, its work would surely be repressed. This in turn would frustrate its mandate to be God's instrument in rapidly resolving the "great controversy."

As the Adventist work of giving the "closing message" extended through the decades following her death in 1915, the counsel of silence in the face of injustice that White gave as an eschatological expedient came to dominate perceptions of her legacy for race relations. The gospel-based racial equality and justice prominent in her earlier exhortations faded into obscurity.[36]

The relationship between church and state became another area of pragmatic accommodation. While the temperance cause harmonized Adventists with the moral-reform agencies of the nation's nineteenth-century Protestant empire, legislative efforts to bolster Sunday observance stirred them to sharp opposition. In the 1880s Sunday-law crackdowns, first in California and then more so in the South, put Adventists on the wrong side of the law (Figure 12.1). Meanwhile, campaigns for national Sunday legislation and a constitutional amendment affirming the sovereignty of Christ gained momentum.[37]

Ellen White viewed these developments in the unsparing light of the "great controversy," which showed the nation's dominant cultural forces to be on the wrong side of the divine law. Paradoxically, this apparently deterministic outlook stimulated Adventists to lobby tirelessly to thwart the anticipated developments in the short-term. White concluded that the

FIGURE 12.1 The convicts in this chain gang, except for the three men standing in front, were Seventh-day Adventists from Rhea County, Tennessee, who were found guilty in 1895 of violating Tennessee Sunday laws by working on their farms. A wave of arrests of Sabbathkeepers for violating Sunday laws led Ellen White to urge Adventists toward activism for religious liberty (reproduced with permission from A. W. Spalding, *Origin and History of Seventh-day* Adventists, vol. 2, Review and Herald Publishing Association, 1962).

church's role in bringing the "great controversy" to an end required a brief but indeterminate time in which every effort should be made to safeguard religious freedom:

> It is our duty, as we see the signs of approaching peril, to arouse to action. Let none sit in calm expectation of the evil, comforting themselves with the belief that this work must go on because prophecy has foretold it, and that the Lord will shelter His people. We are not doing the will of God if we sit in quietude, doing nothing to preserve liberty of conscience.[38]

Bearing such a witness, she wrote in 1887, put the believer on a collision course with the fallen powers of this world, which must be faced with martyr-like resolve: "To stand in the defense of truth and righteousness when the majority forsake us, to fight the battles of the Lord when champions are few,—this will be our test....The nation will be on the side of the great rebel leader."[39]

In a manner resembling her response to the race question, however, White later tried to defer the kind of confrontation with the authorities envisioned in her stirring exhortations. During the 1890s she urged Alonzo T. Jones, the denomination's foremost public advocate for religious liberty, to moderate several of his positions and soften his confrontational style. Jones, for example, believed that faithful witness to "present truth" required non-compliance with Sunday rest laws by openly engaging in work on that day. White opposed him directly on this, counseling Adventists to avoid conflict with the authorities by not working on Sundays. She also admonished Jones to back away from stringent opposition to reading the Bible in public schools.[40]

The most striking instance of pragmatism regarding separation of church and state came in 1894 when Cecil Rhodes' British South Africa Land Company offered the Adventist church a gift of twelve thousand acres of land. In the first edition of *The Great Controversy* (1888), White had declared: "The union of the church with the State, be the degree never [sic] so slight, while it may appear to bring the world nearer to the church, does in reality but bring the church nearer to the world." Seeking to follow that clear standard, Jones and the other editors of the *American Sentinel*, the church's religious liberty periodical, contended that accepting land from an instrument of British colonial authority would bring the Adventist church into the same kind of corrupt union with the state it had long and loudly denounced, not to mention collusion with an imperialist land grab.[41]

Writing from her temporary home in Australia, White rebuked Jones for his inflammatory rhetoric and misguided zeal in carrying principles to their logical extreme. "Sharp thrusts" in denominational periodicals such as Jones had directed against Rhodes and imperialism in southern Africa could, she warned, unnecessarily antagonize authorities and "bring on the time of trouble before its time." While the church is still in the world, she maintained, God may move the hearts of rulers toward benevolence on behalf of the people of God, and the church "need not sacrifice one principle of truth while taking advantage of every opportunity to advance the cause of God."[42] As new opportunities for advance as well as new fronts of resistance emerged in the heat of the "great controversy," the prophet refused to be tightly bound by her own previous marching orders.

Drama Deferred

Ellen White envisioned a "great controversy" ending in high drama, with demonic conspiracies, heroic stands for truth and righteousness, and finally the thrilling divine intervention and a world made new. Until then she discouraged theatrical confrontation with temporal powers. Rather, her approach was to build up a people loyal to God's government while avoiding direct, noisy threats to the power systems governing in the present age. She did not hesitate to denounce evils—both present and anticipated—perpetrated by such powers. But she would encourage no "masterly efforts" to smash them. Indeed she wanted her people to be known most for Christ-like benevolence and healing in their interaction with the society around them. Accordingly, she called for constructive activism to advance liberty, to bring lasting hope to the poor and oppressed, and to realize manifold societal benefits through enactment of prohibition.

In all of this, however, reform of American society was not her main goal. She consistently aimed to nurture a people loyal to divine law, co-workers with Christ in the final struggle of the "great controversy." In the interests of that cause, she at times avoided or even counseled silence on complex and controversial issues of structural injustice, woman rights, racial oppression, and militarism that some Christian leaders courageously addressed. Some observers may see in this practice craven compromise, constricted piety, and quietist irresponsibility. Others may detect

wise, pragmatic flexibility in the service of faithfulness—refusal to collapse her movement's eschatology into an idolatrous civil millennialism,
while, in the course of promoting a holistic mission, finding ways to make
a substantial impact on the public realm. Something like the latter was
what she tried for, drawing orientation from the promised outcome of the
"great controversy": the triumph of the kingdom of Christ and the establishment of a government that "would use no force" and whose "subjects
would know no oppression."[43]

NOTES

1. Ellen G. White, *Life Sketches of Ellen G. White* (Mountain View, CA: Pacific
   Press, 1915), 162. Unless otherwise indicated, citations of the works of Ellen
   White reference "The Complete Published Writings of Ellen G. White," *Legacy
   of Light* CD-ROM (Silver Spring, MD: Ellen G. White Estate, 1998). Full text
   of "The Complete Published Writings" is also accessible online at "The Ellen
   G. White Estate, Inc." web site, http://www.whiteestate.org.
2. Herbert Butterfield, *The Whig Interpretation of History* (New York: W. W. Norton,
   1931), 34–46; Ellen G. White, *The Great Controversy between Christ and Satan*
   (Mountain View, CA: Pacific Press, 1888), 442–50.
3. Ellen G. White, *The Desire of Ages: The Conflict of the Ages as Illustrated in the Life
   of Christ* (Mountain View, CA: Pacific Press, 1898), 21–22, 759; Ellen G. White,
   *The Story of Patriarchs and Prophets: The Conflict of the Ages Illustrated in the Lives
   of Holy Men of Old* (Mountain View, CA: Pacific Press, 1890), 34, 42, 48–49.
4. Ellen G. White, *Education* (Mountain View, CA: Pacific Press, 1903), 254; Ellen
   G. White, *The Acts of the Apostles in the Proclamation of the Gospel of Jesus Christ*
   (Mountain View, CA: Pacific Press, 1911), 68–69.
5. White, *Education*, 238.
6. White, *Patriarchs and Prophets*, 34; Ellen G. White, "Converted Men Needed in
   All Departments of the Work," (MS 29, 1895) in *Manuscript Releases*, 21 vols.
   (Silver Spring, MD: Ellen G. White Estate, 1981–1993) 3:37–38.
7. Timothy L. Smith, *Revivalism and Social Reform: American Protestantism
   on the Eve of the Civil War* (Nashville, TN: Abingdon Press, 1957); Donald
   W. Dayton, *Discovering an Evangelical Heritage* (Peabody, MA: Hendrickson
   Publishers, 1988).
8. James White, ed., *A Word to the Little Flock* (Brunswick, ME: James White,
   1847), 20.
9. Henry Mayer, *All on Fire: William Lloyd Garrison and the Abolition of Slavery*
   (New York: St. Martin's Press, 1998), 263–264, 456–457, 563–571; J. N.
   Andrews, "Slavery," *Review and Herald* 22 (1864): 172; Sydney E. Ahlstrom,
   A Religious History of the American People (New Haven: Yale University Press,

1972), 867–870; Thomas R. Pegram, *Battling Demon Rum: The Struggle for a Dry America, 1800–1933* (Chicago: Ivan R. Dee, 1998), 32–42, 52–83.

10. Arthur L. White, *Ellen G. White*, 6 vols. (Washington, DC: Review and Herald Publishing Assn., 1981–1986), 2:326–337; Ellen G. White, "The Temperance Work," MS 79, 16 Aug. 1907 in *Loma Linda Messages* (Loma Linda, CA: College of Medical Evangelists, 1918), 237–238; Ellen G. White, *Testimonies for the Church*, 9 vols. (Mountain View, CA: Pacific Press, 1948) 4:275–276 (Testimony No. 28, 1879).

11. Arthur L. White, *Ellen G. White*, 6 vols. (Washington, DC, and Hagerstown, MD: Review and Herald Publishing Assn., 1981–1986) 3:159–160.

12. Ellen G. White, "Temperance and the License Law," *Review and Herald* 19 (1881): 289–290; Ellen G. White, "Daniel a Temperance Reformer," *Signs of the Times* 18 (March 2, 1882).

13. Pegram, *Battling Demon Rum*, 71–72.

14. See George M. Marsden, *Fundamentalism and American Culture* (New York: Oxford University Press, 2006), 49–51; A. T. Jones, "Misdirected Enthusiasm," *American Sentinel* (Feb. 1888): 12–13. See also James H. Moorehead's *World without End: Mainstream American Protestant Visions of the Last Things, 1880–1925* (Bloomington: Indiana University Press, 1999).

15. Ellen G. White, "Drunkenness and Crime," *Review and Herald* 43 (1906); "Drunkenness and Crime" (concluded), *Signs of the Times* 49 (1907): 6.

16. Ellen G. White, "Notes of Travel—Meeting in Chicago," *Review and Herald* 6 (1885): 81–82; Ellen G. White, "Notes of Travel—Marshalltown, Iowa," *Review and Herald* 42 (1884): 657–658; Ellen G. White, "Notes of Travel—No. 5, Visit to San Pasqual and Escondido," *Review and Herald* 35 (1907): 7–8; Ellen G. White to A.T. Jones, Apr. 18, 1900, in *Manuscript Releases*, 7: 167–170; Ellen G. White to J. A. Burden, Sept. 2, 1907, in White, *Loma Linda Messages*, 258–260.

17. Ellen G. White to S.M.I. Henry, Dec. 1, 1898, in White, *Loma Linda Messages*, 232–233.

18. On the significance Adventists attached to national Sunday legislation, see Douglas Morgan, *Adventism and the American Republic: The Public Involvement of a Major Apocalyptic Movement* (Knoxville: University of Tennessee Press, 2001), 45–51. Ellen White remarks quoted in a report of the "American Health and Temperance Association, Fifth Annual Session," *Review and Herald* 7 (1888): 11–12.

19. Ellen G. White, Letter "To Whom It May Concern," July 29, 1898; Ellen G. White to A. T. Jones, Aug. 1, 1898; unless otherwise indicated, unpublished letters from Ellen White are in the archives of the Ellen G. White Estate, Silver Spring, MD. The letter of July 29 was mailed to Jones, according to White Estate personnel.

20. Quoted in Ruth Bordin, *Frances Willard: A Biography* (Chapel Hill: University of North Carolina Press, 1986), 6.

242   ELLEN HARMON WHITE: AMERICAN PROPHET

21. See Lawrence Goodwyn, *The Populist Moment: A Short History of the Agrarian Revolt in America* (New York: Oxford University Press, 1978), 234–235.

22. Michael Kazin, *A Godly Hero: The Life of Williams Jennings Bryan* (New York: Knopf, 2006), 69; Ellen G. White, "A Warning against Political Entanglements," in *Special Testimonies to Ministers and Workers*, Series A, No. 8 (1897) in *Testimonies to Ministers and Gospel Workers* (Mountain View, CA: Pacific Press, 1923), 330–331.

23. Ellen G. White, "Special Testimony Relating to Politics" (June 16, 1899), *Fundamentals of Christian Education* (Nashville, TN: Southern Publishing Assn., 1923), 477. Her Battle Creek College address of 1883 appeared in two parts under the title "Importance of Education" in the *Review and Herald* (Aug. 19 and 26): 529–530, 545–546; reprinted in *Fundamentals of Christian Education*, 82–91.

24. Ellen G. White, *The Ministry of Healing* (Mountain View, CA: Pacific Press, 1905), 183–87.

25. White, *Patriarchs and Prophets*, 534–35; White, *Ministry of Healing*, 184–186.

26. White, *Patriarchs and Prophets*, 533–536.

27. Ellen G. White, Letter to Brother and Sister J.A. Burden, 10 Dec. 1902, in *Manuscript Releases*, 4:75–76. For another example, see White, *Testimonies*, 9:12–13 (Testimony No. 37, 1909).

28. See White, *Ministry of Healing*, 185–186, 190–194, 205–206.

29. George R. Knight, *Organizing to Beat the Devil: The Development of Adventist Church Structure* (Hagerstown, MD: Review and Herald Publishing Assn., 2001), 110.

30. Richard W. Schwarz, "John Harvey Kellogg: Adventism's Social Gospel Advocate," *Spectrum: Journal of the Association of Adventist Forums* 1 (Spring 1969): 15–27, hereafter referred to as *Spectrum*; Jonathan Butler, "Ellen G. White and the Chicago Mission," *Spectrum* 2 (Winter 1970): 41–51.

31. Ellen G. White, "Health, Philanthropic, and Medical Missionary Work" (pamphlet, ca. 1896), 51–52; White, *Testimonies*, 7:110–114 (Testimony 35, 1902).

32. Butler, "Ellen G. White and the Chicago Mission," 46–51.

33. White, *Education*, 110; White, *Testimonies*, 8:184–185 (Testimony 36, 1904).

34. George Marsden analyzes Moody's outlook on premillennialism and social involvement in *Fundamentalism and American Culture*, 36–37.

35. Richard W. Schwarz and Floyd Greanleaf, *Light Bearers: A History of the Seventh-day Adventist Church*, rev. ed. (Silver Spring, MD: Department of Education, General Conference of Seventh-day Adventists, 2000), 234; C. Vann Woodward, *The Strange Career of Jim Crow*, rev. 3rd ed. (New York: Oxford University Press, 1974), 67–109; Rayford P. Logan, *The Betrayal of the Negro from Rutherford B. Hayes to Woodrow Wilson* (New York: Di Capo Press, 1965).

36. For major examples of White's racial counsels in a more progressive, egalitarian mode, see White, *Testimonies* 7:220–230, and, in an overall sense, Ellen G. White, *The Southern Work* (Washington, DC: Review and Herald Publishing

Assn., 1966). For later examples of the use of excerpts from White, *Testimonies*, vol. 9, to justify segregation in the church decades, see Frank W. Hale, Jr., *Angels Watching over Me* (Nashville, TN: James C. Winston Publishing Co., 1996), 157–211; and Samuel G. London, Jr., *Seventh-day Adventists and the Civil Rights Movement* (Jackson: University Press of Mississippi, 2009), 110–111.

37. Morgan, *Adventism and the American Republic*, 38–51.

38. White, *Testimonies* 5:713–14 (Testimony 33, 1889).

39. Ellen G. White, "Our Duty in the Present and Coming Crisis," *Review and Herald* 2 (1887): 17–18; Richard W. Schwarz, "The Perils of Growth, 1886–1905," in *Adventism in America: A History*, ed. Gary Land (Grand Rapids, MI: William B. Eerdmans, 1986), 96–97.

40. See George R. Knight, *From 1888 to Apostasy: The Case of A.T. Jones* (Hagerstown, MD: Review and Herald Publishing Assn., 1987), 83–84, 121–127.

41. White, *The Great Controversy*, 297; Knight, *From 1888 to Apostasy*, 127–131.

42. Ellen G. White, "Special Testimonies to Ministers and Workers," Series A, No. 3 (1895); Letter to S.N. Haskell, Jan. 30, 1895, in *Manuscript Releases* 16:157–166.

43. Ellen G. White, "The Kingdom of Christ," *Review and Herald* 33 (1896): 513.

13

Culture

Benjamin McArthur

WHEN ELLEN GOULD Harmon entered the world in November 1827, Charles Finney was carrying his fervent evangelistic efforts into the burgeoning cities of the East. Finney's successful endeavors helped define the Second Great Awakening. Ellen Harmon's formative years thus coincided with evangelical Christianity's imprint on American culture. She came of age assuming a religious culture that was socially dominant, indeed still unchallenged by the later appeals of mass culture.

When Ellen G. White died in July 1915, the Great War in Europe had been raging nearly a year. The self-assurance of Western Civilization had taken a hit (though the United States was yet to feel the brunt of barbarism's outbreak). More tellingly, that year witnessed the appearance of the final slim volumes of *The Fundamentals*. This influential series of popular theology, inaugurated in 1910, announced a new religious impulse: Protestant Fundamentalism. White's final years saw an American Christianity no longer abuzz with anticipation of success but instead frantic about ways to neutralize the corrosive acids of higher criticism, evolution, and liberal theology in general. A mid-nineteenth-century America idealized by John Greenleaf Whittier verse and Currier & Ives prints had clearly given way to an emerging mass society characterized by O. Henry stories and Art Nouveaux posters. Ellen White's America was changing almost beyond recognition.

The ten decades of White's life witnessed the evolution of an urban and commercialized culture that increasingly defined America. Americans threw themselves enthusiastically into sports and commercial entertainments of many sorts. Christians were not immune to these enticements, as the enthusiastic embrace of sports at Battle Creek College and the Avondale school in Australia testified. White never came to terms with what in her mind was cultural declension. Thus, among the essential functions in her mature ministry was securing her church family against an abundance of secular temptations. In the process she also shaped a set of Adventist attitudes about recreation and culture that endured for decades.

White was raised a Methodist. This historical accident had huge implications for the future of Adventism. The distinctives of that religious subculture were, through White, firmly imprinted on emerging Adventism. Methodism sought sanctified perfection for its members. Accomplishing this meant avoiding those popular songs, stories, and most forms of commercial entertainments that could only serve to degrade minds. Fiction of any sort remained suspect through much of the nineteenth century. In 1877 the Methodist *Discipline* implemented an amusement ban that threatened reproof—or even expulsion—for attending such amusements as the theater. Idealized Methodist culture also stressed the possibilities of every moment. Even times of relaxation, the *Methodist Quarterly Review* (*MQR*) advised, should be made "tributary to our mental and moral improvement" (what the Puritans had earlier termed "redeeming the time").[1]

The anxiety-ridden rhetoric of the *MQR* and of Ellen White could at times be indistinguishable. An "appetite for fiction," one Methodist writer penned, may become "more and more craving, and finally so morbid that it requires the abominable trash which corrupts and blasts whatever it touches." Compare this to White's admonition: "If you have been in the habit of reading storybooks, will you consider whether it is right to spend your time with these books, which merely occupy your time and amuse you, but give you no mental or moral strength? If you are reading them, and find that they create a morbid craving for exciting novels, if they lead you to dislike the Bible, and cast it aside, if they involve you in darkness and backsliding from God,–if this is the influence they have over you, stop right where you are."[2]

The point is not to attribute literary influence but rather to grasp a shared sensibility. White carried into emerging Adventism a thorough-going moralism that was shaped by culturally middle-brow Methodism. This can be seen most directly in her subscription to the *Ladies' Repository*. This mid-nineteenth-century women's magazine, founded and edited by Methodist Bishop Leonidas Hamline, sought to provide cues for a life of enhanced sophistication while remaining safely within acceptable religious bounds.[3]

The Methodist community, older and more established than Adventism, typified American upward mobility and cultural accommodation. The more comfortable among them patronized resorts at Saratoga or Long Branch, and a few even ventured to Europe. This desire for refinement, what one historian has called "consecrated respectability," was reflected in the pages of the MQR. In the latter half of the nineteenth century arguments in favor of quality literature began to be seen, even attempting, according to literary scholar John O. Waller, "a theoretical groundwork for a Christian esthetic of prose fiction criticism."[4]

But Ellen White and her Adventist community expressed little concern with wedding gentility to piety. Adventists had traveled fewer miles down the path of "Culture." They remained a largely small-town and agrarian people of modest education. Their cultural suspicions more resembled those of the emerging Pentecostal tradition (though the latter's adherents were probably even more adamant in their forsaking the world's cultural allures). Further, White did not bow–nor would she ever–to the strenuous demands made by Victorian arbiters of taste on those who sought an aura of refinement. Dilettantism had no part in a people with eyes set firmly on impending last days. Cultural uplift for its own sake was a hollow distraction. In any event, the limitations of White's education precluded sophisticated aesthetic taste. She would not read Henry James; she quite possibly never heard of him.[5]

Ellen White on the Arts

The Advent movement was born amidst the Dionysian impulses of the Burned-over District. Apocalyptic visions, religious frenzies, and subsequent public disrepute characterized the various forms of Ultraism in antebellum America. Such upheaval would seem fertile soil in which art could flourish, giving creative expression of the divine order. For the Shaker and Mormon traditions, this seems to have been true. But for Seventh-day Adventism, one of the most enduring religious movements to emerge from this time, no artistic tradition developed (music partly excepted). How do we explain this? In part, at least, one must look to the influence of the church's prophet, Ellen White.

White held a utilitarian view of the arts. They were to be useful either in cultivating spirituality and moral discernment or in inculcating values such as hard work and thriftiness that promoted success. There was no place for mere aestheticism or amusement. She wrote considerably more about literature than about music or the plastic arts. This may be because she was herself a writer. She also had more exposure to writers than to the efforts of painters, sculptors, or musicians. And words conveyed ideas more directly than did the other arts. There seemed more at stake with written works, both for good and ill. "Novel and story-book reading are the greatest evils in which youth can indulge. Novel and love-story readers always fail to make good, practical mothers," she wrote. "They are dwarfed in intellect, although they may flatter themselves that they are superior in mind and manners."[6] This statement of White's (the likes of which could fill many pages) captures her prevailing tone and message regarding literature: a tendency toward absolute–even hyperbolic–statements ("the greatest evils," "always fail," "dwarfed in intellect") and an unremitting stress on moral danger. For reasons discussed below, she returned to fiction's dangers again and again, particularly in regard to the proper education of children. Perhaps no other of her admonitions became more thoroughly ensconced in Adventism than this one.

What were her primary objections? First, fiction makes addictive readers unfit for life, seeking as they do romance and thrill rather than reality and the quiet pleasure of real accomplishment. Second, it carries direct hazards to mental and physical health. "The memory is greatly injured by ill-chosen reading, which has a tendency to unbalance the reasoning powers, and to create nervousness, weariness of the brain, and prostration of the entire system." (White held a view of the mind that posited a finite amount of memory capacity; too much knowledge of any sort will fill it up. For her, "Much less information with a mind well disciplined, would be of far greater value.") Third, even useful moral lessons from literature, such as might be afforded by classical writers, require too much dredging through "superstition, specious reasoning, and error." "Why should we wade through the mass of error contained in the works of pagans and infidels, for the sake of obtaining the benefit of a few intellectual truths, when all truth is at our command" (in Scripture)? And, finally, the artificial excitement of romance causes the Bible to pale. "My dear young friends ... do you not find the Book of God uninteresting? The charm of that love story is upon the mind, destroying its healthy tone, and making it impossible for you to fix the attention upon the important, solemn truths that concern your eternal welfare."[7]

Twenty-first-century readers who find these comments extreme should recall the cultural backdrop against which they were penned. America was experiencing a revolution in publishing. The end of the nineteenth century witnessed the new power of the steam press and the creation of a national reading market that elicited an outpouring of popular fiction. Dime novels were the best known products of the day: westerns, romances, and adventures that were printed and purchased in the hundreds of thousands. Weekly and monthly fiction magazines further fed the hungry maw of an enlarged urban populace. In fairness, some well-known works appeared alongside the ephemera, including such religious best-sellers as Lew Wallace's *Ben Hur* and Henryk Sienkewicz's *Quo Vadis*. But, on balance, one must judge the outpouring of fiction as a gush of formulaic pap, the nineteenth-century predecessor to the inanities of multi-channel cable TV programming of the next century.[8]

Thus, when White wrote that much of her day's reading "like the frogs of Egypt, are overspreading the land," and are "not merely commonplace, idle, and enervating, but unclean and degrading," she was exaggerating only in the last two adjectives. Nor was she alone in her condemnation. Christian moralists widely shared her opinion. Few expressed the outrage more colorfully than T. DeWitt Talmage, popular pastor of a Brooklyn church and a leading Christian controversialist. "The longest rail train that ever ran over the Erie or Hudson tracks," he wrote in 1888, "was not long enough nor large enough to carry the beastliness and the putrefaction which have been gathered up in bad books and newspapers of the land in the last twenty years."[9]

But if White's writings could not match the rhetorical flourishes of Talmage, she was perhaps even more categorical in her judgments. Talmage, like most educated Christian writers of his age, respected the potential of great writing. "There are novels that are pure, good, Christian, elevating to the heart," he admitted. No such concession came from White, whose resistance to the genre was unremitting, a salient so critical to the Advent war against the diversions of modern culture that it could not be surrendered.[10]

Even so, White's practice was more complex than her statements would suggest. Beginning in the 1850s she began compiling large scrapbooks of stories, brief homilies, and interesting scraps of information about science, health, and history from religious periodicals. These were originally for her children's edification. But in the mid-1870s she and husband, James, saw wider possibilities for them. They soon produced a series of twenty small volumes, each just sixteen pages between colored paper covers. These were advertised by the church's press at two cents each for children ages five to twelve. The stories blended moralism with exhortations to work and thriftiness, typifying the moral economy of Victorian youth literature. But this was only the beginning. A more ambitious four-volume series, *Sabbath Readings for the Home Circle,* followed over the next few years. These were substantial volumes, each around four hundred pages, the early volumes for youth, the last one appealing to more adult tastes. Care was taken to avoid "anything of a sectarian or denominational character" so that a broad Christian market might be reached (the project was undertaken partly to boost the newly established Pacific Press).[11]

By testimony of her husband, Ellen White made all the selections. And significantly, all the stories appear to be fictional. Not that White ever used the "f" word; she preferred the more neutral "story." But there is little question that despite White's many animadversions against fiction, she had no scruples about recommending a certain type as an appropriate Sabbath-afternoon activity. To the Whites, these homely tales (which "will inculcate principles of obedience to parents, kindness and affection to brothers and sisters and youthful associates, benevolence to the poor, and the requirements of the gospel") had nothing in common with fiction as they knew it. Although she never made the analogy explicit, White probably viewed the stories much like biblical parables, containing truths that transcended facticity. What the Adventist public believed about the stories cannot be known. Readers likely assumed that if their prophet was involved, factual authenticity was assured.[12]

White had rather less to say about music and the visual arts. Her comments on music were generally more nuanced and positive than those about literature. White understood music to be part of the core of worship. "Music was made to serve a holy purpose, to lift the thoughts to that which is pure, noble, and elevating," she rhapsodized, "and to awaken in the soul devotion and gratitude to God." She found scriptural warrant for her opinion, citing the Israelites' experience as they prepared to enter Canaan, singing "the songs that had cheered the wilderness wandering." In an extra-scriptural insight, she even described the joyful singing of young Jesus. While acknowledging that good music could be "a blessing," she worried that Satan often made it one of his "most attractive agencies to ensnare souls," thus turning it into "a terrible curse."[13]

Adventists, firmly in the Protestant tradition, were from their beginning people of the word. Representations of divinity seemed uncomfortably close to violation of the Second Commandment; religious art of any sort smacked of Catholicism. When evangelical Protestant churches began seeking through the various arts a common religious culture for America, Adventists resisted, seeing in this another example of mainstream apostasy. During White's travels about Europe in 1885, she took the opportunity to visit both Versailles and some cathedrals. The magnificence of the Milan Cathedral especially impressed her. "I never saw such a gorgeous combination of colors," she marveled. But it was, finally, a monument to idolatry. Nonetheless, Adventist church leaders early discovered the power of iconography, most clearly, of course, in prophetic charts. Acceptable art taught religious truth.[14]

Something of a turning point in the Adventist embrace of art came in the early 1870s when medical pioneer Merritt G. Kellogg brought to James White's attention an allegorical illustration called *The Way of Life*. The busy composition presented the story of man's fall and redemption. "Read" from left to right, it showed Adam and Eve being driven from the Garden with the coming of sin, the ceremonial sacrifices of the Old Testament, Jesus and the disciples, the Cross, and future glory. It conveyed the "Great Controversy" in a nutshell. James White saw an opportunity. Currier & Ives lithographs, which became in these decades the very definition of middle-class domestic art, included some prints with religious themes. Should not Adventism find its own visual voice for church members' homes and for evangelistic use? Thus began an interesting publication history. First appearing in 1874, *The Way of Life: From Paradise Lost to Paradise Restored* went through several renderings, which tell of both a new awareness of art's legitimacy and of important theological development in Adventism. The original sketch put the Ten Commandments front and center, dwarfing the Cross, reflecting Adventism's early stress on the persistence of God's law (Figure 13.1). But in the early 1880s James reconsidered the emphasis. He traveled to New York City in 1881 to commission Thomas Moran, one of America's leading artists (best known for his heroic landscape canvases) to redesign the illustration. James died before the project could be concluded, but Ellen saw it to completion. Now titled *Christ the Way of Life*, Moran's rendition has Christ on the Cross dwarfing all other details (Figure 13.2). Ellen White's new theological emphasis on Christ's work and God's love for mankind found pictorial statement well before her major work on the life of Jesus, *Desire of Ages* (1898), appeared in print. Thousands of copies of the various versions were engraved.[15]

FIGURE 13.1 *The Way of Life: From Paradise Lost to Paradise Restored* was designed by James White in 1876, and it reflects Adventist emphasis in the 1870s on the centrality of God's law (Courtesy of the Center for Adventist Research, Andrews University).

FIGURE 13.2 In 1881 James White commissioned the well-known American artist Thomas Moran to produce this print, *Christ the Way of Life*. It was published in 1883, two years after James's death, and Ellen White owned the copyright (Courtesy of the Center for Adventist Research, Andrews University).

Historian David Morgan sees *The Way of Life* series as bespeaking an important moment in Adventist artistic as well as theological sensibilities. James White, cash-strapped as always, was willing to pay $1,100 to Moran to obtain the engraved plate. In the "Key," which accompanied the purchased illustration, James White wrote, "when Art is employed in the fulfillment of her Heaven-born mission," it is "of heavenly origin" and becomes "a benefactor of mankind." A "tidal change" in Adventist use of art was under way, Morgan notes. Ellen White and her church were having to come to terms with the fact that America was becoming a "visually rich print culture." Adventism began adapting its methods to appeal to "the theatrical illusionism so much a part of twentieth-century popular culture." In the 1890s illustrated editions of White's books began to appear, though she remained conflicted about this development. On the one hand, she objected to any poor-quality art, thinking it demeaned her message; on the other hand, she fretted that illustrations were driving up the price of her books, making them less accessible to some. In one extreme example, an 1899 morocco leather-bound edition of *The Great Controversy* was issued for $7.00 (about $194.00 in 2013 dollars).[16]

Ellen White on Recreation

As with the arts, recreation had the potential for good or ill. Ellen White herself was not one for vigorous outdoor recreation; nor did she attend concerts (save the occasional religious performance at a school), the theater, sporting events, or other commercial amusements of the day, which she avoided on principle. For relaxation, she sought periodic rest in country retreats, enjoyed outdoor walks and an afternoon in a comfortable chair in the sunshine. One might even say she partook of early American tourism through her many cross-country train journeys and travels to Europe and Australia. But her priorities were always clear: life was serious, the end of time was near, and recreation was purely instrumental. White held firmly to the medieval origin of the word. "Recreation" was to refresh or cure. "When true to its name, re-creation, tends to strengthen and build up," she noted. To this end she exhorted members of her Adventist community to provide their children with "innocent recreation, to lead them in pleasant paths where there is no danger." Family outings were essential. "Parents should become children with their children. . . . Let the whole day be given to recreation." The criterion for proper amusements, then, was the degree to which they restored the Christian to full powers for the urgent work at hand.[17]

In her predisposition toward rural, outdoor recreation, Ellen White shared a Jeffersonian impulse that powerfully affected American culture. The inexorable urban and industrial landscape toward which America marched was matched by a nostalgic longing for earlier, simpler times. "In this age life has become artificial, and men have degenerated," White concluded, a judgment that the sage of Monticello himself might have penned had he survived another 70 years. White imagined instead an ideal that reached back to biblical times. "In early ages, with the people who were under God's direction, life was simple. They lived close to the heart of nature. Their children shared in the labor of the parents and studied the beauties and mysteries of nature's treasure house." It was God's "design that we shall be happy in the charms of nature."[18]

Anything else, mere "amusements," was a diversion—or worse. The worse included virtually all forms of theatricals. For her, theaters ranked "among the most dangerous resorts for pleasure." Rather than being a school for morality, White saw the theater as "the very hotbed of immorality. Vicious habits and sinful propensities are strengthened and confirmed by these entertainments. Low songs, lewd gestures, expressions, and attitudes deprave the imagination and debase the morals. Every youth who habitually attends such exhibitions will be corrupted in principle." The theater in Shakespeare's metaphorical sense as a stage for the enactment of the cosmic drama, however, appealed to White. "The world is a theater," she wrote; "the actors, its inhabitants, are preparing to act their part in the last great drama." But commercial entertainments of most kinds—circuses, billiards, dance halls, saloons, the usual suspects of the religious community—were not to be considered. So far as we know, White never witnessed a commercial theatrical, which may have contributed to her hyperbole. But her stridency also came from living the final decades of her life during a time of explosive growth in American theatricals, including vaudeville, the legitimate stage as well as the new motion pictures. These cultural threats to religious values were clear.[19]

A sense of apocalyptic urgency could not well coexist with the multiplying amusements tempting Adventist youth. Ellen White's reputation within Adventism as an opponent of sports and games is well earned. Her counsel was pointed, and it was repeated across the decades in many compilations. One should "shun the false and artificial, discarding horse racing, card playing, lotteries, prize fights, liquor drinking, and tobacco using." Chess and checkers also came in for disapproving comment: "Heaven condemns them."[20]

Participatory sports, though, would seem to be in a different category, combining exercise and the outdoors. Why did they likewise earn White's disapprobation? Because of the overwhelming threat she perceived in them. Context is everything here. The late nineteenth century witnessed the greatest profusion of organized spectator sports since the days of Rome. As Americans left the farms for the cities their need for periodic release from the confinements of city life found various outlets. Professional baseball and college football were the most prominent of the many sports Americans watched and played. The twenty-first-century American baseball fan, used to gleaming ball parks and middle-class family attendance, would have difficulty imagining the male-dominated, hard-drinking, profane atmosphere of nineteenth-century venues. And today's college football players, though faster, larger, and capable of even harder hits, enjoy protective equipment that their counterparts of a century past never knew. There were a handful of deaths each year in college football, a mayhem so scandalous that President Theodore Roosevelt threatened to ban the game. Ellen White perceived Satan's hand in all this: "He has invented sports and games, into which men enter with such intensity that one would suppose a crown of life was to reward the winner."[21]

The passion for sport infected the fledgling Adventist colleges. The boys of Battle Creek College organized a school football team in 1893 and began playing other Michigan college teams. A rah-rah spirit pervaded the campus. When word of this reached Ellen White in Australia, she sent a message to college leaders: Students "act as if the school were a place where they were to perfect themselves in sports, as if this was an important branch of their education. . . . This is wrong from beginning to end." Throughout the decade other Adventist colleges confronted student bodies clamoring for organized sports. From Union College in Nebraska came complaints about the nonsensical cheers set up by spectators. The Keene Institute (Texas) broom-shop manager fretted to her that football and baseball were luring away his workers. Where were the watchmen, White sadly asked in response, when these "unseemly games and athletic sports" were occurring?[22]

But athletic trouble was also brewing right in White's backyard of Australia (where she spent most of the 1890s). Students at young Avondale College shared the proverbial national passion for sports. A Founder's Day afternoon picnic included organized games of cricket and tennis. White, who had just that morning delivered an address to students and faculty about their high calling, was severely dismayed. School leaders were rebuked for encouraging a "species of idolatry," where the forces of the enemy gained a decided victory, and God was dishonored. In this case, school leaders became defensive, feeling that White had overreacted to innocent games. But in the end they submitted to the "voice of prophecy" among them.[23]

What would she have them do for fun? Students needed breaks from their studies, she conceded. "I do not condemn the simple exercise of playing ball," she wrote. But she would have preferred youth to find their need for physical exertion in a manual-labor program. Let "useful employment take the place of selfish pleasure."[24] Indeed, she carried a larger concern that games were going to interfere with the structured manual labor that she deemed an important part of education. White may have been guilty of confusing the impulse to play, so strong in the young, with the sheer physicality of hard work. She had put tremendous effort into the creation of Avondale as a model Adventist school. To see its young charges so soon capering about the playing fields was akin to Moses's finding his people dancing before a golden calf the moment he descended from the mount.

Casting a Long Shadow

What difference did Ellen White's writings on culture make to the Adventist community then or now? One cannot quantify such influence, but historical testimony and personal observation based on involvement in the community suggest it was considerable. This should not be surprising. Her admonitions about the arts and recreation were aimed at a fellowship that already shared her inclinations. New members largely came from other Christian traditions with similar strictures, and much of rural or small-town America, the source of most Adventists then, was outside the orbit of intensive commercial entertainments (one recalls the whiff of scandal that a threatened pool hall brought to Meredith Willson's imaginary River City).[25] In short, White reinforced cultural standards, which, while weakening and often honored in the breach, nonetheless continued to enjoy resonance in the memory of many Americans. Certainly other emerging American religious traditions, such as the Holiness and Pentecostal churches, would find much in common.

But what differentiated Adventism under White's influence from its nearest religious kin, the Methodists, was the former's lack of structured debate over cultural matters. White was, after all, a prophet, and in matters of behavior her words carried unique sanction. By contrast, the Methodist sub-culture was becoming more socially assimilated. Its church leaders, unrestrained by an oracular presence, carried on lively debates over church standards. For several decades general conference sessions occasioned discussion of how specific the *Discipline* should be regarding unacceptable behavior. The 1872 *Discipline* for the first time enumerated a list of activities the devout should avoid: "dancing, playing at games of chance, attending theaters, horse races, circuses, dancing parties, or patronizing dancing schools, or taking such other amusements as are obviously of misleading or questionable moral tendency." But even from the beginning there were some in church leadership who felt this behavioral labeling was wrong-headed, undermining the sort of moral reasoning a mature Christian should nurture. It was "a grave blunder of ecclesiastical legislation," one Methodist divine wrote. Yet the moralist party successfully warded off change in the *Discipline*. "If the theater is an evil institution," wrote Henry Brown, "if it is degrading in its influence, hurtful to society, and an enemy to the Church of Christ" ("gilded nastiness" in the creative phrase of another churchman), why should prohibitions against it not continue? Not until 1924, during that secular, culturally rebellious decade, would the amusement ban be lifted, a concession no doubt to the changing practice of too many members.[26]

To say that no respected voice within Adventism demurred from Ellen White's counsel on arts or recreation is not to say that behavior always followed. Collegiate youth loved their sports; other Adventists no doubt read novels, attended plays, or found the popular syncopated rhythms of ragtime enticing. But to enjoy the forbidden fruit of modern literature in the quiet of one's home was one thing, to indulge in the very public act of theater or cabaret attendance quite another. Adventism was marked for much of its history by a high degree of adherence to those recreational behavioral norms defined by Ellen White. The enforcement of such norms proceeded through the informal but powerful system of peer influence, beginning with the socialization that took place in the expanding elementary, secondary, and collegiate school system.

The very insistence with which *Review and Herald* editors approached the subject of amusements suggests that temptations persisted. Pastor William P. Pearce wrote two lengthy diatribes in 1902 against card playing and theater. Both were heavily adorned with quotations by notables of the Western tradition, from Plato to John Milton to Joseph Addison, against the reckless misspending of time. The appeal to such writers rang ironic, given that nothing in the Adventist tradition encouraged lending credence to the classics. Indeed, even after other cultural prohibitions attenuated, anti-intellectualism persisted. White's lack of education and narrow religious concerns encouraged a disengagement of Adventism from the world of culture and ideas. She repeatedly warned against sitting at the feet of those "exalted as the world's educators." Individuals turning to them were "in danger of accepting the vile with the precious."[27]

Two things remain notable about Ellen White's influence on Adventist attitudes toward popular culture: how long her influence persisted and, once slippage began, how quickly her influence dissipated. Through much of the twentieth century her counsel retained prescriptive force. Socialization of Adventist youth included warnings of dangers in fast music and all theatricals (though oddly the sanctions were greater against movies than live theater). The teaching of fiction in denominational schools remained circumspect. As late as the mid-1970s the issue remained so vexing that Adventist English scholars collaborated on a large work dedicated to defining a proper place for literature in education. Five of the fourteen chapters dealt directly with White's statements on fiction. A veteran Adventist scholar counseled caution in assigning literature to students. "The deep convictions and the souls of our students are involved." In music a similar story was seen. In 1972 the General Conference of the Seventh-day Adventist Church, troubled by the growing presence of popular musical idioms in worship services, organized a Task Force on the Philosophy of Music. This blue-ribbon committee of musicians and church officials began their work with a thorough review of Ellen White's comments on music. Her statements on "Desirable Qualities" and "Undesirable Qualities" helped shape the task force's conclusions. Given the strident debates in Adventism about the probity of drums or guitars in worship, Ellen White's words about the "bedlam of noise" at the 1900 Indiana camp meeting and her comment that "Satan works amid the din and confusion of such music" were a godsend to traditionalists within the denomination, who wished to drive out any hint of folk or rock influence.[28]

But the floodgates opened during the last quarter of the century. In the mysterious ways of cultural change, prophetic sanction lost its force, save for the most conservative elements of the church. Bans on movie attendance fell (never formally, simply through disregard); indeed, Adventist colleges began film programs, graduating students who found jobs in the Hollywood industry. Contemporary—even provocative—works of fiction began appearing in college literature syllabi. Popular music of every genre made its way into academy and collegiate performances. Courses on twentieth-century art and tours of leading galleries became part of college curricula. And in the realm of sports, a long-standing and principled refusal to participate in inter-varsity athletic leagues gave way to small but ambitious programs at both the secondary and collegiate level, some of them offering athletic scholarships.

These changes were never described as repudiations of White's counsel. Rather, they were couched in terms of seeking the principles behind the message. Competitive sports were acceptable so long as notions of a healthy, balanced life and sportsmanship were emphasized. Cinema could be redeemed as a useful medium for propagating a Christian message to contemporary society. Literature was upheld as a window into the mind of an age, critical for Christian understanding of the world it confronts. Adventism had moved into a new age, more attuned to society. But if Ellen White's influence in matters of culture was severely compromised, it was not effaced. And while her admonitions no longer carried their original prescriptive authority, they nonetheless could be appreciated for their pointed critique of the recreational and artistic blandishments of an emerging mass society.

NOTES

1. John O. Waller, "The Methodist Quarterly Review and Fiction, 1818–1906," *Bulletin of the New York Public Library* 71 (1967): 575–76; Benjamin McArthur, *Actors and American Culture, 1880–1920* (Philadelphia: Temple University Press, 1984), 130–31.

2. Waller, "The Methodist Quarterly Review," 581, quoting the *MQR*; Ellen G. White, "Danger of Reading Fiction and Infidel Books," *Youth's Instructor* 32 (1884), 145–46, in Ellen G. White, *Fundamentals of Christian Education* (Nashville, TN: Southern Publishing Assn., 1923), 92.

3. Kathryn T. Long, "Consecrated Respectability: Phoebe Palmer and the Refinement of American Methodism," in *Methodism and the Shaping of American Culture*, ed. Nathan O. Hatch and John H. Wigger (Nashville, TN: Kingswood Books, 2001), 294.

4. William Warren Sweet, *Methodism in American History*, rev. ed. (Nashville, TN: Abingdon Press, 1954), 336–37; Nathan O. Hatch, "The Puzzle of American Methodism," in *Methodism and the Shaping of American Culture*, 36; Long, "Consecrated Respectability," 281; Waller, "Methodist Quarterly Review and Fiction," 586.

5. On Pentecostalism's responses to culture, see Grant Wacker, *Heaven Below: Early Pentecostals and American Culture* (Cambridge, MA: Harvard University Press, 2001), 124–25, 128–29.

6. Ellen G. White, *Testimonies for the Church*, 9 vols. (Mountain View, CA: Pacific Press, 1948), 3:152 (Testimony 22, 1872).

7. White, *Testimonies*, 4:497-8 (Testimony 29, 1880); Ellen G. White, "Books in Our Schools," *Advent Review and Sabbath Herald* 44 (1891): 527–28 (hereafter referred to as *Review and Herald*), reprinted in White, *Fundamentals of Christian Education*, 171, 167; Ellen G. White, "What Shall We Read?" *Youth's Instructor* 50 (1902): 552, in Ellen G. White, *Messages to Young People* (Nashville, TN: Southern Publishing Assn., 1930), 273.

8. James D. Hart, *The Popular Book: A History of America's Literary Taste* (New York: Oxford University Press, 1950); John Wood, "The Trashy Novel Revisited: Popular Fiction in the Age of Ellen White," *Spectrum: Journal of the Association of Adventist Forums* 7 (April 1976): 16–24, hereafter referred to as *Spectrum*.

9. Ellen G. White, *Education* (Mountain View, CA: Pacific Press, 1903), 289–90; Thomas DeWitt Talmage, *Social Dynamite; or, The Wickedness of Modern Society* (Chicago: Standard Publishing, 1888), 172.

10. Talmage, *Social Dynamite*, 173. George R. Knight argues that White never formulated anything approaching a systematic view of literature in *Myths in Adventism: An Interpretive Study of Ellen White, Education, and Related Issues* (Hagerstown, MD: Review and Herald Publishing Assn., 1985), 153–74.

11. The story of the Golden Grain and Sabbath Readings for the Home Circle books is told by Arthur L. White in *Ellen G. White*, 6 vols. (Hagerstown, MD: Review and Herald Publishing Assn., 1981–1987), 3: 52–55.

12. In the mid-twentieth century L. W. Cobb wrote a pamphlet evidently widely circulated and now preserved in the White Estate arguing that all of the stories in the *Sabbath Readings* were factual; see his "Give Attendance to Reading," (n.p.: n.p.), 41. In contrast, John Waller concluded, first, that she could not have ascertained the veracity of most of the stories, and, second, that the form the stories took, relying on highly improbable coincidences, clearly partook of the sentimental melodramatic formula of the age; see Waller, "The Question of Fiction in Five Scrapbooks of Mrs. Ellen G. White," typescript, Ellen G. White Estate.

13. Ellen G. White, *Patriarchs and Prophets; or, The Great Conflict between Good and Evil, as Illustrated in the Lives of Holy Men of Old* (Oakland, CA: Pacific Press, 1890), 594 (holy purpose); White, *Education*, 142 (Israelites); Ellen G. White, *The Ministry of Healing* (Mountain View, CA: Pacific Press, 1905).

14. David Morgan's *Protestants and Pictures: Religion, Visual Culture and the Age of American Mass Production* (New York: Oxford University Press, 1999), explores these themes in depth. See also Malcolm Bull and Keith Lockhart,

Seeking a Sanctuary: Seventh-day Adventism and the American Dream, 2nd ed. (Bloomington: Indiana University Press, 2007), 238–39; and D. A. Delafield, *Ellen G. White in Europe* (Washington, DC: Review and Herald Publishing Assn., 1975), 229–30, 175–76.

15. A reproduction of *Christ the Way of Life* can be found in Morgan, *Protestants and Pictures*, 191. The first offering of the illustration appeared in *Review and Herald*, 43 (February 17, 1874).

16. Morgan, *Protestants and Pictures*, 195–97.

17. White, *Education*, 207; Ellen G. White, "Sabbath-School Reunion at Healdsburg, Cal.," *Review and Herald* 5 (1884): 74, reprinted in Ellen G. White, *The Adventist Home* (Nashville, TN: Southern Publishing Assn., 1952), 498, 501.

18. On the Jeffersonian influence, see Morton White, *The Intellectual versus the City* (New York: New American Library, 1962), chapter 2; White, *Education*, 211; Ellen G. White, "Christian Recreation," *Review and Herald* 21 (1886): 45, reprinted in White, *Adventist Home*, 502. Like Jefferson, whose advocacy of simple, agrarian values was frequently belied by his unacknowledged sybaritic tastes, White's apostrophes to rural simplicity failed to recognize how her resolute institution building would create a bureaucratized, urban church.

19. Ellen G. White, *Counsels to Parents, Teachers and Students Regarding Christian Education* (Mountain View, CA: Pacific Press, 1913), 327–28, reprinted in White, *Adventist Home*, 516; White, *Testimonies*, 8:27–29 (Testimony 36, 1904). The context of her statements within the larger religious community's posture toward theatricals can be found in McArthur, *Actors and American Culture*, chapter 5.

20. White, *Adventist Home*, 498–99.

21. Ellen G. White, "No Other Gods before Me," *Review and Herald* 37 (1901): 1.

22. White, *Ellen G. White*, 6: 374; Ellen White to F. Howe, May 21, 1895, Ellen G. White Estate.

23. White, *Counsels to Parents, Teachers and Students*, 350–51.

24. Ellen G. White, *Selected Messages*, 3 vols. (Washington, DC: Review and Herald Publishing Assn., 1958, 1980), 2: 322; White, *Counsels to Parents, Teachers and Students*, 354.

25. Meredith Willson, *The Music Man* (New York: G. P. Putnam Sons, 1958).

26. Henry Brown, *The Impending Peril; or, Methodism and Amusements* (Cincinnati: Jennings and Pye, 1904), 70, 222, 227; Karen B. Westerfield Tucker, *American Methodist Worship* (New York: Oxford University Press, 2001), 46.

27. William P. Pearce, "Do I Believe in Card-Playing?" *Review and Herald* 4 (1902): 50; William P. Pearce, "Facts and Fictions of the Theater," *Review and Herald* 17 (1902): 9; Ellen G. White, "Books in Our Schools," *Review and Herald* 44 (1891): 690, in White, *Fundamentals of Christian Education*, 171.

28. Robert Dunn, ed., "Seventh-day Adventists on Literature," typescript, Department of English, Loma Linda University, 1974; John O. Waller, "A

Contextual Study of Ellen G. White's Counsel Concerning Fiction," ibid., 61; "Music: Its Role, Qualities, and Influence, as Set Forth in the Writings of Ellen G. White," a compilation of materials assembled for the 1972 Task Force on the Philosophy of Music" (Takoma Park, MD: Ellen G. White Estate, 1972).

14

War, Slavery, and Race

Eric Anderson

BOTH ELLEN HARMON White's critics and her followers have distorted her statements about the American Civil War and its aftermath, including the issues of race and reunion that remained significant at her death in 1915. Too often her comments, assumptions, and expectations have been wrested from any appropriate historical context and conscripted into the service of such polemical purposes as proving either that she was a "false prophet" or a truly inspired one.

But a twenty-first-century historian might profitably begin the study of a nineteenth-century visionary by noticing where the official apologists and the angry heretics agree. They all assume, for example, that slavery and the Civil War were centrally important topics to Ellen White, as intrinsically important to her as to later observers. They agree that her credibility would be damaged if she could be shown to be a "racist" by today's standards. They are also sure that her role as a prophet and sectarian leader was built on prediction of the future, or, at least, unique insight into the events around her.[1] If she was really a prophet, by their assumptions, she should be expected to anticipate the course of events.

What she actually said about the American crisis presents a challenge to both her enemies and her defenders. Her strictly predictive writings turn out to be remarkably secondary to another objective—namely, instructing Adventist believers in their duty. Her commentary on the Civil War and slavery is, in fact, surprisingly spotty. She had nothing to say about the Fugitive Slave Law until nearly a decade after its enactment, when the law was already a dead letter in key areas of the North. Her private correspondence yields not a single reference to the name of Lincoln, a leader about whom the historian expects her to have definite and quotable opinions. After a flurry of comments about slavery and disunion between 1858 and 1863, she drops the subject, giving no evaluation of the Emancipation Proclamation, the employment of black troops, or the decisive victories of Grant and Sherman.[2] She does not return to the Civil War issues until the 1890s, when Adventist efforts to evangelize black southerners encountered ferocious opposition, compelling a mostly northern church to consider (belatedly) the troubling matter of ecclesiastical segregation. Once again, she offers little in the way of prediction.

If we put aside our ideas about what Mrs. White "should have said," and try to understand her world view on its own terms, perhaps we will be less surprised. We will find, I believe, a woman who was first and last a preacher of the second coming of Christ, an apocalyptic prophet who interpreted everything around her as a "sign of the times." She approached the War of the Rebellion and related matters not as an historical analyst or a political activist, but as an evangelist preaching the end of her world. Slavery, race, secession, and the war were important topics, to be sure, but subjects to be taken up or discarded as they helped to explain biblical prophecy and God's requirements for his faithful "remnant people." Her ideas about war, American nationality, "the Afro-American character and destiny" (to borrow George M. Fredrickson's phrase) were all shaped by the more fundamental matter of the mission of Seventh-day Adventism.[3]

Civil War

Ellen White's historical context is not easily recovered. Indeed, only a painstaking exercise of historical imagination can re-create her world, the Adventist world of the Civil War era. When Confederate artillery opened fire on Fort Sumter and its tiny Federal garrison in April 1861, there were few believers in "present truth"—no more than 4,000 Seventh-day Adventists in the entire world, almost all of them residing in the northern part of the United States. This group was not yet organized into a national denomination. The very name "Seventh-day Adventist" was new, the brethren having agreed upon it only eight months earlier.

These scattered believers were evolving into fully recognizable Seventh-day Adventists, but in crucial respects they were different from the species as it exists today. They were remarkably united, however, on their view of America, a nation they saw as rapidly declining from its original greatness, undone by the sin of slavery. As preacher J. H. Waggoner said, the nation's "*democratic* professions" were inconsistent with its "*slaveocratic* practices." Although the Adventists opposed slavery, at the same time they were certain that slavery would never be abolished, since, by their reading, the book of Revelation taught that slavery would exist at the time of the Second Coming. Uriah Smith, editor of the *Review and Herald*, took the unusual step of reprinting Lincoln's "House Divided" speech in 1858, but rejected Lincoln's views as hopelessly unrealistic: "He who looks for good, or hopes for reform in the legislative or executive departments of this government, is doomed, we think, to utter and hopeless disappointment." Ellen White's husband, James, accurately summarized the Adventist position in 1862: "For the past ten years the Review has taught that the United States of America were [sic] a subject of prophecy, and that slavery is pointed out in the prophetic word as the darkest and most damning sin upon this nation."[4]

Once the fighting began, Adventists expected the worst, believing that the conflict in the United States could well be the herald of earth's final crisis. "What then will be the end of these things?" asked Uriah Smith early in 1862, as the Army of the Potomac prepared for its spring offensive. "One of the two things must follow: either a continuation of our national difficulties, or a peace upon dishonorable and disgraceful terms." In his thinking, a clear victory for the Union was simply not a possibility.[5]

A few months later, as Northern armies were finally advancing on Richmond, J. H. Waggoner was equally glum. "As a question of rights," he wrote, the slaves were entitled both to freedom and an education that would "restore the capability" to properly use their rights. "In my opinion, education and gradual emancipation would be the best for all parties. But who has any hope for such a thing?"[6]

"The hope which animates others," wrote James White, "that the war will soon terminate with the freedom of the millions of 'bond-men and bond-women' of North America, and that a period of peace of millennial glory is to follow, we do not cherish." He proceeded to explain the Adventist understanding of Revelation, especially chapter six in which the prophet describes kings, mighty men, chief captains, bond-men and free men, all calling for the rocks and mountains to fall on them in the day of the Lord's wrath. "We think we see, though the prophetic word," explained White, "the continuation of slavery down to the end of all earthly governments." As White demonstrated that biblical prophecy predicted the continuation of slavery, his timing was unfortunate: President Lincoln had already decided to issue an emancipation proclamation. Indeed, a confidential draft of this document lay in the President's desk, awaiting a Union victory to be activated.[7]

Despite their condemnation of slavery, Adventists did not reject America. Even as they despaired of the future of the United States' experiment in democracy, they did not embrace an ideology that saw the nation as flawed from the start or inherently oppressive. Even in the darkest days of the Civil War, they believed that America had "the best government under heaven," and that, "with the exception of those enactments pressed upon it by the slave power, its laws are good." Like Lincoln, they saw the United States as the last, best hope of earth; unlike him, they were certain that the last hope was failing, that the nation was degenerate, rapidly departing from "the wisdom and virtue of its founders."[8]

Although they lamented the failure of the federal government to move immediately against slavery, Adventists' sympathies were, "as far as they are enlisted,...on the side of the government." The South's campaign for independence was simply a rebellion, "one of the most causeless and wicked that ever was incited," comparable to the "hellish rebellion" of Satan and his angels. With slight hyperbole James White declared: "We know of not one man among Seventh-day Adventists who has the least sympathy for secession."[9]

Such was the consensus among Adventists. There is no evidence that Ellen G. White deviated from this consensus. Indeed her visions and prophetic utterances served to confirm the judgments of her fellow believers about the providential significance of the Civil War. She placed a divine imprimatur on their insights that slavery was wrong, that the war was about slavery, and that the North's early missteps were based on a failure to act on these truths. Neither she, nor any other Seventh-day Adventist, expected the war to end in a "new birth of freedom" or a period of national prosperity, peace, and expansion.

Slavery

Like many other opponents of slavery, Ellen White focused her comments more on the sins of the slaveholders than on the aspirations of the enslaved. At times she so emphasized the damaging impact of slavery on black people that she risked dehumanizing them. As early as 1858, she blamed the owners of slaves for treating human beings as brutes, and creating circumstances in which slaves could not justly be held accountable for their moral choices. "I saw that the slave-master would have to answer for the soul of his slave whom he had kept in ignorance," she wrote, adding that the slave who was too ignorant of the Bible to be saved, would be "as though he had not been." But apparently not all slaves were so benighted. At the same time, she predicted that the "last call" would reach some slaves.[10]

In 1859, she urged Adventists to disobey the Fugitive Slave Law and "abide the consequences for violating this law." (Unlike Henry David Thoreau, however, she had no expectation that disobedience would bring about significant reform.) "The slave is not the property of any man," she declared. "God is his rightful master."[11]

Even before the opening guns of the war, in January 1861, she warned the Parkville, Michigan, congregation that the nation would endure a terrible war. She had seen in vision, she said, the marshaling of huge armies, followed by ferocious combat and families in "distress and anguish."[12] After the defeat at the first battle of Bull Run, she said: "God is punishing this nation for the high crime of slavery. He has the destiny of the nation in his hands. He will punish the South for the sin of slavery, and the North for so long suffering its overreaching and overbearing influence." Although some devout Christians explained the Union defeat as God's punishment for the North's initiating combat on Sunday, Ellen White insisted that the Northern armies had failed at Bull Run because God "would suffer no victories to be gained faster than He ordained." Indeed, if the Union forces had not panicked as the direct result of divine intervention, the defeat would have been worse.[13]

In a "testimony" published in pamphlet form in 1862, Mrs. White offered wide-ranging comments on the war, attributing most of her insights to specific visions.[14] "I was shown," "I saw," "This scene was presented before me," "I had a view," and similar expressions are sprinkled throughout her testimony. She asserted that the "accursed system of slavery," and it alone, lay "at the foundation of the war." Even if the North now succeeded in quelling the rebellion, she warned, it had not dealt with the central issue. "The system of slavery, which has ruined our nation, is left to live and stir up another rebellion."

"It seems impossible to have the war conducted successfully," she wrote, because so many Union leaders were proslavery. Accepting the assumptions (if not the prescriptions) of the Radical faction within the

Republican party, her comments on current events had a distinctly partisan flavor. Those who, like the war Democrats, wanted to preserve the Union but "despised" abolitionists, she described as "rebels at heart." Perhaps thinking of General George McClellan's scrupulous respect for the rights of slave masters, she strongly condemned those who denied freedom to runaway slaves or even "sent them back to their cruel masters."

No doubt her fellow Adventists recognized her references, direct and indirect, to recent events. She eloquently rejected, for example, the Lincoln administration's call for a day of fasting and prayer on Thanksgiving, 1861, as "an insult to Jehovah." Without naming the battle, she also referred to the embarrassing Union defeat on October 21, 1861 in the minor battle of Ball's Bluff, an event central to the Radical case that disloyal officers were weakening the war effort. After a small force under the command of General Charles Stone was repulsed with heavy loss, Congress created the Joint Committee on the Conduct of the War to investigate the humiliating failure, especially the death of a promising Republican officer, former Senator Edward Baker. Under a cloud of suspicion, General Stone was arrested and held in prison for six months.[15] The Adventist prophet referred to the incident by reminding her readers of the biblical story of Uriah: "Valuable men have thus been sacrificed to get rid of their strong antislavery influence. Some of the very men whom the North most need [sic] in this critical time, whose services would be of the highest value, *are not*. They have been wantonly sacrificed."

Ellen White offered little in the way of specific predictions. She did anticipate great and increasing distress, including famine and ultimately (after a "little time of peace") "strife, war, bloodshed, with famine and pestilence" that included "other nations." She expected the United States to be "humbled into the dust." She phrased most of her comments in contingent or qualified language: "It looked to me like an impossibility now for slavery to be done away." "Had our nation remained united it would have had strength, but divided it must fall." "When England does declare war, all nations will have an interest of their own to serve, and there will be general war, general confusion."[16] She did not foretell the outcome of particular battles or campaigns or identify crucial turning points.

If she seldom revealed the future in unmistakable clarity, she did have strong and definite counsel about the duty of Seventh-day Adventists, especially after a debate about military service broke out in the summer and fall of 1862. This debate was set off by James White's editorial "The Nation," which appeared in the August 12, 1862, issue of the *Review and*

Herald. Published at a low point in the Northern war effort, the editorial dealt with how Adventists should respond to the impending military draft. Although the fledgling denomination opposed slavery and secession, "our people have not taken that part in the present conflict that others have," White admitted. Adventists declined to volunteer, he wrote, because they believed that the Bible predicted that slavery would never be abolished. In addition, the Adventist affirmation of the "perpetuity and sacredness of the law of God" clashed with certain of the "requirements of war." It was not possible, he asserted, to serve as a soldier and yet obey the divine injunctions against Sabbath-breaking and killing.[17]

White moved onto controversial ground with his next statement, which proved to be the most explosive two sentences in the entire history of the official church publication: "But in the case of drafting, the government assumes the responsibility of the violation of the law of God, and it would be madness to resist. He who would resist until, in the administration of military law, he was shot down, goes too far, we think, in taking the responsibility of suicide." Although believers "might call into question" the policies of "our amiable president, his cabinet, or of military officers" (especially the decision to keep "the precious blacks" out of battle, while sending "the valueless white man" to "fall in battle by thousands"), they still had an obligation to honor "every good law of our land." Adventists had no need to flee the country "or stand trembling in their shoes for fear of a military draft," White concluded. Believers needed to trust in God's mighty power.[18]

In the intense discussion that followed, one reader declared that White's editorial had "grieved and astonished" him, leaving his faith "terribly shaken." The claim that the government bore the responsibility when a conscripted soldier violated God's law struck him as a "dangerous and untenable" position. If the government can "assume the responsibility now for the violation" of the fourth and sixth commandments, "and we go clear," he asked, "why may not the same government assume the responsibility...and we go clear" at the end of time when Adventists expected national legislation requiring Sunday worship.[19]

M.E. Cornell pithily summarized the Adventist consensus on the war: "The cause of the North is just, but there are too many Achans in the camp," a reference to Israel's defeat at Ai, caused by the secret disobedience of Achan (Joshua 7:10–26). Although he rejected an interpretation of "Thou shalt not kill" that forbade all warfare, he still objected to "voluntary service in this war," since soldiers could not keep the Sabbath and were exposed to corrupt "camp associations" such as swearing and card playing. Another reader insisted: "We should move in reference to the shortness of time.... We cannot now move as good Christians did in reference to the revolutionary war." If we really believe that "this generation" will witness "the fall and dissolution of all earthly governments," we will not act as if we expected an indefinite extension of "probationary time." Therefore, he fully endorsed White's editorial.[20]

A few Adventists were ready to move farther away from pacifism. One brother ready to fight was Joseph Clarke, a man who "almost fancied that the time might come when a regiment of Sabbath-keepers would strike this rebellion a staggering blow." Although his imagination was "full of Gideons, Jephthahs, and fighting Davids," even Clarke did not expect "the full destruction of slavery."[21]

In response to this controversy about conscription, Ellen White's leadership role—or her "role as a prophet" —was manifested most clearly. If her comments on the war had been neither original nor predictive, she now made unmistakably clear statements about the obligations of "God's people." Writing in early 1863, she began by noting "the dreadful state of our nation." The key issue for her was spiritual, not political or military. "The one all-important inquiry which should now engross the mind of everyone is: Am I prepared for the day of God?" She warned Adventists of the dangers of excess, repeatedly employing words such as "caution," "discretion," and "quiet," while rejecting "fanaticism" and agitation and indiscretion. Since their failure to volunteer made some people think that they were Rebel sympathizers, Adventists needed to be very quiet about "refusing to obey a draft." She counseled her fellow believers to let the denomination's "true sentiments in relation to slavery and the Rebellion to be made known." At the same time, she made it clear that Adventists should not volunteer to fight. "I was shown that God's people...cannot engage in this perplexing war, for it is opposed to every principle of their faith." Without specifically commenting on the debate about the sixth commandment and killing in war, she warned of worldly officers, and the "requirements of rulers" that conflict with the Ten Commandments.[22]

If volunteering for the Union Army was one extreme, the other was political sympathy with the South. Ellen White rebuked an Adventist from upstate New York for his "indiscreet course" in supporting the South and defending the institution of slavery. "Your views of slavery cannot harmonize with the sacred, important truths for this time. You must yield your views" or be expelled from the Advent fellowship, she warned.[23]

Her own political views remained resolutely Radical Republican, at least in analysis. She never went beyond what Jonathan Butler has described as "paper radicalism" to advocate diverting any time or money to campaigning for Republican politicians or legislation. It was too late for that. "Everything is preparing for the great day of the God," she wrote, and time would last only "a little longer." She thus interpreted the Democratic gains in the 1862 Congressional elections as the Radicals would: "Many were blinded and grossly deceived in the last election, and their influence was used to place in authority men who would wink at evil...who are Southern sympathizers, and would preserve slavery as it is." She continued to interpret Union military failure as the Radicals did, blaming highly placed "rebel sympathizers" and proslavery "professed Union men." In a claim with particular power for Adventists, she asserted that many Union generals were influenced by spiritualism, which she believed was Satanic. "These leading men" were often led to defeat, she said, by following the instructions of evil spirits posing as great warriors of the past.[24]

In a clear reference to the Union defeat at Second Bull Run (1862), she wrote: "In some cases when generals have been in most terrible conflict, where their men have fallen like rain, a reinforcement at the right time would have given them a victory. But other generals cared nothing how many lives were lost, and...withheld necessary aid, fearing that their brother general would receive the honor of successfully repulsing the enemy." As Ellen White's readers were likely to know, this was precisely the accusation against General Fitz-John Porter, who faced a court-martial after Second Bull Run for failing to obey orders. An admirer of McClellan and a proslavery Democrat, Porter had first taken little initiative to help John Pope, the blustery antislavery general who had superseded McClellan, and then moved slowly to obey direct orders. In private, both Porter and McClellan were pleased to see Pope discomfited.[25]

And there Ellen White left the subject. She could muster no optimism beyond this faint hope: "I saw that God would not give the Northern army wholly into the hands of a rebellious people, to be utterly destroyed by their enemies." After early 1863, she had nothing more to say about the nation's fiery ordeal. Having endorsed the emerging consensus that condemned both volunteering and Confederate sympathies, she left the details of dealing with the state and federal government to the brethren. As the scholarly John N. Andrews and others negotiated a legal exemption from combat for Adventist conscripts, she was silent. She had already moved on to other subjects, including health reform, dress reform, and wrong use of her testimonies.[26]

Race and Reconstruction

She did venture a strange, off-handed statement about race (or more precisely, races) in 1864 that has provoked considerable controversy ever since.[27] In the third volume of *Spiritual Gifts*, Ellen White retold the history of ancient Israel, as presented in Genesis and Exodus. In describing the crimes of antediluvian man, including idolatry, polygamy, and cruelty, she declared: "But if there was one sin above another which called for the destruction of the race [i.e., the human race] by the flood, it was the base crime of amalgamation of man and beast which defaced the image of God [in man], and caused confusion everywhere." In this intriguing statement, which stands without elaboration, her reference was to the human race in general. She added a second comment a few pages later, however, that applied to the post-Flood world and *races*: "Since the flood there has been amalgamation of man and beast, as may be seen in the almost endless varieties of species of animals, and in certain races of men."[28]

These statements provoked significant debate among Seventh-day Adventists, with critics charging that she believed Negroes were not human and defenders insisting that she meant no such thing. A strong Adventist consensus rejected theories of polygenesis (which asserted that some humans were not descendants of Adam and Eve), as well as any other religious or scientific justification for slavery.[29] Uriah Smith defended Mrs. White by noting that she was, after all, discussing "races of men," and therefore *human by definition*. At the same time he was certain that certain primitive groups were low "in the scale of humanity," mentioning "the wild Bushmen of Africa, some tribes of Hottentots, and perhaps the Digger Indians of our own country" as examples.[30] For Smith (and White), it should be noted, "race" was a looser term than it is in today's usage, which would not label a particular tribe or discrete ethnic group as a "race." Significantly, Smith did not mention the recently freed African Americans as an example of the lowest or most backward groups.

Ellen White no doubt knew what Smith was saying in her defense, and there is no evidence that she objected to it. It is reasonable, in fact, to assume that she agreed with him. For either Smith or White, the discovery of some particularly backward tribe, far from Battle Creek, would not justify American slavery or diminish the philanthropic and evangelistic obligations of Christians. In Smith's words, "What has the ancient sin of amalgamation to do with any race or people at the present time?" "Has any one a right," he asked, "to try to use it to their prejudice?"[31]

Neither the prophet nor other church leaders were changed greatly by the crisis of the house divided. In the light of a sweeping Union victory and the end of slavery, Adventists might have re-examined their interpretation of prophecy, their suspicion of political activism, and their certainty that their nation was rapidly declining. Instead, they reacted to the crises of Reconstruction much as they had to the conflicts of the Civil War.

As Andrew Johnson, in effect, broke diplomatic relations with the Republican party, and promoted his own mild form of Reconstruction, Adventist leaders hardly remained neutral. "The President is a rebel and traitor," declared the *Review and Herald* early in 1866. In the next issue, the editors continued to cite Republican denunciations of Johnson and even quoted a speech from the old abolitionist warrior, William Lloyd Garrison. At the same time the editors rejected direct political involvement, insisting that Adventists should "keep aloof from political matters." Although they might note "these commotions, as signs of the times," they should not "drink into their spirit," commented the *Review and Herald*, adding, "We are pilgrims and strangers here, and our citizenship is in a better country over which the Prince of Peace shall reign." Just before the autumn congressional elections, the church paper published an appeal from a sympathetic non-Adventist calling upon Adventists to join other Christians in opposing Johnson's dangerous policies. Editor Smith commented that he was "in sympathy with the sentiments it expresses," but emphatically rejected political action: "For our own part, we feel less and less inclined to have any connection with political matters."[32]

Ellen White returned to the issue of race only when it was necessary to do so. For a long time Seventh-day Adventists had virtually no black adherents. As late as the 1890s, there were "not over twenty colored Seventh-day Adventists south of Mason and Dixon's line." Then prompted by the prophet herself, Adventist evangelists (black and white) began a "mission to black America," with the result that by 1907 some 700 African Americans had become Adventists (out of a North American membership of roughly 60,000). She urged Adventists to develop schools for blacks in the South, including Oakwood Industrial School (Figure 14.1).[33]

The prophet's return to the subject came at a time of increasing white prejudice against black Americans. As Adventists (including Ellen White's

FIGURE 14.1 Ellen White at Oakwood Industrial School (now Oakwood University), a historically black Seventh-day Adventist institution in Huntsville, Alabama, that she helped found. She is flanked in the front row by her sons James Edson (on her right) and William C. (Courtesy of the Ellen G. White Estate, Inc.).

son Edson) sought to evangelize black southerners, the white South was moving to undo the achievements of Reconstruction.[34] By 1910 every Southern state had, by one method or another, disfranchised the vast majority of black voters and codified a system of radical racial segregation. There was little effective resistance from the federal government or northern public opinion. (Indeed, with the election of Woodrow Wilson in 1912, many of the leaders in this southern campaign against blacks came to national prominence.)

During the last years of Ellen White's life, shrill white fanatics commanded unprecedented attention and respect. A person could win elections or sell novels or pack lecture halls by insisting that blacks had no future in America, not even a rigidly segregated America, and that Negroes were a dangerous group steadily reverting to barbarism. In this unpromising context, Ellen White returned to her admonitions of the Civil War era, emphasizing both the degradation of "the colored race" and the duties of Adventists. "Though the colored people have been freed from political slavery, many of them are still in the slavery of ignorance and sin," she wrote. She described Christ and his angels weeping at the sight of "a people unable, because of their past slavery, to help themselves." If such language strikes a modern ear as infelicitous or "insensitive," her basic message distinctly rejected the Negrophobic excesses of her time. She had instruction from the Lord: Remember the colored people's "providential deliverance from slavery, their *common relationship to us by creation and redemption*, and their right to the blessings of freedom."[35]

In the last volume of her *Testimonies*, published in 1909, Mrs. White noted sorrowfully the existence of "strong prejudice against the Negro race," a hostile feeling that was "growing stronger and still stronger." Although she was clear in affirming that "the religion of the Bible recognizes no caste or color," she also insisted that "the time has not come for us to work as if there were no prejudice." The "problem of the color line" needed to handled differently "in different places and under varying circumstances," she wrote, noting that if northern practices were employed in the South, Adventist evangelism would be completely stifled. "No one is capable of clearly defining the proper position of the colored people," she said, adding: "So far as possible the color line question should be allowed to rest."[36]

She remained an apocalyptic preacher, quick to invoke phrases such as "we have no time now." She wrote, "While men are trying to settle the question of the color line, time rolls on, and souls go down into the grave, unwarned and unsaved." Adventists needed to act in light of the impending "time of trouble." Satan was trying to keep "Christians occupied in controversies among themselves." For the time being ("until the Lord shows us a better way"), "let as little as possible be said about the color line, and let the colored people work chiefly for those of their own race."[37]

As in the earlier case of the Civil War, her statements focused on current responsibilities rather than distant prospects. She did not foresee large-scale black migration to the North nor anticipate the ultimate restoration of black voting rights nor project the end of the Jim Crow system. She expected the radical racism of her day to grow "stronger as the Spirit of God" was "withdrawn from the world."[38] There is no hint in her writings on race that the black church would ever have a decisive role in undoing the southern system of 1910.

"Did Ellen White contradict herself?" Ronald D. Graybill asked in an important study published four decades ago. Written at a time when Seventh-day Adventists were coming to terms with the Civil Rights movement, *Ellen G. White and Church Race Relations* answered the question in the negative. Graybill emphasized the historical context of rising "racial tensions" to explain the shift from her 1891 statement ("You have no license from God to exclude the colored people from your places of worship") to her 1908 admonition ("the colored people should not urge that they be placed on an equality with white people").[39]

As far as it goes, his point remains valid. Placed in the appropriate context, Ellen White cannot accurately be described as a proslavery apologist, a polygenist thinker, a champion of Negrophobia, or a principled defender of segregation—all plausible options for some white religious leaders in her lifetime. True, she saw certain groups of people as backward and degraded, but that did make her a racist any more than W.E.B. DuBois, the black scholar-activist, was a racist when he declared in 1909 that the Sudan was a thousand years behind France in terms of cultural evolution.[40] She consistently refused to explain the ignorance and poverty of southern freedmen as the result of inherent inferiority, choosing instead to emphasize an oppressive environment and sinful discrimination.

Historians need to move beyond either iconoclasm or apologetics to understand that her words and actions on the Civil War and its aftermath, including the recurring debate over "the color line," had a larger context. Ellen White had little interest in "human theories" about the color line, American reform movements, or the political meaning of equality.[41] She was an *Adventist*, focused on the end of time and the Last Judgment above all else. Her leadership was not based on an ability to predict the future in detail, but to inspire action. She had a charismatic power to persuade readers and hearers that the "Blessed Hope" was more important than anything else.

NOTES

1. See, for example, John N. Loughborough, *The Great Second Advent Movement: Its Rise and Progress* (Washington, DC: Review and Herald Publishing Assn., 1909), 338–42; Dudley M. Canright, *The Life of Mrs. E. G. White, Seventh-day Adventist Prophet: Her False Claims Refuted* (Cincinnati: Standard Publishing Co., 1919), 233–43. Arthur L. White's official biography emphasizes the predictive element in his grandmother's comments on the Civil War; *Ellen G. White*, 6 vols. (Washington, DC: Review and Herald Publishing Assn., 1981–1986), 2:39, 46–47.

2. James White, in contrast, made a significant comment on emancipation and the successes of Generals Grant and Sherman; [James White], "Can God Work?" *Advent Review and Sabbath Herald* 25 (1865): 116; hereafter cited as *Review and Herald*.

3. George M. Fredrickson, *The Black Image in the White Mind: The Debate on Afro-American Character and Destiny, 1817–1914* (New York: Harper & Row, 1971).

4. J. H. Waggoner, "National Degeneracy," *Review and Herald* 12 (1858): 160–61; [Uriah Smith], "Republican Principles," ibid., 12 (1858): 126–27; [James White], "The Nation," ibid., 20 (1862): 84.

5. Uriah Smith, "Traitors in Power," *Review and Herald* 19 (1862): 77–78. Seventh-day Adventists were far from unique in describing the war in apocalyptic language. See Terrie Dopp Aamodt, *Righteous Armies, Holy Cause: Apocalyptic Imagery and the Civil War* (Macon, GA: Mercer University Press, 2002).

6. J. H. Waggoner, "Questions," *Review and Herald* 19 (1862): 182.

7. [White], "The Nation," 84, published on Aug. 12, 1862. Lincoln discussed the first draft of the Emancipation Proclamation with his cabinet on July 22, 1862. See Allen C. Guelzo, *Lincoln's Emancipation Proclamation: The End of Slavery in America* (New York: Simon and Schuster, 2004), 117–23.

8. [White], "The Nation," 84; Editorial, "The Degeneracy of the United States," *Review and Herald* 15 (1860): 132. See also Jonathan Butler, "Adventism and the American Experience," in *The Rise of Adventism: Religion and Society in Mid-Nineteenth Century America* ed. Edwin S. Gaustad (New York: Harper & Row, 1974), 185.

9. [James White], "Letter to Bro. Carver," *Review and Herald* 20 (1862): 167; [White], "The Nation," 84.

10. Ellen G. White, *Spiritual Gifts*, 4 vols. (Battle Creek, MI: James White, 1858–1864), 1:193–96.

11. Ellen G. White, *Testimonies for the Church*, 9 vols. (Mountain View, CA: Pacific Press, 1948), 1:202. After the war began, she wrote (ibid., 264): "The fugitive slave law was calculated to crush out of man every noble, generous feeling of sympathy that should arise in his heart for the oppressed and suffering slave."

12. Forty-five years later, Adventism's first chronicler, J. N. Loughborough, remembered that White had warned that some of those present in the Parkville meeting would lose sons, though there is no contemporary confirmation of this dramatic prediction. See Loughborough, *Great Second Advent Movement*, 338, 340.

13. Ellen G. White, "Communication from Sister White," *Review and Herald*, 18 (1861): 100–2; White, *Testimonies*, 1:266–67. For a response to the Sunday battles claim, see *Review and Herald* 20 (1862): 76. See also George C. Rable, *God's Almost Chosen Peoples: A Religious History of the American Civil War* (Chapel Hill: University of North Carolina Press, 2010), 78.

14. White, *Testimonies*, 1:253–60.

15. Recent scholars reject the charge that Stone was a traitor. See, e.g., Bruce Tap, *Over Lincoln's Shoulder: The Committee on the Conduct of the War* (Lawrence: University Press of Kansas, 1998), 55–79.

16. White, *Testimonies*, 1: 259–60, 266–68.

17. [White], "The Nation," 84.

18. Ibid.

19. Henry E. Carver, "The War," *Review and Herald* 20 (1862): 166–67.
20. M. E. Cornell, "Extremes," *Review and Herald* 20 (1862): 163; D. T. Bourdeau, "The Present War," ibid., 20 (1862): 154–55.
21. Joseph Clarke, "The War! The War!!," *Review and Herald* 20 (1862): 134.
22. White, *Testimonies*, 1:55–68.
23. Ibid., 1:359.
24. Butler, "Adventism and the American Experience," 187; White, *Testimonies*, 1:363. I know of only one Union general who had some interest in spiritualism: Ethan Allen Hitchcock. He had many conversations with spiritualist mediums and concluded that they were honest and were "assisted in some peculiar way." See his *Fifty Years in Camp and Field: Diary of Major-General Ethan Allen Hitchcock, U.S.A.*, ed. W. A. Croffut (New York: G. P. Putnam's Sons, 1909), 426, 484–86.
25. For the judgment of a careful modern scholar, see Tap, *Over Lincoln's Shoulder*, 166. Lincoln's view of the matter was similar to that of Ellen White's; see ibid., 153.
26. White, *Testimonies*, 1:365. On the wrong use of her testimonies, see ibid., 1:119–20, 1:327–29, 1:382–83, 1:369.
27. From opposite ends of the Adventist spectrum, two recent contributions to this discussion are T. Joe Willey, *A Beast in the Garden: Who Were the Confused "Races of Men" Created by Amalgamation of Man and Beast* ([Loma Linda, CA]: Aegis Group, 2009); David C. Read, *Dinosaurs–An Adventist View* (Keene, TX: Clarion Call Books, 2009). See also Ronald Osborn's judicious essay "True Blood: Race, Science, and Early Adventist Amalgamation Theory Revisited." *Spectrum*, 38 (Fall 2010): 16–29; and Chapter 11 of this book.
28. White, *Spiritual Gifts*, 3: 64, 75.
29. See [Uriah Smith?], "Negroes before Adam!," *Review and Herald* 17 (1861): 88, for an ironic comment on polygenesis.
30. Uriah Smith, *The Visions of Mrs. E. G. White: A Manifestation of Spiritual Gifts According to Scriptures* (Battle Creek, MI: Seventh-day Adventist Publishing Assn., 1868), 45–46.
31. Smith, *Visions of Mrs. E. G. White*, 45. Contrary to the claim of a later apologist, Francis D. Nichol, that her statement was meant to read "amalgamation of man and [of] beast," Ellen White never offered such an interpretation. See Nichol, *Ellen G. White and Her Critics* (Takoma Park, MD: Review and Herald Publishing Assn., 1951), 309.
32. Untitled Editorial, *Review and Herald* 27 (1866): 104 (rebel and traitor); William Lloyd Garrison, "The President's Motives and Aspirations," ibid., 112; Editorial, "The Country's Peril," ibid., 112; Ethan Lanphaer, "To the Seventh-day Adventist Brethren in the United States," ibid. 28 (1866): 146–47; [Uriah Smith], "Note," ibid., 147. Despite these emphatic repudiations of political involvement, some Adventist scholar-activists have striven to find in Ellen White and

other pioneers a more usable past; see, e.g., Douglas Morgan, *Adventism and the American Republic: The Public Involvement of a Major Apocalyptic Movement* (Knoxville: University of Tennessee Press, 2001).

33. White, *Testimonies*, 9:225; Gary Land, ed., *Adventism in America* (Grand Rapids, MI: William B. Eerdmans, 1986), 252.

34. Ronald Graybill, *Mission to Black America: The True Story of Edson White and the Riverboat Morning Star* (Mountain View, CA: Pacific Press, 1971).

35. White, *Testimonies*, 7: 222–23 (first published in 1902, emphasis added). On the extremists, see Joel Williamson, *The Crucible of Race: Black-White Relations in the American South since Emancipation* (New York: Oxford University Press, 1984).

36. White, *Testimonies*, 9: 213–15, 223. In a 1901 sermon to "the church for the colored in Vicksburg," White made the odd statement that "In heaven there will be no color line; for all will be as white as Christ himself." See Ellen G. White, "Trust in God," *Gospel Herald* 3 (1901): 22. T. Joe Willey kindly brought this statement to my attention.

37. White, *Testimonies*, 9: 206, 210–11, 216.

38. Ibid., 205.

39. Ronald D. Graybill, *Ellen G. White and Church Race Relations* (Washington, DC: Review and Herald Publishing Assn., 1970), 13–16, 117.

40. Eric Anderson, "Black Responses to Darwinism, 1859-1915," in *Disseminating Darwinism: The Role of Place, Race, Religion, and Gender*, ed. Ronald L. Numbers and John Stenhouse (Cambridge: Cambridge University Press, 1999), 250–51.

41. White, *Testimonies*, 9:213.

15

Gender

Laura Vance

FOUR YEARS AFTER her first vision, Ellen White attended a gathering of fifty sabbatarian Adventists with her husband, James. The group, a remnant of William Miller's millennial movement, discussed the nature of Ellen White's visions, which they determined were divine; and while in attendance at the conference, Ellen received a vision directing that James should commence printing a "little paper," which they titled *The Present Truth* and later the *Second Advent Review and Sabbath Herald*. In the same year, in Seneca Falls, New York, a group led by Lucretia Mott and Elizabeth Cady Stanton voted its support for the Declaration of Sentiments, which advocated the extension of rights to women—including property, marital, divorce, educational, and voting rights. While the gathering of sabbatarian Adventists attracted little attention, the Seneca Falls convention was widely noted and ridiculed in the press; Seneca Falls participants were accused of "unwomanly behavior" and the convention was called the "most shocking and unnatural incident ever recorded in the history of womanity."[1]

As a female religious leader writing in a cultural-historical context in which the prevailing ideology relegated women to the domestic realm, and in which women who participated in public work were denied access to positions of authority, Ellen White held a precarious position. If she promoted women's participation in socially proscribed roles too adamantly, she might be seen both as addressing the question of the legitimacy of her own leadership and as self-promoting. As a young prophet White had been subjected by her followers to physical tests of her authenticity, such as having heavy weights placed on her outstretched arms and being deprived of oxygen while in vision, something to which nineteenth-century male prophets such as John Humphrey Noyes, Joseph Smith, and others were not subjected. Adventist history indicates that God selected White as a prophet after other potential prophets failed in the task. Even James, Ellen's husband, demonstrated some reluctance early in the life of the movement to promote his wife's visions when between 1851 and 1855 he restricted their publication.[2] Unpublished, her visions dwindled until in 1855 sabbatarian leaders encouraged greater attention to White's visions and replaced James as editor of the *Review and Herald*. Never again would her visions be denied an audience or place of reverence among committed Adventists. Still, White left primary defense of her prophetic role to male religious leaders. Her apparent reluctance to speak in defense of her legitimate claim to public religious leadership may have manifested itself further in her unwillingness to make specific claims on women's religious authority, such as a clear statement of support for women's ordination.

Nonetheless, White's writings provided clear support for women's active participation in diverse religious work. She did not hesitate to call on women to serve in a variety of capacities—as colporteurs who sold Adventist books, Bible instructors who prepared people for baptism, missionaries, and as ministerial assistants working with their minister husbands. The imminent advent necessitated the involvement of not only women, but of all Adventists. White asked women to "take their places in his work at this crisis," promising that "if they are imbued with a sense of their duty, and labor under the Holy Spirit, they will have the self-possession required for this time. The Savior will reflect upon these self-sacrificing women the light of his countenance, and will give them a power that exceeds that of men."[3]

American society in 1848 defined men and women as fundamentally distinct, though complementary, and as responsible for different spheres. Barbara Welter has described this distinction as one that divided spheres and concomitant responsibilities into the public and private, and relegated men to the former and women to the latter. The realm of men existed primarily outside of the home, in the harsh and competitive public sphere, which included business, politics, education, law, journalism, and religious leadership. Women's realm—the home—was therefore to be a haven into which men could retreat in order to be replenished and find refuge. The home was widely recognized as a sanctuary, the moral center of the society, and it was women's responsibility—through their child care, nurturing, and domestic efforts—to keep it so. This ideology of separate spheres and responsibilities, though not always realized, especially by disprivileged women, was used to justify women's exclusion from voting, employment in most occupations, equal participation in higher education, or access to religious authority. So strong was the cultural proscription against women's participation in public work or leadership that in 1837 Congregational ministers in Massachusetts called the public speaking of the sisters Sarah and Angelina Grimké "unnatural," warning that such activities would lead to "widespread and permanent injury."[4] By 1848 the cult of domesticity was deeply entrenched in American life. Married women had no legal right to property ownership—even to wages that they earned, or to custody of their children if they divorced, and divorce itself was extremely difficult for women to attain. Women could not vote; and, according to a U.S. Supreme Court decision, husbands could "chastise" their wives in order to safeguard the order of the home, and thereby society.[5]

The suffrage campaign's call for fuller and more equitable participation of women in public life was met with derision; even the Seneca Falls delegates only reluctantly supported female suffrage. Lucretia Mott warned Elizabeth Cady Stanton that her support for suffrage "will make us ridiculous. We must go slowly."[6] One major·branch of the movement, the American Woman Suffrage Association, relied on the ideology and rhetoric of the cult of domesticity to assert that women should vote in order thereby to exert their moral influence more broadly. In short, in the same decades in which Ellen White emerged as the leader of what would become a worldwide Christian denomination, many early advocates of women's rights embraced the ideals of the cult of domesticity. Ellen White focused on a variety of topics in her writings on women—their duties, training and employment as physicians, pay, their family responsibilities, marital relationships and obligations, adornment, modesty, and sexual temptation—and in so doing recognized a sphere for women that was not limited to the domestic realm. The common theme uniting these writings was an emphasis on gathering and preparing souls for the Second Coming of Jesus. Though she remained ambiguous in delimiting the specific parameters of women's access to authority—via ordination, especially—she unequivocally and repeatedly called all Adventists to religious work, to the work of hastening and preparing for the advent in a variety of capacities.

White clearly indicated the import of women's participation in religious work: "Whenever a great and decisive work is to be done, God chooses men and women to do this work, and it will feel the loss if the talents of both are not combined." In another context she wrote: "Women can be the instruments of righteousness, rendering holy service. It was Mary that first preached a risen Jesus.... If there were twenty women where now there is one, who would make this holy mission their cherished work, we should see many more converted to truth."[7]

White insisted in her writings that women were essential to the work of Adventism in a variety of capacities—as ministers, teachers, and physicians. "Women as well as men are needed in the work that must be done," she wrote at the end of the nineteenth century. A decade or so later she recalled that the "Lord has shown me that women teachers are just as greatly needed to do the work to which He has appointed them as are men." Continuing, she wrote that the Lord had "instructed me that our sisters who have received a training that has fitted them for positions of responsibility are to serve with faithfulness and discernment in their calling, using their influence wisely and, with their brethren in the faith, obtaining an experience that will fit them for still greater usefulness."[8]

White advocated for women's participation in the work of Adventism to increase the success of that work, not as an explicit challenge to the prevailing gender ideology. Though her support for women's religious work encouraged women's participation outside of the domestic realm, she did not contest the notion of an essential difference between genders; indeed, she saw women workers as more appropriately (especially in the case of female physicians) and effectively working with other women. "I have felt recently," White wrote in 1911, "that it should be so arranged that women have greater responsibilities. It is their privilege to be educated in some lines of work just as thoroughly as the men are educated. In Bible times the women always took charge of the women.... [Women and men are] not to mix and mingle right together...." In order to maintain modesty, female physicians were to treat women, and male physicians, men. Female physicians "should utterly refuse to look upon the secret parts of men." Women should be thoroughly educated to work for women, and men to work for men. Let men know that they must go to their own sex and not apply to lady physicians."[9]

It is important to emphasize the context in which Ellen White called for women's participation in religious work. In 1873 the U.S. Supreme Court, in *Bradwell v. Illinois*, held that Illinois could exclude even women who had passed the state bar from practicing law in the state in order to preserve "respective spheres of man and woman." While some women were employed for pay within (as laundresses and wet nurses, for example) and outside the home, protective legislation served greatly to restrict women's paid work to low-prestige, low-paying jobs, and the dominant ideology maintained that women be relegated to the domestic sphere. In marked contrast, Ellen White told women that they "should not feel that they are excused because of their domestic cares." Instead they should do the "utmost of their ability in the work of God." For Adventists, in the process of building what would become one of the largest and most extensive systems of religious educational, publishing, and healthcare institutions, this call to religious service involved varied contributions—as teachers, administrators, nurses, physicians, writers, editors, and publishers. In the *Review and Herald* in 1899 Ellen White wrote: "teach this, my sister. You have many ways opened before you. Address the crowd whenever you can; hold every jot of influence you can by any association that can be made the means of introducing the leaven to the meal. Every man and every woman has a work to do for the master." Ellen White urged women to "take any post that might be offered—as superintendents, Sabbath school teachers, Bible workers," physicians, and teachers.[10]

Moreover, White frequently emphasized that women engaged in the work of Adventism should be paid: the "conference should have the wisdom to understand the justice of her receiving wages." She consistently and adamantly supported fair remuneration of Adventist women involved in the work from church tithes. "I was instructed," wrote Ellen White, that "injustice has been done to women who labor just as devotedly as their husbands. The method of paying men laborers and not their wives is a plan not after the Lord's order. Injustice is thus done. A mistake is made." She repeatedly called for equitable remuneration for women and, when adequate pay for female workers was not forthcoming, she used her personal tithes to establish a fund for their payment.[11]

Ellen White encouraged women's participation in public religious work not at the expense of women's domestic responsibilities, but in addition to those, allowing that women might hire others to assist them in the home. Calling on Adventists not to "belittle women's work," White suggested the propriety of a "woman [putting] her housework in the hands of a faithful, prudent helper, and [leaving] her children in good care, while she engages in the work."[12] With a domestic staff of her own, she insisted on the value of and respect for paid domestic workers, who could help women to free them for religious work.

Although she encouraged women to participate in religious work, including public religious work, White did so in a way that was not entirely at odds with feminine ideals embedded in her larger socio-historical context. Though she told women to have "staunch, noble independence of character [and to be] reliable and true as steel," White also cautioned modesty and humility for women and men engaged in Adventism's work, writing that "women are needed who are not self-important, but gentle in manners and lowly of heart." She warned that "wives and mothers should in no case neglect their husbands and their children"; they could "do much without neglecting home duties."[13]

Contemporary controversy surrounding women's roles in Adventism focuses especially on the propriety of ordaining women to serve as pastors. In 1888 the Disciples of Christ became the first Christian denomination to institute women's ordination via a change in denominational rules. Less than a decade later, White wrote that women engaged in "service of the Lord" should "be set apart to this work by prayer and laying on of hands." At a time when it was not socially acceptable for women to speak publicly, White wrote that "not a hand should be bound, not a soul discouraged, not a voice should be hushed; let every individual labor, privately or publicly, to help forward this grand work. Place the burdens upon men and women of the church." In a period when higher education was just beginning to become widely available to American women, White called on women to prepare for religious work by cultivating their intellect, urging them to "take advantage of schools that have been established for the purpose of imparting the best of knowledge."[14] Still, there is no question of the ambiguity surrounding Ellen White's position regarding ordination of women, in spite of her obvious support for women's participation in and remuneration for public religious work. Before 1860, in her first decade as a religious leader (though prior to the formal organization of Seventh-day Adventism), White remained silent about the ordination of women.

Given both the socio-historical prejudices against women's participation in public work, especially in positions of authority, and the precarious position this young and emerging female religious leader held, this is not surprising. After formal organization (1863), Adventists, increasingly attentive to who should publicly represent the new denomination, began to train and license (and pay) women as ministers. In the late 1870s White began advocating women's participation in public religious work, and in 1881 the General Conference introduced a resolution in support of women's ordination. White, mourning the recent death of her husband, was not in attendance and never took a public position on the resolution, which said that "females possessing the necessary qualifications to fill that position may, with perfect propriety, be set apart by ordination to the work of Christian ministry." After discussion, the resolution was tabled before coming up for a vote. The failure of the resolution did not prevent Adventism from encouraging women to evangelize and minister throughout the 1880s.[15]

Expansion of the ministry to include those trained in other fields, such as healthcare, increased opportunities for participation in Adventist evangelical work by women. In the face of economic difficulties that Adventism confronted in 1891, White encouraged diversely trained Adventists to evangelize as they provided practical assistance in their work. As medical evangelists commenced "Christian help work," both women and men were ordained to the new work. According to Bert Haloviak, "it was the 'ministry of compassion' that naturally brought women to a prominent role in ... ministerial team efforts."[16]

Late in her life, in 1911, Ellen White wrote in the *Review and Herald* that the "Lord ordained me as His messenger," describing herself as a "channel for the communication of light." Historical documents indicate that she saw ordination by men as unnecessary for herself. At various times both local conferences and the General Conference gave her ministerial credentials, but these documents did not consistently indicate whether or not she was considered ordained (Figure 15.1).[17] White and her followers understood her to have unique access to the divine, though she did not insist on being labeled a prophet: "To claim to be a prophet is something that I have never done. If others call me by that name, I have no controversy with them. But my work has covered so many lines that I cannot call myself other than a messenger."[18]

As a female nineteenth-century charismatic religious leader, White was not unique, but the long-term success of the movement that she helped found was extraordinary. With approximately 18 million adult members, Seventh-day Adventism's membership has now surpassed that of The Church of Christ, Scientist (Christian Science), and the Church of Jesus Christ of Latter-day Saints (Mormons) as a worldwide Christian denomination with origins in nineteenth-century America. Though her lifetime saw legal advances for women, White died five years prior to the ratification of the nineteenth amendment extending suffrage to American women. She lived in a culture in which attempts to improve opportunities for women were never without controversy, often evoking ridicule and disdain. As a female leader within an emerging religious organization—one

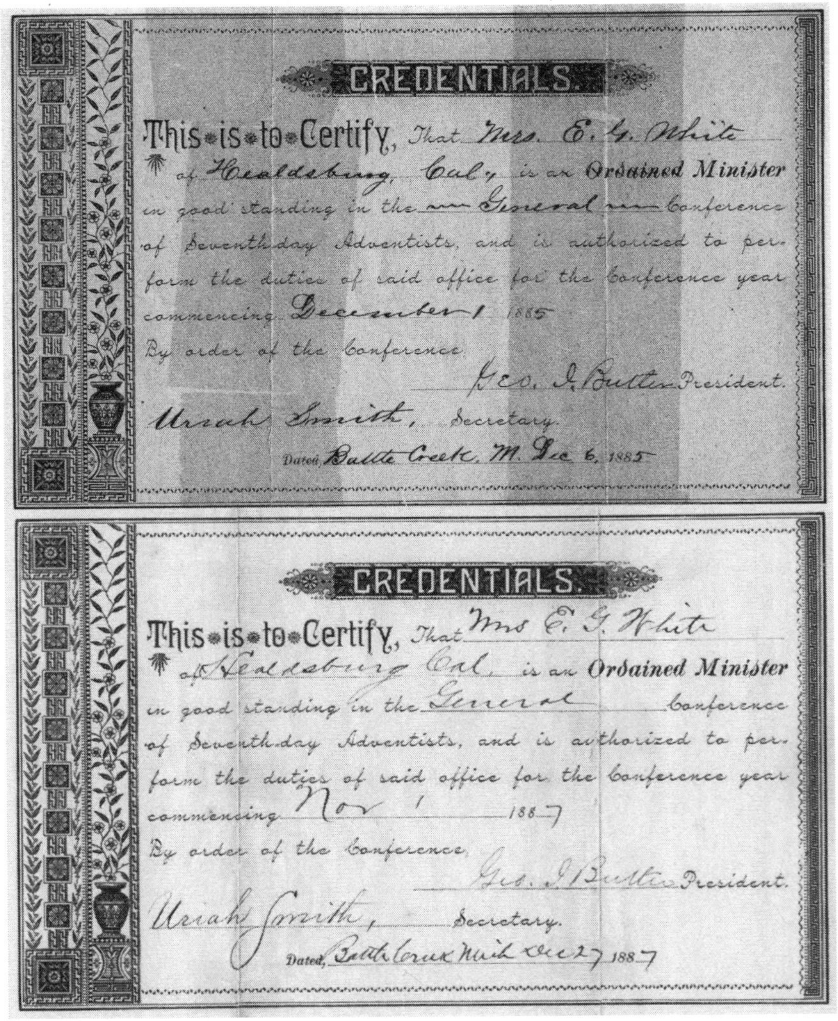

CREDENTIALS.

This is to Certify, That Mrs. E. G. White of Healdsburg, Cal, is an Ordained Minister in good standing in the General Conference of Seventh-day Adventists, and is authorized to perform the duties of said office for the Conference year commencing December 1 1885

By order of the Conference.

Geo. I. Butler President.

Uriah Smith, Secretary.

Dated, Battle Creek, M. Dec 6, 1885

CREDENTIALS.

This is to Certify, That Mrs E. G. White of Healdsburg Cal. is an Ordained Minister in good standing in the General Conference of Seventh-day Adventists, and is authorized to perform the duties of said office for the Conference year commencing Nov 1 1887

By order of the Conference.

Geo. I. Butler President.

Uriah Smith, Secretary.

Dated, Battle Creek Mich Dec 27 1887

FIGURE 15.1 At various times during her life, Ellen White was credentialed as a Seventh-day Adventist minister by both local conferences and the General Conference. These are her General Conference ministerial credentials for 1885 and 1887. Note that in the 1885 copy (top), the word "ordained" is crossed out (Courtesy of the Ellen G. White Estate, Inc.).

rising from failed millennial predictions and public scorn—in a society in which the prevailing gender ideology advocated women's relegation to the domestic realm, the very fact of White's role attracted notice. The Congregationalists first ordained a woman in 1853, and fourteen additional denominations (some very small) allowed women some access to ordination by the beginning of the 1900s.[19] While White actively promoted women's participation in public religious work, she may have perceived advocacy of women's ordination as excessively controversial.

In addition to dealing with the question of Adventist women's roles, Ellen White addressed three major nineteenth-century women's reform movements: suffrage, temperance, and dress reform (see also Chapter 12). Regarding the first, White did "not recommend that woman should seek to become a voter or office-holder." Given widespread Adventist reluctance to vote or participate in politics in the nineteenth century, this is not surprising. Nevertheless, White consistently supported temperance and encouraged Adventist participation in the Woman's Christian Temperance Union (WCTU). White saw the WCTU advancing important goals concomitant with her own health message and identified the WCTU as "in some matters...far in advance of our leaders."[20] Though many members of the WCTU endorsed women's suffrage, in part as a tool by which to implement temperance reform, the temperance movement did not challenge nineteenth-century gender ideals in the same way that suffrage did; to many, temperance appeared as an effort to protect the domestic realm from harms associated with alcohol consumption, such as domestic violence. Suffrage directly challenged women's domestic role.

The third nineteenth-century reform movement in which White became involved, dress reform, also threatened the prevailing gender ideology. The reform dress, a combination of a knee-length skirt worn over ballooning pantaloons that gathered at the ankles with a short ruffle, was introduced in the United States in 1851 by Elizabeth Smith Miller, Elizabeth Cady Stanton's cousin, who had encountered the outfit while traveling in Europe. Miller, Stanton, and other suffragists saw the outfit as providing significant health, comfort, and safety advantages over the then-fashionable women's clothing. In the mid-nineteenth century most fashion-conscious women wore corsets made of whalebone, often tied so tightly as to restrict breathing, under layers of long, heavy, petticoats. The pantaloon outfit became widely known after Amelia Bloomer described it in *Lily*, a women's magazine, and then published sewing instructions, prompting hundreds of women to write to the magazine requesting additional information. Women who donned the outfit met ridicule and found themselves targeted with eggs and stones thrown by men and boys.[21]

In 1863 White connected the reform dress with her health message, though she initially indicated divine disapproval: "God would not have his people adopt the so-called reform dress." Adventist women "who feel called out to join the movement in favor of women's rights and the so-called reform dress," she declared, "might as well sever all connection with the third angel's message." Pants made "women in their dress and appearance as near like the other sex as possible," something "God pronounces [an] abomination." White linked the reform dress with spiritualists and suffragists, leading her to express concern that Adventists, by adopting dress reform, might be associated with those and lose their efficacy in evangelism: "Christians should not take pains to make themselves a gazing-stock by dressing differently from the world."[22]

Nonetheless, during an 1864 stay at the "Home on the Hillside" in Dansville, New York, White became intrigued by the "American costume" worn by female physicians and some patients at the facility. She wrote to friends at Battle Creek:

> They have all styles of dress here. Some are very becoming, if not so short. We shall get patterns from this place, and I think we can get a style of dress more healthful than we now wear, and yet not be bloomer or the "American costume."...I am going to get up a style of dress on my own hook which will accord perfectly with that which has been shown me. Health demands it. Our feeble women must dispense with heavy skirts and tight waists if they value health.[23]

Guidelines for female dress outlined in Ellen White's sixth pamphlet on health reform in 1865 couched the need for dress reform with references to health and safety (Figure 15.2). The "female form" wrote Ellen White, "should not be compressed in the least with corsets and whalebones." Recalling her vision, White described a dress shorter than that normally worn by women, which should "reach somewhat below the top of the boot." Somewhat modifying the American costume, she recommended that her dress be worn in combination with "lined pants gathered into a band and fastened about the ankle, or made full and tapering at the bottom...long enough to meet the shoe."[24]

White's proposed modification in women's dress, especially her incorporation of pants, met fierce resistance from Adventists. In a testimony she described a "strange spirit of blind and bitter opposition" to the outfit. In the face of this opposition, White initially defended the propriety of women's pants: "We advocate that the limbs of women should not be exposed, but sensibly, neatly, and comfortably, clad. Is this immodest? Many say that they have no objections to the length of the dress, but they

THE DRESS REFORM.

AN APPEAL TO THE PEOPLE IN ITS BEHALF.

WE are not Spiritualists. We are Christian women, believing all that the Scriptures say concerning man's creation, his fall, his sufferings and woes on account of continued transgression, of his hope of redemption thro' Christ, and of his duty to glorify God in his body and spirit which are his, in order to be saved. We do not wear the style of dress here represented to be odd,—that we may attract notice. We do not differ from the common style of woman's dress for any

FIGURE 15.2 Ellen White's model reform dress is shown here as an illustration on the cover of her pamphlet, *The Dress Reform* (1868).

could never put on the pants."[25] For a period of time she wore the outfit herself (Figure 15.3).

White insisted that reform dress was worn not to "be odd" or "attract notice," but instead should be donned out of a "sense of duty" and because the reform dress—including pants—was the "most convenient, the most truly modest, and most healthful style of dress worn by woman." In the face of continuing opposition, "that which was given as a blessing was turned into a curse, [and] the burden of advocating reform dress was removed." In 1897, when some Adventist women wished to promote the reform dress, White wrote a letter in which she indicated that "some have supposed that the very pattern given was the pattern that all were to adopt. This is not so.... No one precise style has been given to me as the exact rule to guide all in their dress." She eventually opposed women's pants as "objectionable" and "extreme."[26]

Although White took a position on dress reform at variance with prevailing nineteenth-century gender norms, persistent Adventist opposition

FIGURE 15.3 When James and Ellen White visited the expanded facility of the Western Health Reform Institute, ca. 1874 (see inset), she wore her reform dress (Courtesy of the Ellen G. White Estate, Inc.).

to the shortened dress and pants eventually led her in the end merely to advocate "modest, convenient, and healthful" dress for women. Her support for the WCTU did not conflict with the predominant gender ideology. The WCTU may have allowed for women's participation in leadership of a social movement and supported suffrage as a mechanism for implementation of temperance, but preventing men from drinking was understood and presented as a way for women to protect the home and family. White did not actively oppose women's suffrage but discouraged Adventists from working for women's vote. Thus in her positions on three major nineteenth-century reform movements, White did not radically challenge gender norms, except in her support for reform dress, and she retreated from the controversial components of this when resistance to it proved intransigent.

White defied major nineteenth-century gender expectations and ideals only inconsistently. She sometimes employed the language of the cult of domesticity to describe women's role, writing, for example, that "God has assigned woman her mission; and if she, in her humble way, yet to the best of her ability, makes a heaven of her home, faithfully and lovingly performing her duties to her husband and children, continually seeking to let a holy light shine from her useful, pure, and virtuous life to brighten all around her, she is doing the work left her of the Master." She also wrote that "A young woman may dispense with a knowledge of French and algebra or even piano, but it is indispensable that she learn to make good bread, to fashion neatly fitting garments, and to perform efficiently the many duties that pertain to homemaking." Like other proponents of domesticity, White saw women's influence extending to society, especially through their children. "The mother's influence," she contended, "never ceases. It is ever active, either for good or for evil." There is no indication, however, that she advocated limiting women's activities to the domestic sphere. While acknowledging and valuing women's domestic work, White at the same time asked Adventist women to consider that "society also has claims upon" them: "Women and men are not fulfilling the design of God when they simply express affection for their own family circle." Reminding women that they "should not feel that they are excused because of their domestic cares," White encouraged them to "become intelligent as to how they can work most effectively and methodically in bringing souls to Christ."[27]

White wrote much less about men than women. In her few statements she departed from nineteenth-century gender ideals. She referred to married men as "house-bands" and promoted men's "practical usefulness" in a variety of household responsibilities, but she also emphasized the husband's "authority" and his role as the family's "lawmaker." Especially in her later writings, she emphasized that a man should "love and cherish his wife" and "should never correct his children while impatient or fretful, or while under the influence of passion."[28]

White's position as a nineteenth-century female prophet may have been unusual but it was not unique: Mary Baker Eddy, and earlier, Jemima Wilkinson and Ann Lee, had visions and religious messages that they shared with followers. But the movement that White nurtured has prospered the most. Indeed, Seventh-day Adventism today exceeds in number of adherents some American religious movements founded by nineteenth-century men. Despite this, White is largely forgotten except by Adventists, and women in Adventism in the twenty-first century continue to confront a world church opposed to their ordination.[29]

NOTES

1. Andrew G. Mustard, *James White and SDA Organization: Historical Development, 1844–1881* (Berrien Springs, MI: Andrews University Press, 1988), 99; Harriet Sigerman, "An Unfinished Battle: 1848–1865," in *No Small Courage: A History of Women in the United States*, ed. Nancy Cott (New York: Oxford University Press, 2000), 237 (womanity).

2. Ronald L. Numbers, *Prophetess of Health: A Study of Ellen G. White*, 3rd ed. (Grand Rapids, MI: William B. Eerdmans, 2008), 62, 61, 72.

3. Bert Haloviak, "Longing for the Pastorate: Ministry in 19th Century Adventism," Unpublished Paper, Center for Adventist Research, James White Library, Andrews University, Berrien Springs, MI (1988):15; "Ellen G. White and Women Physicians" in *Manuscript Releases*, 21 vols. (Silver Spring, MD: Ellen G. White Estate, 1990), 7: 335–336; Ellen White, "Words to Lay Ministers," *Advent Review and Sabbath Herald* (hereafter referred to as *Review and Herald*) 34 (1902):7.

4. Barbara Welter, "The Cult of True Womanhood: 1820–1860," *American Quarterly* 18 (Summer 1966): 170–72; Michael Goldberg, "Breaking New Ground: 1800–1848," in *No Small Courage: A History of Women in the United States*, ed., Cott, 231.

5. As recently as 1910 the U.S. Supreme Court, in *Thompson v. Thompson*, ruled that a "wife had no cause for action on an assault and battery charge against her husband because it 'would open the doors of the courts to accusations of all sorts of one spouse against the other and bring into public notice complaints for assaults, slander and libel.' " "Abuse-Women-Worldwide-Issue-American Traditions," in libraryindex.com/pages/2031.

6. Goldberg, "Breaking New Ground," 236.

7. Ellen G. White to E. J. and Jessie Waggoner, Aug. 26, 1898, in Ellen G. White, *Evangelism* (Takoma Park, MD: Review and Herald Publishing Assn., 1946), 469; White, "Address and Appeal, Setting Forth the Importance of Missionary Work," *Review and Herald* 53 (1879): 1.

8. Ellen G. White, Manuscript 149, 1899, in White, *Evangelism*, 493; "Ellen G. White to Ministers, Physicians, and Counsellors at Loma Linda, May 7, 1911," in Ellen G. White, *Daughters of God: Messages Especially for Women* (Hagerstown, MD: Review and Herald, 1998), 94.

9. Manuscript 2, 1911, in White, *Manuscript Releases*, 13: 114; White, *Daughters of God*, 96–97; Ellen G. White to A. G. Daniells, Sept. 1, 1910, in Ellen G. White, *Medical Ministry* (Mountain View, CA: Pacific Press, 1932), 140; Ellen G. White, "The Work of Christian Physicians," June 3, 1904, in White, Special Testimonies, Series B.15 (1903–1913), 14.

10. The Oyez Project, *Bradwell v. Illinois*, 83 U.S. 130 (1873) available at: http://oyez.org/cases/1851-1900/1872/1872_0; Ellen G. White, "Women as Christian

Laborers," *Signs of the Times* 12 (1886), 66; Ellen G. White, "The Excellency of the Soul," *Review and Herald* 76 (1899), 293; White, *Evangelism*, 473–74.

11. White, *Manuscript Releases*, 5: 324, 12: 164; White, *Daughters of God*, 111.

12. White, *Manuscript Releases*, 5: 324.

13. Ellen G. White to Brethren and Sisters at Fresno, July 7, 1888, Letter 41a, Ellen White Estate; Ellen G. White, "Women as Christian Laborers," *Signs of the Times* 12 (1886), 561–62.

14. Mark Chaves, *Ordaining Women: Culture and Conflict in Religious Organizations* (Cambridge, MA: Harvard University Press, 1999), 16; Ellen G. White, "The Duty of the Minister and the People," *Review and Herald* 72 (1895), 433–34; Ellen G. White, *Messages to Young People* (Nashville, TN: Southern Publishing Assn., 1930), 185; White, *Manuscript Releases*, 10:74. See also Steve Daily, "The Irony of Adventism: The Role of Ellen G. White and Other Adventist Women in Nineteenth Century America," (Ph.D. diss., School of Theology at Claremont, 1985), 228; and Haloviak, "Longing for the Pastorate," 3–4.

15. White, *Daughters of God*, 248; Bert Haloviak, "Ellen White Endorsed Adventist Women Ministers," *Spectrum: Journal of the Association of Adventist Forums* 19 (July 1989): 34 (hereafter referred to as *Spectrum*).

16. Bert Haloviak, "Route to the Ordination of Women in the Seventh-day Adventist Church: Two Paths," Unpublished Paper (1985), 30, Center for Adventist Research; Haloviak, "Longing for the Pastorate," 23–24.

17. For additional information on Ellen White's ministerial credentials, see the Ellen G. White Estate document, "Records Pertaining to Ellen G. White's Ministerial/Ordination Credentials," at http://www.whiteestate.org/issues/egw_credentials/egw_credentials.htm.

18. Ellen G. White, "An Appeal to Our Churches throughout the United States," *Review and Herald* 20 (1911):142; Richard Bowen Ferret, *Charisma and Routinisation in a Millennialist Community* (Lewiston, NY: Edwin Mellen Press, 2008), 72.

19. Chaves, *Ordaining Women*, 16. See also Rosemary Skinner Keller and Rosemary Radford Ruether, eds., *Encyclopedia of Women and Religion in North America* (Bloomington: Indiana University Press, 2006), 376.

20. White, "Women as Christian Laborers," in White, *Daughters of God*, 253; Ellen G. White to J. A. Burden, Sept. 2, 1907, in Ellen G. White, *Welfare Ministry* (Washington, DC: Review and Herald Publishing Assn., 1952), 163, 162; Ellen G. White to J. A. Burden, September 2, 1907, in Ellen G. White, *Gospel Workers* (Washington, DC: Review and Herald Publishing Assn., 1915), 384.

21. Sigerman, "An Unfinished Battle," 249–250.

22. Ellen G. White, *Testimonies for the Church*, 9 vols. (Mountain View, CA: Pacific Press, 1948), 1: 424 (Testimony 10, 1864), 1: 457–458 (Testimony 11, 1867). The fullest historical account of White and the reform dress appears in Numbers, *Prophetess of Health*, 184–202.

23. White, "Ellen G. White and Women Physicians," *Manuscript Releases*, 5: 380.

24. Ibid.; Ellen G. White, *Health; or, How to Live* (Battle Creek, MI: Steam Press of the Seventh-day Adventist Publishing Assn., 1865), No. 6: 36; White, *Testimonies*, 1: 460.

25. Quoted in Arthur L. White, *Ellen G. White*, 6 vols. (Hagerstown, MD: Review and Herald Publishing Assn., 1981–1986), 2: 182; Ellen G. White, "The Reform Dress," *Health Reformer* 7 (1872): 154–156.

26. White, "The Reform Dress," 156; Dores E. Robinson, *The Story of Our Health Message* (Nashville, TN: Southern Publishing Assn., 1943), 441; Ellen G. White to J. H. Haughey, July 4, 1897, in Ellen G. White, *Child Guidance* (Washington, DC: Review and Herald Publishing Assn., 1954), 419; White, *Testimonies*, 4: 639 (Testimony 30, 1881); White, *Testimonies*, 1: 459 (Testimony 11, 1867).

27. White, *Testimonies*, 2: 439 (Testimony 18, 1870); Ellen G. White, "Influence of Women," *Good Health: A Journal of Hygiene* 15 (1880): 174–175; Ellen G. White, "Character Tested by Small Occurrences," *Review and Herald* 42 (1895): 299; White, "Women as Christian Laborers," in White, *Welfare Ministry*, 158–159, 165.

28. White, "Family Government Is to Be Maintained," *Review and Herald* 71 (1894): 161–171; Ellen G. White, "The Father in the Family," *Signs of the Times* 19 (1892): 329; Ellen White to Brother Alchin, circa 1870, in White, *Manuscript Releases*, 5: 293; Ellen G. White, Manuscript 161, 1902, in White, *Manuscript Releases*, 18: 121.

29. See also Mark Chaves, "The Symbolic Significance of Women's Ordination," *Journal of Religion* 77 (1):89; and Laura Vance, *Seventh-day Adventism in Crisis: Gender and Sectarian Change in an Emerging Religion* (Urbana: University of Illinois Press, 1999), 101–130.

16

Death and Burial

T. Joe Willey

ON FEBRUARY 25, 1915, Elder W. C. (Willie) White, the youngest son of Ellen White, announced in *The Advent Review and Sabbath Herald* (*Review and Herald*) that his aging mother, who no longer recognized those around her, had fallen in her St. Helena, California, home, causing an intracapsular fracture of the left femur. For the next five months Mrs. White received constant care from three assistants: her nurse Carrie Hangerford, her grandniece May Walling, and her traveling companion and faithful secretary Sara McEnterfer. As Ellen White weakened, Willie promised his brother, Edson, in Michigan, to keep him informed about their mother's progress. On July 12 Willie wrote: "Mother getting worst cannot keep food down.... I will ask you to take charge of the matter of having the grave dug and securing an undertaker and conveyance." A few days later the nurse discontinued her "treatments." Thereafter Mrs. White's breathing became slower and more irregular until she stopped breathing altogether. She passed away at 3:40 during the afternoon of Friday, July 16, at 87 years of age. As the end approached, Willie thought he heard his mother whisper "I know in whom I have believed." Later he described her passing as "Like the burning out of a candle, so quiet."[1]

As White grew weaker and more incoherent, her staff drew up plans for her funeral and prepared biographical materials for release. Some Adventists, however, remained unconvinced that God would allow his messenger to die. At the 1913 General Conference Willie was asked whether his mother expected to die. He replied: "The Lord has not told her how long she will live. He has not told her in a positive way that she is to die; but she expects to rest in the grave a little time before the Lord comes."[2] Willie went on to relate a telling incident about fifteen years earlier: "in one of her night visions, she came out of a very dark place into the bright light, and father was with her. When he saw her by his side he exclaimed in great surprise, 'What, have you been there too, Ellen?' She always understood that to mean that the Lord would let her rest in the grave a little while before the Lord comes."[3]

Three Funerals

Ellen White's first funeral was an informal affair, held Sunday afternoon, two days after her death, on the lawn at Elmshaven under the elm trees.[4] Then her family and associates took her remains by train to Richmond (near Oakland), where the California Conference of Seventh-day Adventists was holding its annual camp meeting. On Monday morning at 10:30 an estimated one thousand people attended a second funeral, led by the president of the Pacific Union Conference. At 3:30 in the afternoon, Willie White and Sara McEnterfer accompanied the casket on a Northwestern train heading to Chicago, expecting to reach Battle Creek Thursday evening. Because the train arrived in Battle Creek later than expected, there were few persons at the depot to greet them, making it necessary to call on the baggage men loitering around the platform to lift Mrs. White's casket into the hearse.[5] All day Friday the casket remained in George R. Israel's home on Garrison Avenue (Figure 16.1).

The General Conference headquarters in Takoma Park, Maryland, sent out more than a thousand funeral invitations. The mayor and city commissioners of Battle Creek received special offers to sit directly behind the White family on the platform in the Tabernacle Church. Carefully prepared news releases went to selected editors and reporters in Battle Creek, "to prevent," as Willie said, "the publication of a lot of derogatory matter."[6]

On Saturday, July 24, nearby Adventist churches in Michigan discharged their members to attend the funeral. Kalamazoo sent a score of delegates. Others came from as far away as Washington, Boston, Chicago, and Detroit. Three thousand people crowded into the Battle Creek Tabernacle Church and another thousand milled outside on the lawn or in the hallways, unable to squeeze in. From eight o'clock until half-past ten in the morning, the throng of friends and acquaintances filed past the open casket in front of the pulpit.

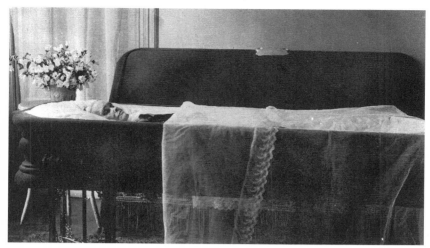

FIGURE 16.1 Ellen White in her casket, 1915 (Courtesy of the Ellen G. White Estate, Inc.).

The funeral service began at eleven o'clock with music, prayer, and a lengthy life sketch by Elder A. G. Daniells, president of the General Conference. Elder S. N. Haskell then preached a sermon, noting that "Precious in the sight of the Lord is the death of his saints." Haskell had known White for more than fifty years, "under nearly every circumstance of life." As a widower in 1894, he had proposed marriage to her. After praying about the matter, she declined. One of the most important of her reasons was her desire to retain her own byline on her books and articles. Even though Haskell had married someone else, a large photograph of him occupied a special place in Mrs. White's bedroom in Elmshaven.[7]

Following the sermon, a double quartet sang "We Shall Meet," a song from *Hymns and Tunes*, the Seventh-day Adventist hymnal. After the closing prayer the coffin was removed to the vestibule at the Van Buren Street entrance so that everyone would have an "opportunity to view the face of Sister White."[8] Hundreds of people who had been unable to find seats in the Tabernacle Church passed by this second open-casket viewing. The casket was then sealed and the remains taken by carriage to the Oak Hill Cemetery. More than a hundred automobiles and nine city streetcars, chartered by the church, followed the procession down Main Street, crossing over to South Avenue to end at the cemetery. The sky grew overcast with a threat of thunderstorms as the temperature warmed to 80 degrees.

The early afternoon services at the graveside were brief. The double quartet sang again, this time "We Shall Sleep, But Not Forever." Elder I. H. Evans read a passage from the Bible and Elder G. B. Thompson offered prayer. At that time, according to both the *Review and Herald* and the *Battle Creek Enquirer*, "The remains of our dear sister were tenderly and silently lowered into the grave to rest beside the body of her husband, Elder James White." A ten-page funeral insert in the *Review and Herald* showed a photograph taken before the casket was lowered in the grave, accompanied by the caption "Just before the grave was filled."[9]

A Secret Interruption

What happened after the crowd of mourners dispersed has remained a closely held secret for nearly a century. It began to unravel in 1973 when Alta Robinson, the wife of Virgil Robinson, a great-grandson of Ellen White, stumbled onto a bewildering letter written October 15, 1915, by Edson White to his brother, Willie.[10]

> There were some matters mentioned in your letter of September 17 which I have not answered.[11] You asked in regard to mother's burial. I think I explained this to you fully stating that we went to the grounds about three weeks after the funeral and we saw her placed in the grave that had been prepared for her. Of course her face had changed considerably, and yet she was preserved as well as I could expect. When we went to the cemetery Sister Isreal [sic] took me over in her auto, and we were glad to meet Mr. and Mrs. R. C. Gardner, Mrs. E. B. Jones and Mrs. L. V. Barton. They are all our people and happened to be at the grave just at the time that the change was made from the vault to the grave. Everything went off smoothly, and occupied but little time. [12]

Ten days later Willie replied to Edson: "In your letter of October 15, you tell me about the removal of Mother's body from the vault to the grave. We also have the bill from the sexton."[13]

Like most other Adventists, Mrs. Robinson understood that Ellen White had been buried in full view of the mourners on July 24, 1915. That was what the *Review and Herald* had reported and what was described in the funeral pamphlet, *In Memoriam*, sent to devotees unable to attend the funeral. Launching an investigation, Robinson wrote to the sexton of the Battle Creek Cemetery, asking him if he knew "whether or not Sister White was buried on the day of her funeral." Because the sexton had no personal knowledge of the matter, he passed the Robinson inquiry on to Mark L. Bovee, a grandson of Uriah Smith. At the time Bovee, press secretary for the Battle Creek Tabernacle Church, was actively collecting Adventist history related to his grandfather and other church pioneers. As a frequent contributor to the Battle Creek newspapers on church and community affairs, Bovee had interviewed several elderly people who still had lucid memories of the 1915 burial.

L.C. Coulsten, 94 years old, told Bovee that he "distinctly remembers that Sister White was buried on the spot, immediately following gravesite service." Ninety-year-old Edith Childs, "very alert and [with] a keen memory," also assured Bovee "that Sister White was buried immediately after close of graveside service. Not only that, but she said she saw the casket being lowered and dirt was thrown on it, as is sometimes the custom."[14] Bovee told Robinson that he hoped these two eyewitnesses were adequate to verify that Mrs. White had been buried July 24. He suspected that Edson White's letter was "in error." Perhaps, Bovee speculated, Edson had confused his mother's burial "with the burial of Elder James White, in 1881."

Bovee, it turns out, had recently obtained several diaries of William H. Hall, formerly chief steward of the Battle Creek Sanitarium. In them he noticed a peculiar entry for August 23, 1881: "Tonight I went to [sic] J. E. White and others to Oak Hill Cemetery and WE MOVED THE REMAINS OF ELD. WHITE FROM THE VAULT TO THE GRAVE. We opened the casket and took a last look until the morn of the resurrection. Rest in peace, war worn soldier—sleep on."[15] This comment led Bovee to speculate that Edson's letter to Willie in 1915 must have confused the ten-day delayed interment of his father, back in 1881, with a delay in his mother's burial. "Maybe the reason for this delay was because James White had passed away suddenly and the family did not own the cemetery burial lot," surmised Bovee. "So his coffin was removed from the grave and stored in a vault until the lot could be purchased."

When Robinson read Bovee's speculation, she immediately recognized a problem with his proposition. At the time of James White's death two of White's children were already buried in the family plot along with his parents. In fact, the Whites had purchased Burial Lot 320 for twelve dollars twenty years earlier, on February 12, 1861. Recognizing that both parents had experienced delayed interments, Robinson candidly informed Bovee: "Well, that only compounds the confusion in my mind."

Arthur White's Reaction

By November, 1974, Arthur L. White (1907–1991), a grandson of James and Ellen White and secretary of the Ellen G. White Estate, had become aware of the interrupted burials of his grandparents. Like his father, Willie, Arthur White devoted his life to maintaining a positive memory of Ellen White. After seeing the evidence from the Robinson and Bovee communications, White recognized the shadowy implications of these interruptions, as he noted in an internal memorandum kept in the vault of the White Estate.[16] White recounted hearing "rumors that Ellen G. White was not buried in the Oak Hill Cemetery on the day of her funeral." When such reports surfaced, he had "categorically denied that her burial was any different than what might have been anticipated. In other words, that she was buried in the Oak Hill Cemetery on the day of her funeral." Without revealing how much effort he had spent in investigating the matter, he wrote "We are unable to track down any other information that would support the J. E. White statement.... At no time was this matter discussed by W. C. White [Arthur White's father] in his conversations with me. I have never heard it mentioned in the family." Although he admitted that Edson's letter "cannot be dismissed," he preferred to believe the traditional account: "Seventh-day Adventist[s] have accepted on the basis of those who were present at the funeral and the reports which appeared in the *Review and Herald* and the news media that Ellen White in her casket was lowered into the grave in the White plot at the Battle Creek cemetery on the Sabbath of the funeral, and thus having been laid to rest had not been disturbed."

White speculated that if the casket had indeed been removed to the cemetery vault, it had been "to prevent possible exhuming by the curious, particularly Dr. John Harvey Kellogg, for an examination of her brain." However, there is no evidence that Kellogg planned to autopsy or examine the brain of the decedent. He did not even attend White's funeral, because he was making arrangements to travel to San Francisco the next day to attend the Pan American Exhibition and participate in a Race Betterment Conference. [17]

Within a few months after Arthur White drafted his memorandum Bovee returned to the Oak Hill Cemetery to examine the burial records of Ellen White. After pulling up the leather-bound volume for 1915, Bovee discovered that Edson had been correct. According to the official cemetery records, Ellen White's casket was transferred to the vault on July 24 and remained there until August 26. Thus, the actual date for the interment of Ellen White was not July 24, as reported by the *Review and Herald* and the newspapers, but rather 34 days later. The cemetery also recorded the primary cause of death as "chronic myocarditis" ("arterio-sclerosis" being listed as secondary), not a broken hip.[18] Bovee made photographic copies of these cemetery records and sent them to the White Estate.[19]

After receiving this evidence, Arthur White sent Bovee a feeble thank you letter: "You write of the fact that Ellen White was not placed in the grave until about three weeks after her funeral. I appreciate the data you have sent to us on this. The whole thing was rather incredible to me, but I think there is ample evidence to support what seem to be the facts. Thank you for going to the trouble to investigate the matter thoroughly there."[20] At the time of his exchange with Bovee, Arthur White was writing a six-volume biography of Ellen White. Surprisingly, he made no mention of the interrupted burials of either grandparent, not even in a footnote.[21]

What Happened?

Why, then, were the caskets containing the remains of James and Ellen White secretly extracted from their graves and removed to temporary storage above ground? Several possible explanations come to mind. During the winter coffins were sometimes stored in the vault until the ground thawed, but this was obviously not the case in summer. On other occasions, when family members were absent, the decedent might be held in the vault to allow a final viewing before burial. Again, this was not an issue with the Whites. Both funerals were held a week after death to allow time for family and friends to come from out of town. Despite the evidence, Arthur White continued to state "categorically" that his grandmother had been buried on Sabbath afternoon at the end of her funeral.

The most likely explanation for the delayed burials is theological. Adventists have long taught that at the Second Coming the righteous dead will rise from their graves in their original physical forms and ascend to heaven and everlasting life. Until then, their bodies—there are no separate souls in Adventism—remain unconscious in their graves. But Adventists also believe that a few special humans have already arisen to heaven. The strongest support for this belief comes from the writings of Ellen White, who claimed to have "visited" heaven in vision on several occasions. While there she personally met Jesus and other humans, including Enoch,

Moses, and Elijah.[22] Ellen White also taught that at the time of Christ's resurrection a multitude of righteous individuals had come forth from their graves and ascended into heaven: "They were those who had been co-laborers with God, and who at the cost of their lives had borne testimony to the truth. Now they were to be witnesses for Him who had raised them from the dead."[23] Knowing that a chosen few had already gone to heaven, Edson and Willie White might well have believed that their worthy parents deserved the same unbridled benefit.

At the time of James White's death in 1881 an Adventist elder had urged Ellen White to appeal to God to raise her husband from the dead. "Do not let them bury him," one of the leading brethren implored, "but pray to the Lord, that He may bring him to life again." After reflecting on the request, Mrs. White declined, saying, "He had done his work. . . . Would I have him suffer all this over again? No, no. I would in no case call him from his restful sleep to a life of toil and pain. He will rest until the morning of the resurrection," which she, of course, believed was not far off.[24]

Edson assumed the lead in planning the secret interruptions, since he was most involved in the delayed burials of both his parents. From his own testimony we know that he was the one who, accompanied by trusted witnesses, checked their caskets for the physical remains before resealing the coffins and burying them in private. Younger brother Willie was also aware of what Edson was doing, and together they must have allowed their imagination to triumph over death. If their parents, known as "co-laborers with God," were taken to heaven, it would ultimately mean that they also might have a chance to escape the grave. Of course, this interpretation could be wrong—we have no direct evidence. Both brothers kept their actions and motivations a secret.

NOTES

I want to thank the following for their assistance in the preparation of this chapter: Janice Little and Patricia Chapman, Department of Archives and Special Collections, Del E. Webb Memorial Library, Loma Linda University; Merlin D. Burt, director, Center for Adventist Research, James White Library, Andrews University; Debra E. Stanley, office manager, Oak Hill Cemetery, Battle Creek, Michigan; and Ronald L. Numbers, University of Wisconsin-Madison.

1. W. C. White to J. E. White, June 25, 1915, E. G. White Estate, Silver Springs, MD, hereafter cited as White Estate; W. C. White to Edson White, July 10, 1915, quoted by Arthur L. White, *Ellen G. White*, 6 vols. (Washington, DC: Review

and Herald Publishing Assn., 1981–86), 6:431. For a slightly different version of White's last words, see ibid., 3:173.

2. W. C. White, "Opening Session," *General Conference Bulletin* 7:1 (1913), 6; and "Confidence in God," 7:14 (1913), 219.

3. W. C. White, "Confidence in God," *General Conference Bulletin* 7:14 (1913), 219, quoted in White, 6:445.

4. Sometime on Sunday, July 18, an undertaker in nearby St. Helena embalmed the body for burial.

5. "Out of Town People Will be at Funeral," *Battle Creek Evening News*, July 23, 1915.

6. Ibid.; W. C. White to Edson White, July 10, 1915, Loma Linda University Heritage Research Center, Del E. Webb Memorial Library; hereafter cited as LLU Heritage Research Center.

7. Gilbert M. Valentine, *W. W. Prescott: Forgotten Giant of Adventism's Second Generation* (Hagerstown, MD: Review and Herald Publishing Assn., 2005), 236. White addressed more letters to Haskell than to any other person outside her immediate family.

8. "The Final Funeral Services of Mrs. Ellen G. White," *Advent Review and Sabbath Herald* 38 (1915): 10; hereafter cited as *Review and Herald*.

9. "Thousand Attend Funeral Service," *Review and Herald* 38 (1915), 12. The *Battle Creek Enquirer*, July 25, 1915, noted that "The casket was then lowered in the grave beside that of her husband."

10. Alta Robinson was employed by the Ellen G. White Estate in Washington, D.C., as a research assistant.

11. The September 17 letter has not been discovered in W. C. White's letterbooks or in other sources. The quoted passage is from J. E. White to W. C. White October 15, 1915. I searched unsuccessfully for the September 17 letter in the Andrews and Loma Linda University archives. Jim Nix, director of the White Estate, told me that he had also been unable to locate the letter. May Israel served as Ellen White's bookkeeper in Australia.

12. J. E. White to W. C. White, October 15, 1915, LLU Heritage Research Center.

13. W. C. White to J. E. White, October 25, 1915, White Estate.

14. Mark L. Bovee to Mrs. V. E. Robinson, April 29, 1973, Uriah Smith/Mark Bovee Collection, No. 146, Center for Adventist Research, James White Library, Andrews University, Berrien Springs, MI.

15. Quoted ibid.

16. Arthur L. White, memorandum titled "Ellen G. White—Question of Deferred Burial," November 4, 1974, LLU Heritage Research Center.

17. "Dr. Kellogg Planning to Attend Pan American Exhibition in San Francisco," *Battle Creek Inquirer*, July 23, 1915.

18. The death certificate, a copy of which can be found in the LLU Heritage Research Center, was signed by her physician, Dr. G. E. Klingerman, who was affiliated with the Saint Helena Sanitarium.

19. Mark Bovee to Ron Graybill, March 14, 1975, Center for Adventist Research.

20. Arthur White to Mark Bovee, April 1, 1976, Center for Adventist Research.

21. White, *Ellen G. White*. Virgil Robinson, *James White* (Washington, DC: Review & Herald Publishing Assn., 1976), also did not mention James's delayed burial.

22. Ellen G. White, *A Sketch of the Christian Experience and Views of Ellen G. White* (Saratoga Springs, NY: James White, 1851), 16.

23. Ellen G. White, *The Desire of Ages* (Mountain View, CA: Pacific Press, 1898), 785.

24. Ellen White, *Manuscript Releases from the Files of the Letters and Manuscripts Written by Ellen G. White*, 21 vols. (Silver Spring, MD: Ellen G. White Estate, 1981–1993), 7: 419. See also White's letter to "Sister Belden," December 25, 1906, White Estate; and Ellen G. White's posthumously published *The Retirement Years* (Hagerstown, MD: Review & Herald Publishing Assn., 1990), 164.

17

Legacy

Paul McGraw and Gilbert Valentine

NEWS OF ELLEN G. White's death on July 16, 1915, at age 87, near St. Helena, California, did not shock those closest to her. There was deep sadness but little surprise. Since 1913 her son W. C White had been alerting church leaders to her increasing frailty and the likelihood of her demise. Friends and colleagues began to expect the worst after a fall broke her hip on February 13, 1915, and they received with anxious concern each new update on her deteriorating condition. But adjusting to the idea that they would now have to await the second coming of Jesus in her absence presented a real challenge for Adventism.

Adventist leaders, however, had already started thinking about the implications of life without the prophet. With her son W. C. White, they had talked about what would happen after his mother was gone. How the church might best handle the loss of its most influential voice posed a problem that had been on their agenda for some time. How would the church relate to the writings of a dead prophet? Among the core leadership, at least, a consensus developed that the church should shift from emphasizing the prophetic charisma to building up and strengthening the "apostolic gifts and all the other gifts in the church."[1] But making this transition produced conflict and tension.

Although Battle Creek, Michigan, no longer remained the center of Adventism, it was where the denomination said its final goodbyes to Ellen White. An estimated four thousand mourners attended the funeral (see Chapter 16). During the eulogy, General Conference President Arthur G. Daniells spoke of the legacy he believed Ellen White would leave. "Her voice is silent; her pen is laid aside. But," he predicted, "the mighty influence of that active, forceful, Spirit-filled life will continue." Like other Adventists, he believed that her life had been closely "linked with the eternal." He asserted that the work she had done had "left a monument that will never crumble nor perish."[2]

The "monument" of which Daniells spoke comprised far more than the legacy of her literary accomplishments. She had also played a vital part in helping establish an enduring international community of faith distinguished by a focus on "the world to come" and a conviction that "this present world" would very soon end. Other teachings of the prophet had developed into a distinctive present-world emphasis on education and health care that had led to the establishment of numerous schools, colleges, and hospitals (see Chapter 7). Not all the institutions survived the exigencies of time and changing circumstances, but most did, and many continued into the twenty-first century. Paradoxically, her emphasis on the imminence of the end of the world helped to create a rapidly expanding movement that at the time of her death was already contributing to the long-term social betterment of many societies.[3]

While both Ellen White's fellow believers and her critics recognized the significance of her personal involvement in shaping her religious community, they saw her extensive writings as her distinctive contribution. This chapter addresses the posthumous role of Ellen White's writings, the people and entities who controlled them, and the authority attributed to them. As we shall see, during the nearly one hundred years since her death, these aspects of her Adventist legacy have been the source of ongoing conflict and debate.

Establishing the Estate

Ellen White herself set the trajectory of her posthumous influence on Adventism. Recognizing the impact her writings had already made on her church, she sought to assure that they would continue to be accessible and respected. She believed that even after her death, "these words that have been given to me by the Lord will still have life and will speak to the people."[4] And they did, although the influence of this legacy has been confined almost entirely to her community of faith. Her writings never found their way into the consciousness of the wider world in the same way as did the writings of a Louisa May Alcott or a Harriet Beecher Stowe.

Although confident about the continuing spiritual value of her writings, Ellen White expressed concern about the future administration and oversight of them. Her son W. C. White noted that in her closing years his mother had sought legal advice about the framing of an appropriate will and the appointment of trustees.[5] Finding a balance between family interests and church priorities proved difficult. In her first will, drafted just before departing for Australia in 1891, she left the care of her property and her writings almost exclusively in the care of W. C. White.[6] Ten years later, following her return to the United States in 1900, she drew up and signed another will, dated October 16, 1901. This document left her estate in the care of both her sons, Edson and W. C., with substantial bequests to denominational work in the southern states of America, where Edson had labored. In a note attached to the will and addressed to her sons, she specified that the literary assets were to be held jointly by Edson, W. C., and long-time family friend Stephen N. Haskell "as a perpetual trust."[7]

In consultations with certain "leading brethren" in Washington, Ellen White signed a third will, drawn up and signed in 1906. This will stipulated that the church officials would appoint the trustees of her estate. According to a handwritten note on the copy of this will in the White Estate files, even this did not satisfy the General Conference officers. So yet another will was prepared in 1909 incorporating similar trustee arrangements but with 70 percent of royalty payments allocated for the repayment of her debts, incurred largely in purchasing the plates of her books from denominational publishers, with whom she had become increasingly unhappy. But worried that appointment of the trustees by the church's General Conference Committee would not securely safeguard the interests of her work, particularly if certain individuals were included, Ellen White never signed this will.[8] Thus in 1912 she revised her will one last time, agreeing to an arrangement that enabled her to name her trustees. This group would then become a self-perpetuating independent body that would appoint their own successors.[9] The initial group of trustees and several members of Ellen White's family (Figure 17.1) would play a crucial role in Ellen White's posthumous legacy.

The five individuals chosen to administer the trust were W. C. White, Ellen White's younger son; C. C. Crisler, a valued aide at Elmshaven for many years; Arthur G. Daniells, president of the General Conference of Seventh-day Adventists from 1901 to 1922 and also a close friend and confidant; Charles F. Jones, manager of the Pacific Press; and Francis M. Wilcox, editor of the *Review and Herald*. These trustees, appointed for

FIGURE 17.1 Ellen White and her family at her home, Elmshaven, in St. Helena, California, 1913. *Back Row:* Herbert White, Henry White, Wilfred Workman, Mabel White-Workman; *Middle Row:* William C. White, May White, Ellen G. White, Ella Mae White-Robinson, Dores E. Robinson; *Front Row:* Grace White, Arthur White, Mabel Robinson, Virgil Robinson (Courtesy of the Ellen G. White Estate, Inc.).

life, would administer everything from the disposition of her property to the future publication of her writings. The will set aside a portion of the royalties from White's books to defray the expenses of the trustees.

But things did not quite work out as Ellen White had hoped. Upon her death, the large liabilities that encumbered the estate unexpectedly complicated establishment of the trusteeship and resulted in an embarrassed General Conference agreeing to assume responsibility for the many debts by extending a large loan to liquidate them.[10] The General Conference was concerned to protect creditors and at least informally carry out the intention of the will in setting up a trusteeship even if the probate court did not. By mutual agreement the trustees assigned to the General Conference all real and personal property in the estate as equity against the loan until the loan was repaid through assumed future royalty income from publications. In fact, in the eyes of the probate court, this transaction was a simple sale, with the General Conference purchasing the estate.[11]

In 1938, following the death of W. C. White, the trust completed a move of the Estate offices with its vaults and manuscript files from California to the General Conference offices in Washington, D. C., where it became formally identified as the Ellen G. White Estate. Legal and financial issues, however, continued to trouble the relationship between the General Conference and the Estate until 1941. For various reasons, including poor accounting, the loan was not fully repaid to the General Conference until the 1950s.[12]

Posthumous Publications and Unpublished Material

After Ellen White died, the newly appointed trustees were uncertain about what to do with the large collection of letters and other manuscripts. At their first meetings they agreed that nothing should be published that had not already been printed. Daniells and other church leaders did not know what might be in personal letters to others, but what they did know about letters to themselves led them to be very cautious. They wanted to keep White's personal correspondence unpublished to avoid any negative reflection on individuals. They felt it would be much safer if the vault were simply locked up. Church leaders among the trustees were also concerned that Elmshaven should not become an independent competing publishing agency for new books. For already published works, continued publication, translation, and promotion would be no problem. But even this would require authorization from the General Conference treasurer, for there was to be no further incurring of debt. To reduce the large expense at Elmshaven, staff were let go and the activities of the Estate wound down.[13]

During her final years White and her editorial staff focused on completing her five-volume *Conflict of the Ages* series, a devotional commentary on the Bible, subsequent Christian history, and the events of the end-times. The process had involved her assistants selecting material from earlier works (articles, manuscripts, and letters) and supplementing the themes with new material (see Chapter 5). The last volume of this series, *Prophets and Kings,* still incomplete at her death, was finalized by the staff and published posthumously in 1917. With this work completed the remaining editorial staff found reassignment, and W C. White alone stayed on to serve as custodian. [14]

W.C. White worked under severe financial constraints during the first decade after his mother's death and felt frustrated with the ambiguity surrounding his role. He recounted to a friend that his mother had instructed him: "While I live, I want you to do all you can to hasten the publication of my writings in the English language, and after I die, I want you to labor for their translation and publication in foreign languages." Daniells, who understood and appreciated the role of "agent" White had played in fostering his mother's work, acknowledged White's frustration. As he explained later, he knew Ellen White "feared that no one, except perhaps her son, Elder W. C. White, would adequately realize the need of bringing forth at the proper time such unprinted manuscripts as contained certain cautions and warnings the Lord had given her which would be needed in the closing years of our work." During this decade many in leadership believed that the "canon" of Ellen White's writings should be closed. These men of "strong conviction," reported Daniells, felt that "not one sentence should be made public by the trustees unless it had been printed in some form while Mrs. White was alive." Thus the General Conference was reluctant to give W. C. White free rein with his mother's writings. As Daniells explained later, the trustees faced "a difficult challenge" and did not at the time "fully understand their responsibility nor comprehend how best to undertake it."[15]

As time passed, however, attitudes began to change. Daniells, as the senior trustee, began to moderate his own position and sought the agreement of others in leadership. He thought a "new understanding" could be reached, and in 1925 the Autumn Council of the General Conference conceded the right of publication decisions to the trustees. W. C. White wrote his daughter that the General Conference Committee had "come across" and "set free the trustees." B. E. Bedoe, assistant secretary of the General Conference, "In behalf of the Committee," spelled out the new arrangement in a letter to W. C. White. The committee had been persuaded, noted Bedoe, that "the trustees should bear full responsibilities in this matter" regarding the publication of his mother's writings. It had also budgeted enough money for the White Estate to hire some clerical and editorial assistance. But Bedoe also carefully noted that the concession had been "without record"; that is, the committee had intentionally chosen not to record minutes of the action, indicating either some residual hesitancy or perhaps awkwardness over its earlier opposition. At any rate, W. C. White felt free to begin preparing some new compilations drawing on unpublished sources. The "freedom" he anticipated, however, turned out to be something of a chimera, for it was seriously curtailed by the General Conference's insistence on authorizing any new publications.[16]

Apprehensions about the release of unpublished material continued because church leaders wondered if W. C. White and his small group of trustees were best qualified to understand the spiritual needs of the church; after all, W. C. White did not have his mother's gift of insight. Was this responsibility the proper role of the trustees? Were they the inheritors of the "gift," or was their role simply the task of physical custodianship of the writings? It took another decade or so for the church to resolve these questions.[17]

Meanwhile, a backstage struggle developed between the independent-minded and increasingly uncooperative W. C. White at Elmshaven and the General Conference leaders in Washington, leading to uncomfortable confrontations in 1932 and years to follow. To resolve the tension the General Conference finally found it necessary to assert more formal control of the White Estate properties. This was achieved through what was from W. C. White's perspective as a trustee a forced transfer of the Estate literary properties by the trustees to the General Conference. The vehicle was a contentious "Bill of Sale." Although the parties signed the sale in 1932, some of the terms continued to generate negotiation for another seven years.[18]

During these tumultuous times, unauthorized releases of unpublished material by W. C. White continued to perplex General Conference leaders. Some material, published even without the permission of his fellow trustees, was directed specifically at church leadership and was deemed highly offensive because of its severely critical tone. Who, reasoned church leaders, gave W. C. White such a burden to call out his colleagues? Was this not an abuse of his role as a trustee? The effrontery, exacerbated by White's active involvement in independent entities that often criticized and undermined the General Conference, angered administrators. The church could not afford to have "a super-administrative committee," as veteran leader W. A. Spicer labeled the trustees, for a community warring against itself would never be strong. The practical but theological question to resolve was whether the "charisma" of Ellen White had been placed in a family or in the community of the church.[19]

The confrontations produced a church-appointed "Spirit of Prophecy" committee that coordinated efforts of the White Estate Trustees and church officials. This arrangement provided a clear path for the posthumous release of unpublished materials, and soon a stream of compilations emerged, built around specific themes and drawing on Ellen White's previously published works and unpublished manuscripts.[20] The downside of some of these volumes was that the selective arrangement of material could easily reflect the particular interests and biases of compilers rather than White's original intent. By the 1970s the Estate had became increasingly aware of the value of releasing complete manuscripts and documents as they had been originally written, with historical context added when needed. By the twenty-first century the Estate was investing in an extensive research and publishing project to situate Ellen White's writings in their historical context and was committed to digitizing her entire corpus, both published and unpublished, and making it publicly available.[21]

Conflicts over Status and Authority

Meanwhile, the no-release policy of the first decade following Ellen White's death angered vocal opponents of Daniells and his colleagues in church leadership. Men such as Claude Holmes, a Linotype operator at the Review and Herald, and J. S. Washburn, a Maryland-based evangelist, represented a substantial segment of church opinion that suspected Daniells and his associates had been reproved in Ellen White's letters and were leading the church away from authentic Adventism. Believing that exposure of the reproofs would lead to the election of new, more orthodox leadership, Holmes gained covert access to Daniells' files in the General Conference vault in 1917 and made illicit copies of some of the correspondence. During the next two years, he and Washburn used the material in a pamphlet war against the Daniells administration.[22] Holmes and Washburn, who held an inerrantist view of Ellen White's writings, believed that leaders such as Daniells diminished the status of the "Spirit of Prophecy" not only by limiting the availability of her writings to the general public but by taking a non-inerrantist view of them. The struggle over these matters revealed a deepening fissure within Adventism through the years of the Great War.

As soon as the war ended, Adventist leaders who sought to maintain a cohesive Adventist theology organized a Bible conference in Takoma Park, Maryland, for its leading thinkers. The meeting convened in 1919, the same year that anti-modernist Protestants organized the World's Christian Fundamentals Association and a number of Bible conferences. Discussion at the Adventist conference reflected the fundamentalist themes then coursing through conservative American Christianity. Immediately following the Bible conference, a group of denominational college Bible and history teachers remained for a further meeting with church leaders (but not W. C. White) to discuss various educational issues.

Although not initially scheduled on the program, questions about the nature and authority of the Ellen White corpus became a major focus of discussion at these later meetings. General Conference president A. G. Daniells and other moderate leaders, along with a number of the teachers attending, openly advocated a reduced and contextually nuanced view of Ellen White's authority.[23]

Having worked closely with Ellen White for many years, Daniells felt he had a much more factual, realistic understanding of her role and authority than those who tended to oversimplify, idealize, and absolutize her work. Like any good Protestant, he insisted that the Bible could be understood "without resorting to the *Testimonies*" to unlock its meaning. He also asserted that Ellen White herself had not held an inerrantist view of her own work. "As I understand it," he declared, "Sister White never claimed to be an authority on history, and never claimed to be a dogmatic teacher on theology," but had stood ready to correct and revise statements that needed to be corrected. William W. Prescott, who had served as president of several Adventist colleges, and H. Camden Lacey, a religion teacher at Washington Foreign Mission Seminary in Takoma Park, echoed Daniells, with Lacey arguing that the worth of the "spirit of prophecy" lay in "its spiritual value rather than its historical accuracy." This viewpoint found support in the 1911 revised version of *The Great Controversy*, which, with Ellen White's approval, had incorporated corrections of historical information suggested by several Adventist scholars. Nevertheless, Daniells, aware that his was a minority viewpoint highly suspect to traditionalists, expressed a pastoral concern to say not "one word that will destroy confidence in this gift to this people," that would "create doubts," or would "in any way depreciate the value of the writings of the spirit of prophecy." (Consequently, access to the transcripts of these conferences remained restricted and virtually unknown until the 1970s.)[24]

Suggesting that Ellen White's writings were not inerrant troubled many far beyond the circle of Holmes and Washburn, who, along with W. C. White, had not attended the conferences. As one knowledgeable participant reminded the attendees, the inerrantist view had spread throughout the denomination. Many Adventists, he noted, believed that every "word that Sister White has written was to be received as infallible truth."[25]

Prescott attributed what he considered the growing misunderstanding about Ellen White's authority to W. C. White and his associates, who were fostering an over-idealized and less than honest view of the way his mother's books and articles had been prepared for publication. Shortly before Ellen White's death in 1915 Prescott had remonstrated with her son over the issue, warning that the misperceptions, if not corrected, would create a crisis in the community. He urged the Elmshaven staff to be more open and honest about Ellen White's manner of work.[26]

The Adventist controversy over Ellen White's authority paralleled the broader theological debate between fundamentalists and modernists in American Protestantism. Reflecting the spirit of fundamentalism, Adventist inerrentists insisted that the methods of so-called "higher criticism" should not be applied the writings of Ellen White any more than to the Bible. Despite considerable resistance to this inerrentist view, over the years it became normative within Adventism. Although Adventists would theoretically reject the idea of verbal inspiration and the notion of inerrancy based on it, they nevertheless adopted a position of what could be called "practical inerrancy." Not surprisingly, this attitude undermined Daniells' reputation and figured prominently in his not being reelected to office in 1922. Afterwards he felt his "standing" was not "good enough" to even write a preface or endorsement for a new compilation of unpublished Ellen White material. His later volume *The Abiding Gift of Prophecy* (1936) comprehensively affirmed his confidence in the validity and usefulness of Ellen White's unique spiritual gift—even if it was not inerrant.[27]

The Debate Resumes

Debates over the nature of Ellen White's authority wound down during the 1930s, as the "practical inerrancy" perspective rose to a position of orthodoxy.[28] That position remained dominant until the 1970s, when controversy again broke out about the role of White's writings in the life of the church, particularly in resolving disputes related to theology. Once again Adventist leaders began wrestling with the question of Ellen White's primary legacy. Was it to be found in the power of her writings for spiritual development or in their authority to determine the specifics of doctrinal teaching? If the latter, how did that mesh with the church's professed Protestant stance that held the Bible to be the sole authority for determining doctrine?

These questions became especially divisive following the publication in 1957 of a collaborative volume titled *Seventh-day Adventists Answer Questions on Doctrine*. The appearance of this book, which grew out of discussions with evangelical Christians over the orthodoxy of Adventists, gave rise to heated church-wide controversies over the nature of Christ, the Trinity, and means of salvation.[29] Because quotations from Ellen White were used to support almost every conceivable perspective, some commentators began referring to her "wax nose," which rendered her determinative role untenable.[30]

The 1970s produced several studies by newly minted Adventist scholars (typically trained outside the church) that further demonstrated the inadequacy of "practical inerrancy" as a framework for interpreting the life and work of Ellen White (see Chapter 18). These publications added challenging new perspectives and much new information but cost several of the scholars their denominational employment. The revisionist view of a fallible Ellen White found some vindication in the accidental discovery of the uncatalogued transcripts of the 1919 Bible conference in the General Conference Archives. The publication of these "lost" notes by the lay-Adventist journal *Spectrum* in 1979 brought the perspective of Daniells and other early-twentieth-century moderates back into the discussion.[31]

Debates about the place of White's legacy and the authority assigned to her writings intensified throughout the 1980s, especially in the controversy that erupted over Desmond Ford's teachings. Ford, a prominent Adventist academic and influential preacher, argued that the distinctive doctrine of the "investigative judgment," used to explain the Millerite "disappointment" of 1844, was not biblical. Questioning this central tenet of Adventist eschatology, so closely linked with the denomination's self-identity and endorsed by Ellen White, created a firestorm. A meeting between Ford and denominational leaders in Glacier View, Colorado, in 1980 upheld the traditional Adventist stance, and Ford subsequently lost church employment. The key issue in this controversy was whether Ellen White's doctrinal pronouncements should be determinative or be considered as "formative" and spiritual in a pastoral sense. In spite of mounting evidence and strong arguments for the contrary view, church authorities continued to opt for the "determinative" perspective.[32]

The tensions surrounding the Ford controversy intensified further in 1982 when, in a polemical volume entitled *The White Lie*, Walter Rea, an Adventist pastor, gave wide publicity to the charge that Ellen White frequently and knowingly plagiarized in her published work. While Rea's basic charges were not new, the extent of her pattern of literary indebtedness surprised church leaders and alarmed church members. Responding to the allegations, church authorities at first seemed willing to relate constructively to the increasing weight of evidence and the expanding array of

scholarly studies that presented Ellen White in a more human light than
had been common. In 1982 they convened an International Prophetic
Guidance Workshop to review much of the new evidence. A consensus
emerged that an education program was needed to encourage a more
nuanced and accurate assessment of Ellen White's role and authority to
replace the unrealistically inflated notions that had become commonplace
in the denomination. The church also sponsored a major study by Fred
Veltman on literary sources in the *Desire of Ages* (see Chapter 5) and published studies by two White Estate staffers, Ronald Graybill and Robert
W. Olson, that probed possibilities for a broader understanding of inspiration and revelation in the context of the Ellen White corpus. For a moment
it seemed that the church was finding ways of gradually shifting ground.
But the challenges proved too daunting, and the education program never
materialized.[33]

Meanwhile a number of Adventist historians continued the effort
to contextualize Ellen White and Adventism. George R. Knight's *Myths
in Adventism* (1985) was followed by two volumes edited by Gary Land,
Adventism in America and *The World of Ellen G. White*. These works, two of
which were brought out by denominational publishers, tried to move away
from the contention and hyperbole associated with books such as Walter
Rea's *The White Lie*—and created virtually no controversy.[34]

By the end of the century White's legacy and its influence in the life
of the church were changing in other ways. Although official Adventism
still affirmed her authority as a prophet, fewer and fewer church members in the rapidly expanding denomination, located largely in developing
countries and speaking languages other than English, actually read her
writings. Continuing arguments over her role appeared restricted largely
to special interest groups within westernized Adventism. In contrast to
the observation in 1919 that many Adventists believed every word of Ellen
White "was to be received as infallible truth," early twenty-first-century
Adventists appeared little concerned about her words at all. This was
especially true of young Adventists. Recent surveys tracking the changing values of Adventist youth report seriously declining numbers who
acknowledge her prophetic authority or who actually read her books.[35]

In response to the decreasing engagement with Ellen White's legacy,
White Estate trustees and church administrators initiated programs to
heighten her profile and to generate greater circulation of her writings. As
early as 1969 the church orchestrated a worldwide reading-and-study campaign, the "Testimony Countdown Series," to introduce modern readers

to White's early instruction to the church. Similar initiatives have promoted *Steps to Christ, The Desire of Ages,* and *The Ministry of Healing.* Early in 2012 the president of the General Conference, Ted Wilson, launched a world-wide campaign to distribute "more than 170 million copies" of Ellen White's eschatological classic, *The Great Controversy,* substantially condensed and renamed *The Great Hope* to appeal to contemporary readers. The developing awareness among the trustees that White's nineteenth-century worldview and language present a barrier to modern readers has led to similar revisions, such as the extensively rewritten reissue of White's *The Desire of Ages,* an 1898 biography of Christ, as *Messiah.*[36]

Divergent perspectives on the role and authority of the Ellen White writings continue to compete in the church. New scholarly studies attempt to understand Ellen White in her context, valuing her contribution to the building of the movement but underscoring the pragmatic and time-conditioned nature of that contribution. On the other hand, among conservatives there is increasing evidence of a subtle trend to "canonize" her writings by formally associating them with or including them in the publication of scripture. *The Clear Word Bible,* an Adventist paraphrase by Jack Blanco published in 1994 by the Review and Herald Publishing Association, unapologetically incorporates White's insights into scripture and is widely read in churches.[37] The *Remnant Study Bible,* published by Remnant Publications and sold widely in Adventist Book Centers, uniquely combines special comments by Ellen White with the text of the King James Version. One in four columns on each double page of scripture is given to E. G. White statements. These diverse approaches to White's legacy and their attendant tensions will become increasingly significant as the denomination experiences more acutely the tensions between science and religion in the debates over creationism and evolution and reconsiders gender issues. In 1907 Ellen White said presciently, "Whether or not my life is spared, my writings will constantly speak, and their work will go forward as long as time shall last."[38] Relating to the legacy and authority of White's writings will continue to create tensions and engage the thinking of the church as it seeks to fulfill its mission and engage a world that has not yet ended.

NOTES

1. *General Conference Bulletin,* 1913, 5, 6, 275; W. C. White to A. G. Daniells, December 31, 1913, Ellen G. White Estate, Silver Spring, MD. Except where

attributed to another collection, all correspondence and manuscripts are in either the White Estate or the General Conference Archives, also in Silver Spring, MD.

2. "The Final Funeral Services of Mrs. Ellen G. White...," *Advent Review and Sabbath Herald* 92 (1915): 4, hereafter referred to as *Review and Herald*; A. G. Daniells, "Life Sketch of Sister E. G. White...," *Review and Herald* 92 (1915): 6.

3. Worldwide membership at the time of her death was 136,000; see *The Fifty-third Annual Statistical Report Year Ending December 31, 1915*. In 2012 it was approximately 18 million; see www.adventistarchives.org.

4. Ellen G. White, *Selected Messages from the Writings of Ellen G. White*, 3 vols. (Washington, DC: Review and Herald Publishing Assn., 1958, 1980), 1:55; Arthur L. White, *Ellen G. White*, 6 vols. (Washington, DC: Review and Herald Publishing Assn., 1982), 6:404, 445.

5. There are four extant wills prepared by or for Ellen White during the last 24 years of her life. An account of the framing of the wills and the rationale for establishing her estate is found in Gilbert M. Valentine, *The Struggle for the Prophetic Heritage: Issues in the Conflict for Control of the Ellen G. White Publications, 1930–1939* (Muak Lek, Thailand: Institute Press, 2006), 41–48.

6. W. C. White, Statement, January 27, 1933, 5.

7. W. C. White noted in 1933 that this will had been drawn up without the knowledge of either him or his brother and that it had been framed at a time "when the administration of the General Conference affairs did not stand high in her estimation." W. C. White, handwritten statement attached to 1901 will and dated January 22, 1933.

8. W. C. White to A. G. Daniells, January 31, 1912; W. C. White, Statement, January 27, 1933, 5. Ellen White named these men to W. C. White, stressing that "none of these should have anything to do with the affairs of her books." W. C. White identified them in this 1933 document by positions they had held both before and after his mother's death. See Valentine, *Struggle for the Prophetic Heritage*, 53.

9. W. C. White, Statement, January 27, 1933. See also James R. Nix "A History of the White Estate," unpublished MS, 7–9. Should the will be "attacked" (potentially by Edson White or other heirs) the estate would revert to W. C. White as the "residual devisee."

10. Liabilities totaled $87,000, equivalent to 93 years of an annual salary for an ordained minister at the time ($963.00), which had been the rate of Ellen White's own annual remuneration.

11. W. C. White to W. T Knox, October 2, 1916, General Conference Corporation Minutes, November 17, 1916. In 1922 the White Estate Trustees viewed the General Conference as a "friendly mortgagee" because of its large loan to the Estate. White Estate Board Minutes, July 25, 1922, 3.

12. General Conference Committee minutes, November 17, 1915, General Conference Archives, Silver Spring, MD. In 1989 the General Conference

offices were moved from Washington, DC, to Silver Spring, MD. See also Valentine, *Struggle for the Prophetic Heritage*, 44–47, 130.

13. Valentine, *Struggle for the Prophetic Heritage*, 49.

14. W. C. White to "Dear Friend," October 20, 1915.

15. Ibid.; A. G. Daniells, "Mrs. White's Legacy to the Trustees," March 11, 1935 (MR 68), General Conference Archives, Silver Spring, MD.

16. A. G. Daniells to W. C. White, July 22, 1925; W. C. White to Ella May Robinson, December 8, 1925; B. E. Beddoe to W. C. White, November 19, 1925; Valentine, *Struggle for the Prophetic Heritage*, 81.

17. Valentine, *Struggle for the Prophetic Heritage*, 135–136.

18. Ibid., 87–97. In view of the fact that the General Conference already technically owned the properties, this 1932 transfer by a "Bill of Sale" was more for the benefit of the church's own internal records. As Attorney Jere Fox has called to our attention, the probate court had in fact already dealt with the transaction as a sale back in 1916.

19. Ibid., 75–76.

20. During the early 1930s W. C. White had prepared several compilations on medical and temperance work and circulated them without the authorization of even his fellow estate trustees. Following the agreement, the Estate produced *Medical Ministry*, the first book that relied heavily on previously unpublished material. Later volumes included *Counsels on Diet and Foods* (1938), *Counsels on Stewardship* (1940), *Evangelism* (1946), *Temperance* (1949), *Welfare Ministry* (1952), *The Adventist Home* (1952), and *Child Guidance* (1954).

21. http://www.whiteestate.org/search/collections.asp

22. Holmes was dismissed from employment after he refused to return copies of the purloined documents; General Conference Committee Minutes, March 27, 1917, General Conference Archives. He continued to agitate vigorously against Daniells and his colleagues. For details of the affair, see Bert Haloviak, "In the Shadow of the 'Daily': Background and Aftermath of the 1919 Bible and History Teachers' Conference," unpublished paper, 1979. http://www.adventistarchives. org/docs/AST/Ast1979.pdf#view=fit (accessed July 29, 2012). See also LeRoy E. Froom, Reference Files, 1920s–1930s, Claude E. Holmes Folder, General Conference Archives.

23. For an extended analysis of the 1919 Bible conferences, see Michael W. Campbell, "The 1919 Bible Conference and Its Significance for Seventh-day Adventist History and Theology" (Ph.D. dissertation, Seventh-day Adventist Theological Seminary, Andrews University, 2008); abstract in *Andrews University Seminary Studies* 46 (2008): 258. See also Paul McGraw, "Without a Living Prophet," *Ministry: International Journal for Pastors* 73 (December 2000): 11–15.

24. Molleurus Couperus, ed., "The Bible Conference of 1919," *Spectrum: Journal of the Association of Adventist Forums* 10 (May 1979), 23–57, esp. 27 (destroy confidence), 30 (without resorting), 34 (authority), 38 (Lacey), 54–56 (Great

Controversy); hereafter referred to as *Spectrum*. Transcripts of the conferences are now available on the Web site of the Office of Archives and Statistics, General Conference of Seventh-day Adventists.

25. Couperus, "The Bible Conference of 1919," 49. For Claude E. Holmes's reaction to the 1919 conferences, see "Have We an Infallible Spirit of Prophecy?" tract written to J. S. Washburn, April 1, 1920, Document File 352, White Estate. In a letter to W. C. White, October 31, 1926, Holmes wrote: "I love your mother's writings. They are all scripture to me."

26. For a discussion of Prescott's 1915 letter highlighting misperceptions of Ellen White in the church, see Gilbert M. Valentine, "The Church 'Drifting toward a Crisis': Prescott's 1915 Letter to William White," *Catalyst* 2 (November 2007): 32–94. On Prescott, see Gilbert M. Valentine, *W. W. Prescott: Forgotten Giant of Adventism's Second Generation* (Hagerstown, MD: Review and Herald Publishing Assn., 2005).

27. A. G. Daniells to W. C. White, September 25, 1923; A G. Daniells, *The Abiding Gift of Prophecy* (Mountain View, CA: Pacific Press, 1936).

28. For influential expressions of this position, see W. H. Branson, *In Defense of the Faith: The Truth about Seventh-day Adventists; A Reply to Canright* (Washington, DC: Review and Herald Publishing Assn., 1933); and Francis D. Nichol, *Ellen G. White and Her Critics* (Washington, DC: Review and Herald Publishing Assn., 1951).

29. *Seventh-day Adventists Answer Questions on Doctrine* (Washington, DC: Review and Herald Publishing Assn., 1957). In 2003 George R. Knight brought out an annotated version of *Questions on Doctrine* (Berrien Springs, MI: Andrews University Press, 2003.)

30. Geoffrey Paxton seems to have introduced the phrase in *The Shaking of Adventism* (Wilmington, DE: Zenith Publishers, 1977), 156.

31. See Donald R. McAdams, "Shifting Views of Inspiration: Ellen White Studies in the 1970s," *Spectrum* 10, No. 4 (1980): 27–41; Molleurus Couperus, "The Bible Conference of 1919," *Spectrum* 10, no. 1 (1979), 23–57; Jonathan M. Butler, "Introduction: The Historian as Heretic," Ronald L. Numbers, *Prophetess of Health: Ellen G. White and the Origins of Seventh-day Adventist Health Reform* (Knoxville: University of Tennessee Press, 1992), xxv–lxviii. See also Ronald L. Numbers, "Preface," *Prophetess of Health: A Study of Ellen G. White*, 3rd ed. (Grand Rapids, MI: Eerdmans, 2008).

32. On the Ford controversy in Australia and New Zealand, see Peter H. Ballis, *Leaving the Adventist Ministry: A Study of the Process of Exiting* (Westport, CT: Praeger, 1999).

33. Walter T. Rea, *The White Lie* (Turlock, CA: M & R Publications, 1982); Arthur N. Patrick, "Contextualising Recent Tensions in Seventh-day Adventism: A Constant Process of Struggle and Rebirth"? *Journal of Religious History* 34 (2010): 272–288. See also Patrick, "Seventh-day Adventist History

in the South Pacific: A Review of Sources," *Journal of Religious History* 14 (1987): 307–26.

34. George R. Knight, *Myths in Adventism: An Interpretive Study of Ellen White, Education, and Related Issues* (Washington, DC: Review and Herald Publishing Assn., 1985); Gary Land, ed., *Adventism in America: A History* (Grand Rapids, MI.: William B. Eerdmans, 1986); Gary Land, ed., *The World of Ellen G. White* (Washington, DC: Review and Herald Publishing Assn., 1987).

35. This trend was noted in a 1979 article, "The Use of the Spirit of Prophecy in Our Teaching of Bible and History," *Spectrum* 10 (May (1979): 37, 38. In 1992 Roger L. Dudley and V. Bailey Gillespie surveyed over 11,000 students in North American Adventist elementary and secondary schools and reported that 42% never read Ellen White and 24% read her writings less than once a month. See Dudley and Gillespie, *Valuegenesis: Faith in the Balance* (Riverside, CA: La Sierra University Press, 1992), 120. See also V. Bailey Gillespie and Michael J. Donahue with Ed Boyatt and Barry Gane, *Valuegenesis Ten Years Later: A Study of Two Generations* (Riverside, CA: La Sierra University Press, 2004).

36. "Testimony Countdown," *Ministry* 42 (April 1969): 24–27; "2012: Big Year for the Great Controversy," at www.reviewandherald.com/index.php/news/article/33rhpa; Jerry D. Thomas, *Messiah: A Contemporary Adaptation of the Classic Work on Jesus' Life, the Desire of Ages* (Nampa, ID: Pacific Press, 2002).

37. Following criticism of the title, the publishing house deleted the word "Bible" from the original title *The Clear Word Bible*, and the words "An Expanded Paraphrase" were added in subsequent printings. The text of the paraphrase utilizes fragments, quotes, and paraphrases from the writings of Ellen G. White.

38. Ellen G. White, *Selected Messages from the Writings of Ellen G. White*, 3 vols. (Washington, DC: Review and Herald Publishing Assn., 1958, 1980), 1: 55.

18

Biographies

Gary Land

DESPITE HER ROLE in developing the Seventh-day Adventist Church, Ellen G. White has received relatively little attention from historians outside her religious tradition. Within her communion, however, an apologetic approach to her biography went almost unchallenged over a period of about one hundred years. Although there were a few precedents, beginning in the 1970s historians with connections to the denomination began reexamining her life and writings, asking questions about her relationship to nineteenth- century society and culture, the sources of her ideas, and her methods as an author. About the same time that this critical approach emerged, scholars outside the church began including Ellen White in their histories of nineteenth-century American religion, women, and reform. Because of the influence of Ronald L. Numbers's *Prophetess of Health: A Study of Ellen G. White*, however, they usually emphasized her role as a health reformer and gave little emphasis to her other activities.

Establishing the Adventist Interpretation, 1850s–1910s

Two works laid the foundation for the historical picture of Ellen G. White: Ellen White's own autobiography, which went through three editions between 1851 and 1880, with a fourth edition published after her death, and John N. Loughborough's *Rise and Progress of Seventh-day Adventists*, published in 1892. These works established the centrality of White's role as a "messenger" of God, particularly through recounting her visionary experiences.[1]

In the first version of her autobiography, *A Sketch of the Christian Experience and Views of Ellen G. White,* the author briefly described her conversion at about age thirteen, her attendance at Millerite meetings, and her "hungering and thirsting" after full salvation. But from that point on, the book mainly recounted some fifteen visions that she had experienced between December 1844 and May 1851, written "with the hope that it will cheer and strengthen the humble, trusting children of God" and the belief "that the Lord required it of me."[2]

Whereas her first autobiography seems to have been primarily a vehicle for the publication of her visions, White's second version, published in 1860, had a broader apologetic purpose. In the preface she noted that she was writing to show that she had never been a Mormon, as some had accused her of being, and "felt anxious that my brethren should know *what* my experience has been, and *where* it has been." (There was indeed a tenuous connection: in 1835 one of her second cousins, Agnes Moulton Coolbrith, had married Don Carlos Smith, Joseph Smith's younger brother, and after the death of Don Carlos, Agnes in 1842 had become one of the prophet's plural wives.) But beyond responding to accusations of Mormonism, the volume also addressed criticisms that she was receiving within the Adventist movement. To establish the accuracy of her reporting, she included quotations from letters and accounts by persons who had observed her in vision. She closed the volume by asking those who could "testify to other facts stated in this book" to send her their statements. Subsequent printings of the book included several pages of these "testimonies." She also asked for corrections of any errors, though later printings made no mention of these.[3]

This second autobiography gave many more personal details than her earlier book. Beginning with the story of the childhood injury that forced her to leave school at an early age, it described her family's expulsion from the Methodist church because of their Millerite beliefs and her first vision some two months after the "Great Disappointment." She told of fighting fanaticism in Maine, sacrificing her own interests to advance the sabbatarian cause, defeating opposition within the sabbatarian ranks, and struggling with her own and her husband's ill health. In addition, she recounted other episodes that became staples in subsequent Adventist accounts of her life, including a story of holding a large family Bible in her outstretched hand while in vision. The third version of her autobiography, *Life Sketches* (1880), continued the story of her life past 1860, emphasizing the continuing role of her visions and dreams and her extensive travels in promoting the church.[4]

After Ellen White's death in 1915, C. C. Crisler, who had served as her secretary, added an account of her life after 1881. Testifying to the large role that Ellen had come to play in the denomination after the death of her husband, this posthumous book deleted James's autobiographical story. Made up largely of quotations from her writings, Crisler's new section continued the description of her camp-meeting travels and years in Europe and Australia. It noted her role in the development of Adventist institutions, including the establishment of the Avondale School in Australia, the 1901 reorganization of the General Conference and its subsequent move to Washington, DC, and the beginnings of the medical school in Loma Linda, California. Crisler also drew attention to what Adventists believed was evidence that Ellen White's visions were supernaturally inspired.[5]

In contrast to Ellen White books, which emphasized the content of her visions, John N. Loughborough's *Rise and Progress of the Seventh-day Adventists* (1892) described her physical manifestations while in vision, drawing on his own memories and those of eyewitnesses. A thoroughgoing supernaturalist, he wrote to demonstrate that the visionary phenomena were genuine and could only be explained through divine agency. Loughborough claimed to have seen White in vision over fifty times and to have been present while physicians examined her. "I esteem it a pleasure to bear testimony to what I have seen and know," he wrote. Impressed by the physical phenomena accompanying her visions, he stated that White typically shouted "Glory!" three times as she went into vision and after a brief swoon exhibited superhuman strength, moving her hands and arms frequently and gracefully. Although she had no noticeable breath while in vision, her heart beat regularly. To support these observations, Loughborough provided several statements from eyewitnesses. Loughborough also offered "Proofs of Divine Agency," including stories of her holding the large Bible while in vision and a report of her having seen the moons of Jupiter, Saturn, and Uranus, astronomical knowledge that had convinced Joseph Bates of her divine inspiration. In addition, he put forward theological rules for determining "genuine manifestations of the Spirit of God."[6]

More than a decade later, Loughborough published a new version of his book under the title *The Great Second Advent Movement: Its Rise and Progress* (1905). Casting his discussion of Ellen White as an apologetic for belief in her divine inspiration, he cited additional eyewitnesses to the physical phenomena accompanying her visions as well as twenty-one associates who affirmed that she had not taught the shut-door doctrine, which held that the door of salvation had been closed permanently in 1844. He identified several of Ellen White's predictions that, he believed, had come true, among which was the San Francisco earthquake.[7] Together, Ellen White's autobiographies and J. N. Loughborough's histories established the foundation for an Adventist historical understanding of Ellen White.

The Middle Period: The Image Consolidated, 1920s–1970s

Although Seventh-day Adventists produced several books on Ellen White during the four decades after her death, most of them concentrated on affirming White's role as a prophet rather than developing increased biographical and historical understanding. While some of the writers had known Ellen White personally, most of them were a generation or more younger than the founders of the church. Addressing a denominational membership that had had little or no personal contact with White, they played an important role in consolidating the image and meaning of the prophet.

Arthur G. Daniells, who had worked with Ellen White in Australia in the 1890s and served as president of the General Conference between 1901 and 1922, wrote *The Abiding Gift of Prophecy* shortly before his death in 1935. The first half of the book traced the development of prophecy from the Old Testament through the history of the Christian Church, arguing that God uses prophets to reveal Himself. Daniells believed that false visions had occurred during the Millerite movement, but with Ellen White the "true manifestation came at the appointed hour." Commenting on the declining frequency of her visions during the latter part of her life, he explained that the change occurred through God's providence:

> In later years when it was possible to judge her claims by the character and content of her published works and labors, wholly apart from the physical evidence, these physical phenomena were no longer necessary to faith, and her public visions became less frequent, and finally ceased.[8]

William A. Spicer, who followed Daniells into the presidency of the General Conference, serving from 1922 to 1930, wrote several faith-affirming books on Adventist history. In *The Spirit of Prophecy in the Advent Movement,* published in 1937, he stated that with Ellen White God had called an "agent through whom He should speak messages to the people of the rising movement." He believed that divine inspiration provided the only adequate explanation for her writings. "With the call to that young woman in 1844 to take up this burden," he wrote, "there came strength and gifts to do the work required." Consequently, "The writings of the Spirit of prophecy [that is, Ellen White] carry their own credentials."[9]

Meanwhile, the denomination published its first general history, M. E. Olsen's *A History of the Origin and Progress of Seventh-day Adventists* (1925), which drew extensively on White's own writings and Loughborough's histories. Only the second Adventist to earn a Ph.D. (in 1909 from the University of Michigan's literary department), Olsen said very little about supernatural influences and, unlike Loughborough, apparently felt no need to defend White against her critics. He suggested that White had helped to unify the early Adventists and pushed them into such activities as publishing and education. With regard to health reform, he said that she "took different ground from contemporary hygienists in laying stress upon the moral influence of health reform."[10] Olsen largely eschewed interpretation in favor of description.

That the denomination was consciously promoting a particular image of Ellen White became clear when the Adventist Missionary Volunteer Society asked Everett Dick, a teacher at Union College, an Adventist school in Lincoln, Nebraska, who had earned a Ph.D. in history from the University of Wisconsin in 1930, to write a book for young people about early Adventist leaders. His original manuscript included a discussion of the ill health of both James and Ellen White and their involvement in the shut-door doctrine, but he found his sponsors unwilling to publish such information.[11] Concerned about his reputation as a historian, he stated in his foreword that

It has been my purpose to present the inspirational incidents in the lives of these leaders without any attempt to discover their human weaknesses or foibles. I make no claim that the volume is a critical, scientific history, but have frankly attempted to produce a popular work which will inspire to nobler living and great self-sacrifice the young people of this denomination, which the founders gave their all to establish.[12]

Despite the restrictions on content, Dick discussed Ellen White in strictly historical terms, eschewing the supernatural explanations that generally governed denominational interpretation. For instance, in writing about her vision that settled the question of whether the Sabbath was to be observed beginning at 6:00 p.m. or sundown on Friday, he stated: "In time of crisis, when division was apparent, her counsel and messages were recognized as the voice of God, and strong men yielded points of difference and gave way to the messages." He also noted White's changing function in the church over time, observing that while James was alive "her place was that of one who is the dynamic power behind the leaders" but that after her husband's death "she came more to the foreground in the denominational consciousness."[13]

Dick's historical approach garnered few followers. Both general histories and works on Ellen White that appeared from the 1940s to the early 1970s maintained the supernatural and apologetic approach of earlier books. Typical was the work of Dores Eugene Robinson, a former secretary of Ellen White's who had married one of her granddaughters and written *The Story of Our Health Message* (1943). Unlike most Adventist writers, Robinson wrote extensively about White's historical context, in particular the health-reform movement of the mid-nineteenth century. But he believed that she had functioned independently of that influence, arguing that the basic principles of her 1863 vision "were in advance of the general knowledge of the time" because her source was God, not other reformers.[14]

By the 1970s the Adventist denomination had established an image of Ellen G. White that compared her favorably with the prophets of the Bible, regarded her doctrinal positions as biblically sound, saw her as indispensable to the development of the many lines of Adventist endeavor, believed that she wrote under the influence of divine inspiration, and portrayed her as an attractive personality. Within this image, there was little room for contemporary influences, development and change in her thinking, errors, or personal ambition. This idealized Ellen White nearly transcended her time and place.

The Image Challenged

As Ellen White acknowledged, she had had her critics from the beginning of her ministry. It is not surprising, therefore, that these criticisms began to appear in biographical and historical accounts of early Adventism. Just as the developing Seventh-day Adventist image of Ellen White was grounded in the theological conviction that she was God's messenger, so the writings of Isaac Wellcome, Dudley M. Canright, and Louis R. Conradi, who contributed to the first stage of critical response to this developing image, rested on the rejection of that notion. The historical record served as fodder for theological polemics.

Wellcome, a writer and publisher in the Advent Christian denomination, another Millerite descendent, published his *History of the Second Advent Message* in 1874 to demonstrate that his church, rather than the Seventh-day Adventists, was the legitimate heir of William Miller's movement. An associate of the Whites in the early aftermath of the "Great Disappointment" of 1844, Wellcome drew on his memory to argue that Ellen had been a proponent of the shut-door theology, asserting that her visions "were but the echoes of Eld. [Joseph] Turner and others' preaching [of the shut-door], and we regarded them as the product of the over-excited imagination of her mind, and not as facts." He argued that as time passed, the theological content of Ellen's visions had changed and that James had attempted to suppress her earliest publications, which supported the shut-door on the basis of visions. Wellcome also attacked the Whites for arguing that they had opposed the post-Disappointment fanaticism in Maine. He scornfully commented that "if this were true then the Christian people of Maine would need a new dictionary to inform them of the proper definition of fanaticism."[15]

Dudley M. Canright had been ordained a Seventh-day Adventist minister in 1865, but in 1873 he began having problems personally with James and Ellen White and ultimately with Adventist theology (Figure 18.1). After moving in and out of the ministry several times, he resigned his membership permanently in February 1887 and shortly thereafter received ordination as a Baptist minister. In 1888 he published *Seventh-day Adventism Renounced*, a volume that became a standard source for later critics of the denomination. Although he criticized Ellen White in that volume, he developed his critique more fully in *Life of Mrs. E. G. White* (1919). Comparing White with Mary Baker Eddy, Canright argued that her early dreams and visions resulted from the interaction of her overly excited religious environment with "her physical and mental condition," which produced "hallucinations of her own mind." He attributed the cessation of her visions in the 1870s to "the change of life common to women." Canright's most serious criticisms addressed White's writings. He argued that her literary assistants had gathered "the greater portion of the material for her larger and most important books." Furthermore, he accused her of copying "extensively from other writers without giving credit," a practice that

FIGURE 18.1 Among the colleagues of Ellen White who shaped her reputation was Dudley M. Canright, who eventually became an outspoken critic (Courtesy of the Ellen G. White Estate, Inc.).

he attributed to her being "so anxious to make books, so possessed with the idea of her own self-importance, and so desirous of appearing something that she was not, that she ignored the rights of others, purloined from their writings, and became a pronounced literary kleptomaniac."[16]

Twenty years later, Louis R. Conradi, a former Adventist minister and administrator who had left the denomination in the early 1930s and joined the Seventh Day Baptists, published a pamphlet titled *The Founders of the Seventh Day Adventist Denomination*. Dismissing Ellen White as a "hysterical girl" who had "fanciful" visions, he accused her of being an imposter who had based two of her early visions on the Millerite preacher Enoch Jacobs and on her associate Joseph Bates. She and James, he charged, had committed "pious fraud" when they allegedly changed the chronological order of the early visions and omitted references to the shut-door.[17]

Except for William H. Branson's *Reply to Canright* (1933) and Francis D. Nichol's *Ellen G. White and Her Critics* (1951), Seventh-day Adventists did not take much notice of Wellcome, Canright, or Conradi. [18] Although their criticisms may have affected individual believers and, particularly in Canright's case, provided important sources for other critics of Adventism, these works had little discernable influence on the development of Seventh-day Adventist thinking regarding Ellen White.

Ellen White scholarship changed dramatically in the 1970s, when a small group of young Adventist scholars in history and religion launched a quest to discover the historical Ellen White. Almost all the participants had attended non-Adventist graduate schools in the 1960s and returned to teach in Adventist institutions, where they applied their critical methodologies to the writings of Ellen White. Many of the group had also been instrumental in establishing the Association of Adventist Forums in 1967, which two years later began publishing *Spectrum*, an independent journal devoted to discussion of Adventism that offered an outlet for new thinking about Ellen White. [19]

Spectrum fired the opening salvo in its autumn 1970 issue. Herold Weiss (Ph.D. Duke) and Roy Branson (Ph.D. Harvard), two young professors at the Seventh-day Adventist Theological Seminary, called for Adventist scholars to examine Ellen White's relationship to other authors, the intellectual and social milieu of her time, and her own intellectual development. In the same issue, William S. Peterson (Ph.D. Northwestern), an Andrews University English professor, tackled the question of White's relationship to other authors by arguing that *The Great Controversy* largely drew on the works of Sir Walter Scott and James A. Wylie. "It simply will not suffice to say that God showed her the broad outline of events and she then filled in the gap with her readings," Peterson stated. "In the case of the French Revolution, there was no 'broad outline' until she had read the historians." Offered the opportunity to respond, W. Paul Bradley of the White Estate said that critical scholarship was not needed, for "no reinterpretation is required to make us know God's messages for us." Furthermore, "one must doubt whether historical criticism will have a preponderance of weight. There will always have to be present a strong element of faith." Discussion continued until Ronald Graybill, a researcher at the White Estate who had studied with Branson, demonstrated that White had actually drawn her material second-hand from Uriah Smith, editor of the *Review and Herald*, who had used the historians in writing his commentary *Thoughts on Daniel and Revelation*. [20]

Up to this point, discussion of Ellen White and her sources remained limited largely to the readers of *Spectrum*. In 1976, however, Ronald L. Numbers, a Berkeley-trained historian of science and medicine who had taught briefly at both Andrews University and Loma Linda University before joining the faculty of the University of Wisconsin, published *Prophetess of Health*, which examined Ellen White's development as a health reformer. Noting that he differed from most Adventist writers in avoiding use of "divine inspiration as an historical explanation," Numbers developed two major themes. First, he argued that Ellen White had drawn on contemporary health reformers for many of her ideas. Writing about her essay "How to Live," he stated that "even the casual reader must agree that a striking similarity does exist between Mrs. White's ideas and those commonly expressed by the health reformers." Examining other of her writings, he placed in parallel columns quotations from White, Horace Mann, and L. B. Coles, commenting that "often she appropriated passages from them with only cosmetic changes." Second, Numbers demonstrated that Ellen White's ideas regarding health had changed or developed over time. In 1849, for instance, she had advised Adventists to rely on prayer rather than go to physicians, but by 1860 was recommending the use of doctors and denying that she had ever taught otherwise. Perhaps more significant, although she consistently advocated a vegetarian diet beginning in the 1860s, her rationale shifted from the alleged "animalizing tendencies" of a carnivorous diet to its transmission of disease and its cruelty to animals.[21]

Prophetess of Health caused an uproar within Adventism. The denomination, which had initially sought to prevent publication by Harper & Row, rushed out a paperback edition of Robinson's *Story of Our Health Message* while the White Estate sent speakers to Adventist centers and published extensive critiques of the volume. The controversy even prompted a *Time* magazine article. The fundamental issue between Numbers and his critics was methodological. The Estate, under the leadership of White's grandson Arthur L. White, argued that if divine inspiration is excluded *a priori*, then one is left with nothing but a secularist-historicist interpretation of Ellen White's life and an implicit denial of the validity or truthfulness of her claim to divine inspiration. The Estate's widely circulated report concluded that "this late-hour attack upon the validity of her messages does not stand the test of history nor the judgment through the years of the church's trusted spiritual leaders."[22]

Meanwhile, Donald R. McAdams (Ph.D. Duke), who taught history at Andrews University, examined White's use of sources in writing her chapter on John Hus in *The Great Controversy*. McAdams concluded that

The historical portions of *The Great Controversy* that I have examined are selective abridgements and adaptations of historians. Ellen

White was not just borrowing paragraphs here and there that she ran across in her reading, but in fact following the historians page after page, leaving out much material, but using their sequence, some of their ideas, and often their words.

Rather than releasing his paper publicly, McAdams presented it to the White Estate, which pursued a similar study of the chapter on Luther and reached similar conclusions. The implications of such scholarship could hardly be avoided. As the young historian Benjamin McArthur, who had just earned a doctorate in history at the University of Chicago, observed, "If Mrs. White's writings are shown to be historically conditioned, they will lose their traditional authority....Adventist identity itself will be threatened."[23]

Trained scholars who sought a degree of objectivity dominated the new critical study of Ellen White.[24] But in 1982 they were joined by Walter Rea, a senior Adventist minister in California. After years of ardently promoting the Spirit of Prophecy, as Adventists often called the writings of Ellen White, he had begun a close examination of *Patriarchs and Prophets, Prophets and Kings,* and *The Desire of Ages* only to discover that they were based largely on works by Alfred Edersheim, Daniel March, William Hanna, and other nineteenth-century writers on the Bible. In what was becoming something of a tradition among critics of Ellen White, Rea devoted much of his polemic, *The White Lie,* to columns that paralleled excerpts from White's works with their alleged sources. As his title suggested, Rea was concerned not only with the fact of White's literary borrowing but also with what he believed had been the denomination's cover-up of this fact. "[T]he information revealing the extent of her literary dependence has been deliberately kept from lay members," he alleged, "until independent researchers began to make the facts public." Based on the information he and others had brought to light, Rea concluded that rather than being divinely inspired, White wrote under very human influence and therefore could not be accepted as a religious authority. He called on Adventism to come to grips with this situation.[25]

The Denomination Responds

Rea's exposé prompted a vigorous response from the church.[26] The General Conference commissioned Fred Veltman, a New Testament scholar teaching at Pacific Union College, to examine White's use of literary sources in her writing of *The Desire of Ages*. Analyzing fifteen chapters, Veltman and his assistants concluded that about 31 percent of this material was "in some degree clearly dependent upon material appearing in our 500-plus literary sources." Although White's emphasis was frequently different from that of her sources, Veltman concluded that her writing exhibited little that was unique. "We found source parallels," he stated, "for theological, devotional, narrative, descriptive, and spiritual materials, whether in reference to biblical or extrabiblical content." He observed that study needed to be given to White's own "understanding of inspiration and of her role as a prophet" within the context of nineteenth-century understandings.[27] Clearly, the more-or-less official denominational understanding of Ellen White had changed considerably since these issues had erupted in the early 1970s.

Additional evidence of the impact of the new scholarship in the church's thinking appeared in an authorized college-level textbook on denominational history, *Light Bearers to the Remnant* (1979) by Richard W. Schwarz, chair of the history department at Andrews University who had once hired both Numbers and McAdams. Schwarz approached Ellen White largely through her own self-understanding, quoting extensively from her accounts of her visions. Like other traditionalists, he stated that she did not introduce new doctrines but rather provided encouragement and assurance to the Adventist believers. Although he was not allowed to cite *Prophetess of Health* in his chapter bibliographies, Numbers's book influenced his interpretation of White's 1863 vision. "All the major points emphasized had been discovered by persons like Graham, Coles, and Trall," Schwarz wrote. "The vision did convey to Seventh-day Adventists the divine approval of natural remedies over drugs and of a balanced health program including diet, exercise, fresh air, rest, sunshine, and the curative powers of water."[28]

Meanwhile, Arthur L. White had embarked on a multi-volume biography of his grandmother, *Ellen G. White* (1981–86). In many respects a throwback to older approaches to Ellen White, this biography relied on extensive quotations from her letters and other writings. The author rarely addressed the issues that Adventist scholars had been dealing with in recent years, downplaying the issues of literary dependency and the role of her literary assistants. Although the biography provided considerable factual information about Ellen White's life and was therefore useful for reference purposes, it offered little in the way of analysis. Equally apologetical was Herbert E. Douglass's hefty *Messenger of the Lord: The Prophetic Ministry of Ellen G. White* (1998).[29]

Elsewhere there were signs of change. Most significant were the publications of George R. Knight, who taught successively in the school of education and the theological seminary at Andrews University and who between 1982 and 2010 wrote more than thirty books on Adventist theology and history. In them he sought to present a realistic view of Ellen White and yet maintain a positive tone. Minimizing her contributions to theology, he emphasized her roles in shaping an Adventist "lifestyle" and in expanding the denomination's vision regarding such things as reorganization and missions. Although denominational publishers brought out all of his books, Knight succeeded in presenting White "as a human being who had her own trials and disappointments as well as victories and accomplishments." In discussing the debate over White that had begun in the 1970s, Knight explicitly rejected both her verbal inspiration and inerrancy, suggesting instead that she had changed over time and that she must be understood within her historical context. This was believer's history but written with nuance and caution.[30]

The View from Outside

Little of the discussion of Ellen White reached beyond Adventist boundaries and, therefore, it did not catch the attention of scholars outside the church. Furthermore, up to the mid-1960s most research and writing in American church history concentrated on "mainstream" Christianity rather than marginal groups. As David W. Lotz has pointed out, this was a period of theologically motivated "church history" that examined the "church catholic."[31] The late 1960s saw the emergence of a broader religious history that focused less on institutions and doctrines and more on the diversity of religious experience. Once marginal traditions, such as Mormons, Adventists, and Christian Scientists, now found themselves welcomed to the historical mainstream.

Although Adventist historian Everett N. Dick had written an entry on White for the *Dictionary of American Biography*, published in 1937, from the 1930s through the 1960s non-Adventist historians rarely mentioned Ellen White. Surveys of American church history by William Warren Sweet and Jerald Brauer, who emphasized mainstream Christianity, briefly discussed Millerism and the emergence of Seventh-day Adventists but did not mention Ellen G. White. A more specialized study of social history, Whitney R. Cross's *The Burned-Over District*, placed Ellen White at the center of the "Seventh-day Church" that emerged out of Millerism. Winthop Hudson's *Religion in America*, published fifteen years later, similarly stated that Ellen White had taught "that Christ's failure to appear was due to a neglect of proper Sabbath observance." In 1972, Sydney Ahlstrom's encyclopedic *Religious History of the American People*, widely regarded as marking the end of an era in the writing of church history, noted White only in passing, describing her nine-volume *Testimonies to the Church* as the denomination's "chief unifying factor."[32]

Interest from academics began increasing in the 1970s through the convergence of four elements. First, the publication of Ronald L. Numbers's *Prophetess of Health* by a major trade publisher brought increasing recognition of White as an historical figure, especially in reference books and surveys of American religion. Second, growing interest in women's history prompted a number of scholars to weave previously obscure women into the historical record. Peter W. Williams commented that "the entry of large numbers of women into the historical profession" shifted the "matrix" through which the careers of controversial women such as Ellen White were interpreted. Third, as mentioned above, research into the history of American religion shifted from a theologically oriented mainstream Protestant synthesis to a more pluralist paradigm. Finally, historians became increasingly interested in the history of reform, particularly in the areas of temperance, health, and fitness.[33]

In 1972–1973 Numbers and Vern Carner, who were teaching at Loma Linda University, organized a series of lectures that addressed the social and religious context of early Adventism. Edwin Gaustad, of the nearby University of California, Riverside, edited the lectures for publication by Harper & Row under the title *The Rise of Adventism* (1974). Ellen White appeared briefly in John B. Blake's discussion of health reform, but Jonathan Butler's "Adventism and the American Experience" gave much more attention to White as it creatively explored the changing thrust of Adventist eschatology. In 1858, Butler stated, she took a position of "political apocalypticism" that eschewed all political activity, writing of slavery and its support by the churches as "a chief indication of a decaying world," and looked forward to the pouring out of God's wrath on the nation. Some two decades later, however, "the prophetess was midwife for the new eschatology," which he termed "political prophetic," as she "urged Adventists to be, in effect, a tiny political cadre doing their part to prolong the American future so the Adventist message could go forth and flourish." In later publications, Butler firmly placed Ellen White and her thought within the context of her time, a view that was potentially damaging to her religious authority within Adventism but received little attention there.[34]

In the mid-1970s, Numbers led out in developing a scholarly history of the Seventh-day Adventist Church that came to fruition with the publication of *Adventism in America: A History* (1986), which I edited. As a general history of the denomination written by Adventist scholars, this volume discussed Ellen White largely in terms of institutional growth and development. In contrast to earlier Adventist histories, *Adventism in America* also examined debates over White that occurred during her own lifetime as well as those of the 1970s.[35] Although the volume offered no new interpretations of Ellen White, it was the first serious history of Seventh-day Adventism to be published by a non-denominational publisher, William B. Eerdmans, and thus was distributed to a wide market, including academic libraries.

As Numbers continued his extraordinarily productive career as a scholar, he did not leave Ellen White behind. In his book *The Creationists*, published by Alfred A. Knopf in 1982, he traced the history of "scientific creationism" back to Adventist writer George McCready Price, who in turn had based his ideas on White's "suggestion that the deluge and related events had buried the fossils." Numbers returned to White again in a 2003 essay in which he argued that John Harvey Kellogg had translated "White's sexual warnings, born of visions and bred in a culture of religious and medical sectarianism, into arguably the most widely circulated medical text on sex in the years spanning the last two decades of the nineteenth century and first two decades of the twentieth century." In these works on creationism and sex, as well as other publications, Numbers demonstrated that Ellen White had a cultural and social significance that reached far beyond Seventh-day Adventism.[36]

The growth of Ellen White studies among Adventist scholars coincided with the explosion of interest in women's history among historians generally. The landmark collection of biographies in *Notable American Women* (1971), which included an entry on Ellen White by historian of religion C. C. Goen, asserted that White's biblical interpretations "largely...determined Seventh-day Adventist orthodoxy." A few years later Janet Wilson James, a coeditor of *Notable American Women*, included Ann Lee, Jemima Wilkinson, and Ellen White among a "motley company of extremists" who "offered healing, comfort, and love, release from anxiety, guilt, and subservience, and a millennium close at hand." She described "the cults" founded by these women as providing a refuge for the rootless, and for women without families and those trapped in intolerable marriages." Later writers tended to take a more sympathetic view of these rebellious outsiders, often explaining their dissent as a response to male dominance in the mainstream churches.[37]

By the late 1970s and early 1980s Ellen White's name was frequently appearing in reference works and surveys of religion in America, often in her role as a health reformer. For example, in his widely read *Pilgrims in Their Own Land: 500 Years of Religion in America*, Martin Marty described her as the "virtual founder of the modern health-minded cause of Seventh-day Adventism," a woman who possessed the "genius" for connecting health cures with "a whole plan of salvation."[38]

Ellen White also benefited from the growing interest in "new" or "outsider" religions, previously relegated to the margins of American religious history. R. Laurence Moore, who had contributed a chapter to *The Rise of Adventism*, took the lead in his pathbreaking *Religious Outsiders and the Making of Americans* (1986), which devoted a number of pages to Adventism and White. Moore emphasized her role as a health reformer but also commented on her views about public issues. Noting White's opposition to strikes, emphasis on self-help, and generally *laissez faire* economic philosophy, he commented that, despite her outsider religious position, "she said things that placed her more on the side of the haves than the have-nots." Paul Conkin followed Moore with his *American Originals: Homemade Varieties of Christianity* (1997). In a long chapter titled "Apocalyptic Christianity," Conkin stated that "one of the most fascinating themes in Seventh-day Adventism is how this movement used Ellen G. White to serve the ends of a religion that came to symbolize obedience and good order, not enthusiasm and ecstasy." Although, according to Conkin, she assumed "the prophetic role too often," she was "humane and irenic" and politically skillful, particularly after her husband's death, but left her denomination a tension-filled legacy, not least of which was conclusively defining her prophetic role, an issue that Conkin believed "remains unresolved." Nevertheless, he placed her along with Ann Lee and Mary Baker Eddy, "in the great trinity of female prophets in American Christianity."[39]

This interest in the history of American religions, including those outside the mainstream, provided the opportunity for two British authors with Adventist backgrounds to publish *Seeking A Sanctuary* (1989). Sociological in perspective and thematic in structure, this volume offered perhaps the best and freshest interpretation of Adventism but did not give a systematic account of Ellen White. Rather than studying White biographically, Bull and Lockhart focused on her significance for shaping the contemporary Adventist ethos and thus frequently referred to her writings as they examined Adventist views of such subjects as religious liberty, women, and race. They concluded that for Adventists White was increasingly one authority among many—so much so that "in the 1970s an open season on Ellen White research made reason and the Bible her two judges."[40]

In *Adventism and the American Republic* (2001), which originated as a University of Chicago dissertation, Douglas Morgan featured Ellen White's influence on Adventists' understanding of their relationship to the state. Maintaining that she influenced "all aspects of Seventh-day Adventist belief and life," he examined the political implications of her Great Controversy theology, which regarded "freedom as central to God's government of the universe and the great controversy as challenge to and vindication of God's rule." Expecting that the government would soon turn against God's people, White counseled Adventists to stand apart from political parties but at the same time urged involvement in reform issues such as temperance. Seeing White as essentially pragmatic in her church-state views, Morgan concluded that she "sought to ensure that Adventist separatism would not be so radical as to cut the church off from appropriate opportunities to build itself up as a source of good in the world."[41]

Except for the work of Numbers, Butler, Morgan, and a few other Adventist scholars, virtually all of the writing about Ellen White that appeared outside denominational publications rested on secondary sources.[42] A major exception was a study by Ann Taves, a historian of religion at the Claremont School of Theology and Claremont Graduate School, who subsequently moved to the University of California, Santa Barbara. In her book *Fits, Trances, & Visions* (1999) Taves examined White's early visionary experiences, connecting her with the "shouting Methodist" tradition. Drawing on the recently discovered 1845 transcript of the Israel Dammon trial, which described Ellen as an indecorous young prophet, Taves commented that "we can see evidence of both the development of the visionary currents within the shout tradition and what La Roy Sunderland [a mid-nineteenth-century psychologist of religion] would have called clairvoyant somnambulism," a term referring to assessment of individual character while in a trance. Explaining how White, who was one of several visionaries in the wake of the Great Disappointment, overcame her rivals, Taves stated that her visions not only better met the needs of the sabbatarian movement than the prophetic experiences of her contemporaries but received the support and promotion of her husband James. As Ronald Numbers once observed, "Seventh-day Adventism would not have been the same without Ellen White; it would not have existed without James."[43]

During the past forty years, Ellen G. White has moved from a position of virtual invisibility to a faint shadow in historians' understanding of nineteenth-century American culture. With the developing interest in the history of women and alternative religions, part of the more general multicultural thrust of the late twentieth century, several historians have concluded that she creatively engaged her times in a unique and significant way. Except for Ann Taves, however, these historians have viewed White almost exclusively in terms of her health reform advocacy.[44] Meanwhile, many Seventh-day Adventist scholars have fixated on the issue of her literary indebtedness and have given little attention to the broader dimensions of her relationship to nineteenth-century America. Although both groups have considerably advanced knowledge of Ellen G. White, they have only set the stage for a fuller examination of this religious leader that includes her work as a devotional author, religious thinker, public speaker, and developer of institutions. Beyond that of most other nineteenth-century women, she has left a legacy both in America and abroad that remains to be more extensively explored and more completely understood. The present book is a step in that direction.[45]

NOTES

1. Although it was the first book, apart from her own autobiography, published about Ellen White, Uriah Smith's *The Visions of Mrs. E. G. White: A Manifestation of Spiritual Gifts according to the Scriptures* (Battle Creek, MI: Steam Press of the Seventh-day Adventist Publishing Assoc., 1868) contained virtually no biographical information.
2. Ellen G. White, *A Sketch of the Christian Experience and Views of Ellen G. White* (Saratoga Springs, NY: James White, 1851).
3. Ellen G. White, *Spiritual Gifts*, vol. 2: *My Christian Experience, Views and Labors in Connection with the Rise and Progress of the Third Angel's Message* (Battle Creek, MI: James White, 1860), iv, 294–304.
4. James White and Ellen G. White, *Life Sketches: Ancestry, Early Life, Christian Experience, and Extensive Labors of Elder James White and His Wife, Mrs. Ellen G. White* (Battle Creek, MI: Steam Press of the Seventh-day Adventist Publishing

Association, 1880), 131–342. See also the comments of Jerry Moon on these various editions in "Historical Introduction," James White, *Life Incidents* (Berrien Springs, MI: Andrews University Press, 2003), ix, xiv. In 1878 a biographical sketch of Ellen White, probably written by her niece Mary Clough, appeared in *American Biographical History of Eminent and Self-Made Men, Michigan Volume* (Cincinnati, OH: Western Biographical Publishing Co., 1878), 107–8.

5. Ellen G. White and C. C. Crisler, *Life Sketches of Ellen G. White: Being a Narrative of Her Experience to 1881 as Written by Herself: With a Sketch of Her Subsequent Labors and of Her Last Sickness* (Mountain View, CA: Pacific Press, 1915), 255–449.

6. J. N. Loughborough, *Rise and Progress of the Seventh-day Adventists* (Battle Creek, MI: General Conference Association of Seventh-day Adventists, 1892), 93–97, 103–4, 126, 181–83.

7. J. N. Loughborough, *The Great Second Advent Movement: Its Rise and Progress* (Washington, DC: Review and Herald Publishing Assn., 1905), 208–11, 226–27, 443–61.

8. Arthur Grosvenor Daniells, *The Abiding Gift of Prophecy* (Mountain View, CA: Pacific Press, 1936), 250, 273.

9. W. A. Spicer, *The Spirit of Prophecy in the Advent Movement* (Washington, DC: Review and Herald Publishing Assn., 1937), 26, 36, 48. See also William A. Spicer, *Pioneer Days of the Advent Movement with Notes on Pioneer Workers and Early Experiences* (Washington, DC: Review and Herald Publishing Assn., 1941).

10. Mahlon Ellsworth Olsen, *A History of the Origin and Progress of Seventh-day Adventists* (Washington, DC: Review and Herald Publishing Assn., 1925), 265; Michael Campbell, "Adventism's Earliest Generation of Adventist Historians," May 2, 2007, at http: adventisthistorian.com. Two denominational histories written for young people during this period were those by Matilda Erickson Andross, *Story of the Advent Message* (Takoma Park, MD: Review and Herald Publishing Assn., 1926) and Emma E. Howell, *The Great Advent Movement* (Washington, DC: Review and Herald Publishing Assn., 1935).

11. Everett N. Dick, interview by author, Berrien Springs, MI, August 12, 1976. See also Jonathan M. Butler and Ronald L. Numbers, "Introduction," in *The Disappointed: Millerism and Millenarianism in the Nineteenth Century*, ed. Ronald L. Numbers and Jonathan M. Butler (Bloomington: Indiana University Press, 1987), xvi; and Gary Land, "Foreword," in Everett N. Dick, *William Miller and the Advent Crisis, 1831–1844*, ed. Gary Land, (Berrien Springs, MI: Andrews University Press, 1994), viii.

12. Everett Dick, *Founders of the Message* (Washington, DC: Review and Herald Publishing Assn., 1938), 9–10.

13. Ibid., 235, 246.

14. Dores Eugene Robinson, *The Story of Our Health Message* (Nashville, TN: Southern Publishing Assn., 1943), 69–73.

15. Isaac C. Wellcome, *History of the Second Advent Message and Mission, Doctrine and People* (Yarmouth, ME: I. C. Wellcome, 1874); reprinted with a "Historical Introduction" by Gary Land (Berrien Springs, MI: Andrews University Press, 2008), 402, 408.

16. D. M. Canright, *Seventh-day Adventism Renounced after an Experience of Twenty-eight Years* (Kalamazoo, MI: Kalamazoo Publishing Co., 1888); D. M. Canright, *Life of Mrs. E. G. White, Seventh-day Adventist Prophet: Her False Claims Refuted* (Cincinnati, OH: Standard, 1919), 48, 57–58, 187, 84–85, 193, 205–6.

17. L. R. Conradi, *The Founders of the Seventh Day Adventist Denomination* (n.p.: By the author, 1939), 12, 26, 29, 35, 54, 66.

18. William H. Branson, *Reply to Canright: The Truth about Seventh-day Adventists* (Washington, DC: Review and Herald Publishing Assn., 1933); Francis D. Nichol, *Ellen G. White and Her Critics: An Answer to the Major Charges that Critics Have Brought Against Mrs. Ellen G. White* (Washington, DC: Review and Herald Publishing Assn., 1951).

19. Much of the following discussion draws on Gary Land, "Coping with Change, 1960–1980," in *Adventism in America: A History*, ed. Gary Land (Grand Rapids, MI: William B. Eerdmans, 1986), 219–23. For a non-Adventist's view of these developments, see Stephen J. Stein, "History, Historians, and the Historiography of Indigenous Sectarian Religious Movements in America," in *Religious Diversity and American Religious History: Studies in Traditions and Culture*, ed. Walter H. Conser, Jr. and Sumner B. Twiss (Athens: University of Georgia Press, 1997), 135–36.

20. Herold Weiss and Roy Branson, "Ellen White: A Subject for Adventist Scholarship," *Spectrum: Journal of the Association of Adventist Forums* 2 (Autumn 1970): 30–33, hereafter referred to as *Spectrum*; William S. Peterson, "A Textual and Historical Study of Ellen G. White's Account of the French Revolution," ibid., 66; W. Paul Bradley, "Ellen G. White and Her Writings," ibid. 3 (Spring 1971): 48, 61; Ronald D. Graybill, "How Did Ellen White Choose and Use Historical Sources?" ibid., 4 (Summer 1972): 49–53. About the same time that this critical discussion was developing, Rene Noorbergen, an Adventist journalist, published a peculiar book that compared Ellen White with psychics, arguing that essentially she was the true psychic; see his *Ellen G. White: Prophet of Destiny* (New Canaan, CT: Keats, 1972).

21. Ronald L. Numbers, *Prophetess of Health: A Study of Ellen G. White* (New York: Harper and Row, 1976), xi, 95, 155–56, 35–36, 174, a third expanded edition of which appeared in 2008 (Grand Rapids, MI: William B. Eerdmans). Several articles dealing with Numbers's book appeared in *Spectrum* 8 (January 1977): 2–36. Twenty-five years later, the journal published retrospective reviews. See Gary Land, "An Ambiguous Legacy" and Herbert E. Douglass, "Reexamining the Way God Speaks to His Messengers," *Spectrum* 29 (Autumn, 2001): 23–32.

22. Ellen G. White Estate, "*A Critique of Prophetess of Health* (Washington, DC: Ellen G. White Estate, 1976), 10, 93. For a review of this volume, see Gary Land, "Faith, History and Ellen White," *Spectrum* 9 (March 1978): 51–55.

23. Donald R. McAdams, "Shifting Views of Inspiration: Ellen G. White Studies in the 1970's," *Spectrum* 10 (March 1980): 34, 37; Benjamin McArthur, "Where Are Historians Taking the Church?" ibid., 10 (November 1979): 13. McAdams's essay on *The Great Controversy* chapters remains unpublished, but see Eric D. Anderson, "Ellen White and Reformation Historians," ibid., 9 (July 1978): 23–26.

24. One controversy focused on White and the shut-door doctrine. Ingemar Lindén's *The Last Trump: A Historico-Genetical Study of Some Important Chapters in the Making and Development of the Seventh-day Adventist Church* (Frankfort am Main: Peter Lang, 1978), 93–102, and *1844 and the Shut-Door Problem* (Uppsala: By the author, 1982) argued that Ellen White supported the shut-door theology of Joseph Turner on the basis of her visions. P. Gerard Damsteegt, *Foundations of the Seventh-day Adventist Message and Mission* (Grand Rapids, MI: William B. Eerdmans, 1977), 149–63, referred to Turner's concept of the shut door as the "extreme" view and argued that White adhered to a more moderate version.

25. Walter T. Rea, *The White Lie* (Turlock, CA: M & R Publications, 1982), prologue, n.p. See also Walter Rea, "The Making of a Prophet," *Adventist Currents* (March 1987), 30–31, 33. Rea also raised the issue of the role of her literary assistants, but gave it only brief attention; see *White Lie*, 199. A fuller analysis of the role of these assistants appeared in Alice Elizabeth Gregg's "The Unfinished Story of Fannie Bolton and Marian Davis: Part I, Fannie's Folly," *Adventist Currents* 1 (October, 1983), 24–27, 34–35, and "The Unfinished Story of Fannie Bolton and Marian Davis: Part II, Marian the 'Bookmaker,'" ibid. (February 1984), 23–25, 29.

26. See, for example, John J. Robertson, *The White Truth* (Mountain View, CA: Pacific Press, 1981), which argues, among other things, that Ellen White's use of other authors reflected contemporary practice and fits within biblical concepts of inspiration.

27. Fred Veltman, "The *Desire of Ages* Project: Part 1, The Data," *Ministry* 62 (October 1990), 6; Fred Veltman, "The *Desire of Ages* Project: Part 2, The Conclusions," ibid. (December 1990), 12.

28. Richard W. Schwarz, *Light Bearers to the Remnant: Denomination History Textbook for Seventh-day Adventist College Classes* (Mountain View, CA: Pacific Press, 1979), 108. A later edition of this book included *Prophetess of Health* in its bibliography for a chapter entitled "The Twentieth-Century Debate over Fundamentals." See Richard W. Schwarz and Floyd Greenleaf, *Light Bearers: A History of the Seventh-day Adventist Church*, rev. ed. (Nampa, ID: Pacific Press, 2000), 646.

29. Arthur L. White, *Ellen G. White*, 6 vols. (Hagerstown, MD: Review and Herald, 1981–86). A one-volume abridgement of this biography appeared as Arthur L. White, *Ellen G. White: Woman of Vision* (Hagerstown, MD: Review and Herald, 2000). See also Herbert E. Douglass, *Messenger of the Lord: The Prophetic Ministry of Ellen G. White* (Nampa, ID: Pacific Press, 1998), an apologetical work; and Jerry Allen Moon, *W. C. White and Ellen G. White: The Relationship between the Prophet and Her Son* (Berrien Springs, MI: Andrews University Press, 1993), which offered a scholarly and analytical approach to the Whites.

30. For example, see George R. Knight, "Ellen G. White: Prophet," in *Early Adventist Educators*, ed. George R. Knight (Berrien Springs, MI: Andrews University Press, 1982), 26–49; George R. Knight, *A Search for Identity: The Development of Seventh-day Adventist Beliefs* (Hagerstown, MD: Review and Herald Publishing Assn., 2000); George R. Knight, *Myths in Adventism: An Interpretive Study of Ellen White, Education, and Related Issues* (Hagerstown, MD: Review and Herald Publishing Assn., 1985); George R. Knight, *Walking with Ellen White: The Human Interest Story* (Hagerstown, MD: Review and Herald Publishing Assn., 1999).

31. David W. Lotz, "A Changing Historiography: From Church History to Religious History," in *Altered Landscapes: Christianity in America, 1935–1985* (Grand Rapids, MI: William B. Eerdmans, 1989), 312. See also Kevin M. Schultz and Paul Harvey, "Everywhere and Nowhere: Recent Trends in American Religious History and Historiography," *Journal of the American Academy of Religion* 78 (March 2010): 135–39.

32. E. N. D[ick]., "White, Ellen Gould Harmon," in *Dictionary of American Biography*, ed. Dumas Malone, vol. 20 (New York: Charles Scribner's Sons, 1937), 98–99; William Warren Sweet, *The Story of Religion in America* (New York: Harper & Brothers, 1939), 401–4; William Warren Sweet, *Religion in the Development of American Culture, 1764–1840* (New York: Charles Scribner's Sons, 1952), 306–11; Jerald C. Brauer, *Protestantism in America: A Narrative History* (Philadelphia: Westminster, 1953), 160–63; Whitney R. Cross, *The Burned-Over District: The Social and Intellectual History of Enthusiastic Religion in Western New York, 1800-1850* (Ithaca, NY: Cornell University Press, 1950), 316–17; and Sydney E. Ahlstrom, *A Religious History of the American People* (New Haven, CT: Yale University Press, 1972), 481.

33. Peter W. Williams, "Introduction," to *Perspectives on American Religion and Culture*, ed. Peter W. Williams (Oxford, UK: Blackwell), 289; Lotz, "Changing Historiography," 334. In their historiographical analysis, Schultz and Harvey briefly note that "America's culture of health and fitness is not only quasi-religious, but even has religious origins"; see "Everywhere and Nowhere," 144.

34. John B. Blake, "Health Reform," in *The Rise of Adventism: A Commentary on the Social and Religious Ferment of Mid-Nineteenth Century America*, ed. Edwin Scott Gaustad (New York: Harper & Row, 1974), 30, 46; Jonathan Butler, "Adventism

and the American Experience," ibid., 184, 192–93; Jonathan M. Butler and Rennie B. Schoepflin, "Charismatic Women and Health: Mary Baker Eddy, Ellen G. White, and Aimee Semple McPherson," in *Women, Health, and Medicine in America: A Historical Handbook*, ed. Rima D. Apple (New York: Garland, 1990), 337–65; Jonathan M. Butler, "The World of E. G. White and the End of the World," *Spectrum* 10 (August 1979): 2–13; Jonathan M. Butler, "Prophecy, Gender, and Culture: Ellen Gould Harmon [White] and the Roots of Seventh-day Adventism," *Religion and American Culture* 1 (1991), 3–29.

35. Land, *Adventism in America.*

36. Ronald L. Numbers, *The Creationists* (New York: Knopf, 1992), 75; Ronald L. Numbers, "Sex, Science, and Salvation: The Sexual Advice of Ellen G. White and John Harvey Kellogg," in *Right Living: An Anglo-American Tradition of Self-Help Medicine and Hygiene*, ed. Charles E. Rosenberg (Baltimore, MD: Johns Hopkins University Press, 2003), 207. See also Ronald L. Numbers and Rennie B. Schoepflin, "Ministries of Healing: Mary Baker Eddy, Ellen G. White, and the Religion of Health," in *Women and Health in America: Historical Readings*, ed. Judith Walzer Leavitt (Madison: University of Wisconsin Press, 1984), 376–89; Ronald L. Numbers, "White, Ellen Gould," in *The Encyclopedia of Religion*, ed. Mircea Eliade et al., vol. 15 (New York: Macmillan, 1987), 377–79; and Ronald L. Numbers, "Ellen G. White and the Gospel of Health," in *Eerdmans' Handbook to Christianity in America*, ed. Mark Noll et al. (Grand Rapids, MI: William B. Eerdmans, 1983), 197–99.

37. Janet Wilson James, "Women in American Religious History: An Overview," in *Women in American Religion*, ed. Janet Wilson James (Philadelphia: University of Pennsylvania Press, 1980), 856.

38. Martin E. Marty, *Pilgrims in Their Own Land: 500 Years of Religion in America* (Boston: Little, Brown, 1984), 321–24. See also Marty's comments on White in *Righteous Empire: The Protestant Experience in America* (New York: Dial, 1970), 124, and in *Modern American Religion*, vol. 1: *The Irony of It All, 1893-1919* (Chicago: University of Chicago Press, 1986), 156.

39. R. Laurence Moore, *Religious Outsiders and the Making of Americans* (New York: Oxford University Press, 1986), 135; Paul K. Conkin, *American Originals: Homemade Varieties of Christianity* (Chapel Hill: University of North Carolina Press, 1997), 130, 132, 137, 142.

40. Malcolm Bull and Keith Lockhart, *Seeking a Sanctuary: Seventh-day Adventism and the American Dream* (San Francisco: Harper & Row, 1989), 31.

41. Douglas Morgan, *Adventism and the American Republic: The Public Involvement of a Major Apocalyptic Movement*, Foreword by Martin Marty (Knoxville: University of Tennessee Press, 2001), 24, 52, 56–57.

42. One exception was David Morgan's *Protestants & Pictures: Religion, Visual Culture, and the Age of American Mass Production* (New York: Oxford University Press, 1999), 192–97, which discussed the theological significance of White's

endorsement of a Thomas Moran print, "Christ, the Way of Life," that had been commissioned by her husband, as well as her questioning of the illustrated editions of her books produced during the last few years of her life. See also David F. Holland, *Sacred Borders: Continuing Revelation and Canonical Restraint in Early America* (New York: Oxford University Press, 2011), esp. 157-69.

43. Ann Taves, *Fits, Trances, & Visions: Experiencing Religion and Explaining Experience from Wesley to James* (Princeton, NJ: Princeton University Press, 1999), 160, 163; Numbers, *Prophetess of Health,* 3rd ed., 243.

44. For an incomplete list of references to Ellen White's promotion of health reform, see Numbers, *Prophetess of Health,* 3rd ed., xxi–xxii.

45. Although published after the writing of this chapter, two significant books on Ellen White should be noted: Gilbert M. Valentine, *The Prophet and the Presidents* (Nampa, ID: Pacific Press, 2011) and Jerry Moon and Denis Fortin, eds., *The Ellen G. White Encyclopedia* (Hagerstown, MD: Review and Herald Publishing Assn., 2014).

Index

Great Disappointment, 6, 32, 38–40,
45, 54–55, 152, 166, 179, 181, 315, 323,
328, 339
Grimké, Angelina, 111, 281
Grimké, Sarah, 281
Groveland (Massachusetts), 110–111, 116

Hall, Lucinda, 15–16
Hall, William H., 299
Hamlin, Mary, 40, 124n.5
Hamline, Leonidas, 245–246
Hangerford, Carrie, 295
Hanna, William, 332
Harmon, Elizabeth, 75, 80
Harmon, John, 75
Harmon, Mary, 80
Harmon, Robert, 75–76
Harmon, Sarah, 75–76
Haskell, Stephen N., 297, 307
Hastings, H. L., 151
Hastings, Leonard, 168
Haverhill (Massachusetts), 110, 116
Hawkins, Minnie, 137
Haywood (North Carolina), 121
Healdsburg (California), 118
Healdsburg College (Pacific Union
College), 133, 333
Healdsburg Enterprise (publication), 99
healing, 15, 202, 207–208, 213
health: development of Adventist health
institutions, 129–132, 183, 204; and
dress, 288–290; drugless healing,
129–130, 198; Ellen White's particular
interest in, xi, xiii, 196, 234–235;
exercise, 198; health care for the
poor, 234; health food, 204; health
reform, 12, 14, 22, 86–87, 113, 115,
131–132, 161, 198–205, 217, 271, 306,
326, 339; and medical education, 137;
mental health, xi, 205, 209–212, 247;
and participation of Adventist
women, 285; public health, 133;
and sexual purity, 199–203;

vegetarianism, 198, 201, 203–204;
and water cure, 129, 204
Health Reformer (publication), 128, 131,
141n.24, 205, 210
Henry, O., 244
Henry, S. M. I., 118, 230
Herbert, John, 13
higher criticism, 244, 313
Himes, Joshua V., 38, 40, 182
Hitchcock, Gen. Ethan Allen, 277n.24
holiness, 43
Holmes, Claude, 312–313
holy kissing, 7
"Holy Flesh" Movement, 21
Holy Spirit, 3, 21, 38, 43–44, 52, 97, 99,
122, 168–169, 172, 182, 206, 213, 274, 324
Homer, Winslow, x
hospitals, ix
Howson, John Saul, 103
Hudson, Winthrop, xi, 335
Huntsville (Alabama), 120
humoral theory. *See* medicine
Hus, John, 96, 331
hygiene, 196, 326
Hygeo-Therapeutic College (New
Jersey), 132
hydropathy, 129–132, 204
hymns, 34, 297
hypnotism, 207

Illinois, 282
immigration, 185, 224
immortality, 9
Indiana, 21, 113
inerrancy, xii
industrialization, ix, 224, 234
inspiration. *See* revelation
International Prophetic Guidance
Workshop, 316
Iowa, 122
Irwin, George A., 94, 118–119
Israel, 4, 185, 268
Israel, George, 296

Printed in the USA/Agawam, MA
May 6, 2014

588928.064